The Postwar Challenge

Studies of the German Historical Institute London

GENERAL EDITOR: Hagen Schulze

The Postwar Challenge
Cultural, Social, and Political Change in Western Europe, 1945–58

EDITED BY

DOMINIK GEPPERT

GERMAN HISTORICAL INSTITUTE LONDON

OXFORD
UNIVERSITY PRESS

OXFORD
UNIVERSITY PRESS

Great Clarendon Street, Oxford OX2 6DP
Oxford University Press is a department of the University of Oxford.
It furthers the University's objective of excellence in research, scholarship,
and education by publishing worldwide in
Oxford New York
Auckland Bangkok Buenos Aires Cape Town Chennai
Dar es Salaam Delhi Hong Kong Istanbul Karachi Kolkata
Kuala Lumpur Madrid Melbourne Mexico City Mumbai Nairobi
São Paulo Shanghai Singapore Taipei Tokyo Toronto
with an associated company in Berlin

Oxford is a registered trade mark of Oxford University Press
in the UK and certain other countries

Published in the United States
by Oxford University Press Inc., New York

© The German Historical Institute London 2003

The moral rights of the authors have been asserted
Database right Oxford University Press (maker)

First published 2003

British Library Cataloguing in Publication Data
Data available
Library of Congress Cataloging in Publication Data
Data available
ISBN 0-19-926665-4

1 3 5 7 9 10 8 6 4 2

Typeset by John Saunders Design & Production, Oxford OX13 5HU
Printed in Great Britain
on acid-free paper by
Biddles Ltd., Guildford and King's Lynn

Foreword

An increasing awareness of globalization and the ever-closer links between the nations of Europe have led to a growing methodological interest in comparative, international, and transnational perspectives on historical developments. At the same time, modern and especially contemporary history have been rather slow to match these methodological considerations with the production of empirical studies. In historical research and writing, more often than not the national paradigm prevails—if only for practical reasons, such as limited resources of time and knowledge. The problem of comparative projects is, of course, that few historians are equally at home in two, three, or even four national historiographies, especially such rapidly expanding ones as British, German, Italian, and French contemporary history. Hence the best chance of enhancing our knowledge of Europe's postwar history is to gather contributions by specialists from different countries. That is what this volume has set out to do.

The volume grew out of an international conference which the German Historical Institute London held at Cumberland Lodge in Windsor Great Park on 6–8 July 2001. The aim of the conference was to bring together experts from Britain, France, Germany, Italy, and the USA to investigate, in an explicitly comparative perspective, some of the most important changes that took place in Western Europe during the first thirteen years after the Second World War—in the period, say, between the fall of Berlin in 1945 and the coming into force of the Treaty of Rome. Most of the essays in this volume are revised versions of papers presented at the Cumberland Lodge conference; the contributions by Pieter Lagrou, David Gilgen, Dominik Geppert, and Toby Thacker were added at a later stage to complete the comparative perspective. The essays look at the many challenges which Western European nations faced during this period: the psychological and material aftermath of the war; the need for economic and social restructuring; and the impact of the Cold War on domestic political, social, and cultural developments.

Apart from the contributors, I should like to take this opportunity to thank a number of individuals who helped to make our conference a success. Professor Kathleen Burk (London), Professor William D. Rubinstein (Aberystwyth), Professor David Reynolds (Cambridge), and Professor Axel Schildt (Hamburg) greatly stimulated the discussions which they chaired. I am also grateful to Dr Mark Mazower (London) who gave an inspiring Keynote Speech and to Professor Detlef Junker who gave a paper on 'The USA and Germany in the Age of the Cold War, 1945–90'. I should also like to thank those, like Dr Angus Calder, Professor Hartmut Kaelble (Berlin), Professor Jens Petersen (Rome), and Professor Keith Robbins (Lampeter) who stimulated our debates during the conference. The expert advice and critical comments of Professor Harold James (Princeton), Professor Anthony J. Nicholls (Oxford), and Professor Lothar Kettenacker (London) were extremely helpful. J. A. Underwood translated one of the French and Aelmuire Helen Cleary one of the Italian essays into English. Angela Davies had the arduous task of revising the English of all other texts; many thanks go to her for her precise and conscientious work in preparing the manuscript for publication. The relationship between the GHIL and Oxford University Press dates back many years and many volumes; my thanks go to Ms Anne Ashby for her expertise. Finally, however, the main credit for organizing the conference and editing this volume is due to Dominik Geppert, and I should like to express my thanks to him.

Hagen Schulze

London
May 2003

Contents

List of Tables

1

Introduction

DOMINIK GEPPERT

A bird's-eye view of what Eric Hobsbawm called the Short Twentieth Century shows that the thirteen years from 1945 to 1958 are central in more than chronological terms.[1] The years between the fall of Berlin and the Treaties of Rome are also a key period for understanding Europe's development from a war-torn, economically and politically unstable continent, in which most countries were governed by dictatorial regimes, to a relatively peaceful, prosperous, and democratic region of the world. In political terms, the immediate post-1945 years seem to represent a 'lost step' between the calamities of the 1930s and the subsequent democratic transitions in southern and eastern Europe in the 1970s, 1980s, and 1990s, as Tom Buchanan and Martin Conway have recently written. One of the great challenges for historians, Buchanan and Conway argue, is to ask 'why a very particular parliamentary model of democracy was so successfully implanted (with a few notable exceptions) in Western Europe after 1945'.[2] In economic terms, the period witnessed the gradual emergence of a regulated welfare capitalism based on an implicit understanding between the government, employers, and trade unions about the core principles of economic management, namely, the predominance of the private sector of the economy combined with a goal of (almost) full employment, some degree of public ownership, and state involvement. At the same time, the long boom began that was not only the foundation of Western Europe's growing prosperity and political stability but the main underlying cause of the enormous socio-cultural transformations that were to

I am grateful to my colleagues Lutz Klinkhammer (German Historical Institute Rome) and Stefan Martens (German Historical Institute Paris), who read this introduction and offered their expert advice on current Italian and French historiography.

[1] Eric Hobsbawm, *Age of Extremes: The Short Twentieth Century, 1914–1991* (London, 1994).
[2] Tom Buchanan and Martin Conway, 'The Politics of Democracy in Twentieth Century Europe: Introduction', *European History Quarterly*, 32/1 (2002), 7–12, at 10–11.

follow.[3] Thus, in social and cultural terms, the immediate post-war period was the hinge between a more traditional, deferential, and authoritarian past and the pluralistic, meritocratic, and leisure-orientated consumer society of the present day.

These are generalizations, of course, which tend to neglect important continuing differences between individual nations and societies. The expansion of the welfare state, for example, was a feature common to the whole of Western Europe in the 1950s and 1960s; and yet, the actual forms of welfare provision were shaped not so much by external influences or the transfer of knowledge between countries as by national traditions.[4] Much the same can be said about the management of the economy. Everywhere in Western Europe the unrestricted capitalism of the inter-war period was 'tamed' after the Second World War, but the extent of state intervention, the mechanisms of control, and the instruments of planning differed from country to country.[5] Keynesian macro-economic management, for instance, was widely accepted and applied both in France and in Britain in the 1950s, whereas in Germany it only became government practice in the second half of the 1960s.[6]

In order to explore the development of postwar societies in Western Europe, one needs to combine transnational and national perspectives.[7] Thus the four sections of this volume compare key developmental processes in the postwar societies of the four biggest Western European nations—Britain, France,

[3] Hartmut Kaelble, *Der Boom 1948–1973: Gesellschaftliche und wirtschaftliche Folgen in der Bundesrepublik Deutschland und in Europa* (Opladen, 1992).

[4] Gøsta Esping-Andersen, *The Three Worlds of Welfare Capitalism* (Cambridge, 1990); Hans Günter Hockerts (ed.), *Drei Wege deutscher Sozialstaatlichkeit: NS-Diktatur, Bundesrepublik und DDR im Vergleich* (Munich, 1998), 8–10; see also Kees van Kersbergen, *Social Capitalism: A Study of Christian Democracy and the Welfare State* (London, 1995).

[5] Richard Vinen, *A History in Fragments: Europe in the Twentieth Century* (London, 2000), 368.

[6] Peter Hall (ed.), *The Political Power of Economic Ideas: Keynesianism across Nations* (Princeton, 1989).

[7] Until recently, contemporary historians have mainly concentrated on the latter; see Philipp Gassert's complaint about the lack of comparative work in German contemporary history: 'Die Bundesrepublik, Europa und der Westen', in Jörg Baberowski et al., *Geschichte ist immer Gegenwart: Vier Thesen zur Zeitgeschichte* (Stuttgart, 2001), 67–89, esp. 83–9; in similar vein Sebastian Conrad, 'Doppelte Marginalisierung: Plädoyer für eine transnationale Perspektive auf die deutsche Geschichte', *Geschichte und Gesellschaft*, 28 (2002), 145–69, at 145. For Britain see Geoff Eley, 'Playing it Safe: How is History Represented?', *History Workshop*, 35 (1993), 206–20; with a European perspective from Austria, Michael Gehler, 'Zeitgeschichte zwischen Europäisierung und Globalisierung', *Aus Politik und Zeitgeschichte*, B 51–2 (2003), 23–35.

Italy, and West Germany.[8] These nations share a number of important characteristics which render them attractive for a comparative approach. After 1945 they all were or became capitalist economies and parliamentary democracies. Regarding size and population, they were roughly in the same league. They had all been belligerents in the Second World War and later became members of the North Atlantic alliance.

At the same time, however, Britain, France, Italy, and West Germany are sufficiently different to represent the diversity which is Europe's hallmark. In Britain and France, the political systems had survived the travails of the interwar period; in Italy and Germany, liberal democracies had been replaced by fascist and National Socialist dictatorships. Germany lost the war and Britain won it; France and Italy did neither. After 1945 Britain remained a monarchy, whereas France, Italy, and Germany were or became republics. Federalism was a prominent feature in postwar Germany, but not in France. Moreover, the Italian and French economies were still much more dominated by agriculture than the German and British ones.

The first two sections of this volume ask how these different nations came to terms with their most recent history, and how they discussed the challenges of economic and social restructuring after the war. A solely comparative approach along national lines, however, does not do justice to the historical reality of societies which were not hermetically sealed national units, but inextricably intertwined with one another through individual and institutional contacts and the transfer of goods and ideas. The third section examines an area in which these links between countries and the limits of the nation-state had become most obvious after 1945, namely, the debates about the beginnings of supranational integration in Europe. The fourth section, which focuses on the influence of the USA on the social and cultural reorganization of Western Europe, abandons national subdivisions altogether and examines some agents of American influence in Western Europe.

[8] See e.g. Heinz-Gerhard Hauptmann and Jürgen Kocka (eds.), *Geschichte und Vergleich: Ansätze und Ergebnisse international vergleichender Geschichtsschreibung* (Frankfurt am Main, 1996); Hartmut Kaelble, 'Vergleichende Sozialgeschichte des 19. und 20. Jahrhunderts: Forschungen europäischer Historiker', *Jahrbuch für Wirtschaftsgeschichte*, 1993, no. 1, 173–200; A. A. van den Braembussche, 'Historical Explanation and Comparative Method: Towards a Theory of the History of Society', *History and Theory: Studies in the Philosophy of History*, 28 (1989), 1–24; and the essays by Jürgen Osterhammel, Susanne-Sophia Spiliotis, and Albert Wirz in *Geschichte und Gesellschaft*, 27 (2001), 464–98.

The volume thus seeks to combine two methodological approaches: international comparison and intercultural transfer.[9] A challenge faced by all historians dealing with the beginning of the postwar period is the impact which the end of that period had on their profession. The implosion of the Soviet empire not only brought about the end of Communist rule in Eastern Europe, but also altered the perception which Western European societies had of themselves and their history. Conceptual categories and scholarly priorities have changed accordingly. One must be careful, of course, not to over-emphasize the significance of the world-political turning point of 1989–91 for the re-orientation of European historiography over the past twelve years. Historical research is a long-term business. The roots of many changes go back to the late 1980s or even further. But it is obvious, on the other hand, that the end of the bipolar international order has immensely affected the work of historians. It has led to the opening of archives in many Central and East European states which had hitherto been firmly closed. Assumptions of the antagonistic nature of every aspect of life in East and West have been called into question.[10] In retrospect, the Cold War seems to lose some of its frightfulness and apocalyptic aura. Diplomatic crises and military confrontation are no longer seen as its only defining features; an astonishing amount of stability and a remarkable reliability appear as equally important characteristics. At the same time, the cultural dimension of the conflict, not only between the two blocs, but also inside them, is attracting the attention of historians. Art, music, literature, high and popular culture in general, have been discovered as important battlefields. Historians ask how ideology and propaganda contributed to a Cold War mentality in East and West.

[9] Cf. Johannes Paulmann, 'Internationaler Vergleich und interkultureller Transfer: Zwei Forschungsansätze zur europäischen Geschichte des 18. bis 20. Jahrhunderts', *Historische Zeitschrift*, 267 (1998), 649–85; Michelle Espagne, 'Sur les limites du comparatisme en histoire culturelle', *Genèses*, 17 (1994), 112–21.

[10] There have been several attempts to view the history of postwar Europe as a whole, even though it was divided by the Cold War; see for example Mark Mazower, *Dark Continent: Europe's Twentieth Century* (Harmondsworth, 1998); Vinen, *A History in Fragments*. In April 2001 the German History Society in association with the History Department of the University of Wales in Swansea organized a Regional Conference on the topic 'Social History of Central European Politics, 1945–53', which brought together historians working on East Germany, Austria, Hungary, and Czechoslovakia. The explicit aim was to explore 'common experiences and phenomena in the whole region, especially on both sides of the Iron Curtain'.

Furthermore, neo-Hegelians who proclaimed the 'end of history' have been proven wrong.[11] On the contrary, the notion of historical change has been put back on the agenda. Many historians, at least in the Western world, who were born around 1945 'took it for granted that history stopped when their own lives began', as Richard Vinen has put it.[12] Few will share that view today. One effect of the changed perception is the calling into question of the traditional periodization, especially the notion of *Stunde Null*, the 'zero hour' when the war ended and supposedly something completely new began. Hence, the caesura of 1945 has become increasingly blurred. More and more historians are exploring the impact of the people's wartime experience on the postwar era. Historians have become increasingly interested, for instance, in the long-term impact of the experience of war upon soldiers' attitudes and mentalities in postwar societies.[13] Moreover, numerous studies of gender history and the history of everyday life have shown that the end of the war did not constitute the decisive break in people's experience which historians have long stressed.[14]

But if 1945 does not mark a magic Zero Hour, it nevertheless does mark the end of the Second World War and a complete change in the circumstances under which policy could be conducted. The postwar challenges, therefore, differed sharply from the requirements of wartime. The same applies, to a certain extent, to the year 1958, with which this volume ends. The coming into force of the Treaties of Rome, the fall of the Fourth Republic in France, the take-off of the economic miracle in Italy, the increasing domestic difficulties of the centre-right governments and the revitalization of Social Democracy in West Germany and Britain, growing private affluence in all Western

[11] Francis Fukuyama, *The End of History and the Last Man* (London, 1992).

[12] Vinen, *A History in Fragments*, 2–3.

[13] This is a field that has been well researched in regard to the First World War, but is still in its infancy in respect to the Second World War; cf. Peter Schrijvers, *The Crash of Ruin: American Combat Soldiers in Europe During World War II* (London, 1998); Paul Addison and Angus Calder (eds.), *Time to Kill: The Soldiers' Experience of War in the West, 1939–45* (London, 1997). For the First World War see Hans Mommsen (ed.), *Der Erste Weltkrieg und die europäische Nachkriegsordnung: Sozialer Wandel und Formveränderung der Politik* (Cologne, 2000).

[14] See e.g. the survey by Mark Mazower, 'Changing Trends in the Historiography of Postwar Europe, East and West', *International Labor and Working-Class History*, 58 (Autumn 2000), 275–82.

European countries, slowly changing attitudes towards the Nazi past in Germany—none of these events and developments in itself justifies the notion of a decisive caesura. Taken together, however, they indicate a tectonic shift in the cultural, social, and political landscapes.

With the wall that used to divide the past from the present finally torn down, there is an increasing awareness amongst historians of the social and psychological repercussions which the war (and even the pre-war period, for that matter) had on post-war societies. At least three different aspects of the legacy of the past need to be considered: the effects of wartime migration and the displacement of large groups of people; the question of how exponents and sympathizers of the old dictatorships should be treated and how they could be integrated into postwar societies; and public and private recollections of the Nazi (and fascist) dictatorship and the memorialization of the war in literature, art, monuments, and public speeches. The first problem has only quite recently become the focus of renewed attention. The fate of German expellees from Silesia, Pomerania, East Prussia, and the Sudeten area and the suffering of the Poles, who were forced to leave their homes in East Poland and settle in the former Reich territories, were long treated as taboo subjects.[15] This kind of wartime migration affected central and eastern Europe immensely more than the western or southern parts of the Continent. But countries such as France and Italy also had to come to terms with the dislocation of large groups of their populations. Two million French citizens were transferred to Nazi Germany as prisoners of war or forced labourers; hundreds of thousands fled from the German occupied areas in the east and north to the southern and western parts of France.[16] Not dissimilar was the fate of 700,000 Italian soldiers, who ended up in German prisoner-of-war camps; almost the same number again were imprisoned by Allied forces in Africa and Russia.[17] Even in

---

[15] Cf. Dierk Hoffmann et al. (eds.), *Vertriebene in Deutschland: Interdisziplinäre Ergebnisse und Forschungsperspektiven* (Munich, 2000). The success of Günter Grass's novel *Im Krebsgang*, which deals with the Soviet navy's sinking of the refugee ship *Wilhelm Gustloff* in January 1945, reflects the changed mood not only in the scientific community, but in a wider public; cf. Günter Grass, *Im Krebsgang* (Göttingen, 2002). The Hamburg news magazine *Der Spiegel* devoted two of its front-page stories to the subject in the first quarter of 2002 alone; cf. *Der Spiegel*, 2002, nos. 6 and 13.

[16] See Pieter Lagrou's essay in this volume.

[17] See Filippo Focardi's contribution to this volume.

Britain, some sixty million changes of address were registered during the war as the result of wartime dislocation and chaos.[18] In every case, the integration of those uprooted groups posed a formidable challenge to postwar societies and their political leaders.[19]

Another inheritance from the recent past—politically and morally more delicate—were the surviving exponents of the National Socialist and fascist dictatorships plus millions of sympathizers, collaborators, and fellow-travellers. The question of how the supporters of the old regimes were treated and what mechanisms were used finally to integrate them into German, French, and Italian postwar society, has been studied extensively for the last decade or so.[20] The task was most difficult in Germany, where the vast majority of the people accepted the NS dictatorship until the bitter end. Thus in the first four years after the end of the war the victorious powers pursued an ambitious policy of purging. But in the following years, until about 1955, exactly the opposite policy was implemented towards former Nazi functionaries in the newly founded West German state. In his contribution Norbert Frei describes this new attitude as *Vergangenheitspolitik* (politics of the past), which he sums up as: 'amnesty', 'integration', and 'demarcation'. In practical terms this meant that former Nazis were no longer pursued by the courts, and those already sentenced were given an amnesty and integrated into postwar society. At the same time, in political rhetoric a clear line of demarcation was drawn between the Bonn republic and the Nazi regime. Not until the end of the 1950s did a more critical approach to the 'unmastered past' emerge, and in the 1960s this led to Nazi criminals being pursued by the courts. By this time the integration of former

[18] Mazower, *Dark Continent*, 188.

[19] For the German case see Pertti Ahonen, 'Domestic Constraints on West German Ostpolitik: The Role of the Expellee Organizations in the Adenauer Era', *Central European History*, 31 (1998), 31–64.

[20] Cf. Klaus-Dietmar Henke and Hans Woller (eds.), *Politische Säuberung in Europa: Die Abrechnung mit Faschismus und Kollaboration nach dem zweiten Weltkrieg* (Munich, 1991). For Italy also see Hans Woller, *Die Abrechnung mit dem Faschismus in Italien, 1943–8* (Munich, 1996); J. Dunnage (ed.), *After the War: Violence, Justice, Continuity and Renewal in Italian Society* (Hull, 1999). For Germany see Norbert Frei, *Adenauer's Germany and the Nazi Past: The Politics of Amnesty and Integration*, trans. Joel Golb (New York, 2002). For France, the Netherlands, and Belgium see Pieter Lagrou, *The Legacy of Nazi Occupation: Patriotic Memory and National Recovery in Western Europe, 1945–1965* (Cambridge, 2000).

Nazis into West German society had more or less been accomplished and a younger generation of Germans, who had grown up after the war and had not themselves been entangled with the NS system, started to ask awkward questions. The attitude of postwar societies towards former supporters of the old regimes is inextricably linked with the question of how these societies recalled their own past during the years of NS domination and war.[21] Filippo Focardi demonstrates in his chapter how a collective memory of the Second World War developed in Italy. He presents this process as a battle between two competing narratives, the anti-fascist and the fascist. Between 1943 and 1947 the Italian anti-fascists managed to establish their interpretation in the nation's collective memory: the Italians were the victims of fascism and of a war perpetrated by Mussolini and Germany. It was only the heroic struggle against Nazi Germany at the side of the Allies after 1943 that revealed the Italians' true feelings. This interpretation became less firmly rooted in the following five years once the anti-fascist coalition had been disbanded and the Cold War had set in, but nothing was found to replace it. It was therefore possible to revive it at the end of the 1950s and for a long time it remained the dominant form of collective memory.

By the 1990s, however, a decisive shift had taken place, not only in Italy, but also in France and other European countries, such as Switzerland, Portugal, Sweden, and Poland, which abandoned 'the founding myths of the postwar era'.[22] The German and the Italian publics, for instance, were both confronted with the unpleasant truth that the notion of a decent and respectable army, as opposed to a criminal political leadership, was a myth.[23]

---

[21] For the attitude of the German public to the Nazi past see Axel Schildt, 'Der Umgang mit der NS-Vergangenheit in der Öffentlichkeit der Nachkriegszeit', in Wilfried Loth and Bernd A. Rusinek (eds.), *Verwandlungspolitik: NS-Eliten in der Nachkriegszeit* (Frankfurt am Main, 1998), 19–54; for France see Henry Rousso, *Le Syndrome de Vichy de 1944 à nos jours* (2nd edn.; Paris, 1990); id., *Vichy: L'événement, la mémoire, l'histoire* (Paris, 2000); Eric Conan and Henry Rousso, *Vichy, un passé qui ne passe* (Paris, 1994). For Italy see Enzo Collotti and Lutz Klinkhammer, *Il fascismo e l'Italia in guerra: Una conversazione tra storia e storiografia* (Rome, 1996); Jens Petersen, 'Der Ort der Resistenza in Geschichte und Gegenwart Italiens', *Quellen und Forschungen aus italienischen Archiven und Bibliotheken*, 72 (1992), 550–71.
[22] Michael Jeismann, *Auf Wiedersehen Gestern: Die deutsche Vergangenheit und die Politik von morgen* (Stuttgart, 2001), 59.
[23] Cf. Filippo Focardi, 'La questione della punizione dei criminali di guerra in Italia dopo la fine del secondo conflitto mondiale', *Quellen und Forschungen aus italienischen Archiven*

French historians now emphasized the extent of popular support for the Vichy regime, its agreement with parts of NS ideology, its involvement in Nazi crimes, especially the persecution of French Jews, and the limited scope of the purge after the war. Postwar France, the revisionist argument runs, grossly exaggerated its contribution to the Allied victory over Germany and reinvented itself as a nation of resistance fighters united in its struggle against the enemy. In his chapter, Pieter Lagrou argues that this sceptical reading of the country's relationship to its past itself distorts historical facts by unduly concentrating on commemoration by Gaullists and Communists, both of whom were forces on the fringes of the political spectrum between 1946 and 1958. The memory of suffering and persecution in postwar representations, Lagrou claims, was as important as remembering the resistance—the more so as it was related to the immediate task of dealing with the social consequences of the war faced by French politicians of the Fourth Republic.

Developments in Britain were different. Unlike in Germany, the defeat of National Socialism did not call British national traditions into question, but confirmed them. Unlike in Italy, memory of the war did not divide the nation, but united it. Unlike France, Britain did not suffer occupation and the national humiliation that went with it. Thus after 1945 the British produced their own idiosyncratic recollections of the Second World War. They mostly revolved around the 'Dunkirk spirit', which supposedly led not only to victory over Nazism and fascism, but also to the reforms of the Attlee government and the establishment of the welfare state. Self-assertion, progress, and prosperity were linked to the values of common sacrifice and national solidarity. The war thus entered British collective memory 'as a narrative of popular democratic accomplishment'.[24] As in other European countries, revisionist historians

und Bibliotheken, 80 (2000), 543–624; Gerhard Schreiber, *Deutsche Kriegsverbrechen in Italien: Täter, Opfer, Strafverfolgung* (Munich, 1996); Lutz Klinkhammer, *Stragi naziste in Italia* (Rome, 1997); Gerd R. Ueberschär (ed.), *Orte des Grauens: Verbrechen im Zweiten Weltkrieg* (Darmstadt, 2003). See also Wolfram Wette, 'Das Bild der Wehrmacht-Elite nach 1945', in Gerd Ueberschär (ed.), *Hitlers militärische Elite*, ii: *Vom Kriegsbeginn bis zum Weltkriegsende* (Darmstadt, 1998), 293–308; Detlef Bald *et al.*, *Mythos Wehrmacht: Nachkriegsdebatten und Traditionspflege* (Berlin, 2001).

[24] Geoff Eley, 'Finding the People's War: Film, British Collective Memory, and World War II', *American Historical Review*, 106/3 (2001), 818–38, at 821. For this kind of interpretation see Paul Addison, *The Road to 1945: British Politics and the Second World War* (London,

increasingly challenged this kind of postwar interpretation. Some stressed activities such as looting, black market activities, absenteeism, and strikes, which did not easily fit into the image of a nation united in its fight against a common enemy; some doubted that popular support for the reforms of the Labour administration was as widespread as was often claimed.[25] Others argued that from the point of view of *realpolitik* both the war against Hitler and the ensuing socialist reforms were mistakes, which put Britain's long-term interests as a great power at risk.[26]

What was different was the extent to which the myth of war and victory has remained substantially unchallenged in British public opinion. 'According to folk memory', it still is 'our last great collective achievement as a nation', as the historian Peter Hennessy put it in 1992.[27] Nick Hewitt, who in his chapter examines commemoration of the war using British war memorials, goes so far as to argue that remembrance of the Second World War plays a more important role today than it did fifty years ago. According to Hewitt official commemoration of the Second World War in Britain immediately after 1945 had nothing to do with class or party affiliation, but embraced all classes and views. The most important dividing line Hewitt can perceive was between different generations—between those who had fought in the First World War and the soldiers of the Second World War. Hewitt describes these younger men as a 'sceptical generation' since in numerous questionnaires they rejected the idea of impressive war memorials—of the type erected to commemorate the First World War—preferring instead 'utilitarian' memorials like public swimming baths or housing for wounded veterans. Only decades later, when the veterans of the Second World War had grown old, did they forget about their earlier feelings towards memorials and urgently demand the

1975); Kenneth O. Morgan, *Britain since 1945: The People's Peace* (2nd edn.; Oxford, 2001); Stephen Brooke, *Labour's War* (London, 1992).

[25] Cf. Geoffrey Field, 'Social Patriotism and the British Working Class: Appearance and Disappearance of a Tradition', *International Labor and Working-Class History*, 42 (1992), 20–39, at 27; Angus Calder, *The Myth of the Blitz* (London, 1991); id., *The People's War* (London, 1969); Pete Grafton, *You, You and You: The People out of Step with World War II* (London, 1981).

[26] Cf. Corelli Barnett, *The Audit of War* (London, 1986); id., *The Lost Victory: British Dreams, British Realities, 1945–50* (London, 1995); John Charmley, *Chamberlain and the Lost Peace* (London, 1989); id., *Churchill: The End of Glory* (London, 1993).

[27] Peter Hennessy, *Never Again: Britain 1945–51* (London, 1992), 6.

erection of monuments to commemorate their achievements in the war against Hitler's Germany.

But learning the lessons of the Second World War did not mean only looking backwards and coming to terms with the past. Even more urgently needed was a vision for the future. The war and the confrontation with Nazism, as Mark Mazower writes in his history of Europe's twentieth century, 'acted as a catalyst inside and outside the continent for a renewed attempt to define the place of the democratic nation-state in the modern world . . . What was to become the wartime consensus rested upon the belief that in order to survive in Europe, democracy would have to be reinterpreted.'[28] Immediately after the war, this reinterpretation seemed to favour socialist solutions almost everywhere in Western Europe. In Germany, where discussions were dominated by memories of the world economic crisis of the inter-war period and the experience of the Nazi command economy, there was agreement between the major parties that any new economic and political system had to be judged by its ability to prevent catastrophes of this kind from happening again. As David Gilgen demonstrates in his chapter, both the Christian Democrats and the Social Democrats thus initially demanded socialist measures such as state control of strategic industries, the nationalization of raw material extraction (especially mining), and some form of central planning (though this last measure was much more weakly developed in the CDU concept). Only after the summer of 1947 did the Christian Democrats under the leadership of Konrad Adenauer turn their backs on socialism and advocate the idiosyncratic mixture of ordo-liberalism and welfare politics that came to be known as the German Social Market Economy.

Similarly, in Britain socialism had the floor after 1945. Jose Harris rejects the view that the Second World War hardly had any effect on postwar British society. Challenging a major trend of recent research, which suggests that the structure of British government and society was not fundamentally changed by the impact of the war, she stresses the significance of the Second World War as a caesura in British history. She maintains that the ideas of 'war socialism' were more important, more influen-

---

[28] Mazower, *Dark Continent*, 185, 187.

tial, and more radical than is generally assumed today. The notion that successful planning methods used during the war could be transferred to management of the national economy was not, according to Harris, exclusive to the political Left, but was also supported by members of the Conservative Party. The belief that some sort of state collectivism should be part of the future was generally shared. A main difference between West Germany and Britain was that in Britain the Labour government under Clement Attlee was in a position to realize far-reaching reform measures, whereas in Germany the Social Democrats were prevented from doing the same—first because of Allied occupation, and later, after September 1949, because a coalition of Christian Democrats and Free Liberals formed the government. As a result, the 'Attlee consensus'[29] on which post-war Britain was built included large-scale nationalizations of key industries as well as the establishment of a tax-financed national health system. In the Federal Republic on the other hand, the ordo-liberalism of men like economic minister Ludwig Erhard and his advisers Franz Böhm, Alfred Müller-Armack, and Walter Eucken prevailed.

Another major difference was the degree of American involvement in the restructuring processes of the postwar years. Nowhere in Western Europe was US influence as strong as in West Germany, where the USA did not have to rely solely on persuasion or economic and diplomatic pressure, but could directly implement reforming measures in its capacity as one of the occupation powers. Even after the end of occupation rule in 1949, the American High Commissioner in Germany, together with his British and French colleagues, retained considerable rights and responsibilities regarding disarmament, the break-up of cartels, the question of reparations, foreign relations in general, and the monitoring of foreign trade and foreign exchange in particular. In Britain on the other hand, American influence was especially weak, ironically not least because of the special relationship between the two countries, which ruled out any direct American involvement in British domestic affairs. Apart from that, the idea of deliberately modernizing the country did not occur to either Britons or Americans at that time.

---

[29] Addison, *The Road to 1945*.

Victory over Germany and the feeling this created that Britain was in the vanguard of modernity prevented such matters from ever being considered.

The situation was completely different in France. Here the defeat of 1940 and the subsequent collaboration of many French people with Nazi Germany convinced the economic and political élites of the need for a thorough modernization, as Gérard Bossuat demonstrates in his contribution. Initially, however, it was not clear what should serve as the model for modernity. Since the Soviet way was out of the question for all parties except the Communists, three basic models were discussed: the much-admired German model of state organization and powerful cartels; the socialist British welfare state, which was being established across the Channel; and the US model, not much admired to start with, based on mass consumption, mass production, and free trade. And then there was, of course, France's own mercantilist tradition of active state involvement in the economy. In the end, Bossuat concludes, a 'Franco-American modernization model' emerged, which was marked by interventionism, state socialism, nationalizations, on the one hand, and a far-reaching programme of social justice as well as social dialogue in the workplace, balanced public finances, an export drive, material comfort for wage-earners, and high performance in technology on the other. To be sure, American financial aid to France and Jean Monnet's personal role as transatlantic intermediary were crucial in bringing about important socio-economic changes. Bossuat doubts, however, whether American involvement really was responsible for a new social and economic order in France after 1945. He emphasizes the specifically French roots of many seemingly new developments and stresses the limits of American influence.

With regard to economic and monetary policy in postwar Italy, the 'importance of the foreign constraint' cannot be over-estimated, as Luciano Segreto argues in his chapter. Decisions taken outside Italy, either in Washington or in Brussels, were crucial in determining Italian policy in those fields and in over-coming domestic obstacles to reform. This domestic situation was characterized not only by a powerful Communist Party, the influence of the Vatican on Italian domestic policy, and a weak state tradition, but also by a very traditional economic structure, dominated by small family firms and the economic legacy of fascism in the form of state-controlled big enterprises, especially the banking system, and the shipbuilding, energy, and steel industries. Segreto shows how technocratic managers in this powerful state sector adopted American concepts of deregulation, favoured free trade and a reorganization of the Italian economy, and eventually partly prevailed over politicians and civil servants, many of whom were sceptical about the market economy. American economic models, however, were only adopted up to a point, the point at which real social change would have started. Attempts to go beyond this failed.

In the third section, which deals with discussions about the future of the nation-state and the beginning of European integration, the contributions once again centre on the fine balance between American influence and independent development in Western Europe. Traditionally, American influence was deemed to be of very great importance.[30] Only in the 1980s, with the opening of European archives, did another school of historians challenge this assertion by stressing that economic recovery in Europe had already begun before the Marshall Plan was implemented and that European nations did not simply follow the American lead, but acted out of clear-sighted self-interest.[31] A second leading question, which runs through the section, concerns the motivation of the foreign policy élites who took part in the discussions. Were they driven by supranational idealism and a desire to purge the Continent of the threat of war and the nationalist excesses of the past?[32] Or did traditional notions of national interest and *Staatsräson* guide their behaviour, as historians of the realist school of historiography continue to argue?[33] A

---

[30] See e.g. the revealing title of the memoirs of the former US Secretary of State Dean Acheson, *Present at the Creation* (2nd edn.; New York, 1987). More recent examples of this historiographical school include John Killick, *The United States and European Reconstruction, 1945–1960* (Edinburgh, 1997), and Geir Lundestad, *'Empire' by Integration: The United States and European Integration, 1945–1997* (New York, 1998).

[31] Particularly influential were two studies by Alan Milward, *The Reconstruction of Western Europe, 1945–1951* (London, 1984) and *The European Rescue of the Nation-State* (2nd edn.; London, 1999). See also Werner Abelshauser, *Wirtschaft in Westdeutschland, 1945–1948* (Frankfurt am Main, 1983).

[32] A classic example of that school of thought is Walter Lipgens, *A History of European Integration* (Oxford, 1982).

[33] Two influential examples of this interpretation are Franz Knipping and Josef Becker (eds.), *Power in Europe? Great Britain, France, Italy and Germany in a Postwar World* (Berlin, 1986) and Ennio di Nolfo, *Power in Europe II: Great Britain, France, Germany and Italy and the Origins of the EEC* (Berlin, 1992).

third leitmotiv is the question of how important the European federalist movement was in the different countries. What influence did the federalist vision have? How, specifically, was a supranational solution envisaged? How did these ideas change in the course of time?

In his paper on the West German debates, Wilfried Loth emphasizes specifically German motives and objectives. He interprets the popularity of the European movement, especially amongst the young, as a reaction to the loss of orientation after defeat in the war and the bankruptcy of the Nazi regime. Later, he argues, regaining state sovereignty, self-restraint on the part of the Federal Republic and securing peace also became driving forces in West Germany's policy on Europe. Loth stresses that it was unclear which concept of Europe would prevail in Germany—the idea of a socialist Europe as a 'third force' between East and West, as envisaged by Martin Niemöller, Jakob Kaiser, and Eugen Kogon, or Adenauer's concept of integration into the West. The Cold War finally led to the latter being adopted, even though it was initially less popular than its socialist counterpart.

In her chapter on the discussions in France, which focuses on French security interests between the end of the Second World War and the collapse of the European Defence Community (EDC) in 1954, Elisabeth du Réau likewise stresses that the debates were based on specifically French problems and perceived threats. The key problem was the unresolved dichotomy between the need for security—initially against Germany, and then increasingly against the Soviet Union—and the preservation of national sovereignty and self-determination. The second aspect had traditionally played an important role in French security policy. According to du Réau, this was one of the main reasons why the federalist approach, successfully implemented in economic policy by Jean Monnet and Robert Schuman, failed in the case of the EDC, foundering on opposition from inter-governmentalists such as de Gaulle. Even more revealing of the important difference of opinion regarding the process of European construction was, in du Réau's view, the failure of the political community project, which was discussed at the same time by the 'ad hoc Assembly' of the European Coal and Steel Community (ECSC) and the Council of Europe.

Leopoldo Nuti's contribution on the Italian case once again introduces the USA as a central factor in the discussion, though more in a passive than an active role. Italian policy for Europe, he maintains, was designed not least to secure American aid and to establish good relations with the USA. It was easier to communicate this objective to the Italian public in the language of idealistic European rhetoric than by using the concepts of discredited power politics. None the less, historians of the realist school were right, according to Nuti, to emphasize the continuity of traditional diplomacy and *realpolitik* beyond the caesura of 1943–5. This was, of course, a new form of power politics with different methods. Like their German counterparts, Italian politicians and diplomats used the concept of European integration as a means to secure a position of parity in the emerging European state system of the postwar period.

The discussion on Europe in Britain, dealt with by Piers N. Ludlow, was different from the debates in the other three countries because in the 1950s Britain was not involved in nascent European integration. Ludlow therefore focuses on the thesis often used to explain this difference, namely the assertion that missing the opportunity to take part in European integration from the start was the price Britain paid for victory in the Second World War. Ludlow disputes this thesis. He argues that Britain did co-operate politically and economically in many ways in the postwar era. It was a founding member of the Bretton Woods bodies, the United Nations, the General Agreement on Tariffs and Trade (GATT), and the North Atlantic Treaty Organization (NATO), to name but a few. Ludlow argues that the willingness to participate in these endeavours does not fit into the 'price of victory argument', nor do the numerous continuities connecting British foreign policy before 1939 and after 1945. Like Nuti, Ludlow stresses the importance of national interest as far as European integration was concerned. In this respect, according to Ludlow, there was no difference in principle between the British and their continental neighbours—it was just that British national interest, as defined by those in charge of foreign policy, pointed in a direction different from that in France, Italy, or Germany.

The fourth section, finally, deals with the social, political, economic, and cultural influence of the USA in Western Europe during the Cold War. Again, the delicate balance between the impact of the USA and independent European traditions is at the centre of attention. Moreover, although the socio-cultural as well as the political and economic impact of the USA was felt in all European countries, considerable national differences remained. National cultures and the specific political environment in different countries shaped reactions. American decision-makers who dealt with Europe had to adapt their activities to different national situations. They had to take into account strong Communist parties and the polarized political scene in Italy and France; the British experience of a wartime alliance with the USA, but also a remaining latent anti-Americanism; the temptation for Germany—as well as to a lesser degree for Italy and France—to avoid taking sides in the superpower conflict and instead act as a bridge between the two superpowers.[34] Thus it is not sufficient to ask only to what extent European countries became 'Americanized', or how the USA influenced European societies. One also has to look carefully at different fields of American influence (military, financial, economic, cultural) and at the various ways in which influence was exerted (by official government policy or through the unofficial involvement of secret services, via private foundations and/or certain eminent individuals).

In his reinterpretation of the Marshall Plan, Carlo Spagnolo analyses the impact of the US government's European Recovery Programme in Britain, France, Germany, and Italy. In doing so, he demonstrates the degree to which the USA's plans for domestic, security, and economic policy with respect to Western Europe were intertwined.[35] Spagnolo sees the Marshall Plan as part of a comprehensive strategy, ultimately geared towards establishing a new world order under American hegemony. As far as American strategists were concerned, securing peace and saving liberal capitalism went hand in hand. The threat, as they perceived it, came not only from the Soviet Union, but also from

---

[34] With the benefit of hindsight, however, the inclination of Germans to take a neutralist stand in the Cold War was never as great as many of Germany's Western allies feared at the time; cf. Alexander Gallus, *Die Neutralisten: Verfechter eines vereinigten Deutschland zwischen Ost und West 1945–1990* (Düsseldorf, 2001).

[35] For a survey of the most recent research on the topic see Kathleen Burk, 'The Marshall Plan: Filling in Some of the Blanks', *Contemporary European History*, 10/2 (2001), 267–94.

the disastrous consequences of the war in Western Europe. The fact that entire population groups had been driven out and families split up paved the way, as the Americans saw it, for socialism to take over the western half of the continent. That is why it was essential to create a stable political and economic situation. US decision-makers, however, soon found out that the West European recipients of their aid programmes were often awkward partners. More than once, European and American notions of social ideals, the function of the state, and the role of individuals came into conflict with each other. Sometimes it was only the common fear of the Soviet menace that united both sides and kept Euro-American conflicts under control. To this extent, as Spagnolo provocatively puts it, the Cold War might have been necessary to get the Marshall Plan through.

Volker Berghahn adds a further dimension to the picture of American postwar planning for Western Europe: the cultural one.[36] In American eyes the threat posed to Western Europe by the Soviet Union was not confined to the political, military, and economic spheres, but extended to culture as well. 'The Cold War', Berghahn writes, 'was not just about which side had the superior economic-technological and power-political potential for shaping the future. The conflict was also about the power of ideas and the greater creative energy that the two sides could mobilize in cultural terms.' In many respects the cultural counter-offensive was more difficult than most other measures, for although the Western Europeans had reluctantly accepted American political, military, and economic superiority at the end of the 1940s, they were unwilling to give up their own feeling of superiority in cultural matters. For its part, America believed it had won the cultural Cold War against the Soviet Union by the mid-1950s, while attempts to influence Western Europe still had to continue. The ups and downs of US cultural policies in Western Europe, which Berghahn analyses, were partly due to the shift in American domestic politics from the Democratic Truman administration to the Republican Eisenhower government. Berghahn demonstrates that a combination of McCarthyism and the fiscal restraint of the new Eisenhower

---

[36] For a more detailed discussion of the cultural Cold Wars see Dominik Geppert, 'Cultural Aspects of the Cold War', *Bulletin of the German Historical Institute London*, 24/2 (Nov. 2002), 50–71.

administration led to a shift in American cultural policies. The official government channels, which had fed US cultural institutions in Europe, dried up while both unofficial funding by the CIA and the financial involvement of big private foundations gained importance.

Michael Hochgeschwender extends the discussion about the US cultural offensive by presenting an important concrete example: the Congress for Cultural Freedom (CCF). This was an organization of European and American intellectuals financed by the CIA, and later by the Ford Foundation, which interpreted the Cold War primarily as an intellectual conflict. The work of the Congress, which had national branches in the USA as well as in France, Italy, Britain, and the Federal Republic of Germany, was intended to be supranational, but none the less exhibited certain significant national peculiarities. In the Federal Republic and Britain, where there were no strong Communist parties, the focus was on combating national neutralism or Communist fellow-travellers. Apart from that, CCF intellectuals tried to move the Labour Party and the SPD away from left-wing or Marxist dogmatism towards a more centrist position, not least by intensifying communications across the Atlantic with reform-oriented liberals in the USA. In France and Italy, on the other hand, it was more a question of curbing the intellectual influence of the Communists and breaking down anti-American prejudices while at the same time combating anti-liberal, conservative Roman Catholicism.

It was no accident that the CCF's foundation in the summer of 1950 took place at a large public meeting in Berlin of all places. The city played a central role not only as a crisis point in the power-political struggle but as a place of symbolic significance as well. Western propaganda praised Berlin as the 'front-line city of the Cold War', as a 'bastion' or 'bulwark' of freedom.[37] The initiators of Radio Free Europe (RFE), a Munich-based American radio station which was crucial for US propaganda in Eastern Europe, were among the first to utilize the symbolic power of the divided city for their purposes. They commissioned a foundry to cast a bell resembling the American

[37] On Berlin's symbolic role in the Cold War see Andreas W. Daum, 'America's Berlin 1945–2000: Between Myths and Visions', in Frank Trommler (ed.), *Berlin: The New Capital in the East. A Transatlantic Appraisal* (Washington, DC, 2000), 49–73.

liberty bell in Philadelphia. This so-called 'freedom bell' toured through the USA, raising funds for RFE's 'Crusade for Freedom', and was finally sent to Berlin in October 1950, where, in a huge public ceremony, it was put in the belfry of Rathaus Schöneberg, the West Berlin city hall. Through this act, the 'spirit of America' was symbolically transferred to Berlin.[38]

Dominik Geppert uses the history of the freedom bell to analyse the symbolic and rhetorical dimensions of the Cold War. He focuses not only on the people and institutions that were responsible for the project (RFE and the 'National Committee for a Free Europe'/NCFE), but also on the rhetoric of 'freedom versus tyranny' which surrounded the Berlin bell. Like the Congress for Cultural Freedom, the NCFE used the language of anti-totalitarianism to rally support for the US-led struggle against Communism in the USA and in Western Europe. Both the Committee and the Congress were part of the 'state–private network' which Berghahn analyses in his chapter.[39] But there were also a number of important differences. The CCF initially concentrated its efforts on France, Italy, and Britain, whereas RFE and the NCFE assigned Germany and the Communist states of Eastern Europe a central role in their strategy. The Congress tried to attract cultural and intellectual élites by publishing a number of very influential highbrow magazines and by organizing conferences, exhibitions, and seminars. The Committee and its Crusade for Freedom, on the other hand, appealed to a mass audience and tried to mobilize as many people as possible. The CCF members' urban cosmopolitanism differed sharply from the more conservative outlook of the average American or European who supported the Crusade's activities. The former were distinctively liberal and secular in outlook, whereas the latter were often attracted by the traditional or religious overtones in American propaganda. Although the CIA played an important funding role in both cases, its influence on the public statements of the CCF and NCFE's Radio Free Europe seems to have been markedly different. In contrast to the

---

[38] Diethelm Prowe, 'Brennpunkt des Kalten Krieges: Berlin in den deutsch-amerikanischen Beziehungen', in Detlef Junker (ed.), *Die USA und Deutschland im Zeitalter des Kalten Krieges: Ein Handbuch* (Stuttgart, 2001), i. 260–70, at 262.

[39] The term 'state–private network' was coined by Scott Lucas, *Freedom's War: The American Crusade Against the Soviet Union* (New York, 1999).

Congress, the policy of the radio station was influenced, at least temporarily and partially, by the secret service.

It would be wrong, however, to assume that the CIA participated in, or even controlled, every American propaganda effort in the Cold War. Toby Thacker's case study of American music and reorientation in Germany makes clear that the State Department and the American High Commission for Germany (HICOG) played a much more important part in attempts to introduce American music to Germany than the secret service. Thacker does not concentrate on jazz, which has often been used as a symbol for the 'Americanization' of Western Europe and Germany in particular.[40] Instead, he focuses on US efforts to popularize American concert music by various means such as supporting performances, broadcasting recordings as well as live performances, publishing articles, sponsoring lecture tours, and the like. His contribution is a reminder that the usual distinction between the European, especially German, notion of high culture (*Kultur*), which could be attained only by an educated élite, and the American concept of popular culture, was not as clear-cut as is often assumed. The deliberate attempts by US cultural diplomats to popularize American concert music in Germany demonstrate that there were exponents of high culture on the other side of the Atlantic too. Moreover, their efforts are a good example of the American desire to combat the cultural anti-Americanism of the European élites. 'Millions of dollars were spent in this struggle and it may well be that no other hegemonic power in history has ever invested as much as the United States did after World War II in changing foreigners' perception of it as a civilization', as Berghahn has written.[41] But Thacker also reminds us of the limits of this American struggle. He states that by the mid-1950s the programme of introducing American concert music appeared to have been largely unsuccessful—not least because of deep-rooted anti-American prejudices and feelings of cultural superiority in Germany. 'No one country,' Thacker concludes, 'however rich and powerful, can, even if physically occupying another, and in control of its information

---

[40] See e.g. Uta G. Poiger, *Jazz, Rock and Rebels: Cold War Politics and American Culture in a Divided Germany* (Berkeley, 2000).

[41] Volker Berghahn, *America and the Intellectual Cold Wars in Europe: Shepherd Stone between Philanthropy, Academy, and Diplomacy* (Princeton, 2001), 289.

media, simply choose which parts of its culture it wishes to impose upon the other.'

Three closely related themes run through almost all the essays in this volume. First, all essays emphasize the fluidity and uncertainty of the period from 1945 to 1958. The dichotomous character of the Cold War international system did not immediately become apparent to all policy-makers in Western Europe. The political paradigms of the inter-war period still loomed large with many members of the postwar political élite. Nor did the idea of a supranational European alternative to the nationalisms of the past rapidly gain ground in Western Europe after 1945. British statesmen were not alone in their scepticism towards the concept of European integration. In the years up to 1958 there were important changes to be made which decisively shaped future developments.

Second, the precarious balance between American influence and genuinely European driving forces recurs frequently. Some contributors support the thesis of the primacy of the USA; others maintain that the postwar period should no longer be regarded as the end of the European era in world history, but as a pivotal decade in the European twentieth century. In their view, the reorientation of historical research since 1989 means there is a chance 'to give European history back to the Europeans'.[42] Others insist that American influence on Western European history in the second half of the twentieth century cannot be overestimated. Europeans might speak various dialects, they argue, but the common language, which all use, is American English.

The third complex of questions is closely connected with this. How important were national peculiarities when reacting to common challenges—for example, the threat from the USSR, the need for social security in the welfare state, or attitudes to the USA's hegemonic role? And vice versa: to what extent were developments in the postwar societies similar to one another despite national differences? What role was played, for example, by different state traditions in the development of an interventionist and welfare state after 1945?[43] How important was the—

---

[42] As Mark Mazower provocatively put it at the conference on which this volume is based.

[43] Cf. Hans Schauer, *Europäische Identität und demokratische Tradition: Zum Staatsverständnis in Deutschland, Frankreich und Großbritannien* (Munich, 1996).

partly real, partly perceived—menace from the Soviet Union in keeping differences inside the Western camp under control? The concept of national *Sonderwege* does not allow us to deal adequately with questions like these.[44] Its basic flaw is that it implies a comparative approach, which, in the end, it does not deliver. Instead, it will be one of the main tasks of future research to analyse both the converging and the diverging effects of the Cold War.

The essays in this volume do not intend to provide a definitive analysis of these effects, or even a conclusive account of the cultural, social, and political changes in Britain, France, Germany and Italy after the Second World War. Rather, they intend to contribute to ongoing discussions—or in many respects ones that are just beginning. There are many obvious gaps in this volume. The tensions between the nation-state and the regions, for example, are not discussed; nor is the sometimes painful transition that former imperial and/or colonial powers underwent as they entered the post-colonial world. Another limitation is geographical. Britain, France, Italy, and Germany are only a part of Western Europe. But so are the Benelux countries, and wartime neutrals like Spain, Portugal, and Switzerland, which are not covered in this volume. Those countries deserve fuller treatment, but their inclusion would have at least doubled the content of the volume. A further particularly conspicuous gap is gender, for women were allowed to vote for the first time in France in 1945 and in Italy in 1946. In the following years, women voters significantly contributed to the electoral victories of Christian Democratic parties, for example in the Federal Republic of Germany.[45] It has been argued, moreover, that women's distaste for ideology and their loyalty to individual leaders such as Adenauer and de Gaulle did much to shape the specific political style (consensual rather than confrontational) of

---

[44] The concept has recently been revitalized by Heinrich A. Winkler for the case of postwar Germany; cf. Heinrich A. Winkler, *Der lange Weg nach Westen*, ii (Stuttgart, 2001); see also Anselm Doering-Mateuffel, 'Eine politische Nationalgeschichte für die Berliner Republik: Überlegungen zu Heinrich August Winklers "Der lange Weg nach Westen"', *Geschichte und Gesellschaft*, 27 (2001), 446–62, and, more generally, Anthony J. Nicholls, 'The Myth of the German *Sonderweg*', in Cyril Buffet and Beatrice Heuser (eds.), *Haunted by History: Myths in International Relations* (New York, 1998), 209 ff.

[45] Cf. Frank Bösch, *Die Adenauer-CDU: Gründung, Aufstieg und Krise einer Erfolgspartei, 1945–1969* (Stuttgart, 2001).

the postwar era.[46] It might be fruitful to take this hypothesis as a starting point for an analysis of the impact of women voters on the different political systems of Western European states after 1945. If this volume stimulates some of its readers to study these and other aspects of Europe's common, but diversified history in the postwar years, it will have achieved its main purpose.

---

[46] Vinen, *A History in Fragments*, 379.

PART I

Coming to Terms with the Past

2

Coping with the Burdens of the Past: German Politics and Society in the 1950s

Norbert Frei

If we accept that there is such a thing as 'political culture', even the 'political culture of a nation', many Germans and many observers from abroad would probably agree that Germany's political culture is to a large degree characterized by a constant awareness of the past. And, of course, 'the past' here means not just history in general, but almost exclusively the Nazi past. There is even a special word for this German speciality. It is untranslatable and ugly, and highly problematic if taken literally, but was originally meant in an anti-apologetic, self-critical way when it was coined in the late 1950s: *Vergangenheitsbewältigung*, usually rendered as 'coming to terms with the past'. Literally it has the connotation of a process that is done once and for all, but again, this was not the original intention.

A willingness to go on reflecting critically about the period of National Socialism can indeed be seen as a feature specific to the political culture of the present-day Federal Republic. But this has not always been the case, and it was particularly not so during the 1950s.

Historians, it is true, love the *Vorgeschichte*, the story not behind but before the story. In this case, however, it could be argued that this is more than a professional obsession. One cannot properly analyse how the Germans coped with the Nazi past during the 1950s without understanding what had happened in this respect immediately after the war, that is, in the period of direct

Instead of providing footnotes for this essay, I refer the reader to my study, *Vergangenheitspolitik: Die Anfänge der Bundesrepublik und die NS-Vergangenheit* (Munich, 1996; paperback 1999), now available in English as *Adenauer's Germany and the Nazi Past: The Politics of Amnesty and Integration* (New York, 2002).

Allied rule during the second half of the 1940s. In fact, it seems useful to identify three phases which are relevant to how the Germans coped with the Nazi past in the 1950s.

First, and often overlooked, was the period of the politics of purge which lasted from 1945 to the end of direct occupation in 1949 (section I). Secondly, there was the actual period of *Vergangenheitspolitik* (policy of the past), which more or less began with the foundation of the Federal Republic in 1949 and peaked during the mid-1950s (section II). And thirdly, there was the emerging period of *Vergangenheitsbewältigung*, understood as a critical approach to the impact of *Vergangenheitspolitik*. This started late in the 1950s and intensified in the 1960s (Section III).

I. *The Politics of Purge*

With regard to the first phase, the politics of purge, it is historically inadequate to describe those years simply as a period of failed denazification. For between the end of the war and the beginning of the Adenauer government, war criminals were indicted on serious charges, Nazi officials were put into detention camps, and bystanders *(Mitläufer)* were confronted with their political guilt.

Judicial purges were not limited to the Nuremberg Trial of twenty-four top members of the Nazi Party, the state, and the *Wehrmacht*. Before and after the International Military Tribunal, there were military trials in each of the four Zones of Occupation. The French, the British, and the Americans took a total of about 5,000 perpetrators to court. No less than 800 of them were sentenced to death, and about one third were executed. During the Follow-up Trials in Nuremberg, which were held by the Americans alone, about 180 representatives of the German élite were put on trial. Four out of five of them were found guilty, and twelve people were hanged.

Immediately after the end of the war, the Allies started a massive programme of subjecting party officials and SS members to 'automatic arrest'. By the end of 1945 the Americans alone had taken about 100,000 Germans into custody. The overall figure was more than twice as high. And while many experienced this kind of detention only for a couple of weeks or months, a significant number were imprisoned for up to three years, usually in former concentration camps but with better food and treatment.

The endemic problem of the bystanders was addressed in a vigorous policy regarding the German *Berufsbeamtentum* (civil service). After some random dismissals during the first few weeks in order to minimize the potential for political resistance and to break up Nazi networks, every civil servant in the American Zone of Occupation who had been a member of the Nazi Party before May 1937 had to leave his desk. A few hundred thousand German *Beamte* (civil servants) were affected by this, and it is easy to believe that some were right in perceiving themselves to have been unjustly treated.

Most Germans, however, regarded this as typical of the whole process of denazification, which they considered a complete failure. They almost welcomed these flaws as starting points for a far-reaching critique. Thus even before the Federal Republic came into being, the policy of political purge had been fundamentally challenged. When Adenauer took over in 1949, the German public expected a general revision regarding the handling of the past. And in many respects, this was exactly what happened.

II. *The Period of* Vergangenheitspolitik

The meaning of this period could be summed up as *Bewältigung der frühen NS-Bewältigung* (coming to terms with the early attempts to come to terms with the Nazi past). In the early years of the Federal Republic denazification policies were completely abolished, and even more importantly, almost all of those who perceived themselves as victims of a political purge were largely reintegrated. However, counterbalancing these decisions to some extent, the period was also characterized by a general political reaffirmation of the anti-Nazi consensus of the immediate postwar years. In other words, the key elements of *Vergangenheitspolitik* were amnesty, integration, and demarcation.

Immediately after the constitution of the Bundestag calls were made for a *Bundesamnestie*, an amnesty law. In fact, there was no party in the Bonn Parliament which did not press for this law, which came into force at the end of December 1949, despite considerable reservations on the part of the Allied High Commissioners. The law granted an amnesty to everyone charged with offences committed before 15 September 1949 and punishable by up to six months' imprisonment. About 800,000 people benefited from this law. While the majority had committed non-political offences during the period of hunger and black markets, the amnesty also applied to crimes of the Nazi era which had not yet come under the statute of limitations. And a special clause took care of those Nazi officials and SS members who had assumed a false identity in 1945 in order to avoid prosecution. They now had a chance to become 'legal' again.

Official statistics do not tell us how many Nazi perpetrators profited from the amnesty. However, there are indications that the figure was some tens of thousands, and included those who participated in the *Kristallnacht* pogroms of November 1938. Even those who were responsible for deaths may have got away without punishment because the law also granted amnesty in cases of assault and certain degrees of manslaughter.

Neither the public nor the majority of parliamentary deputies were informed about these details, either before or after the law was passed. The bureaucrats of the Ministry of Justice, most of whom had served under Hitler, effectively concealed the dark consequences of their law, and even the Secretary of Justice, Thomas Dehler (Free Democratic Party, FDP), and the other expert lawyers of the Bundestag were not open on this issue. Instead, they talked vaguely about the confusion and lack of justice which had been the result of that 'difficult period' that had only now, in 1949, come to an end. And all of them emphasized how important it was to 'forget about the past'. Thus the amnesty law became a symbol of a *Vergangenheitspolitik* which was only beginning.

This was partly the result of an incorrect but widespread perception that the *Bundesamnestie* was the final political blow against denazification. Only two months after the amnesty law, in February 1950, the FDP managed to force upon the Bundestag a debate about federal guidelines for what was called the 'liquidation' of denazification. While this debate made no sense at all (because the denazification programme was governed by *Länder*, not federal law), all parties in the Bundestag were

happy to display their resentment at any further use of denazification procedures. The Christian Democratic Union (CDU) and
the Social Democratic Party (SPD), which was in opposition, felt
under pressure to compete with the verbal outbursts of the
representatives of right-wing parties such as the Deutsche Partei
(DP) and the FDP who presented themselves as rigorous lobbyists for *Vergangenheitspolitik*. The remarkable result was that for the
second time since the amnesty law, the CDU and SPD joined
forces in order to prevent implementation of the most radical
suggestions of the right-wing parties.

None the less, the debate about the end of denazification and
the amnesty law were publicly perceived as politically legitimizing the idea of a *Schlußstrich* (closing line). And at the same time
the debate delegitimized any further judicial attempts to proceed
against Nazi perpetrators. These attempts had been hampered
for years by the fact that almost all of the judges who had been
fired in 1945 were back in office again. For the civil service in
general and the judicial system in particular, there was no need
for a special law to set in motion the process of reintegrating all
the civil servants who had lost their jobs in 1945. However, a
lenient and integrationist policy towards the past was signalled
when in April 1951 the Bundestag, again without any opposition,
passed the infamous 'Organizational Law to Settle the Judicial
Interests of Persons who are Eligible under Article 131 of the
Basic Law' (*Gesetz zur Regelung der Rechtsverhältnisse der unter Artikel
131 des Grundgesetzes fallenden Personen*). Some ten thousand former
civil servants benefited from this law, despite their Nazi past,
thus clearly pointing to the idea of a *Schlußstrich*. From that
moment on, almost nobody from the old guard of civil servants
who had been forced out of office under Allied Occupation
'suffered' any longer. They were absolved from any further need
to think about their individual and collective failures during the
Third Reich. As it happened, the Federal Republic generously
acknowledged the claims of the servants of the old Reich, and re-
established their former status.

The recklessness of the civil servants' lobby and all their tricks
and manoeuvres, which ultimately meant that even former
members of the Gestapo were able to return to public service,
makes the law relating to Article 131 appear as a turning point.
From 1953 to the mid-1960s, its already mild restrictions were

further relaxed just before every federal election, and the
generosity of this process resulted in a deteriorating public
morality towards the past. With fewer and fewer inhibitions,
almost every Nazi bureaucrat who considered himself eligible
came out of the closet. After a while, even former *Waffen-SS* officers demanded state jobs or pensions. And as far as the public
mood was concerned, it was telling that the term *Wiedergutmachung* had almost lost its original meaning relating to the
efforts regarding the victims of National Socialism. In the early
1950s the alleged victims of denazification perceived themselves
as 'victims of de-Nazification' (*Entnazifizierungsgeschädigte*) and
called for *Wiedergutmachung*.

Small wonder, then, that there were also public pleas for a
General Amnesty. In 1952 a group of right-wing lawyers and
politicians established the Steering Committee for the
Preparation of a General Amnesty. The central figure of the
committee was Ernst Achenbach, a former diplomat and
defence lawyer during the IG Farben Trial in Nuremberg, now
a member of the FDP and a lawyer in Essen with excellent
connections to Ruhr magnates such as Hugo Stinnes, Jr.

Compared with the demands of the most radical *Schlußstrich*
lobbyists, Achenbach, and the SS mastermind behind the
scenes, Werner Best, the relevant parts of the second amnesty
law which the Bundestag passed in the summer of 1954 seemed
almost restrictive. In fact, however, the second amnesty law
went a considerable way further than the first one of 1949.
Again, the conservative coalition and the Social Democrats
made great efforts to balance the law so that every deputy could
accept it. *Vergangenheitspolitik*, it cannot be repeated too often,
relied heavily on a broad political consensus. And although
there were some difficult moments when right-wing liberals
pushed for the Best–Achenbach concept while some Social
Democrats thought that it was too lenient, a symbolic unity was
achieved. With very few dissenters, the Bundestag voted to
repeat the 1949 offer to all those Nazis who had gone underground in 1945. But the 'illegals' were not the only ones to benefit. The 1954 amnesty law also applied to those perpetrators
whose deeds fell into the period from 1 October 1944 to 31 July
1945.

Anybody who could claim that they had acted under the

assumption that it was their official or judicial duty *(Amts-, Dienst- oder Rechtspflicht)* or that they were carrying out an order from above was no longer to be put on trial if the expected punishment did not exceed three years' imprisonment. This, of course, meant that even people indicted for manslaughter got off without a trial if, for example, they had killed innocent people who, in the spring of 1945, had hung out a white flag too early. As a result, the bulk of the crimes of the final period of the Third Reich, the *Endphase-Verbrechen*, were never subject to judicial investigation.

The politics of amnesty meant that the number of new indictments of Nazi criminals dropped to an all-time low. In 1950, the West German justice system had filed accusations against 2,500 suspects; in 1954 there were only 183 new cases. And there were by no means objective reasons for this decline. During the mid-1950s hardly anyone in the Federal Republic had to worry about their Nazi past any longer. The risk that they might be the subject of political or judicial investigation was almost zero.

But *Vergangenheitspolitik* did not stop there. On the contrary, the political bargaining even for those perpetrators who had been convicted of appalling deeds continued. During the immediate postwar period the Catholic and (even more) the Protestant Church had been the main organizers of the protest against the alleged victors' justice of vengeance *(Siegerjustiz)*. But from 1949 on, lobbying on behalf of war criminals became a central task of Bonn's *Vergangenheitspolitik*. Interestingly enough, neither representatives of the Churches, such as the Protestant bishop, Wurm, or the Catholic bishop, Neuhäusler, nor politicians ever argued for clemency on the grounds of a religious disapproval of capital punishment. Most were motivated by nationalist resentment against the Allied War Crimes Trial Programme—a resentment which they were incapable of hiding.

As early as the spring of 1951, the Adenauer government, with the support of virtually all German newspapers, had managed to talk the Allies, and in particular the Americans, into some generous acts of clemency. The best-known single part of this retreat from the earlier programme of punishment was the decision by the American High Commissioner, John McCloy, to release about one third of the remaining eighty-nine inmates of Landsberg prison and to reduce the sentences of another half of them; only five of fifteen pending death sentences were confirmed. However, if the Americans believed that the German agitation against the War Crimes Trial Programme would end after this act of clemency, they were in for a frustrating experience. In fact, McCloy's gesture triggered further demands.

After the Landsberg decision there were only about 1,800 'Germans in Western Allied custody', as Bonn's euphemistic jargon had it. But government officials made enormous efforts to persuade the Allies to accept a radical solution to the problem of war criminals. Some highly sensitive diplomats in the German Foreign Office even spoke of an *Endlösung der Kriegsverbrecherfrage* (final solution to the problem of war criminals)—there can be no doubt that by that time everybody was aware of Nazi terminology.

From the start, the Adenauer government had been more than supportive when the fate of war criminals was at stake. The extent of its support is probably illustrated best by a clear institutional contradiction. The Central Office for the Prosecution of Nazi Crimes (the *Zentrale Stelle der Landesjustizverwaltungen* in Ludwigsburg) was not established until December 1958. By contrast, the Central Office for the Protection of Rights *(Zentrale Rechtsschutzstelle)* had been founded within the Federal Ministry of Justice in 1949—again, with the consent of all parties in the Bundestag. The mission of this office was much clearer than its official name: the *Zentrale Rechtsschutzstelle* had to ensure that every German in foreign custody received a proper defence. While superficially this policy appeared to offer no more than the usual protection that any decent democracy would grant its citizens, in reality it protected Germans who had been accused or convicted of war crimes, whether in foreign countries (such as France, the Netherlands, or Belgium) or during the Allied War Crimes Trial Programme in Germany. In fact, the *Zentrale Rechtsschutzstelle* spent a considerable proportion of its budget on defence lawyers not outside Germany, but on those who were acting for convicted war criminals in the Allied detention centres in Landsberg, Werl, and Wittlich, and, of course, on the *Hauptkriegsverbrecher* (major war criminals) in Spandau.

We do not know what Adenauer's personal feelings on the question of war criminals were, but there is no suggestion that he was personally involved to the extent that many of his cabinet members were. However, Adenauer knew all too well that the German public expected the government to do everything it could to get the war criminals out of Allied custody, and he was aware that these demands, if not taken seriously, could easily be transformed into broader nationalist resentments. And, above all, Adenauer knew that his government had to be successful in order to satisfy the demands of the military circles *(soldatische Kreise)* whose self-esteem had been reinforced by the outbreak of the Korean War. Their basic line had been stated in the famous *Himmeroder Denkschrift* of October 1950 and reinforced by Speidel and Heusinger, Adenauer's military advisers: any German defence contribution is unthinkable so long as German soldiers are imprisoned. During the Western Treaties negotiations in 1953 and 1955 this was reason enough for the Chancellor to put his personal prestige at stake. And in fact, against the resistance of the Allied High Commissioners, Adenauer did achieve a solution of the war criminal issue. As a result, in 1958 the last of those who, ten years previously, had been convicted not as 'ordinary soldiers' but as leaders of SS Special Forces *(Einsatzgruppen)* were released.

The ethical implications of this leniency, which contradicted the public understanding of how fundamentally criminal and murderous the Nazi system and warfare had been, were probably even more important than the actual releases of perpetrators. It seems that ultimately the public struggle for a couple of hundred war criminals had a much deeper meaning. The struggle was about the political morale and self-esteem of millions of soldiers: acknowledgement of the truth about the Nazi *Weltanschauungskrieg* (ideological war) had to be sacrificed in order to strengthen the belief of 'ordinary men' that they had risked their lives in a good cause, and that they had fought for the future of the German people. To achieve this reassurance, an image of the past was needed that would function as a cover-up for the historical facts that had been established by the Allies in the late 1940s.

In order to counterbalance the strategies of amnesty and integration, *Vergangenheitspolitik* involved a third element: the policy of normative demarcation *(normative Abgrenzung)*. To some extent, this anti-Nazi demarcation must be seen as an attempt to fulfil Allied expectations. But it would be unfair to assume that there was no genuine wish on the German side to stabilize the anti-Nazi consensus of the Federal Republic's founding fathers. As amnesty and integration continued, this consensus of 1945 seemed to lose impetus, and because of this a series of reaffirmative executive and judicial actions were taken from 1949. However, they took place at a significantly lower level. Thus, there were a number of cases in which politicians had to agitate for judges to act against neo-Nazism. Generally speaking, public prosecutors and courts took action only against people who openly justified Nazi crimes, in particular, the murder of the Jews, or who seriously criticized the legitimacy of the anti-Hitler resistance movement.

For example, in February 1950 only massive public protests prevented the politician, Wolfgang Hedler, a member of the right-wing DP and a member of the Bundestag, from getting away with insulting Holocaust survivors and the officers of the 20 July 1944 movement, whom he called traitors. At first acquitted by a *Landgericht*, a higher court sent Hedler to prison for nine months. As in the Hedler case, it was largely due to an energetic public prosecutor and political pressure from Bonn that in 1952 Otto Remer, the hero of the Sozialistische Reichspartei (SRP), was put on trial. Remer, who had been in charge of the security battalion Großdeutschland on 20 July 1944, on a number of occasions publicly accused the plotters of breaking their oath of loyalty to Hitler.

The Hedler case and the Remer trial, the latter dominated by the prosecutor general in Brunswick, Fritz Bauer, clearly served to establish the limits of a *Vergangenheitspolitik* which, on the whole, had become generous and extensively integrationist. This was even more true of the decision by the newly established *Bundesverfassungsgericht* (Supreme Court) which, on the request of the Adenauer government, banned the Sozialistische Reichspartei in the autumn of 1952 because of its all too obvious similarities with the Nazi party. While this prohibition had been encouraged by the Allied High Commissioners (particularly John McCloy, who in conversation with Adenauer repeatedly expressed his concerns), the most spectacular action against the threat of growing neo-Nazism was taken by the British High Commissioner without the help of the German authorities. In January 1953 Sir Ivone Kirkpatrick ordered the imprisonment of a group of six former high-ranking Nazis who, according to British Military Intelligence, had infiltrated the FDP in North Rhine–Westphalia and were poised to gain control over the party's political programme. This group was led by Werner Naumann, who had been Goebbels's deputy in the Reich Ministry for Propaganda. Despite evidence suggesting that the group posed a serious political threat, German politicians and public opinion immediately complained that the British had ignored German sovereignty.

Only Adenauer, who had received confidential information from Kirkpatrick, refrained from joining the chorus. Adenauer was aware that Kirkpatrick's coup had been an effective warning to all those who thought that a redefined Nazism could make a political comeback. In fact, the detention of the Naumann group put an end to all speculation about a unified national party to the right of Adenauer's Western-orientated CDU. The 1953 federal election showed that the Chancellor's party was the clear winner both of the action against the Naumann circle and of *Vergangenheitspolitik* in general.

All these acts of anti-Nazi demarcation, of course, occurred only on the far right. However, they served not only as a warning but as a normative definition, defining how far anybody could go before risking access to the political arena. During this process of demarcation any positive ideological acknowledgement of National Socialism and anti-Semitism became taboo. Except for the detention of the Naumann group, all of these acts of demarcation had been carried out by the Germans themselves, but always with the awareness of possible Allied intervention. The argument that Germany was watched over by the Allies (or by the foreign media) was one of the main rhetorical figures of *Vergangenheitspolitik* in the 1950s—and for decades to come.

III. *The Advent of* Vergangenheitsbewältigung

From the mid-1950s on *Vergangenheitspolitik* was questioned because of the moral scandals it had produced and the problems it had left unresolved. Young people, liberal intellectuals, and leftist politicians began more clearly to express their scepticism, leading to the new term *unbewältigte Vergangenheit* (unmastered past).

Fuelled by events like the publication of *The Diary of Anne Frank* or, as early as 1955, protests by students and professors against the appointment of a radical right-wing publisher as Minister of Education and Arts in Lower Saxony, the concept of *Vergangenheitsbewältigung* took shape. A seemingly endless number of scandals about personal and institutional continuities with the Nazi past heightened the increasingly moralizing quest for *Vergangenheitsbewältigung*.

There is much evidence that the GDR provided a crucial impetus for a more critical analysis of Nazi history in the Federal Republic of the late 1950s and early 1960s. A regime which had already retreated to a position of declamatory anti-fascism was discovering that the accusation of an 'unmastered past' was a superb instrument for discrediting the Bonn republic politically and morally. Campaigns against Hans Globke, the head of Adenauer's chancellery, who had written a legal comment on the Nuremberg Race Laws of 1935, and against Theodor Oberländer, the Nazi expert on the East who became Minister for Refugees under Adenauer, undoubtedly had an enormous impact on West German youth and on critical observers in the Western democracies. And this also holds true for tens of thousands of leaflets entitled *Hitler's Murderous Judges in Adenauer's Service*, which East Berlin found ways of distributing in West Germany. The outing of the Nazi careers of many other high-ranking officials, which was largely made possible by files from East Berlin archives, encouraged the circle of those in the Federal Republic calling for *Vergangenheitsbewältigung* to expand.

Intellectuals such as Theodor W. Adorno and Karl Jaspers, a number of liberal journalists, and representatives of the new academic discipline of contemporary history, pushed education about the 'recent past' in the media and in schools. Finally, the scandalous judicial failings of the 1950s also resulted in the perpetrators being looked at more closely. The Auschwitz Trial in Frankfurt, which was instigated by a small group of lawyers around Fritz Bauer in 1963 and decisively supported by survivors of the camp, such as Hermann Langbein, marked a turning-point. From now on, there was a small but highly active network of politicians and lawyers, artists and intellectuals, who effectively opposed the idea of a *Schlußstrich*.

The agonizing Bundestag debates of the 1960s and 1970s,

which ultimately decided that there was no statute of limitations for murder, were as much a testimony to the changed social climate as the critical attitude of the children of the war towards their parents. Future historical research might demonstrate that not only the ubiquitous personal continuities with the Third Reich but also the refusal of parents in the 1950s to talk to the younger generation resulted in the specific profile of the students' revolt of 1968 in Germany.

The most crucial outcome of this long phase of *Vergangenheits-bewältigung*, however, is turning out to be that the central crime of the Nazi period, the murder of the European Jews, entered the public awareness only with a significant delay. Despite all the facts made available by contemporary historians and the media as early as the 1960s, it was the American TV series on the Holocaust, broadcast in 1979 that, as the title of the book of the series points out, 'affected a whole nation'.

3
Reshaping the Past: Collective Memory and the Second World War in Italy, 1945–1955

FILIPPO FOCARDI

This essay argues that between 1943 and 1947 anti-fascist forces in Italy successfully elaborated a collective memory of the war which they imposed as the public memory of the new state and as the dominant social memory. The key features of this narrative were a portrayal of the Italians as 'victims' of fascism and of a war desired by Mussolini, a re-dimensioning of Italian responsibility in the Axis war, the blame for which was laid entirely upon the Duce and the former German ally, and, finally, a glorification of the role played by the Italian people in the struggle against Nazi Germany and its fascist allies after the armistice. This memory was put under considerable strain during the first parliamentary term in the years 1948–53, coinciding with the definitive breakdown in the unity of the anti-fascist forces and the development of the Cold War. Nevertheless, it was not replaced by a dominant alternative memory; on the contrary it was confirmed and re-launched in the mid-1950s, effectively before 1960, which is generally identified by Italian historians as the year in which the anti-fascist memory of the war was revived.[1]

The memory of the war which was confirmed in Republican Italy had its roots in the representation of the conflict which the anti-fascist forces had made immediately after the armistice of 8 September 1943, the day on which Italy had surrendered to the Allied nations, and on which the Nazi occupation had begun.

[1] On this point, see Filippo Focardi, 'La memoria della guerra e della Resistenza nei discorsi commemorativi e nel dibattito politico italiano (1943–2001)', *Novecento*, 5 (2001), 91–128.

This portrayal was triggered by a number of fundamental political requirements shared by the entire anti-fascist front, that is, by the monarchy and the Badoglio government, which had fled from Rome to take refuge in the south of Italy already liberated by the Allies, and by the resurrected parties of the Committee of National Liberation. These were: (1) a need to counter the propaganda of the Italian Social Republic which stigmatized the armistice as a 'betrayal' of the nation and of the German ally, and invited the Italians to continue the struggle alongside the Third Reich; (2) a need to mobilize the country for the struggle against Germany (upon which Victor Emmanuel III had declared war on 13 October 1943); and (3) a need to convince the Allies to overturn Italy's armistice status, since, although recognized as a 'co-belligerent' state alongside the Allied nations, it nevertheless remained a conquered enemy subject to unconditional surrender.

The response to this threefold need took the form of an intensive propaganda effort which hinged primarily on the elaboration of a reading of the past condensed into interpretative slogans and clichés relating to the past experience of fascism, the Italo-German alliance, and Italy's participation in the Axis war. At the same time, it built up into a codified image of the enemy: the Hun.

Who was the traitor? This was the crucial question on which fascism and anti-fascism clashed. Reversing the accusations of 'betrayal' made by the propaganda of Salò,[2] the anti-fascist front retorted that the person who had betrayed the Italians and led the nation to ruin was Mussolini. He had imposed an alliance 'against nature' with Hitler's Germany which everyone opposed, precipitating the country into a war which was 'neither desired nor supported' (this expression was used by Badoglio and later adopted by the entire anti-fascist front).[3] Benedetto Croce, the well-known philosopher and a prominent member of the Liberal Party, spoke, for example, of a 'foolish and ill-omened alliance', the fruit of a 'party pact' running completely counter to the

---

[2] On the propaganda of the republican fascist government cf. Mario Isnenghi (ed.), *1943–45: L'immagine della RSI nella propaganda* (Milan, 1985), and id., 'Autorappresentazioni dell'ultimo fascismo 1943–1945', in Pier Paolo Poggio (ed.), *La Repubblica sociale italiana 1943–45* (Brescia, 1986), 99–111.

[3] Badoglio first used this expression in a speech on Radio Bari on 19 September 1943. Text in Agostino degli Espinosa, *Il Regno del Sud* (Milan, 1995; first edn. 1946), 75–7.

entire national tradition.[4] The judgement of the leader of the Communist Party, Palmiro Togliatti, was the same. He deeply condemned the alliance entered into by the fascists with the 'age-old enemy' of the Italian people—the 'hated Hun'; an alliance signed 'without any consultation and without the consent of the Italian people, contrary to all the traditions and interests of the Italian nation'.[5]

Germany's behaviour was also described as treacherous. Ever since the drawing up of the Pact of Steel, Germany had aimed to link Italy to itself only in order to use it as a political ally in its quest for world domination. In Germany's plans, Italy, too, was to be reduced to a mere satellite of the greater German Reich, and the Duce transformed into one of the Führer's simple *Gauleiter*: treachery, therefore, from the very start in terms of intentions, and later betrayal in actual fact on the battlefield itself. Monarchist propaganda and the anti-fascist press denied the presumed Italo-German camaraderie extolled in fascist propaganda, describing the Germans as untrustworthy allies, supercilious towards the Italian soldiers they considered racially inferior, and ready to betray them, as, it was said, had already happened at El Alamein and on the Don. There the German commanders, in order to save their own troops hard pressed by the advancing enemy, had deliberately sacrificed the Italian contingents. They had abandoned them on foot and without supplies to the tragic destiny of imprisonment or death. Images of Italian soldiers being thrown bodily off the German lorries on to which they had tried to climb, and frozen or wounded Italian soldiers being cast out of the huts of Russian peasants where they had sought refuge had a strong emotional impact on the country. They were presented by the anti-fascist forces as a symbol of the falsity of so-called German comradeship, and a prelude to the violence and hatred which the Germans were to unleash on the Italians after 8 September.[6]

---

[4] Croce's words are taken from the *Manifesto per la chiamata dei volontari*, Naples, 10 October 1943. Text in Benedetto Croce, *Scritti e discorsi politici (1943–1947)*, i (Bari, 1963), 3–7.

[5] These words were pronounced by Togliatti on 29 December 1945 at the Fifth Communist Party Congress. Cf. Palmiro Togliatti, *Opere*, ed. Luciano Gruppi (Rome, 1984), 176–7.

[6] Cf. Filippo Focardi, '"Bravo italiano" e "cattivo tedesco": riflessioni sulla genesi di due immagini incrociate', *Storia e Memoria*, 5 (1996), no. 1, 62–6.

This action, designed to counter the claims of fascist propaganda, was accompanied by the energetic and concerted efforts of the monarchy and the anti-fascist forces to mobilize the country against the German 'invader'. Exploiting the tradition of the Risorgimento and the anti-German memories of the First World War which were still alive, the monarchy and the anti-fascist forces called on the Italians to take up arms against the 'age-old enemy' of the nation, against the 'eternal Teutonic barbarian' who had returned to ensnare them.[7] The martyrs who had fallen in the struggle against the 'beastly German aggressor' were set on a par with those who had fallen in the struggle against Austrian domination; the Neapolitan insurrection against the Germans of September 1943 was compared to the historic *giornate* (days of insurrection) during the nineteenth-century struggles for independence.[8] The war conducted alongside the Allies after the armistice was described in epic terms as a 'Second Risorgimento' of the Italian nation, as a 'war of national liberation' supported by the entire populace rallying around the regular troops and the partisan divisions ('un popolo alla macchia', 'a nation underground', was the eloquent phrase coined by the Communist leader Luigi Longo).[9]

The political and propaganda action undertaken with respect to the Anglo-American victors further influenced this depiction of the war. The fundamental and legitimate anxiety of the anti-fascist ruling class was to avoid a punitive peace for a country which had emerged from the war vanquished. Reviving a position previously assumed by the first Badoglio government, all the governments of national unity which emerged after the agreement between the Committee of National Liberation and the monarchy in the spring of 1944 put at the centre of their international activity the claim for the merit acquired by Italy in the struggle against Germany after 8 September, and thus recognition of the right to alliance on an equal footing with the Allied

---

[7] On the image of the Germans cf. Claudio Pavone, *Una guerra civile: Saggio storico sulla moralità nella Resistenza* (Turin, 1991), 206–20 and Enzo Collotti, 'I tedeschi', in Mario Isnenghi (ed.), *I luoghi della memoria: Personaggi e date dell'Italia unita* (Rome, 1997), 65–86.

[8] On the Resistance in Naples and the popular insurrection of the so-called 'quattro giornate' cf. Gloria Chianese, 'Napoli', in Enzo Collotti, Renato Sandri, and Frediano Sessi (eds.), *Dizionario della Resistenza: Storia e geografia della Liberazione*, vol. i (Turin, 2000), 376–87.

[9] Luigi Longo, *Un popolo alla macchia* (Milan, 1947).

nations. 'Democratic and anti-fascist Italy', they said, should not have to pay for the sins of 'Mussolini's Italy'. To this end, it was essential to make as clear a distinction as possible between the behaviour of Italy and that of Germany, alongside which the nation had, nevertheless, fought for a full three years.[10]

Allied propaganda offered a valid means of support in this enterprise. From the very start of hostilities this propaganda (British, American, and Soviet indiscriminately) had aimed to detach fascist Italy from the alliance with Hitler's Reich. For this purpose, it had distinguished between the responsibility of fascism and that of the Italian people, slaves of the dictatorship, and Italian guilt in general from Germany's much more serious guilt.[11] The anti-fascist front unanimously emphasized this distinction. It presented the Italians as 'victims' of fascism, of 'Mussolini's war' and of the 'hateful Hun'. While the Germans had shown themselves to be fanatical soldiers, disciplined and cruel, the Italians by contrast had taken part in the war without conviction, without hatred for the enemy, capable of silent personal sacrifice but not of cruelty and violence. While the German people had remained loyal to their Führer until the decline of the Reich, the Italian people had risen up against fascism, liberated the country, and executed the Duce. These differences with Germany were real. Nevertheless the representation of Italy as an essentially anti-fascist country was misleading.

The anti-fascist ruling class especially emphasized differences in the behaviour of Italian and German troops in the occupied territories, for example, in Yugoslavia and in Greece. The figure of the *cattivo tedesco* (wicked German), capable of all manner of villainy against the civilian population and the Jews, was contrasted with that of the *bravo italiano* (good Italian).[12] Poorly

---

[10] Cf. Filippo Focardi, 'L'Italia antifascista e la Germania (1943–1945)', *Ventesimo Secolo*, 5 (1995), no. 13, 144 ff.

[11] On British and American propaganda cf. Maura Piccialuti Caprioli, *Radio Londra 1939–1945* (Rome, 1979); Lamberto Mercuri, *Guerra psicologica: La propaganda anglo-americana in Italia 1942–1946* (Rome, 1983); Alejandro Pizarroso Quintero, *Stampa, radio e propaganda: Gli Alleati in Italia 1943–1946* (Milan, 1989). As regards the propaganda from Soviet sources, see Palmiro Togliatti's speeches from Russia: Palmiro Togliatti, *Da Radio Milano-Libertà* (Rome, 1974), and the *Discorsi agli italiani* in Palmiro Togliatti, *Opere*, iv, pt. 2: *1935–1944*, ed. Franco Andreucci and Paolo Spriano (Rome, 1979).

[12] Cf. Focardi, ' "Bravo italiano" e "cattivo tedesco" ' and id., 'La memoria della guerra e il mito del "bravo italiano": Origine e affermazione di un autoritratto collettivo', *Italia Contemporanea* (2000), nos. 220–1, 393–9.

armed, badly dressed, undernourished, catapulted against his will into a disastrous war, the Italian soldier had offered solidarity to the people of the countries he had invaded under Mussolini's orders. He had helped them in their struggle against hunger and poverty, sharing with them the little he had and, above all, had protected them from the abuse and violence of his Germanic comrades in arms, thus saving many lives, as in the case of the thousands of Jews wrenched from the talons of the Teutonic exterminators. As the historian Gaetano Salvemini observed, the Italian soldier's 'innate sense of humanity' was set against the 'cold, mechanical brutality' of the 'Teutonic automaton . . . barbarous and uncivilized'.[13] Here, too, although the description of the Italian soldiers as 'defenders of the oppressed' rested on factual evidence (I refer, for example, to the assistance offered to the Jews),[14] it nevertheless concealed another and much less edifying aspect of reality (also deleterious in terms of the peace treaty). This was the Italian share of responsibility for aggressive warfare and for the grievous crimes committed—by Italian soldiers too—against civilians and partisans, especially in Yugoslavia, including pitiless reprisals, the execution of hostages, the destruction of entire villages, and the deportation of local citizens.[15]

Thus, even before the end of the conflict, the Italian antifascist forces had delineated the storyline of the experience of war and fascism which was to form the basis for the construction

[13] Gaetano Salvemini and Giorgio La Piana, *La sorte dell'Italia* (Rome, 1945), 55.

[14] There is a vast amount of research on the action of the Italian civil and military authorities in defence of the Jews. Cf. e.g. Leon Poliakov and Jacques Sabille, *Gli ebrei sotto l'occupazione italiana* (Milan, 1956); Jonathan Steinberg, *All or Nothing: The Axis and the Holocaust 1941–1943* (London, 1990); Menachem Shelah, *Un debito di gratitudine: Storia dei rapporti tra l'Esercito italiano e gli ebrei in Dalmazia (1941–1943)* (Rome, 1991); Daniel Carpi, *Between Mussolini and Hitler: The Jews and the Italian Authorities in France and Tunisia* (Hanover, 1994).

[15] Cf. Teodoro Sala, 'Guerra ed amministrazione in Jugoslavia 1941–1943: un'ipotesi coloniale', in Bruna Micheletti and Pier Paolo Poggio (eds.), *L'Italia in guerra 1940–1943* (Brescia, 1992), 83–94; Tone Ferenc, *La provincia 'italiana' di Lubiana: Documenti 1941–1942* (Udine, 1994); Enzo Collotti, 'Sulla politica di repressione italiana nei Balcani', in Leonardo Paggi (ed.), *La memoria del nazismo nell'Europa di oggi* (Florence, 1997), 181–208; Brunello Mantelli, 'Die Italiener auf dem Balkan 1941–1943', in Christof Dipper, Lutz Klinkhammer, and Alexander Nützenadel (eds.), *Europäische Sozialgeschichte: Festschrift für Wolfgang Schieder zum 65. Geburtstag* (Berlin, 2000), 57–74; Carlo Spartaco Capogreco, 'Una storia rimossa dell'Italia fascista: L'internamento dei civili jugoslavi (1941–1943)', *Studi Storici*, 42 (2001), no. 1, 203–30; Davide Rodogno, *Il nuovo ordine mediterraneo: Le politiche di occupazione dell'Italia fascista in Europa (1940–1943)* (Turin, 2003).

of a largely self-absolving collective memory, founded on the constant confrontation between Italy and Germany, and the consequent minimization of Italian guilt. In the first two years after the war, that is, during the period when the peace treaty was discussed and the Republican state created, this storyline was confirmed by a powerful press and publicity campaign which produced an 'official story'. In sum, the crucial elements of this account were as follows: the Italian people had been subjected to the fascist dictatorship, and had been dragged by Mussolini and his henchmen into an unpopular war, alongside the detested ally Germany; the Italian soldiers had fought bravely, despite poor conditions and a lack of preparation, finally sacrificing themselves in a war they had never wanted; unlike their German counterparts they had shown humanity to the inhabitants of the occupied countries; they had been betrayed on the battlefield by their German comrades; as soon as Mussolini's dictatorship loosened its grip, the Italian people had revealed their true anti-fascist sentiments; the entire Italian people had participated in the struggle for national liberation, not only the armed forces and the partisans, but also the civilians who had supported the Resistance, paying a high price in terms of human life, as borne out by the numerous massacres perpetrated by the fascists and Germans; the Italians, alongside the Allied troops, had by their own efforts liberated the cities of central and northern Italy, defeating the Germans and their fascist accomplices; from this point of view, Italy should consider itself morally victorious and consequently it deserved a 'just peace'. Certain events and significant dates were immediately singled out and given symbolic importance: 25 July 1943, the day the fascist regime collapsed, 'undermined by twenty years of opposition on the part of the Italian people';[16] 8 September 1943, considered the start of the Resistance,[17] and marked by several crucial episodes such as the defence of Rome against the Germans at Porta San Paolo, the German massacre of the Italian garrison on the Greek island of Cephalonia,[18] and the

---

[16] Cf. Mimmo Franzinelli, 'Il 25 luglio', in Isnenghi (ed.), *I luoghi della memoria*, 219–40.

[17] Cf. Mimmo Franzinelli, 'L'8 settembre', in Isnenghi (ed.), *I luoghi della memoria*, 241–70.

[18] After the armistice, the Italian soldiers of the 'Acqui' division stationed on the island of Cephalonia in the Ionian Sea refused to surrender their arms to the Germans and fought against them for several days. After the Italian forces were forced to surrender

victorious insurrection in Naples; 24 March 1944, the day of the
Fosse Ardeatine massacre, commemorated as the first major
sacrifice of Italian citizens, both civilians and soldiers, Catholics
and Jews, Communists and Monarchists;[19] and finally, 25 April,
the Liberation, the most important date of all, taken as a symbol
of national redemption, and officially established as a national
holiday in 1946.[20]

This official story put the entire responsibility for the fascist
war fought from 10 June 1940 to 8 September 1943 on Mussolini
and the Germans. It smoothed over or minimized the aggressive
character of the conflict, dwelling instead on the humanitarian
behaviour of the 'good Italian soldiers'. Above all, it highlighted
the events of the 'second war' fought by the Italians between 8
September 1943 and 25 April 1945, considered as the real war, in
which the Italian people had been able to reveal their true feelings in a concerted show of force against the hated fascists and
the detested Hun. It was this latter war, the war of the co-
belligerent Italy and of the partisan Resistance, which was celebrated by a political and intellectual class which had taken a
leading part in it, and which drew from it the source of its legitimacy as the country's ruling class.

There is no doubt that such a narrative, although it grew from
legitimate political needs, produced a distorted version of
national history. There were highly significant omissions: for
example, the existence of a popular consensus for fascism; the
enthusiasm with which many Italians had welcomed the
prospect of war alongside Germany in the hope of a rapid
victory;[21] and the civil war character of the Resistance, which
could not be reduced simply to a struggle against the foreigner

(22 September 1943), the German military command ordered mass executions. Cf.
Giorgio Rochat and Marcello Venturi (eds.), *La divisione Acqui a Cefalonia: Settembre 1943*
(Milan, 1993).

[19] On 23 March 1944 in via Rasella in Rome, Communist partisans led an attack on a
column of German troops; 33 German soldiers died. On the following day, 335 Italians
were taken to the Fosse Ardeatine, in the vicinity of Rome, where they were slaughtered.
Cf. Robert Katz, *Death in Rome* (New York, 1967), and Steffen Prauser, 'Mord in Rom?
Der Anschlag in der Via Rasella und die deutsche Vergeltung in den Fosse Ardeatine im
März 1944', *Vierteljahrshefte für Zeitgeschichte*, 50/2 (2002), 269–301.

[20] On the celebration of 25 April as a national holiday cf. Cristina Cenci, 'Rituale e
memoria: le celebrazioni del 25 aprile', in Leonardo Paggi (ed.), *Le memorie della Repubblica*
(Florence, 1999), 325–78.

[21] Cf. Simona Colarizi, *L'opinione degli italiani sotto il regime: 1929–43* (Rome, 1991),
336–9.

and his few fascist 'servants'. Nor was the depiction of the German 'betrayal' on the battlefield entirely truthful. In certain circumstances, the Italian troops too had behaved with a lack of comradeship towards the German ally.[22]

The narrative elaborated by the anti-fascist forces had been developed and consolidated by virtue of the political agreement reached between the monarchy and the parties of the Committee of National Liberation in March–April 1944. This agreement, which had been under constant strain during the months of conflict, was ruptured after the end of the war with the approach of the referendum on the future type of state (republic or monarchy).[23] The confrontation between the supporters of the monarchy and the supporters of the Republic was also translated into a dispute about memory. The Republican supporters, with the left-wing parties in the front line, took up again the arguments which had been consistently present in the pages of the anti-fascist press, and accused the monarchy of having supported the Mussolini regime on the declaration of war, and of having provoked the catastrophe of 8 September by imprudent and unworthy behaviour, culminating in the precipitous flight of the King and the Court from the capital and the abandonment of the armed forces. The monarchy replied, calling into question one of the bulwarks of the narrative developed by the anti-fascist front: the relationship between Mussolini's dictatorship and the Italian people. The Monarchist press maintained that the king had agreed to Italy's entry into the war in order not to counter the bellicose propensities of the Italian people, marshalled behind the figure of the Duce. It also vindicated the role played by the sovereign in the fall of fascism and defended the decision to abandon the capital at the time of the armistice as an appropriate decision which had ensured institutional continuity, and thus the defence of national interests.[24] How did the dispute end? To put it succinctly, the response to the referendum of 2 June 1946 and the victory of the Republic

---

[22] Studying the Russian campaign in the German archives, Alessandro Massignani has discovered that on the German side, the very same accusations were made against the Italian allies as were raised in the Italian anti-fascist press against the German troops: abandonment of the ally, appropriation of supplies, bullying and violence. Cf. Alessandro Massignani, *Alpini e tedeschi sul Don* (Valdagno, 1991).

[23] The referendum was held on 2 June 1946, at the same time as the national elections.

[24] Cf. Pietro Silva, *Io difendo la monarchia* (Rome, 1946), 135–205.

effectively swept the Monarchist arguments under the carpet. From then on condemnation of the King's flight from Rome was a permanent and crucial element in the memory of the war. The assumption of the hostility of the Italian people to Mussolini's war also remained undisputed.

Other areas of friction were the question of responsibility for the catastrophic conduct of the war and the issue of war crimes, which involved eminent members of the military establishment, such as the generals Giovanni Messe and Mario Roatta, who had gone over to the King and Badoglio after the armistice.[25] Condemnation of the behaviour of the 'disloyal' German ally had helped the military echelons who had gone over to Badoglio (and who had been involved in the preceding disasters of the war) to offload on to the Germans the entire responsibility for the crushing defeats inflicted on Italy on various fronts during the war. On the part of the anti-fascist Left there was no hesitation in considering the German 'betrayal' on the battlefields as aggravating the responsibility of the Italian generals, who had shown themselves incapable of preventing such behaviour and of looking after their own troops. The defence of the honour of the Italian soldiers, unjustly accused by the Germans of lacking skill in combat, did not for the Left constitute a let-out for the ineptitude of the upper echelons of command.[26] Within the framework of the projects for purging the armed forces set in motion from the autumn of 1944 on, the tendency of the Left was to put on trial the Italian military commanders who were responsible for the fascist war, accusing them of disastrous mismanagement of the war and of having committed war crimes.[27] And what was

---

[25] Giovanni Messe was in command of the Italian expedition to Russia (CSIR) and organized the final defence of the Axis forces in North Africa. Having been taken prisoner by the English, he was freed at the request of Badoglio and appointed Chief of Defence of the Armed Forces. In the postwar period he was a Christian Democrat senator and subsequently a Monarchist and Liberal MP. Mario Roatta was, before the war, the Chief of the Military Secret Service (SIM). He was the Army Chief of Defence from March 1941 to January 1942, and later Commander of the Second Army in Yugoslavia and of the First Army in Sicily. He was once again Army Chief of Defence from May to November 1943. In November 1944 he was arrested for fascist crimes and tried by the High Court. He fled during his trial in March 1945 and took refuge in Spain under the Franco regime.

[26] Cf. Focardi, ' "Bravo italiano" e "cattivo tedesco" ', 62–3.

[27] Cf. Lamberto Mercuri, *L'epurazione in Italia 1943–1948* (Cuneo, 1983), 51 ff.; Roy Palmer Domenico, *Italian Fascists on Trial* (Chapel Hill, 1991), 64 ff.; Hans Woller, *I conti con il fascismo: L'epurazione in Italia 1943–1948* (Bologna, 1997), 187 ff.

the result? While the criticism of the abysmal military preparation for the war and its inefficient management was tenacious
and consistent, and resulted in the effective discrediting of the
action of the commanders (albeit in moral and not judicial
terms, because no inquest was actually held apart from an
administrative inquiry into the failure to defend Rome), attempts
to bring members of the armed forces to trial for war crimes
were weak and ineffective. This latter aspect deserves to be studied in greater depth.

As has already been mentioned, one of the cornerstones of the
'dominant narrative'[28] elaborated by the anti-fascist front was
praise for the figure of the 'good Italian' as opposed to that of the
'wicked German'. The anti-fascist Left included the common
soldiers within this category of 'good Italian' but excluded both
their supreme commanders and the fascist volunteers who had
been guilty of serious crimes, especially in the Balkans. Between
September 1944 and March 1945 the Left—the Socialists,
Communists, Republicans, and the Partito d'Azione—made various attempts to try those guilty of war crimes. Foremost among
them was General Mario Roatta, former Commander of the
Second Army stationed in Slovenia and Croatia, who had been
arrested and put on trial for crimes committed before the conflict
but not for war crimes. The Left demanded that he also be tried
for war crimes, but without success. On the contrary, Roatta
managed to evade any trial whatsoever by escaping and taking
refuge abroad. The desire to try war criminals was drastically
diminished after the temporary Yugoslavian occupation of
Trieste and Venezia Giulia (1 May–12 June 1945) and the launching of negotiations for the peace treaty which began with the
Potsdam Conference (17 July–2 August 1945). The Communists
alone raised the matter of war crimes during the peace negotiations, demanding the sentencing of those responsible.[29] And only
the Communist press supported, albeit lukewarmly, Yugoslavia's
request for a certain number of supposed Italian war criminals to

---

[28] On the concept of the 'dominant narrative' see Charles Maier, 'Fare giustizia, fare
storia: epurazioni politiche e narrative nazionali dopo il 1945 e il 1989', *Passato e Presente*,
13 (1995) no. 34, 23–32; Stuart J. Woolf, 'Memoria, narrazione egemonica e pluralismo
europeo', ibid. 32–7.

[29] On the Communist attitude and, more generally, the debate in Italy on the question of war criminals, cf. Filippo Focardi, 'La questione della punizione dei criminali di
guerra in Italia dopo la fine del secondo conflitto mondiale', *Quellen und Forschungen aus
italienischen Archiven und Bibliotheken*, 80 (2000), 578 ff.

be handed over. For clear reasons of state none of the other political forces did so, including the Socialists, the Republicans, and
the Partito d'Azione who had in the past been among the most
avid supporters of a purge of the armed forces. After the exclusion of the Left from the government in May 1947, the Socialist
and the Communist press gave coverage to the renewed accusations of war crimes emerging from Belgrade. However no one,
even among the forces of the Left, ever brought the matter up in
Parliament. A Socialist MP, Giusto Tolloy, specifically declared
that this would not have been opportune in terms of 'patriotic
charity' ('carità di patria').[30] Moreover, even the Commission of
Inquiry specially set up in Italy in May 1946 to investigate Italian
war criminals never arrived at any concrete results.[31] The
Commission of Inquiry, upon which members of the Socialist and
Communist parties also served, effectively operated in such a way
as to avoid the handing-over and punishment of those who had
been accused of war crimes. Thus, in the end, the self-absolving
image of the 'good Italian' was preserved intact.

The above-mentioned cases of conflict between the monarchy
and the Republican forces, and between the military establishment and the anti-fascist Left regarding memory which emerged
in the postwar period failed to erode the foundations of the
'dominant narrative' elaborated between 1943 and 1945.

From the immediate postwar period on, however, this official
line was attacked by antagonistic and bitter neo-fascists.[32] They
upheld the reasons for Italy's participation in the war alongside
Germany, confirmed the support of a vast part of the nation for
the 'Axis war', and praised the heroism displayed in combat by
the Italian soldiers (from the El Alamein paratroopers to the
navy raiders' attacks on the ships of the British fleet). Most
crucially, the neo-fascists blamed the anti-fascist forces and, still
earlier, the Crown, responsible for the collapse of the regime on
25 July 1943, for betraying the nation, which had been left at the
mercy of enemy troops. According to this reading, 8 September
represented not the beginning of the nation's redemption as

[30] Cf. ibid. 623.
[31] Cf. Filippo Focardi and Lutz Klinkhammer (eds.), 'La questione dei "criminali di
guerra" italiani e una Commissione di inchiesta dimenticata', *Contemporanea*, 4 (2001), no.
3, 497–528.
[32] Cf. Francesco Germinario, *L'altra memoria: L'estrema destra, Salò e la Resistenza* (Turin,
1999).

maintained by the anti-fascists, but the country's tragic 'moral overthrow'. The Resistance was considered a cruel 'fratricidal war' between Italians, which benefited only foreigners. Above all, after the signing of the peace treaty (10 February 1947) the neo-fascist press underlined the fact that while the Italian Social Republic had had the positive effect of braking the German desire for destruction unleashed against the traitor Italy, the Italy of co-belligerence had not succeeded in avoiding a punitive peace. *I Saved the Homeland* was, for example, the emblematic title of a book by Marshal Graziani, former Supreme Commander of the Armed Forces of the Social Republic.[33] For Graziani the fascist Salò government had prevented Germany from reducing Italy to a 'second Poland'.

These attitudes were not confined to the neo-fascist press and periodicals, which, incidentally, enjoyed a fairly extensive circulation. (For example, *Rivolta ideale*, the major neo-fascist weekly, had a print run of 150,000 and Graziani's book was one of the best-sellers of the time.) Certain neo-fascist themes, such as the celebration of wartime heroism, the nostalgic recall of bygone power, and the criticism of the Resistance as a movement monopolized by the Left, were accepted by broad sectors of Italian public opinion. These included the lower-middle and middle classes in the south, where nostalgic sentiments towards fascism were still widespread,[34] and military veterans, captured by Allied forces in Russia or in Africa, who had been imprisoned in conditions of severe hardship (there were about 650,000 such soldiers, more or less the same number as ended up in prison camps in Germany).[35] The feelings of these broad sectors of public opinion were expressed in periodicals which wielded

---

[33] Graziani's book was published in Milan in 1948 by Garzanti, one of the major Italian publishers.

[34] Cf. Angelo Michele Imbriani, *Vento del sud: Moderati, reazionari, qualunquisti (1943–1948)* (Bologna, 1996).

[35] See the articles in Istituto storico dell Resistenza in Piemonte (ed.), *Una storia di tutti: Prigionieri, internati, deportati italiani nella seconda guerra mondiale* (Milan, 1989). The Italian prisoners suffered particularly harsh treatment in the Russian camps in the Soviet Union, in the French prisoner-of-war camps of North Africa and in various British camps, for example in India. On this subject, see also Romain Rainero (ed.), *I prigionieri italiani durante la seconda guerra mondiale: Aspetti e problemi storici* (Milan, 1985); Flavio Conti, *I prigionieri di guerra italiani (1940–1945)* (Bologna, 1986). On the subject of veterans, still relatively unstudied by historians, see Claudio Pavone, 'Appunti sul problema dei reduci', in Nicola Gallerano (ed.), *L'altro dopoguerra: Roma e il sud 1943–1945* (Milan, 1985), 87–106, and Erika Lorenzoni, 'Il silenzio dei reduci', *Studi e ricerche di storia contemporanea* (2001), no. 56.

considerable influence at the time, such as Renato Angiolillo's *Il Tempo*, and especially in the political movement which grew up around the weekly edited by Guglielmo Giannini, *L'Uomo Qualunque*, which enjoyed considerable success during the early postwar years.[36]

These circles were marked by a widespread intolerance of anti-fascist rhetoric, and, above all, by deep-seated anti-Communist attitudes. In 1946 authoritative exponents of *L'Uomo Qualunque* and monarchist supporters had already made public accusations against the anti-fascists. For example, in February 1946, at the first Congress of the Uomo Qualunque movement, a member of the National Council (Consulta Nazionale), Emilio Patrissi, defined the anti-fascists as 'jackals sneaking in from abroad to tear apart the body of the nation'.[37] The case provoked furious reactions from all the anti-fascist parties, from the Communists to the Liberals.[38] Similar criticisms and analogous, immediate protests came to the fore again several months later when, at the Constituent Assembly in July 1946, the Monarchist General Roberto Bencivenga launched an attack on the governments of the Committee of National Liberation which had been set up by the 'foreigner' and were blamed for the 'tragic conditions' of the country both nationally and internationally.[39] The anti-fascist parties reacted unanimously to the attitudes expressed by Patrissi and Bencivenga, who called patriotism into question, and consequently queried the very political legitimacy of the governments born of the Resistance. Nevertheless, the cohesion of the anti-fascist front was undermined by the anti-Communism which was widespread not only among the neo-fascist Right and among the followers of the Uomo Qualunque movement, but also among the moderate anti-fascist ranks of the Christian Democrats and Liberals.

Anti-Communism was nourished by the violent press campaign launched by the conservative newspapers on the issue

[36] Giannini's weekly reached a circulation of about 800,000, equivalent to the present print-run of major national dailies such as *Il Corriere della Sera* or *La Repubblica*. On the experience of the political movement of L'Uomo Qualunque cf. Sandro Setta, *L'Uomo Qualunque 1944–1948* (Rome, 1975).

[37] Cf. ibid. 139.

[38] Cf. *Atti della Consulta Nazionale: Discussioni dal 25 settembre 1945 al 9 marzo 1946* (Rome, 1946), 762–65.

[39] Cf. *Atti dell'Assemblea Costituente: Discussioni dal 25 giugno al 14 dicembre 1946* (Rome, 1947), 69.

of Italian prisoners of war in the Soviet Union.[40] This campaign accused Moscow of having caused the death of thousands of Italian prisoners, and of still detaining large numbers as 'working slaves'. It came to a head on the occasion of the elections of April 1948. Exploiting popular discontent at the loss of the large number of soldiers who had perished in these tragic circumstances, violent accusations were launched against a number of Italian Communists who had carried out political indoctrination in the Soviet prison camps. One of these, Edoardo D'Onofrio, brought an action against his accusers. In the famous trial which took place between May and July 1949, the latter were, however, acquitted and D'Onofrio was ordered to pay the legal costs. This was a further blow to the prestige of anti-fascism.

The important elections of 18 April 1948 were the occasion for an open rupture in the old anti-fascist front: on one side was the Socialist and Communist Left, and on the other De Gasperi's Christian Democrats, supported by the Catholic Action Committees. This political division also had repercussions on the memory of the war, as revealed by the celebration on 25 April, the festival of Liberation which happened to fall just a few days after the Christian Democrat victory. While the first anniversary of the Liberation in 1946 had been celebrated in a unified manner, with 'solemn demonstrations' in which civil and religious institutions and partisan associations had participated,[41] the Liberation celebrations of 1948 took place in a context of bitter polemic. In February 1948 the De Gasperi government had issued a decree prohibiting the wearing of uniforms in public,[42] intending thereby to prevent public celebrations on 25 April for fear of political exploitation by the Left. The latter reacted by organizing open-air demonstrations, which resulted in clashes with the police. The Left accused the Christian Democrats of having 'betrayed' the Resistance, asserting both the historical significance of the movement for national liberation and its political importance as a movement for the social vindication of the subordinate classes (the Resistance was portrayed as an 'interrupted revolution' which had to be

---

[40] Cf. Roberto Morozzo della Rocca, 'La vicenda dei prigionieri in Russia nella politica italiana 1944–1948', *Storia e Politica*, 22 (1983), no. 3, 480–542.

[41] Cf. Cenci, 'Rituale e memoria', 343–52.

[42] Ibid. 353.

completed).[43] The Christian Democrats, for their part, claimed
the heritage of the Resistance as a 'struggle for independence
and liberty', values which were threatened externally by Soviet
imperialism, and internally by Communist totalitarianism. This
heritage had to be defended not only from the dangers of resur-
gent fascism, but also from the challenge posed by the Marxist
Left.[44]

From the immediate postwar period on the idea, warmly
supported by the veterans of Salò, of 'making peace' between the
fascists and anti-fascists, the victors and the vanquished, played a
significant role in the Italian public debate. 'Reconciliation' was
to be based on a recognition of the sincerity of the intentions
which, after the armistice, had led many young people to ally
themselves with Mussolini to defend national honour. The need
for reconciliation was also shared at this time by the anti-fascist
parties which, in the opposite political field, had attempted to
distinguish between the rank-and-file followers (who in any case
were not the objects of blame) and those who had held positions
of responsibility or command, and were guilty of serious crimes.
The amnesty of June 1946, signed by the Communist Togliatti,
had been proposed in the name of 'national concord', with the
intention of integrating the rank-and-file followers of fascism into
democratic Italy.[45] However, repeated proposals for 'reconciliation' put forward by the Right took on a very different complex-
ion during the first parliamentary term of 1948–53. This was
characterized by a strong ideological contrast between the forces
of the Marxist Left (the Communists and the Socialists) defeated
in the elections of 18 April 1948, and the government guided by
the Christian Democrats. During these years such proposals for
reconciliation effectively took the form of attempts to put fascists
and anti-fascists on the same level. This would inevitably have led
to a devaluation of the Resistance as the legendary foundation of
the Republican state, and of anti-fascism as its essential ideology.

The right-wing proposals for 'reconciliation' were made in a

---

[43] Cf. Marcello Flores, 'L'antifascismo all'opposizione', in Mino Argentieri *et al.*,
Fascismo e antifascismo negli anni della Repubblica (Milan, 1986), 34–61, and Adriano Ballone,
'La Resistenza', in Mario Isnenghi (ed.), *I luoghi della memoria: Strutture ed eventi dell'Italia
unita* (Rome, 1997), 414–16.

[44] Cf. Guido Formigoni, 'La memoria della guerra e della Resistenza nelle culture
politiche del "mondo cattolico" (1945–1955)', *Ricerche di Storia Politica*, 11 (1996), 7–42.

[45] Cf. Woller, *I conti con il fascismo*, 533–49.

context marked by strong tensions. In this period there were many trials of partisans, generally belonging to left-wing formations, charged with crimes performed in wartime: criminal conspiracy, robbery, theft, extortion, and murder.[46] Judicial proceedings were triggered by the need to staunch the flow of political violence unleashed in the postwar period, especially in certain regions such as Emilia Romagna, against ex-fascists or those suspected of being such. Thousands of partisans were placed under investigation, often on the basis of indictments collected during the war by the fascist authorities. The proceedings frequently resulted in several years of preventive detention; many cases never even came to a real trial, and the defendants were almost always acquitted on appeal. The overall effect was nevertheless significant: the Resistance itself was under attack. Particularly relevant from this point of view was the case brought in 1948 against the partisans responsible for the Via Rasella attack in Rome (in which thirty-three German soldiers had died), followed by the Fosse Ardeatine reprisals (in which 335 Italians had been executed). The action was brought by several relatives of Ardeatine victims who considered the partisan action illegitimate, and called those responsible to account for its consequences; the latter included well-known anti-fascists such as Sandro Pertini, Giorgio Amendola, Riccardo Bauer, and Franco Calamandrei. Even though the Court of Rome in 1950 found against the plaintiffs, confirming the legitimacy of the partisan action, the trial itself represented a challenge to the memory of the Resistance.[47]

The ending of the purges directed against the fascists helped to make the political climate of the first parliamentary term even more strained. This process had been triggered by the amnesty of June 1946, which was applied in an extremely elastic manner.[48] Even those who, on account of having held 'high-ranking positions of civil or political administration or military command', were excluded from the amnesty had effectively

---

[46] Cf. Achille Battaglia, 'Giustizia e politica nella giurisprudenza', in id. *et al.*, *Dieci anni dopo: 1945–1955* (Bari, 1955), 360 ff.; Mirco Dondi, *La lunga liberazione: Giustizia e violenza nel dopoguerra italiano* (Rome, 1999).

[47] To the present day, the Via Rasella attack and the Fosse Ardeatine massacre have frequently emerged as the subject of historical and political polemic. Cf. Alessandro Portelli, *L'ordine è stato eseguito: Roma, le Fosse Ardeatine, la memoria* (Rome, 1999).

[48] Cf. Woller, *I conti con il fascismo*, 542–49, and Dondi, *La lunga liberazione*, 59–70.

enjoyed favourable treatment. When the amnesty was signed
there were 12,000 fascists in prison. By the following year the
number had fallen to 2,000, and in 1952 only 266 were still incar-
cerated. The two-year period between 1948 and 1950, in particular, saw the release of many front-line members of the
Republican fascist government, many of whom had been
charged with serious crimes. These included, for example,
Prince Junio Valerio Borghese, chief of the Decima Mas, one of
the fascist military formations involved in the worst crimes; the
former German ambassador Filippo Anfuso (already sentenced
to death in 1945); and Renato Ricci, chief of the fascist National
Guard. In May 1950 the military tribunal of Rome condemned
Marshal Graziani to nineteen years' imprisonment. Various
pardons and amnesties meant that Graziani actually remained in
prison only for a few months; after his release he accepted the
position of Honorary Chairman of the Movimento Sociale
Italiano (Italian Social Movement), the neo-fascist party established in December 1946.

While the parties of the Left protested against the Resistance
being put on trial, and against the rehabilitation of fascism, the
majority party of the government, the Christian Democrats,
emphasized the need for reconciliation after the bitter divisions
of the war. A crucial theme here proved to be homage to those
who had 'fallen in all wars', an expression of Christian piety
towards all the soldiers who had perished on various fronts. This
argument, warmly supported in the first place by the Vatican,
had been shared in the immediate postwar period by all the
political forces of anti-fascism. They had commemorated those
who had fallen in the fascist war as victims of Mussolini at the
same level as those who had fallen in the struggle against Nazi-
fascism. The same argument brought up again in the climate of
the Cold War ran the risk of compromising, or at the very least
undermining, the anti-fascist memory.

Certain politicians' speeches of the period illustrate this attitude. For example, in an address made on 1 March 1953 in Bari,
honouring the Italian soldiers massacred by the Germans in
Cephalonia in Greece, the Vice-Premier Attilio Piccioni invited
Italians to suppress their feelings of outrage and hatred and
instead to remember these martyrs as 'an example of loyal duty
and intrepid and devoted service to the homeland, even to the

point of sacrifice'.[49] Similar sentiments inspired the address celebrating the ten-year anniversary of the Fosse Ardeatine delivered by another Christian Democrat, the Defence Minister Taviani.[50] The sacrifice of 335 defenceless victims, symbolic of the sacrifices faced by Italy during the war, he suggested, should instil the Italians with a desire for reconciliation. 'May Almighty God inspire the Italians,' urged Taviani, 'so that in their celebration of the past they do not delve further into furrows which are already too deep.' In his tribute to the Ardeatine victims, the Communist Giorgio Amendola paid homage to the partisan action in Via Rasella.[51] Taviani, by contrast, had made no reference whatsoever to the Resistance, seeing in the sacrifice of the innocents a 'condemnation of the perversion of every form of totalitarianism' and an example of an absolute devotion to duty. Loyalty to the homeland, a sense of military honour and of duty, the spirit of self-sacrifice; these were the qualities which Taviani himself evoked in November 1954 when he visited the cemetery of El Alamein in Egypt.[52] The qualities which Piccioni had praised the year before in the soldiers of Cephalonia executed by the Germans were the same extolled by Taviani in the Italian soldiers who had fallen in battle alongside the Germans under the attack of Montgomery's troops.

There was a certain similarity between the appeal for reconciliation launched by the neo-fascist circles and the spirit of conciliation which inspired the Christian Democrat politicians. The concept of reconciliation advanced by the neo-fascists comprised a precise political design: this was to replace anti-fascism with anti-Communism as the source of the Republic's legitimacy, and on the basis of this to give credibility to their own position as a potential governing force.[53] The idea of welcoming the extreme Right, of both Monarchist and neo-fascist stamp, into the anti-Communist bloc found support in the Vatican establishment and

---

[49] 'Il riconoscente omaggio della Patria a mille Salme di militari caduti in Grecia', *Il Popolo*, 2 Mar. 1953.

[50] 'Nel decennale del glorioso sacrificio dei 335 Caduti delle Ardeatine, l'Italia ha esaltato i valori della libertà e della rinascita nazionale', *Il Popolo*, 25 Mar. 1954.

[51] Giorgio Amendola, 'Onore agli eroi della Resistenza romana!', *l'Unità*, 24 Mar. 1954.

[52] Cf. Vittorio Bachelet, 'Uniti idealmente i Caduti per la Patria da El Alamein alla città giuliana', *Il Popolo*, 4 Nov. 1954.

[53] Cf. Piero Ignazi, *Il polo escluso: Profilo del Movimento Sociale Italiano* (Bologna, 1989), 53–99.

among the right wing of the Christian Democratic Party.[54] This
became particularly clear after the situation tightened up as a
result of the war in Korea, and after the Movimento Sociale
Italiano opted in favour of the Atlantic Pact in 1951. This political plan was, however, to encounter strong resistance among the
Christian Democrats themselves. The memory of the war
proved to be an insurmountable obstacle.

On the one hand, the Christian Democrats aimed to overcome discord, and to this end watered down the references to
the Resistance. On the other, they were not willing to under-
write the reading of the war which the right wing, and not only
the neo-fascists, was determined to propose. This emerged decisively during the second parliamentary term, which began in
1953 in a political climate characterized by the emergence of
international *détente*, and consequently the weakening of the ideological dichotomy between Communism and anti-Communism.
As has been observed, even the loss of consensus among the
Christian Democrats in the election of 1953 led the leaders of the
Catholic Party towards a 'revival of the Resistance myth'.[55]

Two trials held between the end of 1953 and the first half of
1954 are emblematic. These were the action taken by the
Defence Minister, the Republican Pacciardi, and several Navy
Admirals against the neo-fascist historian and journalist
Antonino Trizzino, and that brought by the Christian Democrat
leader Alcide De Gasperi against the well-known journalist
Giovanni Guareschi.[56] In his book *Navi e poltrone* (Ships and
Seats), Trizzino had attacked the naval commanders, levelling
the umpteenth accusation of betrayal to the British enemy, and a
similar charge had been brought by Guareschi against De
Gasperi, accused of having asked the Allies to bomb Rome. The
question of treachery was, as we have seen, a crucial aspect; it
was not related to an interpretation of the Resistance, but
touched a nerve which even the moderate forces in the anti-
fascist front could not ignore. It is no coincidence that the two

[54] Cf. Andrea Riccardi, *Il 'Partito Romano' nel secondo dopoguerra (1945–1954)* (Brescia,
1983) and Simona Colarizi, *La seconda guerra mondiale e la Repubblica* (Milan, 1996), 623–31.

[55] Cenci, 'Rituale e memoria', 356.

[56] Trizzino's trial was held in Milan between 19 October and 5 December 1953.
Guareschi's was held, again in Milan, from 13 to 15 April 1954. On the significance of the
trials in terms of the affirmation of a 'dominant narrative', cf. Maier, 'Fare giustizia, fare
storia'.

trials were rapidly wound up, with the defendants being sentenced in both cases.[57]

This marked an important moment in the creation of the memory of the war in Italy. It set precise limits to the revisionism promoted by the Right and undermined its attack on the version elaborated by the anti-fascist forces, centred on the value of the struggle for liberation as the basis for the legitimacy of the democratic Republic. While visibly weakened by the strenuous political opposition of the early 1950s, this anti-fascist narrative nevertheless largely held its ground. Shortly afterwards, in fact, it was to be re-launched and ultimately regained dominance.

This was confirmed on the ten-year anniversary of Liberation, celebrated by both chambers of parliament on 22 April 1955 in a plenary session. After the Left accused the Christian Democrats of having betrayed the Resistance (by ousting them from power and thus preventing a true democratic renewal of the country) and the Christian Democrats accused the Communist partisans of cultivating an anti-democratic totalitarian doctrine, the institutional celebration wound up by reconstructing anti-fascist unity and re-proposing an official memory of the war. Of particular significance was the address made by the Chairman of the Chamber of Deputies, Giovanni Gronchi, a prominent figure of Catholic anti-fascism.[58]

In a spirit of reconciliation Gronchi did not fail to recall the many Italians who had fallen 'in the line of duty' in Mussolini's war, but he gave place of honour to the Resistance fighters, 'all those who offered the sacrifice of their own lives for the freedom and independence of the country'. He celebrated the 'struggle for liberation' as an 'authentic popular movement', as a second Risorgimento, thanks to which the nation had redeemed itself from the 'humiliation of dictatorship'. Gronchi added that, in spite of the political divisions which had arisen after the war, the Resistance remained, and should remain, a common point of reference for the democratic forces within the country. The address was greeted by the deafening applause of all the

---

[57] Trizzino was found guilty of offence to the Armed Forces and of persistent calumny in respect of three Admirals, and was consequently sentenced to 2 years 4 months' imprisonment. His book, *Navi e poltrone*, which had provoked the legal action, was confiscated. Guareschi was found guilty of calumny in relation to De Gasperi and was sentenced to one year's imprisonment.

[58] Cf. Giovanni Gronchi, *Discorsi parlamentari* (Rome, 1986), 472–80.

Parliamentary Deputies, with the exception of the neo-fascist Deputies, who, significantly, were absent from the House. By unanimous decision the assembly voted that the text of Gronchi's address be publicly displayed all over Italy. A few days later Giovanni Gronchi was elected President of the Republic.

Since the 1980s, many of the criticisms which the Italian Right had levelled against the dominant anti-fascist narrative in the immediate postwar period have come back into fashion.[59] This process accelerated in the 1990s in connection with changes in the political scene, foremost among them the establishment of a centre-right government which included Alleanza Nazionale, the direct descendants of the Movimento Sociale Italiano, the post-war neo-fascist party. The focus of the attack was the representation of that 'second war', the anti-fascist war, fought after the armistice. Many of its characteristic features have come under fire: 8 September was interpreted as the 'death of the homeland' and not as its symbolic rebirth;[60] authentic popular participation in the Resistance was denied; the war of liberation was seen as a civil war between two armed minorities, each backed by foreign powers and without any real following in the country itself;[61] in relation to the Resistance, not the noble gestures but the bloody internal contrasts, especially the excesses of its Communist component, were highlighted. Finally there was the inevitable appeal for 'reconciliation'. And so one of the two pillars of the anti-fascist memory of the Second World War—that relating to the Resistance, to the war conducted alongside the Allies after the armistice—was severely struck and made to totter (although not yet to fall).[62] The other pillar of this narrative, the story of the fascist war, the Axis war, has, by contrast, remained practically intact. Its postulates, namely, that all guilt and responsibility lay with the Duce and Germany, that the Italian people were against the war alongside the Germans, and that the Italian

---

[59] Cf. Nicola Gallerano, 'Critica e crisi del paradigma antifascista', in Argentieri et al., *Fascismo e antifascismo*, 106–33.

[60] Cf. Ernesto Galli della Loggia, *La morte della patria: La crisi dell'idea di nazione tra Resistenza, antifascismo e Repubblica* (Rome, 1996).

[61] This interpretation has been authoritatively supported by the historian Renzo De Felice. Cf. Renzo De Felice, *Rosso e Nero* (Milan, 1995) and id., *Mussolini l'alleato: La guerra civile 1943–1945* (Turin, 1997).

[62] The President of the Republic, Carlo Azeglio Ciampi, has proved particularly zealous in defence of the memory of the Resistance. For a reconstruction of the 1990s debate and the action of Ciampi, see Focardi, 'La memoria della guerra e della Resistenza'.

soldiers were intent solely upon alleviating the suffering of the invaded peoples, remain unchallenged. This is a sugar-coated and conciliatory version of a dramatic and morally embarrassing historical reality in which the Italians were not victims, but aggressors, a reality with which the country has consistently failed to come to terms.

4

Beyond Memory and Commemoration: Coming to Terms with War and Occupation in France after 1945

PIETER LAGROU

Introduction

In geopolitical terms, the collapse of France in 1940 is one of the most spectacular events of the Second World War. Once Europe's political powerhouse, France lost its military power, its international prestige, its diplomatic leverage, and a good deal of its economic wealth in one brief but decisive battle. The Vichy government's illusion that it could enter into a beneficial collaboration with its conqueror and the calamitous ideological adventure of its 'National Revolution' made France's postwar prospects considerably worse. The *dissidence* that assembled, first in London and then in small parts of the French colonial empire, around the Under-Secretary of State for Defence, Charles de Gaulle—by no means a political heavyweight before the war—experienced major difficulties in having its legitimacy accepted, both abroad and in the occupied country. Yet the impression is that France, and France alone among the defeated, occupied, and collaborating countries, somehow managed to return to the concert of nations, as the fourth of the Big Three, despite its wartime record. It was temporarily restored to its colonial splendour and, with considerable skill, it negotiated a postwar European settlement in which its role was incommensurate with its economic or military weight.[1] Partly, this was a result of the strategic choices made by the victors of the war. Only France, they believed, could lead European reconstruction and contain a defeated Germany, and, to a lesser extent, Italy. However, it is often suggested that France

[1] See esp. William Hitchcock, *France Restored: Cold War Diplomacy and the Quest for Leadership in Europe 1944–1954* (Chapel Hill, 1998).

usurped this position by imposture and denial and that this strategy of 'invented honour' not only served for external use, but also
involved a substantial degree of self-delusion, whereby postwar
France reinvented itself as a triumphant and fighting nation, fully
entitled to its status as a world power. This deception suggests the
main traits of a supposedly typically French memory of the war: a
denial of the extent of support for Vichy and of its consenting
involvement in part of the Nazi ideology, more specifically, in the
anti-Semitic persecutions; the limited scope of the purge; the
myth of a nation united in resistance and the gross exaggeration
of the French contribution to the Allied victory, from Bir Hakeim
in May 1942 to the liberation of Paris in August 1944; the
commemorative hegemony of the Gaullists and the Communists,
who were not only the protagonists of the resistance, but also the
two single most important antagonistic forces in postwar French
politics. In short, for the sake of geopolitics and with a measure of
artful deceit, France was allowed to avoid coming to terms with
its less than glorious past to a much greater extent than most
other European nations.

This very sceptical reading of France's relationship to its past
has, in more or less sophisticated versions, been much more
influential and widely accepted, both in popular culture and in
historiography, than the stereotype it derides, at least since the
early 1980s.[2] However, this essay tries to show, first, that the
stereotype grows out of a political and cultural history of remembrance—and predominantly a history of high politics and high
culture at that. Secondly, this essay suggests that the Fifth
Republic, which saw de Gaulle's return to power in 1958, func-
tioned as a screen to perceptions of French ways of dealing with
the past, as if the two decades that separate 1945 from 1965
constituted one homogenous period. I will argue for a re-evalua-
tion of the debates that raged under the Fourth Republic and
the forces that animated them, debates in which de Gaulle was
relegated to the sidelines after January 1946 and the Communist
Party after May 1947. I will also question the central place of the
resistance in French remembrance and demonstrate the ascen-
dancy of the memory of suffering and persecution in postwar
representations. My focus will change from a history of

---

[2] For a balanced view see Henry Rousso, *Le Syndrome de Vichy* (Paris, 1987), and Eric
Conan and Henry Rousso, *Vichy, un passé qui ne passe pas* (Paris, 1994).

commemorations, monuments, and political discourse to a social history of the consequences of war and occupation as reflected in social policy, legislation, and the self-organization of veterans and victims of the war. By doing so, this essay will draw attention to the enduring legacy of the Great War in French society, into which the legacy of the Second World War was inserted.

In France—and not in France alone—1914 was on everybody's mind in 1940, for obvious reasons: in less than twenty-six years, France had been twice invaded by its German enemy through its northern border. In 1944 and 1945, 1918 was also on many observers' minds—had this new war not ended like its predecessor, in a German defeat? But this time, it was much more difficult to ignore the fundamental differences in France's experiences of the two wars. France's experience with modern warfare had been cumulative. Only the youngest generation which lived through the Second World War had not lived through the First World War. During the inter-war period, French society had been permeated by the remembrance of the Great War and this period had bequeathed a whole universe of monuments, rituals, discourses, vocabulary, organizations, legislation, and institutions for veterans and victims. Adding the names of those who fell in 1940–5 to the monument for those who had fallen in 1914–18 came naturally to the thousands of French municipal councils, and the whole framework developed after 1918 became the obvious setting for dealing with the legacy of this new war. Yet to assimilate the two wars was also politically expedient. When de Gaulle referred to a 'thirty years' war', it was not the European civil war historians of the late twentieth century would write about, but the twentieth-century continuation of the secular conflict between the German and French nations. In this war, France had twice been the victim of aggression, and it had twice triumphed over its enemy. To present the Second World War as an episode in an ongoing military conflict—after all, France had lost a battle, not a war, in 1940—concealed some of French society's most central experiences during the war years. These were occupation and geographical separation from the main theatres of war for most of the time, the Vichy regime's collaboration with the German victor, persecutions, and massive population displacements, to name only the most important. Yet after 1945, these experiences were impossible to ignore.

The Judicial Dimension

For a start, there was the legacy of 'collaboration'.[3] Heinous crimes had been committed during the occupation, including murder, theft, persecution, and deportation, and they had to be punished. The pre-war penal code was unsuitable for trying wartime crimes, since they were not the outcome of individual criminal undertakings, but part of the criminal policy of the occupier and the regime that had accepted the principle and the practice of collaboration. Beyond the crimes committed, the regime that had sanctioned them had to be put on trial. This judicial process was by nature exceptional: it required both new legislation and new judicial institutions. Pre-war legislation contained provisions for different forms of treason, particularly 'espionage' and 'breach of national security'. However, formally, after the signing of the armistice on 22 June 1940, France was no longer at war with Germany. On this basis, de Gaulle had been sentenced to death by Vichy for desertion, while the volunteers in the French Legion of Volunteers (LVF), fighting with the *Wehrmacht* on the Eastern Front, had Vichy's blessing. The Pétain government could only be put on trial if its first act, the armistice, was judged illegitimate. The notion of treason was extended to include acts committed against the Allies of the Free French and denunciation, a crime with murderous consequences under Nazi occupation. The immunity of civil servants carrying out the orders of the government was suspended, and a new punishment of 'deprivation of civil rights' was introduced. This last provision served to strip a large number of minor offenders of their political and professional rights, among them the right to vote and to be elected, without overburdening the prisons.

The purge also required the creation of an extraordinary judicial apparatus. Since judging collaborators was a one-off operation involving hundreds of thousands of cases, it was impossible to entrust it to the normal courts. Nor could they be expanded enormously and shrunk again once the task was finished. Moreover, the normal courts were part of the problem, since they had

---

[3] See a complete update in Henry Rousso, *Vichy: L'événement, la mémoire, l'histoire* (Paris, 2001), esp. ch. 11: 'L'Épuration en France: Une histoire inachevée', first published in *Vingtième Siècle*, 33 (1992).

proved compliant enough with Vichy's anti-republican and anti-Semetic legislation. The delivery of fast and efficient justice was a major challenge in the establishment of a new legitimate regime, in part also in order to cut short any development of popular or 'wild' justice. If the scope of popular vengeance is a measure of the efficiency of an official judiciary, the purge in France was a success. After the liberation, only about 1,200 individuals were killed in retribution. The scope for political violence by the resistance during the war had also been limited, by comparison with the levels of violence to which it was a reaction. There were two to three thousand executions before the Allied landings, and about twice that number in the violent period between 6 June 1944 and the liberation of any given locality (June to November for most of the territory). Unlike many other countries and unlike the Allied powers, France did not opt exclusively for military courts. Instead, the purge was delegated to a four-tier system of extraordinary courts. At the top was the High Court, which tried the 108 top officials of the Vichy regime. Eight officials were sentenced to death: three were executed (among them Prime Minister Laval), and five sentences were commuted to life imprisonment (among them Pétain). Ten officials were sentenced *in absentia*, eight were sentenced to forced labour, and fourteen received prison sentences of varying length. Fifteen others were sentenced to 'deprivation of civil rights'. Seven of them were instantly rehabilitated on the basis of assistance given to the resistance (including Maurice Papon, who had been in charge of the deportation of Jews from Bordeaux, who would be condemned for crimes against humanity at a second trial in 1998). At the second level were the Courts of Justice, which could pronounce the full range of sentences at the disposal of the normal criminal courts. The courts were presided over by a professional judge, who submitted the judgement to a jury of four members, chosen by the local liberation committees set up by the resistance. Lesser offenders were judged by the 'civic chambers', a type of administrative court which alone could pronounce the sentence of 'deprivation of civil rights'. Military courts, finally, judged war crimes and the cases of military personnel (both French and German).

The scope of the purge in France was by no means limited. A total of 350,000 individual files was investigated; 125,000 of them were judged by the Courts of Justice, and only one quarter were acquitted. Of the accused, 50,000 were sentenced to 'deprivation of civil rights'; 44,000 individuals received prison sentences; and 1,500 death penalties were carried out. At the same time, individual measures of clemency very rapidly reduced the number of individuals imprisoned on charges of collaboration. By the end of 1946 there were not more than 29,000. In 1948 the number had decreased further to 18,000. In 1953 parliament voted on a series of far-ranging amnesty laws with collective effect. As a result, in 1954 only about 1,000 of the most serious offenders were still detained, and by 1960 only nine of them were left. As a consequence, limitations on purges as a judicial process in France were chronological, rather than social. In parallel to the courts and civic chambers, different professional bodies also set up purge committees which pronounced professional sanctions—temporary or permanent bans on exercising a profession. The most important process concerned the public administration. According to the most recent estimates, between 20,000 and 30,000 civil servants were punished by internal purge committees in this way.

Individual clemency and collective amnesty were controversial at the time they took effect. There was no silent consensus on forgiveness and national reconciliation, as existed to some extent in Germany, Austria, and even the Netherlands. Although the Vichy regime had enjoyed widespread consent during its first months, over the four years of its existence its effect on French society had been profoundly divisive. In a highly polarized political climate, the amnesty laws faced outright opposition from the Communist Party, and public feelings ran high. The task the governments of the Fourth Republic set themselves was all the more ambitious since they combined the challenge of national reconciliation with that of European reconciliation with the former enemy, Germany. The defeat of the project for a European Defence Community by a hostile parliament and public opinion one year after the amnesty laws were passed testifies to the widespread opposition to a policy of burying the past as quickly as possible less than ten years after the end of the war. Painful memories of the period of the occupation were still very much alive and they were directly related to the human toll of the conflict.

The Social Dimension

The impact on French society of France's dramatic defeat in May–June 1940 was inversely proportional to its impact on France's geopolitical standing. The human cost of the Second World War, during most of which France was not a combatant, was much more limited than that of the First World War.[4] During the first conflict, eight million French soldiers had been mobilized over a total duration of four years, that is 80 per cent of all men of military age. One sixth of them—one and a half million—died, and one million were permanently disabled. The war also widowed 600,000 women and orphaned 760,000 children. During the second conflict, French war-related mortality is officially estimated at 600,000, but that seems about a third too high. Military casualties did not surpass 150,000, two-thirds of whom died in the battle of the invasion of May–June 1940. A majority of French soldiers fighting on the Allied side in North Africa, Italy, and later on the Western Front, were recruited among colonial troops. Their combined losses did not equal those of French citizens from Alsace and Lorraine forcibly enrolled in the German *Wehrmacht* (estimated at 40,000). For an overwhelming majority of French soldiers, the experience of the Second World War was of German captivity: of the one and a half million soldiers taken captive in June 1940, 940,000 would not be liberated until five years later. This long captivity was a crucial war-experience for France, but it was hardly a murderous one (21,000 soldiers died in captivity). A little over 90,000 civilians died in war-related deaths in occupied France, two-thirds of them as victims of Allied bombing. A higher number, probably between 130,000 and 150,000, died after their transfer to Germany and its eastern conquests, among them 75,000 Jews who were deported from France and murdered from the summer of 1942 onwards, non-Jewish concentration camp inmates, prisoners of war, and conscripted workers.

As a result, war-related mortality during the Second World War in France was only one quarter of that during the First

---

[4] See Pieter Lagrou, 'Les Guerres, les morts et le deuil: bilan chiffré', in Stéphane Audouin-Rouzeau, Annette Becker, Christian Ingrao, and Henry Rousso (eds.), *Violences de guerre: Approche comparée des deux conflits mondiaux* (Brussels, 2002).

World War. Among the major European nations only Britain faced a comparable situation. German losses were three to four times higher after 1945 than after 1918, and Italian losses were almost equal in the two world wars. The nature and the highly unequal distribution of this mortality further strengthened the difference. Whereas the casualties of the Great War had been overwhelmingly soldiers of a conscripted army, more or less equally drawn from all social classes and regions, war-related mortality during the Second World War had very specific and discriminatory causes, in particular the genocide, which accounted for one fifth of all war-related deaths in France (compared with, for example, the Netherlands, where genocide accounted for over half of all war-related mortality). One quarter of the pre-war Jewish community in France was killed, with a considerably higher percentage for Jewish residents of foreign nationality. To a lesser extent this also applied to the victims of political persecution and even of Allied bombing, which each targeted specific groups rather than the French population at large. Even military casualties were concentrated in particular areas, such as Alsace, Lorraine, Morocco, and Senegal.

This peculiar geography of death in war made it particularly difficult to assimilate the memory of the Second World War into that of the First World War, a memory in which the triumph and the sacrifice of the French nation had been symbolized by the figure of the soldier. Mortality was only one consequence of the brevity of the military confrontation and the length of the occupation. Another experience central to this war affected the French population on a vastly greater scale: population displacement. During the occupation, more than two million French citizens were transferred to Germany, either as prisoners of war or as workers. The reintegration of these groups, representing approximately 5 per cent of the French population, was a major challenge for the postwar state.[5] It was, moreover, intimately related to the remembrance of this war. How would the humiliation and the suffering of this considerable mass of citizens be integrated into heroic narratives of resistance and victory?

---

[5] See Pieter Lagrou, *The Legacy of Nazi Occupation: Patriotic Memory and National Recovery in Western Europe, 1945–1965* (Cambridge, 2000).

The Generational Dimension

Inter-war French society had been dominated by the 'génération du feu', the generation whose formative experience, including politically, had been the war in the trenches and the firing of guns and artillery—much like German or Italian society, but with a different result. After 1945, obviously, there was no homogeneous 'postwar generation' as there had been after 1918 in France or after 1945 in Poland, the Soviet Union, Yugoslavia, or even Germany, that is, a generation marked by the collective experience of war. After that dramatic moment of social unification through the war in the trenches, the Second World War had dispersed society along the lines of incommensurably different war experiences. In France, the biography of François Mitterrand is often referred to as typical for a generation that came of age during the occupation, yet it is so for the improbable combination which he embodies of *a priori* incompatible experiences. He was a prisoner of war in Germany, a government official in Vichy, a resister in France, and a politician in London and Algiers. The Second World War generation in France is clearly a generation of missing solidarities, divergent experiences, and alienation and suspicion between compeers. As such, it is an intermediate generation, crushed between two other generations unified by war: the glorious generation of the *poilus* of the Great War and the forgotten generation of the conscripts of the Algerian War. This situation is exemplified by the functioning of the French Ministry for War Veterans. Even today, its agenda is set, on the one hand, by that first paradigmatic generation of war veterans who created the institution and the legislation, and invented the rituals, organizations, and discourses—a generation that is only now being extinguished—and, on the other hand, by the second generation, which is reaching retirement age and looks back to a dirty colonial war. The Second World War generation is unhappy and fragmented in this institution, constantly trying to conform to a model that is impossible to emulate.

Divided Memories, Divisive Remembrance

Gaullist remembrance was élitist and abstract. It commemorated the exceptional courage and vision of heroic individuals—the thousand *compagnons de la libération*, the fifteen emblematic fallen soldiers of the monument on the Mont Valérien—rather than the scattered war experiences of the French population in general. The few thousand Free French who had participated in the Gaullist exploit during the war were dispersed all over the French Empire and they did not constitute the political mass base required for political longevity under the Fourth Republic. The 'veterans' of 1939–45 were a disturbing element in the Gaullist discourse. They included, first of all, over a million prisoners of war, contemptuously described as 'les chevaliers de la crosse en l'air', the 'knights of the raised rifle butts', who had ignominiously capitulated after a few weeks of combat. A good many of them had been taken captive before they had even had a chance to fire their first shot at the enemy. The prisoners of war were no match for the heroic generation of 1914–18, over three million of whom had gloriously contributed to the French victory during four long years of military confrontation. De Gaulle despised the organization of the prisoners of war and personally vetoed the creation of a Ministry of War Veterans for them. In his view, they did not deserve the treatment the veterans of the Great War had enjoyed. Next there were the resistance fighters, courageous combatants, but often politically suspect and very hard to identify. Unlike the case of the veterans of the Great War, no rigorous checking of combat records was possible, and to ascertain the merits of each individual required declarations to be issued by their resistance chiefs. This was the last thing de Gaulle and the entire patriotic establishment of 1914–18 veterans were inclined to do. Next still came a long list of civilians who had suffered as a result of France's status as a defeated nation in the years 1940–4: victims of the repression of resistance activities, victims of political persecutions, victims of genocide, victims of labour conscription, and so on. The French nation could not ignore them and had to face the issue of defining whom to recognize as national martyrs and for what reasons.

Since the *levée en masse* transformed subjects into citizens, belonging to the national community has traditionally been defined in terms of common combat. (This was among the justifications for denying political rights to women.) If Dreyfus had been a grocer instead of a captain in the French army, there probably would never have been an affair. Mass participation in warfare during the First World War entailed claims for mass participation in politics after 1918. Even for Vichy, Jewish war veterans somehow constituted an exception to its state-sanctioned anti-Semitism. After 1945, defining who could be considered a 'combatant' implied defining the boundaries of the national community.

Immediately after de Gaulle resigned from power in January 1946, a Ministry for Veterans and War Victims was created. Laurent Casanova, a Communist deputy and war hero, was appointed as its first postwar minister. The administrative merger of war veterans and war victims had an immediate consequence. The different proposals to recognize the rights of former resisters, survivors of concentration camps, victims of German reprisals, and even labour conscripts, which had not made any reference to the post-1918 context of 'combatants' in 1945 now, through administrative logic, conformed to the whole legal and bureaucratic infrastructure of the post-1918 period. Conferring the quality of *ancien combattant* was a very formal matter after 1918 and the 'green card' or *carte de combattant* was much coveted as the ultimate sign of belonging to the great patriotic family. Post-1918 legislation stipulated ninety days of 'effective combat' in order to qualify for the card, and the veterans intended to defend this qualification and resist every possible devaluation of their title of honour. The *Union Française des Anciens Combattants* (UFAC) initially refused to accept prisoners of war. None of them had a record of ninety days of effective combat, since the entire campaign of 1940 had only lasted half that long. François Mitterrand, successor to Casanova and a champion of the interests of prisoners of war, forced through legislation that recognized the period spent in captivity as 'effective combat', to the great resentment of the first *génération du feu*. Acceptance of resistance fighters into the UFAC dragged on for many years. Anti-Communist suspicion that the party and its affiliated organizations would fabricate certificates on a grand scale to polish up its resistance record contributed to the very long delay in drawing up legislation, to its restrictive nature, the imposition of the same token ninety days, and to its late implementation. The first organizations of certified resistance veterans were created in the early 1950s and entered the UFAC, most prominently the *Association Nationale des Anciens Combattants Résistants*, closely affiliated to the Communist Party, and the Gaullist *Confédération Nationale des Combattants Volontaires de la Résistance*.

The most revealing conflict emerged, however, when it came to defining the victims of fascist occupation policies. The Communist Party strongly supported the paradigm of an anti-fascist community of combat and suffering. All political opponents of fascism, and even more all victims of fascism, could subscribe to it and become part of an anti-fascist family in which the Communist Party, currently and historically, played a central role, and where martyrdom and heroism, victims and veterans, intermingled and fraternally shared the heritage of victory. This anti-fascism was a highly inclusive form of patriotic community. Since all victims of fascism were redefined as anti-fascists, ergo militants, ergo combatants, a whole range of victims could enter the combatant family. This included most prominently Jewish victims, arrested, deported, and, with only a few thousand exceptions, massacred because of what the Nazis perceived as their 'race', regardless of their actual political or religious beliefs, and regardless of their attitude towards the occupier. It also included Communist militants arrested by the Daladier government for obstruction of the war effort at the time of the non-aggression pact between Moscow and Berlin, who ended up in Nazi camps after the invasion. It further included anyone arrested for whatever reason, including random retaliation, with the exception of common law offenders, whose common criminality—black marketeering, theft—had been dealt with by the occupier with the uncommon punishment of detention in concentration camps. All these groups deserved special recognition as national martyrs, because of what they had suffered at the hands of the fascist enemy. These victims of fascism, as a target of Nazi Germany and Vichy, after all, largely represented what the latter had defined as 'l'anti-France': Bolsheviks, Jews, foreigners, masons, and terrorists—most often all combined in one and the same person. In addition, the

Communist Party also acknowledged the workers forcibly transferred to the German industrial centres as 'lesser victims', as they
symbolized the fact that the working class had been the first
victim of fascism. The *grande messe* of this Communist anti-fascist
patriotism was the commemoration at Compiègne in August
1946, staged by Casanova. In a four-day-long ceremony, veterans of the Great War, prisoners of war, victims of Nazi persecution, and labour conscripts were honoured on the occasion of the
return to Compiègne of the stone commemorating the German
capitulation in 1918. The monument had been taken to Berlin in
June 1940, when Hitler had requested that the French armistice
be signed on the same spot, in the same railway carriage. The
ceremony mixed traditional patriotism and a reference to 1918
with the most inclusive version of anti-fascist combatant rhetoric
ever displayed on French soil. The Communist Party's antifascist patriotism symbolized its final integration into the French
nation.

This assimilation of all sorts of victims with combatants was
also expressed in organizations and laws conferring the *carte de
combattant* on, for example, victims of Nazi persecution. *Déportés
politiques*, in order to qualify, had to have undergone ninety days
of detention, or execution. Detention in a concentration camp
thus became assimilated with notions of 'effective combat' and
death at the hands of the enemy, even in a context of political or
racial persecution. The status of combatant was no longer exclusively associated with fighting for the liberation of the
Fatherland. Those whom Vichy had defined as 'l'anti-France'
thus became national martyrs and honorary members of the
national community. This represented a thorough revision of the
traditional concepts of a community of combat and of patriotism,
and it harvested a predictable hostile reaction from French patriots in conservative quarters. The UFAC initially rejected the
application for membership of the anti-fascist *Fédération Nationale
des Déportés et Internés Résistants et Patriotes*, since it included Jewish
victims, Communists arrested before the Party's official entry
into the resistance in June 1941, and random victims of retaliation—all groups that had no clear 'combatant' status. It immediately welcomed the rival Gaullist faction into its ranks. This
excluded all survivors of concentration camps arrested for other
reasons than acts of resistance. Anti-Communism was among the

main reasons for this rejection, but anti-Semitism was not absent in the polemics opposing both organizations and both discourses. The pro-Communist organization explicitly defended its inclusion of Jewish victims, while the Gaullist organization most explicitly justified their exclusion. The debate in the National Assembly finally enshrined the distinction between *déportés de la résistance*, courageous combatants who had paid dearly for their heroism, and the unfortunate *déportés politiques*, who suffered all the same but whose national merit was more ambiguous. Yet, in the long run, the inclusive notion gained general acceptance. The Cold War split the inclusive anti-fascist organization into two only a year after the vote on the law in parliament, and the non-Communist, non-resistance members joined with the formerly exclusivist patriots.

After the departure into opposition of the two resistance champions, the Gaullists in January 1946 and the Communists in May 1947, the 'third force' coalitions that steered the Fourth Republic until its dissolution in 1958 strongly identified with 'The Deportation' as a consensual symbol of the memory of the experience of French society during the Second World War in its inclusive version. A national commemorative day was created and a national monument erected on the *île de la Cité* (although the latter was not inaugurated until 1961 by the then president, de Gaulle). This commemoration differed substantially from the one de Gaulle had tried to organize in 1944 and 1945, but it also successfully countered the claims of the Communist Party to a monopoly of martyrdom and resistance. 'Deportation' became a sacred symbol for the experience of the French nation in general. The suffering and persecutions were integrated into a heroic memory of resistance, where the difference between the ideological enemies of Nazi Germany and Jewish victims was deliberately blurred. It was also very explicitly a Cold War memory, mobilizing a 'spiritual resistance', with overtly Christian references, against a 'totalitarian state'.

Conclusion

Denial and deceit are inadequate categories for describing the ways in which postwar French society tried to cope with the legacy of war and occupation. As in most European countries, the resurgence of postwar patriotism was accompanied by some measure of 'invented honour' and combatant rhetoric, but triumphalism was certainly not the dominant mood in the late 1940s or in the grim 1950s. The claim that postwar society had remained 'silent' on the darker sides of the war years is even more improbable. The purge was a multi-faceted process of considerable scope, which involved hundreds of thousands of individuals and contributed to a significant renewal of the political and professional élites. As for the suffering caused by war, occupation, and the Vichy regime, it was the object not of a taboo, but of a set of very selective memories. The place occupied in postwar remembrance by memories of the persecution of the Jews, which has been at the heart of most recent interpretations, is the result not so much of psychological reflexes of suppression as of the conflicting demands made on public attention and state intervention by other war experiences. In much the same way that postwar West German society prioritized *Vertriebene* (expellees) and prisoners of war over Nazi victims in its social policy and in its *Geschichtspolitik* (official attitude to history), public remembrance in France was dominated by the claims made by prisoners of war, conscripted workers, and victims of political persecution.[6]

Even if French society was much less affected by death and displacement than German, Polish, Ukrainian, and Yugoslav societies, the consequences of the upheaval caused by the war for large groups of the population constituted a major challenge. Very little research has been done on the impact of, for example, wartime migrations on postwar society. The transfer of two million French citizens to Germany, the internal displacement of hundreds of thousands of refugees from the Eastern *départements* to the West, from the northern zone to the southern, disrupted local communities. They accelerated the rural exodus, altered occupational patterns, and probably contributed to a lasting increase in the geographical and social mobility of the French population. The difficult reintegration of prisoners of war and workers into their families and villages prompted unknown numbers to change residence. Unknown numbers of individuals

---

[6] See esp. Robert G. Moeller, *War Stories: The Search for a Usable Past in the Federal Republic of Germany* (Berkeley, 2001).

suspected of collaboration, whether or not they had been the object of judicial or professional purges, preferred the anonymity of a new environment to the hostility of their own community. These changes took place against the backdrop of a dramatic transformation of the French economy and French society during the boom years of the *trente glorieuses*, and in a menacing international context, with the almost uninterrupted engagement of French troops in colonial wars, from Indochina to Madagascar and North Africa, and the Cold War looming over Europe. The consequences of war and occupation were part and parcel of these social transformations. At the same time, postwar French politics were much more polarized and unstable than in almost any other European nation, leading, in 1958, to one of the most serious political crises of postwar European history. In spite of the frailty of the political balance, the weakness of the political centre, and the fragmentation of electoral scores, parliamentary democracy has not only survived in France, it has taken much firmer root than at any previous period in French history.[7] Undeniably—and however unsatisfactory the ways in which this was achieved might appear today—this political evolution is partly the result of a successful management of the consequences of war. This includes dealing with collaborators and victims, re-establishing political legitimacy, attaining at least a minimal national reconciliation, and inventing procedures, rituals, and consensual discourses to commemorate a divisive past. The miraculous recovery of the 'sick man of Europe' was based on a considerable degree of reinvention. Yet imposture alone would not have sufficed.

[7] For a broader perspective, see Martin Conway, 'Democracy in Postwar Western Europe: The Triumph of a Political Model', *European History Quarterly*, 32 (2002), 59–84.

5

A Sceptical Generation? War Memorials and the Collective Memory of the Second World War in Britain, 1945–2000

NICK HEWITT

This essay is based primarily on completed survey forms, transcriptions, press cuttings, and photographs held in the UK National Inventory of War Memorials (UKNIWM), a recording project jointly established in 1989 by the Imperial War Museum and English Heritage. It will attempt to show how the war memorials erected in Britain in the years since the Second World War can provide evidence for the existence of a 'sceptical generation'[1] in the UK, and how they can be used as physical markers illustrating that generation's constantly evolving collective memory of its wartime experiences.

I. *First Responses*

In November 1944 a national panel of observers was asked to give its views about what form war memorials should take after the Second World War ended. The panel members were described as mainly middle class and 'more than averagely thoughtful people . . . with all sorts of beliefs and in all sorts of jobs'.[2] The

---

[1] The term 'sceptical generation' was originally applied to the generation of Germans who *grew up* during the Second World War and the early years of the Federal Republic; cf. Helmut Schelsky, *Die skeptische Generation: Eine Soziologie der deutschen Jugend* (Düsseldorf, 1957); Dirk Moses, 'The Forty-Fivers: A Generation between Fascism and Democracy', *German Politics and Society*, 17 (1999), 94–126; Jan Werner Mueller, *Another Country: German Intellectuals, Unification and National Identity* (New Haven, 2000). The author chose to apply it to the generation of Britons who *fought* the Second World War, with specific reference to their attitude to war memorials. In this context, the term is the theme of this chapter.

[2] *Mass Observation Bulletin P.B.6* (Letchworth, Herts, Nov. 1944), 1. Copy held in Imperial War Museum Department of Printed Books.

results of the survey were published as the *Mass Observation Bulletin* for November 1944.

The *Bulletin* opens with a paragraph headed 'No Stone Memorials', and goes on to argue that 'most people wanted a memorial which would be useful or give pleasure to those who outlive the war'.[3] It was clear that commemorative practice at the end of the Second World War was not going to echo that of the First, which had been followed by what was arguably the largest public arts project the country had ever seen. Almost as soon as the guns had stopped in 1918, British communities had begun spontaneously erecting war memorials, ranging from elaborate works of art by prominent artists, to simple crosses by unknown village stonemasons. In contrast, typical anonymous comments in the *Mass Observation Bulletin* include:[4]

- 'Anything but monuments. Memorial funds for scholarships or charity, memorial utility buildings, but not absolutely useless and often ugly memorials.' (civil servant)
- 'First let us have no more stone crosses, war memorials in the 1918 sense of the word.' (soldier)
- 'The only point on which my mind is fully made up is that they should not take the form of stone monstrosities on every street corner and village green and not one penny would I willingly contribute to any scheme to erect such.' (chemist)
- 'Whatever shape memorials take it should not take the form of useless monuments. We are fighting for posterity, so let the memorials be for the use of posterity—libraries, drama schools, playing fields, village halls, they would all serve a useful purpose.' (schoolmistress)

Objection to traditional memorials on aesthetic grounds was coupled with an underlying cynicism about the values and the faith in the future which they represented; as far as war memorials were concerned, this was certainly a 'sceptical generation'. Contrastingly First World War memorials rarely gave any indication of ambiguities in public perceptions of the war. Indeed, it could be argued that nascent doubts about the war's legitimacy only increased the importance of emphasizing that those commemorated did not die in vain. The First World War

---

[3] Ibid.   [4] Ibid.

memorial at Middlewich, Cheshire,[5] for example, is inscribed 'through all eternity their names shall bide, enshrined as heroes who for Empire died'.

Jay Winter, in his 1995 book *Sites of Memory, Sites of Mourning*, comments that

both the political character of the Second World War and some of its horrific consequences made it impossible for many survivors to return to the languages of mourning which grew out of the 1914–18 war when they tried to express their sense of loss after 1945. The sources of this rupture are not hard to find. Many of the commemorative forms created after 1918 were intended to warn; when the warning was not heard . . . that message of hope . . . was bound to fade away.[6]

This was bitterly confirmed by another contributor to the *Mass Observation Bulletin*:

Most of the last war memorials bear inscriptions to the effect that those of that day were satisfied that it was 'the war to end war'. We of this day will, I am sure, be alive to the necessity of putting our hopes into words. Therefore I would suggest that on each memorial there should be placed a neat plaque saying—'this sacrifice was not enough. Another was called for—and was made'. Care should be taken to leave room for the plaque that will be necessary about thirty years hence.[7]

Of course, war-weary cynicism may not provide the only explanation for the restrained approach to commemoration in 1945. The Second World War had placed great emphasis on the civilian contribution to the war effort. This was supported by the reality of bombing, rationing, and war work. Evidence of the strong grip which this imagery of a 'People's War' rapidly established on the collective memory of the Second World War, and of a widespread disillusionment with traditional symbolic war memorials, is provided by a suggestion made in a letter to *The Times* dated 15 August 1944. Signed by a distinguished panel which included David Cecil, Kenneth Clark, T. S. Eliot, and John Maynard Keynes, the letter called for 'a few of our bomb-damaged churches to be preserved in their ruined condition as permanent memorials of this war'. Like the contributors to *Mass*

---

[5] UK National Inventory of War Memorials, Imperial War Museum (hereafter NIWM), record no. 1992.

[6] Jay Winter, *Sites of Memory, Sites of Mourning* (Cambridge, 1995), 9.

[7] *Mass Observation Bulletin*, 2.

Observation, this group of luminaries objected strongly to the memorials of the First World War:

There will probably be a wide measure of agreement that many of the memorials put up after the last war were unworthy of the men whose sacrifice they commemorate. That a vast gulf of feeling should have lain between the experience and the memorials was in any case inevitable. In this war conditions have been different. England has itself been in the battle and London is still in it.[8]

The suggestion for preserving some of the churches was formalized by a 1945 Architectural Press publication entitled *Bombed Churches as War Memorials*, which included some specific case studies, but the idea was not taken up as widely as its proponents wished. Nevertheless, some examples do exist, such as Charles Church in Plymouth and, rather better known, Old Coventry Cathedral.[9]

It can be argued that this perception of a 'People's War' was misguided. According to statistics reproduced in the British Official History of the Second World War, around sixty thousand civilians had been recorded as killed or missing believed killed by 31 July 1945, half of them in London.[10] In contrast, the total number of military casualties recorded as killed or missing presumed killed was around two hundred and seventy thousand.[11] Some 33 per cent of Britons were mobilized into civilian war work, compared to 22 per cent into the Armed Services, but war work effectively abolished the unemployment that had characterized the inter-war years.[12] Rationing combined the principle of fair distribution across the class divide with the chance of avoidance for those prepared to use the black market.

Nevertheless, these perceived hardships rapidly entered the British collective memory, and a sense of shared participation in the 'People's War' led to civilians feeling less obliged publicly to emphasize their gratitude to the military. Furthermore, the material costs of bombing lent support to the argument that money should be used for practical rather than symbolic

---

[8] *Bombed Churches as War Memorials* (Cheam, 1945). The letter originally appeared during the German 'V-weapon' missile offensive against London in 1944, hence the reference to London being 'still in it'.

[9] NIWM 25527 (Charles Church) and NIWM 17718 (Coventry Cathedral).

[10] I. C. B. Dear and M. R. D. Foot (eds.), *The Oxford Companion to the Second World War* (Oxford, 1995), 1136.

[11] Ibid. 1151.   [12] Ibid. 1132.

commemoration, in other words, for rebuilding blitzed cities and rehousing homeless people rather than building monuments. By the end of 1942, some two and a half million Britons were occupying partially repaired bombed houses.[13]

Another explanation for restraint could be a sense of relief: British casualties in the Second World War were fewer than half those of the First, although the armed forces stood at around five million during both conflicts.[14] It may perhaps have been hard not to feel a sense of gratitude that so many returned, and it was certainly impossible to repeat the sense of shock and bewilderment of 1919.

Relief may have been coupled with at least a subconscious awareness of Britain's lesser role in the Second World War compared to the First. Of particular importance were Soviet losses, generally accepted at nearly twenty million,[15] and the enormous material contribution made by the United States,[16] without which victory in 1945 would have been impossible. To indulge in a prolonged period of national mourning over three hundred thousand dead may perhaps have seemed indecent when faced with a global body count of around fifty million. In *Sites of Memory, Sites of Mourning*, Winter comments that Hiroshima and Auschwitz 'raised the possibility that the limits of language had been reached; perhaps there was no way adequately to express the hideousness and scale of the cruelties of the 1939–1945 war'.[17]

The *Mass Observation Bulletin* seems to demonstrate a clear commitment on the part of the generation which fought the Second World War to a utilitarian rather than a symbolic approach to commemoration. Even the artistic establishment seems to have recognized this underlying strength of feeling. In April 1944, *before* the publication of the *Mass Observation Bulletin*,

[13] Ibid. 1135.

[14] *Commonwealth War Graves Commission Annual Report 1997–1998*. The table on p. 36 gives the numbers of war dead for Great Britain and the former colonies (not including the self-governing Dominions) as being 887,282 for the First World War and 382,677 for the Second.

[15] *The Oxford Companion to the Second World War*, 434.

[16] Ibid. 1179–85. The tables show the scale of US economic output. To give just one example, according to a table on p. 1204, by 1944 the USA was producing 85 per cent of Allied merchant ship tonnage, compared to around 12 per cent by the entire British Commonwealth.

[17] Winter, *Sites of Memory*, 9.

the Royal Society of Arts convened a conference with the stated aim of emphasizing 'the need for a high standard of artistic merit and social and cultural value in the memorials of the present war'.[18] As a result, the Royal Society set up a War Memorials Sub-Committee, the findings of which were published in November.

Initially, the report appears deeply out of touch with the sentiments expressed in the Mass Observation Survey. With reference to how best to record names, it argues that: 'Throughout the centuries the art of the sculptor has provided such records, and few things are more satisfactory than a well designed and well cut inscription.'[19] The report goes on to say that monuments should be 'the creation of individual artists well acquainted with or prepared to study the sentiments of the community that commissions them'.[20]

However, despite this apparent commitment to traditional symbolic commemoration, the report does concede that Books of Remembrance would be 'an acceptable alternative' to sculpture. Remarkably, it then goes on to talk almost exclusively of *utilitarian* memorials. No further advice regarding sculptural projects is provided, and the remaining five pages of this eight- page document are devoted entirely to what it calls 'Projects of Social Service'—Gardens of Memory; parks and open spaces; community centres; village halls; hospitals, and so forth.[21]

Of course, utilitarian projects had been proposed and debated after the First World War as well, but ultimately many were rejected in favour of more traditional projects. Indeed, the debates could sometimes become quite acrimonious. Local newspapers in Shropshire chronicle a bitter argument between supporters of monuments and those in favour of an addition to the local hospital. So, on 15 March 1919, Emma Florence Cuncliffe wrote: 'I note that one suggestion is to place a paltry £2,000 towards a memorial and thousands and thousands are to

---

[18] *War Memorials: A Survey made by a Committee of the Royal Society of Arts and published by the War Memorials Advisory Council* (London, 1944), 2.

[19] Ibid. 3.

[20] Ibid.

[21] Ibid. 4–7. Other 'Projects of Social Service' specifically listed include trees, hilltops or viewpoints, bombed churches, buildings of historic interest or architectural importance, and, perhaps the most poignant of all, 'After-care of the Wounded'. With regard to the latter, the document optimistically argues that 'Government, it may confidently be hoped, will make an ampler provision for them than in the past'.

go towards something that would benefit and save money for the living.'[22] But on 4 April a correspondent identified only as 'grateful patient' retaliated in a rival paper:

Sir, is there any chance of stopping the frightful waste of money in little parish war memorials, when the money might be put to help the splendid Town and County memorial of an annexe to the Royal Salop Infirmary . . . one may say why not have both, but that's where the waste of money comes in.[23]

Even when utilitarian memorials were constructed after the First World War, they rarely occurred in isolation and were often accompanied by some sort of more symbolic memorial, as in Teddington, Middlesex, where the Memorial Hospital is accompanied by a monument designed by the architect Francis Doyle Jones.[24]

The evidence provided by the Mass Observation Survey indicates that by 1944 the country had wholeheartedly embraced the concept of utilitarianism, and certainly did not require the blessing of the artistic establishment, as represented by the Royal Society Sub-Committee, which was apparently just trying to catch up with popular opinion. As after the First World War, commemoration was to be driven by the needs and demands of the local communities, a grass-roots movement out of the control of any central body.

II. *Lights, Roofs and Gardens: Memorials of the 1940s,*
1950s, and 1960s

As far as a national war memorial was concerned, the War Memorials Advisory Council had concluded their report by arguing that

London, to which come the imperial pilgrims who visit the mother country, should surely have a special memorial of its own . . . a shrine

---

[22] *Wellington Journal & Shrewsbury News*, 8 Mar. 1919, p. 5, col. 6.

[23] *Shrewsbury Chronicle*, 4 Apr. 1919, p. 4, col. 3. In the event, Shropshire chose a magnificent monument by the artist Allen G. Wyon as its county memorial. It was constructed in the county town, Shrewsbury (NIWM 13913). However, it proved impossible for those of the same opinion as 'grateful patient' to prevent the construction of 'little parish war memorials'; nearly 500 other First World War memorials in Shropshire are recorded on the UKNIWM database.

[24] NIWM 39853 (Teddington Memorial Hospital) and NIWM 39849 (Monument).

that will include in itself memorials to the dead of the fighting services, the Civil Defence Services, and all those who have taken part in this war and deserve to be remembered.[25]

In the event, however, the Government's decision reflected the pragmatic mood of this more sceptical generation. Arguably the most significant memorial created after the Second World War turned out to be the Land Fund,[26] which was created from surplus war funds in 1946 as a memorial to the dead of both world wars. In terms of symbolic commemoration, the nation settled for simply adding the years 1939–45 to the Cenotaph in Whitehall. In addition the Imperial (now Commonwealth) War Graves Commission accepted responsibility for constructing new cemeteries and Memorials to the Missing, such as the magnificent Royal Air Force (RAF) Memorial to the Missing at Runnymede, unveiled by Queen Elizabeth II in 1953.[27]

Throughout the country, local commemoration of the Second World War was much more practical and understated than that of the First, reflecting the sentiments expressed in the *Mass Observation Bulletin*. The names of the dead were still important, but were often quietly added to existing First World War memorials. These additional inscriptions were muted and often confined to a simple addition, generally 'and also the World War 1939–1945'. A particularly unusual example was the rather unsympathetic addition to Albert Toft's impressive First World War memorial sculpture at Oldham, Lancashire, of a Book of Remembrance set into a recess in the plinth and fitted with an electronic page turner.[28]

In Appleby, Cumbria, the Second World War memorial is a swimming pool.[29] In Stone, Staffordshire, 166 acres of downland were purchased and presented to the National Trust as a 'thank offering for victory and as a memorial to those who fell'.[30] In

---

[25] *War Memorials: A Survey made by a Committee of the Royal Society of Arts*, 8.

[26] The Land Fund, government money originally intended for reconstruction, lives on as the National Heritage Memorial Fund, now part of the Heritage Lottery Fund and sponsor of the UK National Inventory of War Memorials.

[27] NIWM 23270. For a definitive history of the Commonwealth War Graves Commission since the First World War, see Philip Longworth, *The Unending Vigil: A History of the Commonwealth War Graves Commission 1917–1984* (London, 1985; first published 1967).

[28] NIWM 10. See also Derek Boorman, *For Your Tomorrow: British Second World War Memorials* (York, 1995), 147–8.

[29] NIWM 3062.   [30] NIWM 13647.

Eastbourne, six houses were built for disabled ex-servicemen and their families, and opened by the Duke of Devonshire on 12 March 1952 as the Eastbourne War Memorial Housing Society.[31]

Some Second World War utilitarian memorials demonstrate even starker efforts to put the practical needs of the living community above aesthetic value. In Kirkby Stephen, Cumbria, a plaque records the fact that those killed in the Second World War were commemorated by the installation of electric lighting in St Stephen's Church.[32] A similar plaque at St James' Church, Higher Broughton, Salford states that 'in memory of all from this church and parish who lost their lives whilst serving with HM Forces and the Merchant Navy or through enemy action at home during the war 1939–1945 the churchyard boundary railings were replaced in the year 1949'. [33]

The inhabitants of Skelton in Cumbria[34] and Studham in Bedfordshire[35] chose bus shelters as their memorials. Both Heaton Methodist Church, Newcastle upon Tyne,[36] and St John's Presbyterian Church at Kenton,[37] in London, chose the installation of hearing aids.

A few new symbolic memorials were constructed after the Second World War. However, in most cases these could be loosely categorized as official or semi-official projects sanctioned and paid for by the nation or the military. Very few were spontaneously erected by communities.

The military memorials mainly commemorated sections of the Armed Forces which either did not exist during 1914–18 or which radically expanded between the two wars, and therefore felt few or no ties to existing memorials. For example, on 4 October 1952 Queen Elizabeth the Queen Mother unveiled the Commando Memorial[38] at Spean Bridge, in the heart of the old Commando training grounds in the Scottish Highlands.

Other Second World War memorials commemorated

[31] NIWM 16984.   [32] NIWM 517.   [33] NIWM 15960.   [34] NIWM 3119.
[35] NIWM 1670.   [36] NIWM 17819.   [37] NIWM 11003.
[38] NIWM 5894. The Commandos, more properly known as the Special Services Brigade, were formed by the British in June 1940. The personnel were all volunteers whose remit was to carry out guerrilla operations against the Germans, initially along the coast of Occupied Europe. Although the name 'Commando' was taken from Boer irregular units who fought the British during the Boer War of 1899–1902, there was no real precedent in the British Army for these 'special forces' units during any earlier conflict.

Britain's allies, in particular those who fought from Britain after their countries were overrun. One of the best-known examples is the Polish Air Force Memorial at RAF Northolt,[39] the work of the exiled Polish sculptor Mieczyslaw Lubelski, which was unveiled on 2 November 1948 by Lord Tedder.

III. Monuments to the Living: Memorial Construction since 1984

Practicality and understated restraint remained the dominant characteristics of the commemorative practice of this sceptical generation for many years. However, the last years of the century saw an unprecedented desire to construct more permanent and obvious memorials relating to the Second World War, and a wave of memorial construction took place during the 1980s and 1990s. By no means all of these memorials constitute great art; indeed many could not really be considered to be art at all.

Thus, for example, memorials commemorating the United States Air Force (USAF) have appeared at former airfield sites all over East Anglia and elsewhere. George Fox's excellent gazetteer, *Eighth Air Force Remembered*,[40] lists hundreds, many of them restored buildings, simple plaques, or restored artefacts. One such commemorates the 355th Fighter Group at RAF Steeple Morden, Cambridgeshire, and takes the form of a mounted propeller from a P-51 Mustang aircraft.[41]

Memorials commemorating the Merchant Navy have been erected in the Welsh ports of Barry[42] and Cardiff.[43] Simple plaques have been erected by campaign veterans groups such as the Burma Star Association. One of the most impressive pieces of figurative art commemorates the Battle of Britain, and was unveiled at Capel-le-Ferne, Kent, on 9 July 1993.[44]

---

[39] NIWM 2276. After the fall of Poland in September 1939, several Polish squadrons were formed in France and the UK. After the fall of France in 1940, surviving elements were subordinated to RAF command. The Polish Air Force expanded steadily as new personnel became available later in the war, and by 1945 it numbered some fifteen operational squadrons and 19,400 personnel.

[40] George H. Fox, *Eighth Air Force Remembered* (London, 1991).

[41] NIWM 8425.   [42] NIWM 6634.   [43] NIWM 13504.

[44] NIWM 1482. The Capel-le-Ferne memorial was the work of the artist Jamie Buchanan, and takes the form of a seated figure of an airman staring out to sea in contemplative mood, set in the hub of an immense three-bladed propeller cut into the chalk hillside.

An ideal location for many war memorials has been the National Memorial Arboretum at Alrewas in Staffordshire, 150 acres area of woodland set aside for a wide range of commemorative projects, not all of them to do with war. Amongst the war memorials is an unusual wooden sculpture of a polar bear, unveiled in June 1998 to commemorate the 49th Infantry Division whose divisional sign it was.[45] Also in the Arboretum are memorials commemorating the First Army; the Royal Logistics Corps; the Royal Tank Regiment; the Italy Star Association; the veterans of the Greek Campaign; and the Far East Prisoners of War.

The last few years have seen more elaborate, large-scale projects. As a result of a fund-raising campaign which followed the fiftieth anniversary of Victory in Europe (VE) Day, the *Evening Standard* newspaper commissioned a memorial to the London Blitz[46] which was unveiled by the Queen Mother on 11 May 1999. High-profile campaigns for memorials to the Women's Services, Civilians, and the fallen from the Indian subcontinent, Africa, and the Caribbean are under way, and in November 1999 a national memorial commemorating Civilian Workers was unveiled in Coventry Cathedral.[47]

How can this recent explosion of Second World War commemoration be explained? First, it is possible to argue that these memorials are not the work of the 'sceptical generation' themselves, and this is certainly true in some cases. For example, according to Fox many of the USAF memorials have been the work of enthusiasts' groups like the Friends of the Eighth or the Buddies of the Ninth, membership of which is largely drawn from 'Britons who were children during or after World War 2'.[48]

This interest on the part of subsequent generations can perhaps in part be attributed to the rising influence of an increasingly war-obsessed press, a phenomenon which was particularly noticeable during first the fortieth and then the fiftieth anniversaries of key wartime events during the 1980s and 1990s.

[45] NIWM 13436.   [46] NIWM 17959.
[47] The Womens' Services Memorial will be figurative, and will be erected outside the Ministry of Defence buildings in Whitehall. The memorial to black and Asian service personnel was to take the form of a £1.8 million set of commemorative gates and posts at Constitution Hill. Objections to the design led to its being amended to the four inscribed pillars only, which were unveiled on 6 November 2002. Many years in the planning, the Civilians' memorial will take the form of a landscaped memorial park on the banks of the River Thames at Hermitage Wharf, Wapping.
[48] Fox, *Eighth Air Force Remembered*, 164.

IV. *The Fifty Year Cycle—Anniversaries since 1945*

A glance through the newspapers since 1945 clearly demonstrates the extent to which this mass observation of key anniversaries is a recent phenomenon. For the purposes of this essay, the examples studied have been the anniversaries of D-Day, the Allied invasion of Occupied France, on 6 June 1944, and Victory in Europe (VE) Day, 8 May 1945, using *The Times* and the *Daily Mirror* as case studies.[49]

The tenth and twentieth anniversaries passed by almost unnoticed. *The Times Index* for all four years contains only brief references to commemorative events, apart from a leading article marking the twentieth anniversary of VE Day on 7 May 1965. the *Daily Mirror* virtually ignored the tenth anniversaries, although the twentieth anniversary of D-Day fared somewhat better, with a short article appearing on page 7. The only reference to the twentieth anniversary of VE Day, on 8 May 1965, was in the television listings.

Media interest in the Second World War seems to have reached an all-time low in the 1970s. VE Day and D-Day were both marked in *The Times* by a short leader and brief articles, but in the *Daily Mirror* on 6 June 1974 the only reference to D-Day was in the book review section, and on 8 May 1975 the *Daily Mirror* was completely bare of any references to the war.

The Times Index for 1984, however, lists an entire column of D-Day related articles, and two columns referring to VE Day, possibly inspired by a spirit of post-Falklands-war jingoism. The *Daily Mirror* was perhaps understandably distracted by the Miners' Strike on 6 June 1984, although it did find time for a short article describing a commemorative visit made by Prince Charles to Normandy. The *Daily Mirror* more than compensated on 8 May, however, with the multi-page *'Victory Remembered'* souvenir issue, featuring 'Eric's War', the story of Normandy veteran Eric Green. Television listings also show commemorative programming throughout the day.

It was the 1990s, however, which saw an explosion of commemorative journalism on a scale which had never been

---

[49] *The Times* and the *Mirror* (formerly the *Daily Mirror*) were studied at the British Newspaper Library, Colindale, London NW9. References are as they appear in the text.

seen before. The fiftieth anniversary of D-Day in 1994 saw a flotilla of warships sail to Normandy accompanied by most of the heads of state of the former wartime allies. *The Times Index* shows four full columns of D-Day related articles. The *Daily Mirror* again ran a commemorative edition, almost entirely given over to photographs and reports from Normandy and around the country. 8 May 1995 saw another *Daily Mirror* commemorative edition, with a banner headline and the words 'see also pages 2, 3, 4, 5, 6, 7, 18, 19 and 24'. *The Times Index* again shows more than four columns of articles, including a front-page headline on 8 May.

It is important to note that not all of this press and public attention met with the approval of veterans, the living representatives of the sceptical generation. Overtly festive behaviour was sometimes roundly condemned: on 10 June 1994, a *Times* article reported that the Heritage Secretary had 'surrendered to veterans' and cancelled a 'D-Day family jamboree' in Hyde Park. Nevertheless, many of the new memorials which accompanied the festivities *were* the work of the wartime generation.

Indeed, some are arguably so taciturn and personal that they would mean very little to those with no knowledge of the history, like the myriad plaques commemorating campaign veterans' groups. How many contemporary Britons understand the true significance of the Burma Star Association, the Normandy Veterans, or the Far East Prisoners of War? At RAF Winthorpe, Nottinghamshire, a memorial commemorates the men of 1661 HCU.[50] Who now knows that this stands for Heavy Conversion Unit other than those who served in it, and who really knows what a Heavy Conversion Unit was? Equally obscure is a tablet, at Brougham Hall in Cumbria, commemorating the men of the 'top secret Canal Defence Light Tank Project'. [51]

Conversely, other new memorials seem to be an attempt to educate the visitor, at times emphasizing the actions of the living and the survivors—the sceptical generation themselves—as much as or even more than the dead. These memorials

[50] NIWM 20012. Heavy Conversion Units were used to retrain aircrew, converting pilots from twin to multi-engined aircraft.

[51] NIWM 4369. Canal Defence Light tanks were obsolete vehicles fitted with powerful searchlights in place of main armament. The title was something of a misnomer in practice, as in combat they were often used offensively, to blind enemy gunners during assault river crossings at night.

commemorate military units, events, and operations, and often
contain detailed historical information at the expense of purely
commemorative text or lists of names. So, on Skitten Airfield,
near Wick, Caithness, a memorial describes 'Operation
Freshman', an obscure commando raid on German heavy water
production plants in Norway,[52] and in St Helier, Jersey, another
memorial gives an account of another commando raid,
'Operation Hardtack 28'.[53] A memorial beside a main road in
Banff commemorates the men and women of the RAF's Banff
Strike Wing,[54] giving details of the types of mission flown and
damage inflicted. The plaque concludes with the words 'Losses
amongst the RAF Commonwealth and Norwegian squadrons
were high. More than eighty aircrew gave their lives flying with
the RAF Banff Strike Wing', but no names are given.

Sometimes, the new memorials seem to veer more towards
triumphalism than 1919 sentiments would have permitted. In
Deenethorpe, Northamptonshire, a roadside memorial commemorates the 401st Bombardment Group, United States Army Air
Force (USAAF).[55] Dedicated in September 1989, it states: 'from
this airfield the gallant men of the 401st flew 254 combat missions
over Germany and occupied Europe in sturdy B-17 aircraft. The
group was awarded two distinguished unit citations and had the
best bombing accuracy record and second lowest loss ratio
amongst B-17 groups in the 8th Air Force. "The Best Damned
Outfit in the USAAF".'

This relatively late conversion to symbolic war monuments by
the sceptical generation has sometimes led to a failure to understand the sentiments of the generation which preceded it, the
generation which fought the First World War. This break in
continuity can sometimes lead to a startling lack of empathy with
earlier memorials. In Merthyr Tydfil, South Wales, the First

---

[52] NIWM 5932. On 19 November 1942 two Horsa gliders towed by Halifax bombers
set off from RAF Skitten, carrying Commandos whose mission was to attack the German
heavy water plant at Vermork, west Norway. This was 'Operation Freshman'. One
bomber flew into a mountain killing the occupants of both aircraft and glider. The other
glider crash landed and the survivors were taken prisoner and executed by the Gestapo.

[53] NIWM 10070. Operation 'Hardtack 28' was a joint British and Free French
commando raid carried out on Occupied Jersey, 25 and 26 December 1943.

[54] NIWM 13403. The multinational Banff Strike Wing was formed in September 1944
and until the end of the war its six squadrons flew strikes against German shipping in the
North Sea and along the Norwegian coast.

[55] NIWM 3743. See also Fox, *Eighth Air Force Remembered*, 36–7 and 80.

World War memorial is a magnificent sculptural group by L. S. Merrifield. It depicts a central allegorical figure of St Tydfil, flanked by a miner (symbolizing a mining community) and a mother with child. No names were listed on the memorial: 'it was found impracticable to place so many names on the memorial and it was decided to include all the names in a beautifully bound and illuminated book.'[56] Although unconventional, Merrifield's design seems to have been popular at the time. For example, Lord Allenby, unveiling the memorial in 1931, specifically referred to the virtues of recognizing 'the share of women . . . in the war; and of children, too'.[57]

Unfortunately, fifty years later Merrifield's work entirely failed to resonate with the sceptical generation. In 1986 a new war memorial, a rather crude Celtic cross in granite, was erected outside Merthyr Law Courts.[58] The official reason given was that Merrifield's memorial was located on a steep site which 'gave problems for ex-servicemen attending Remembrance Day services'.[59] Whilst the demographic ageing of veterans was undoubtedly a factor, an arguably more significant motive for the new memorial was revealed in the *Western Mail* some years before by former Sergeant Major Benny Lee: 'We have a cenotaph which isn't really a cenotaph. It has no names on it, and we thought it was an old colliery disaster memorial . . . We would like a new cenotaph built with the names inscribed on it.'[60]

Further evidence for this lack of empathy between the Second and First World War generations is provided by the issue of adding trophies to war memorials. The addition of captured enemy weaponry or surplus tanks from the War Office to First World War memorials had often met with a less than enthusiastic response. *The Times* of 13 August 1919 describes how four German guns presented to Farnham in Surrey were pitched into the river.[61] In response to the award of a tank to the town of Cheltenham by the National War Savings Committee, an anony-

---

[56] NIWM 2009. File contains an unattributed and undated cutting entitled *History of the Memorial Movement*, which refers to the book scheme.

[57] Angela Gaffney, *Aftermath: Remembering the Great War in Wales* (Cardiff, 1998), 42.

[58] NIWM 6770.

[59] Gaffney, *Aftermath*, 62 (footnote).

[60] *Western Mail*, 26 Nov. 1975. Cutting in UKNIWM file, no page reference.

[61] *The Times*, 6 September 1919, p. 7 (from unpublished M.Litt. dissertation, 'Commemorating the Lost Generation', by Catherine Jamet-Bellier de la Duboisiere, Trinity College, Cambridge, June 1994).

mous correspondent writing under the heading of 'Cheltonian Chatter' wrote that 'Till death do them part, the town and the tank will be inseparable. One rather shudders at a partnership so enduring, for when all is said, tanks are not beautiful.'[62]

In contrast, on 23 October 1998 a restored Cromwell tank was unveiled at Thetford Forest, Norfolk,[63] to commemorate the 7th Armoured Division—the famous Desert Rats—which was stationed there between January and May 1944 whilst preparing for D-Day. The inscription points out that 'this was the only time the division was in the United Kingdom in its entire existence'. Similarly, a 3.7-inch anti-aircraft gun forms a memorial to the Air Defence of Swansea,[64] and was unveiled on 8 May 1995. It was presented by the Royal Artillery Association 'to commemorate the 50th anniversary of the cessation of hostilities in Europe and in memory of the 387 (unnamed) civilian and military personnel who died in the air raids on Swansea'.

V. *Conclusion*

In 1997 Martin Shaw defined memory as 'images, beliefs, and feelings which arise primarily from individual experience, although they are often constructed and reconstructed in terms of tradition and myth'.[65] It is the contention of this chapter that the 'sceptical generation' which lived through the Second World War have indeed reconstructed their collective memory, perhaps partly as a result of the influence of recent myths and traditions. Perhaps this could be called the 'Eric's War' effect. As a result, they appear to have renounced their scepticism, at least as far as war memorials are concerned.

However, this renunciation has arguably led to the creation of a new myth: the myth of an 'Uncommemorated Generation'. Those who fought the Second World War seem to have forgotten their heartfelt cry of 1945: 'No stone memorials.' More than fifty years on they may now be experiencing a renewed sense of the part they played in the tumultuous events of 1939–45,

---

[62] *Cheltenham Chronicle and Gloucestershire Graphic*, undated cutting in UKNIWM files.
[63] NIWM 19590.
[64] NIWM 17706.
[65] Martin Evans and Ken Lunn (eds.), *War and Memory in the Twentieth Century* (Oxford, 1997), 191–2.

reflected by a desire to memorialize which they simply did not feel at the time. As a consequence, war memorials seem to have gained a new lease of life as markers of permanent values, of history, in a postwar world that has experienced technological and social change faster than ever before.

PART II

Blueprints for Change

6

Socialism and Democracy: The Debate about a New Social and Economic Order in West Germany after the Second World War

DAVID GILGEN

Socialism has the floor! (Der Sozialismus hat das Wort!)
Victor Agartz, 1946

The fall of the Berlin Wall on 9 November 1989 was widely interpreted as a victory of the Western market economy over the Eastern model of a centrally planned economy. There was little doubt that the socialist states collapsed partly because their economic system did not work. The division of the world which marked the second half of the twentieth century was a part of the political rivalry characterized by competing economic systems. Was this strict, bipolar political and economic division inevitable? What were the visions of a political and economic order after the Second World War?

A debate about these questions arose in West Germany. This debate continued into the 1950s, although the basic decisions had already been taken two years after the collapse of the Nazi Reich, and had been implemented through the monetary reform and the following liberalization.[1] The two years of debate from 1945 to 1947 were inspired by the hope that a certain space would be given for the development of a specifically German economic style. The discussion was dominated by the Germans' memories of two economic situations and their consequences in the two decades before 1945—the world economic crisis and the Nazi command economy. There was agreement between the

[1] For the following see Werner Abelshauser, 'Freiheitlicher Sozialismus oder Soziale Marktwirtschaft? Die Gutachtertagung über Grundfragen der Wirtschaftsplanung und Wirtschaftslenkung am 21. und 22. Juni 1946', *Vierteljahrshefte für Zeitgeschichte*, 4 (1976), 415.

most important parties that a new economic and political system was needed to prevent any further catastrophes of this sort. However, the interpretation of the causes of these disasters gave rise to two political camps. After two years of debate, these advocated central planning on the one hand, and a market economy on the other.

What concepts for economic order were there in West Germany? What were the demands of the different political parties, and how did their programmes develop? What degree of diversity existed within the political camps and how much agreement was there between the party programmes? In order to answer these questions, the programmes of the Christian Democrats, the Social Democrats, and the Liberal Democrats between mid-1945 and mid-1947 will be examined.

The Christian Democrats between Christian Socialism and Liberal Conservatism

The conservative party combined the greatest variety of different political groups and directions within its organization.[2] The unification process started at the first meeting, held in December 1945 in Bad Godesberg, and continued with the foundation of the Christian Democratic Union (CDU) and the Christian Socialist Union (CSU) working group in February 1947 at the second meeting in Königstein. In Königstein the Executive Board of the Western Zone and Berlin met to improve the organizational structure of the party, which was less effective than that of the Social Democratic Party (SPD).

Six different groups can be identified within the CDU: the Cologne CDU with Konrad Adenauer forming a conservative centre; a socialist and radical group in Berlin with Jakob Kaiser as its main figure; a free-market faction in Hamburg; a particularistic group in Munich;[3] the Christian Democrats in Hesse with Werner Hilpert, Walter Dirks, and Eugen Kogon; and a group in North Rhine–Westphalia with links to the trade unions

---

[2] See different regional centres and foundations in Robert Hofmann, *Geschichte der deutschen Parteien* (Munich, 1993), 195 f.

[3] Ute Schmid, 'Die Christlich Demokratische Union Deutschlands', in Richard Stöss (ed.), *Parteien Handbuch* (Opladen, 1983), 490–660, at 493.

around Johannes Albers and Karl Arnold. This group promoted a 'just social order' (*gerechte Gesellschaftsordnung*) in a Christian sense, but did not want all existing structures to be changed. They did not reject nationalization in principle, but were more reluctant than Kaiser.[4] The group in Hesse gained importance because it published *Frankfurter Hefte*, a journal edited by Kogon and Dirks who were strongly anti-Communist and wanted to strengthen a union of Catholics and workers.[5] Only after the split with the East German CDU in the Soviet Occupied Zone did the CDU move more to the right and acquire a more focused profile.

The strategy of the CDU was similar to that of the SPD, and aimed to open a conservative, Catholic party to wider social groups. A proposal was made to overcome the division between Protestants and Catholics, and to combine secular and religious forces in a single non-socialist party. However, the Catholics of the Left saw the division between Protestants and Catholics as well as that between the working class and the middle class as one of the reasons for the failure of the Weimar Republic. They wanted to include the interests of all four groups in their programme and to co-operate closely with the SPD.

The Catholic Centre Party (Zentrum)[6] did not follow these lines. It was reorganized in the British Zone where it achieved some early local successes before it later disappeared. (One reason for the eventual success of Christian Democracy and the failure of the Centre Party was that the Churches also supported an inter-denominational solution rather than a return to the small, fragmented parties of the Weimar Republic.)

Two main directions existed within the Christian Democratic Party, a Christian socialist branch and a liberal-conservative branch, which, to start with, did not have a very strong conceptual

---

[4] Axel Lehmann, *Der Marshall-Plan und das neue Deutschland: Die Folgen amerikanischer Besatzungspolitik in den Westzonen* (Münster, 2000), 228.

[5] Ibid.

[6] The Zentrum's economic programme was similar to that of the CDU in the early years, demanding a social economic order to help all classes. It called for the dismantling of cartels and monopolies, the nationalization of mining, iron and steel, transport, energy production, banking and insurance, and for large country estates to be reorganized into small and medium-sized farms, but supported private initiative and the protection of private property in the service of public wealth. Uwe Uffelmann, *Wirtschaft und Gesellschaft in der Gründungsphase der Bundesrepublik Deutschland*, iv, pt. 2 (Dortmund, 1984), 44. Id., *Internationale Politik und deutsche Frage 1945–1947* (Düsseldorf, 1976) 177, 178.

basis. Christian socialism was a modernized interpretation of the
Catholic social doctrine (*Soziallehre*) drawn up by the Dominican
Laurentius Siemer and Eberhard Welty from the Walberberg
monastery.[7] Welty called for the state to be constructed in a way
that secured the interests of, and ensured respect for, the working
class. For him, state intervention in the economy and nationalization were potential tools for achieving this aim. The concept of
Christian socialism also included public ownership of key industries by state, regional, and local institutions, and co-determination
by workers in industry. However, in reality, the claims of the
Christian socialists were often less radical, and included civil liberties and security of private property as pillars of their programme.
Supporters like Welty, Kaiser, and others demonstrated that, in
the situation of a new beginning, Christian socialism was based on
more than 'sentiment', as some conservative critics had claimed.

However, there was criticism of the concept of Christian
socialism right from the start. Not only Adenauer, but also others
such as the banker Robert Pferdmenges and Otto Schmidt, a
Protestant with bourgeois political ideas,[8] strongly opposed any
form of socialism. Adenauer in particular never identified with
this concept or with the early programmatic outlines influenced
by Christian socialism. Adenauer remarked that the phrase
'Christian socialism' was not an accurate combination of words.[9]
Moreover, he went on, one should not get used to the idea that
socialism was something bearable in any form, and he claimed
that the word socialism would lose the party more support than
it would gain. Adenauer was asked by CDU and CSU politicians
to tell Kaiser that the phrase 'Christian socialism' should no
longer be used, as it had no content and would only produce
confusion.[10] However, Christian socialism (even though more
than one version existed) was an important notion at a time
when the conservative wing of the CDU had not yet developed a
presentable counter-concept.[11]

In June 1945 the Cologne CDU released its basic principles,

---

[7] For the following see Lehmann, *Der Marshall-Plan*, 226.

[8] Ibid. 230.

[9] Adenauer, minutes of the CDU zone meeting in Neuenkirchen, 26–28 June 1946.
Ibid.

[10] Ibid.

[11] See Gerold Ambrosius, *Die Durchsetzung der Sozialen Marktwirtschaft in Westdeutschland 1945–1949* (Stuttgart, 1977), 217.

proclaiming the introduction of a 'truly Christian socialism' in contrast to a 'wrong' collectivism, which, it claimed, was opposed to human nature.[12] This programme was based on the ideas of Siemer and Welty. Private property was to be secure, but subordinated to the overriding aim of social justice and public welfare. Public ownership could be extended as far as necessary, and the post office, railways, mining, and energy production were seen as part of the public domain anyway. Banks and insurance companies were to be under state control, and all private monopolies and cartels dismantled. The economy should supply basic demands and be organized in small and medium-sized enterprises under private control. Labour should be seen as a moral duty rather than a commodity. Trade unions and various professional associations were to be secure.

At the same time, the founders of the East German CDU Berlin, Andreas Hermes, Jakob Kaiser, and Ernst Lämmer, put forward their vision of a closely linked economic and social policy. Their programme can be seen as a response to their interpretation of the past. They proclaimed that the state required protection against concentrations of economic power and therefore needed to have control over mining and other key industries.[13] The present situation required strict economic planning with no regard to private interest. They called for both resources and monopolies to be state property, or under state control. Private property was allowed, but, rather as in the Cologne basic principles, only on condition that it constituted an inherent social responsibility. Furthermore, the programme prescribed the redistribution of large country estates in order to give as many Germans as possible access to farmland.

During the first party convention in Bad Godesberg in December 1945, a declaration on economic policy was made which demanded 'socialism out of Christian responsibility'.[14] The constituent elements of this type of socialism were nationalization and parity for workers in economic planning. The

---

[12] Rolf Steininger, *Deutsche Geschichte 1945–1961: Darstellung und Dokumente in zwei Bänden* (Frankfurt am Main, 1983), i. 115. 'Kölner Leitsätze der Christlichen Demokraten, Juni 1945.'
[13] 'Aus dem Aufruf der CDU Berlin 26.6.1945', quoted in Uffelmann, *Wirtschaft und Gesellschaft in der Gründungsphase*, iv, pt. 2, 45.
[14] Helga Grebing, Peter Pozorski, and Rainer Schulze, *Die Nachkriegsentwicklung in Westdeutschland 1945–1949* (Stuttgart, 1980) 61.

Christian socialists saw socialism as a necessity for living in a
Christian way, but they tried to make the difference between
their project and that of Marxism and 'class struggle' clear.
However, the East German CDU's attempt to extend its dominance at the party convention failed.[15]

In any case, Adenauer needed to integrate the left wing of the
CDU more strongly, and the 'Essen basic principles' can be seen
as an attempt to do so. Adenauer announced these principles at
the zone meeting in Neunkirchen on 24 August 1946, stressing
the advantages of a capitalist order based on private property as
against the planned nationalizations. Economic planning, which
was seen as necessary, was a task of the state and autonomous
organizations in the economy. The left wing of the party also
demanded workers' participation, equitable income distribution,
and the prevention of concentrations of economic power,
although they expected much more.[16]

In opposition to the Cologne CDU's programme, Adenauer
developed an economic policy in which he proposed economic
planning to be carried out by self-run institutions of employers,
employees, and consumers. He also called for a just distribution
of profits between entrepreneurs and workers.[17] It is remarkable
that the state had little importance in this concept. This can be
seen partly as a reflection of Adenauer's personal background,
closely linked as he was to the economic élite of the Rhine and
Ruhr area, and partly as a reaction to fear of a totalitarian state.
In Cologne, Adenauer gave a speech in which he stressed the
danger of the state interfering directly in the economy. He
pointed out that the state could be a cruel employer, as the
National Socialist regime had shown. Thus nationalization was
not a solution to the problem of economic power and did not
necessarily signify social progress. However, Adenauer pointed
out that the German economy was under Allied control at that
time and therefore the question of nationalization did not arise.
His fear of a totalitarian state went beyond fear of the unwanted

---

[15] Ibid. 227–8, 234.   [16] Ibid. 236.

[17] From 1947 at the latest, Adenauer also expressed a strong aversion to trade unions.
In a letter to Paul Silberberg dated 30 May 1947, he complained about the trade union
claim to rule and that there was little resistance to their far-reaching demands, as many
important employers, he suggested, had 'light brown spots'. He called this dangerous for
the future, not because of the past of leading entrepreneurs but because of the possibilities to which it gave rise for trade union policy. Ibid. 321.

economic effects of nationalization on the dynamics of individual initiatives. A state which centrally controlled the production of coal, iron, steel, and chemical products would be the absolute master of the entire country.[18]

On 1 March 1946 Adenauer became chair of the CDU in the British Zone. His nomination appeared to set the party on a course away from Christian socialism and towards a conservative policy. However, even with Adenauer as head of the most important regional party organization, the internal party struggle for the direction of future economic policy continued. At this stage Adenauer could not successfully promote his aims, which were driven by a strong rejection of all sorts of socialism, support for a capitalist economic order, Western integration, the ambition of regaining national sovereignty, and the desire to establish in society a conservative system of values based on Christian, Western values.

The other centre of the CDU was situated in Berlin. From the end of 1945, Kaiser led the CDU in the Soviet Zone. His concept of an independent Germany as a 'bridge' between East and West also had strong support in the Western Zones. He repeated his idea later at a CDU meeting, and added that Germany must be a bridge for its own sake and that of Europe.[19]

The 'bridge concept' not only had an external dimension and consequences for unification which made it attractive to many people. It also implied that Germany needed to find a third way between the Soviet-style central market planning economy and unbounded capitalism, which was widely seen as one reason for the end of the Weimar Republic and the rise of the National Socialist movement. Open rivalry for the leadership began between Adenauer and the Berlin group of Kaiser and Lemmer. This struggle ended when Kaiser and Lemmer came under pressure from the Soviet Military Administration (SMAD), and eventually had to leave the Soviet Zone.[20]

However, the East German CDU in particular developed ideas contrary to those of Adenauer. For Jakob Kaiser, now

---

[18] Ibid. 231, 321.

[19] Lehmann, *Der Marshall-Plan*, 233. See also Christian Hacke (ed.), *Jakob Kaiser: Wir haben Brücken zu sein* (Cologne, 1988).

[20] Hofmann, *Geschichte der deutschen Parteien*, 197.

head of the CDU in Berlin, the bourgeois era had finished with the Second World War and the rise of socialism was a logical consequence.[21] Therefore he declared that the CDU was not a bourgeois party. In Kaiser's opinion, care for the community took priority over the protection of private property. In order to achieve this, he called for society and the economy to be rebuilt from scratch. In a draft for a speech on 6 February 1946 Kaiser proposed that the East German CDU should support the concept of private property, but not past the point when it starts to constitute a public threat and establishes power over people. He therefore demanded public ownership of natural resources, strict limitation of country estates, and controls on extensive property-holding.[22] To him, it was obvious that all Christians and true democrats would agree with this analysis, which would lead towards socialism. For Kaiser the future of Germany's society and economy was clear: it would be socialist, not in a Marxist way, but based on Christian social ethics. He proclaimed: 'Socialism has the word!'[23] However, Kaiser argued, no party had a monopoly on socialism, and socialism was different from Marxism. He rejected the materialistic ideology of Marxism because freedom and human nature followed their own logic.[24]

When it announced its new chair in Neheim-Hüsten, the CDU in the British Zone also passed its political programme, which came to include private property and the encouragement of individual initiative. The influence of leftist groups in the CDU continued and was also expressed in the party's programmes. The right of equal representation for workers and a new social order with equitable income distribution was called for in order to overcome the spirit of class struggle. However, the left of the CDU did not manage to get their ideas on nationalization into the programme. The CDU programme vaguely suggested preventing economic concentration in the hands of individuals, associations, and private or public organizations, as this could endanger economic or political freedom. The question of nationalization was not addressed at all since the German

---

[21] Hacke (ed.), *Jakob Kaiser*, 88.
[22] Lehmann, *Der Marshall-Plan*, 227.
[23] Ibid. 228. Extract from Jakob Kaiser's speech at the CDU's Berlin conference in 1946.
[24] Ibid. 417.

economy was under Allied control, as the programme stated.[25] The overall impression is of a rather conservative programme which tried to stabilize economic structures and to postpone or conceal decisions about economic policy. The announced goal of medium-sized property as the basis for a democratic state underlines this policy.[26]

Adenauer still had to face strong internal party opposition from Kaiser and Karl Arnold, Minister President of North Rhine–Westphalia, who were supported by a strong Catholic trade union and the CDU working-class vote. They advocated consensus politics and co-operation with the SPD as well as German unity. At that point neither aim was shared by Adenauer.

Pressure from the left wing of the CDU forced Adenauer to make extensive concessions. The result was the 'Ahlen programme' (1–3 February 1947), which followed the direction of the first draft programme passed in Cologne in 1945. The programme starts by saying that the capitalist economic system had failed to serve the state and social interests of the German people. Thus a basic new order was necessary. According to this interpretation, the capitalist system was mainly responsible for the end of the Weimar Republic and for the rise of the National Socialist movement. The most important thing now was not to repair a malfunctioning system, but to look for a whole new order.

Central economic planning was given a central role in the programme, not only at times of hardship, but also under normal circumstances. Furthermore, the programme provided for the nationalization of mining and the iron and steel industry as well as controls over banks and insurance companies. The dismantling of cartels and monopolies was another aim expressed in the programme. However, dismantling was not to be automatic, but to depend on the technical requirements of each industry and the international competition that it faced. In order to break the power of the cartels, the programme aimed to replace them with equal representation models. In addition, the

---

[25] 'Programm der CDU in der britischen Zone (Neheim-Hüsten, 1.3.1946)', in Martin Tabaczek and Johannes Altenberend, *Deutschland nach 1945: Teilung und Einheit im internationalen Kräftefeld* (Paderborn, 1993), 49.

[26] Lehmann, *Der Marshall-Plan*, 322.

private ownership of shares was to be limited. In sum, the programme was a detailed plan for the reorganization of the economy, and gave clear statements concerning all of its different aspects.

Whether the Ahlen programme is seen as the start of a complete transformation of a capitalist society into a socialist one, or whether it is seen as still a far cry from Christian socialism because private property, self-administration, and personal freedom were still part of the programme, depends on one's definition of Christian socialism.[27] However, the Ahlen programme was the last (major) success for the left of the CDU. The programme was a compromise which satisfied demands within all parts of the CDU and distinguished the party from SPD and Zentrum. From this point on, the liberal-conservative camp gained in importance and influence, especially when more practical decisions had to be taken. One year later Adenauer asked for a new economic policy programme to take account of the changed economic situation after the currency reform.[28]

To strengthen the cohesion of party politics was the aim of the conference in Königstein on 5–6 February 1947. A working group was set up to develop a forum for supra-regional exchange. In connection with the party conference the Berlin daily, *Tagesspiegel,* commented on the confrontation between Adenauer and Kaiser, pointing out that the tactician Adenauer had understood that he needed to make concessions without being forced.[29] However, the suspension of Kaiser and Lemmer from their party chairs by the Soviet Military Administration broke the connection with the East German CDU.

With Kaiser and Lemmer no longer chairing the East

[27] The varieties of Christian socialism promoted by the groups in Cologne, Berlin, and Frankfurt differed markedly from each other. While their basic demands were similar, such as the call for confessional and social integration, the claims of the first two groups left more room for compromise. Grebing concluded that Christian socialism tried to reform capitalism, but never questioned the foundation of the capitalist system. Grebing, Pozorski, and Schulze, *Die Nachkriegsentwicklung in Westdeutschland,* 61.

[28] Ibid. 62.

[29] Lehmann, *Der Marshall-Plan,* 237. The semi-radical formulations in the Ahlen programme can be seen as a compromise tactic which prevented the CDU from moving even more to the left, or even splitting up into different parties. Reinhold Billstein, *Neubeginn ohne Neuordnung: Dokumente und Materialien zur politischen Weichenstellung in den Westzonen nach 1945* (Cologne, 1984), 94. At that stage Adenauer's liberal-conservative ideas were not very popular among large sections of society, and thus such a split would have had severe consequences.

German CDU, only Arnold was left as a strong alternative to the conservative group around Adenauer. In a declaration made in North Rhine–Westphalia on 17 June 1947, the end of capitalism and the need for a new order were stressed once again. Capitalism had failed to secure the supply of basic goods, and had caused egoism and exploitation, which had had severe consequences for the state, ending in Germany's total break-down. Thus the declaration called for the end of capitalist ownership of primary industry. However, it also rejected state ownership of these industries as a possible solution.[30] A compromise between individual initiative and 'true' collectivism (co-operative economy) was seen as the solution. However, this compromise was not explored in greater depth. Monopolies in the coal, steel, iron, and chemical industries were to be nationalized. But this did not mean bureaucratic organization by the state. These factories were to continue to operate independently. The government asked the Military Administration for its support for these plans and for the restitution of companies it had seized. This demand was important to the entrepreneur-friendly parts of the CDU, and united employers and employees for a while in the struggle for parity participation rights.[31] The declaration received strong support for its demand for the reduction of public administration and its encouragement of self-administration. In sum, the declaration combined contradictory elements and returned to the vague and open political demands made in the Neheim-Hüsten programme. This meant that the strong statements of Ahlen took a back seat.

From the summer of 1947 the CDU pursued a liberal-conservative policy which was directed towards the medium-sized businesses in the Frankfurt Economic Council. Johannes Semmler, and, from March 1948 on, Ludwig Erhard, symbolized this new policy.[32] Thus the CDU turned away from Christian socialism and drew up a new programme, influenced by the theoretical

[30] 'Die nordrhein-westfälische Landesregierung unter Ministerpräsident Arnold (CDU) zur Neuordnung der Wirtschaft (17.6.1947). 6. Sitzung am 17.6.1947, Regierungserklärung', printed in Billstein, *Neubeginn ohne Neuordnung*, 151–3.

[31] Werner Plumpe, *Vom Markt zum Plan: Wirtschaftsverwaltung und Unternehmerverbände in der britischen Zone* (Düsseldorf, 1987).

[32] Dirk Berg-Schlosser, 'Die Konstituierung des Wirtschaftssystems', in Josef Becker, Theo Stammen, and Peter Waldmann (eds.), *Vorgeschichte der Bundesrepublik Deutschland* (Munich, 1979), 93–123, at 112.

works of Franz Böhm, Adolf Lampe, Walter Eucken, and Alfred
Müller-Armack. The concept of 'ordo-liberalism', developed by
the Freiburg School around Walter Eucken, and Müller-
Armack's programme for an economic system without central
planning and direction of the economy, including limitations
and controls on the market economy, were of special importance.[33] Neither state nor private ownership of monopolies was
to be allowed. Economic policy was reduced to a combination of
monetary, credit, trade, tariff, tax, investment, and social policy
plus other measures to provide for the welfare and basic needs of
the whole population.[34]

The Social Democratic Party: Dogmatism or Pragmatism?

Two main tendencies can be identified within the SPD in the
first year after the war. One insisted on Marxism as the basis of
its political programme. It rejected a capitalist market economy,
private ownership of the means of production, and the market
economy, which was seen as unstable and thus containing the
risk of developments leading towards fascism again. However, its
programme was relatively moderate compared with its radical
analysis of capitalism. The other tendency supported 'liberal
socialism', which was less dogmatic. Gerhard Weisser and
Heinz-Dieter Ortieb represented this type of Social Democrat.
The main target was to secure a sufficient supply of basic goods
and of work, and a just income distribution. Political freedom
was not to be subject to any restrictions. The question of private
property was not answered in general, but a more decentralized
economy was the ideal for a new economic structure, which
required central planning.[35]

Like the CDU, the SPD also had two regional centres which
competed for dominance. The SPD was refounded in the
summer of 1945 in all occupied zones of Germany. Kurt
Schumacher in the British Zone represented the opening of the
SPD to new groups of voters. He was strongly anti-Communist,

---

[33] Lehmann, *Der Marshall-Plan*, 206 f.
[34] Ibid.
[35] Rolf Wenzel, 'Wirtschafts- und Sozialordnung', in Becker, Stammen, and
Waldmann (eds.), *Vorgeschichte der Bundesrepublik Deutschland*, 293–340, at 314 f.

and his aim was to secure German unity. The other centre was Berlin. The SPD in Berlin was founded by Otto Grotewohl, Erich Gniffke, Max Fechner, and Gustav Dahrendorf. The Central Committee called for the nationalization of banks, insurance companies, natural resources, and the mining and energy-producing industries, as well as the elimination of unearned income such as rents derived from land and apartment buildings. The redistribution of large country estates and worker participation in industry were further demands. Calls were also made for strict limits to be imposed on the interest capital could earn, and for all entrepreneurs to keep their businesses under trustee administration. However, the Central Committee also demanded the end of all limits on individual business initiatives so long as no social interests were affected. In short, it wanted democracy in politics and socialism in the economy.[36]

In the summer of 1945 Kurt Schumacher called for the consequences of German politics to be examined. He demanded the end of capitalist exploitation, and called for the nationalization of private investment and economic planning according to principles which served the economy and not just private interests.[37] Planning and directing the economy should not be confused with socialism, he argued; they were a precondition for socialism. Furthermore, he declared that the nationalization of large-scale industry, large-scale enterprises in the financial sector, and large country estates was an absolute necessity.[38] Property which was not used for capitalist exploitation should not be nationalized because owners of small properties must be seen as on the side of those without possessions.[39] As the SPD economic principles proclaimed, there were no plans to nationalize small properties like farms and craft workshops in which the owner's work was the essential element of the business.[40] It was an important

---

[36] 'Aus dem Aufruf des Zentralausschusses der SPD 15.6.1945', in Ossip K. Flechtheim (ed.), *Dokumente zur parteipolitischen Entwicklung in Deutschland seit 1945*, vol. iii: *Programmatik der deutschen Parteien*, pt. 2 (Berlin, 1963), 2–4, at 2.

[37] Lehmann, *Der Marshall-Plan*, 289.

[38] 'Was wollen die Sozialdemokraten? Neubau, nicht Wiederaufbau!', speech given by Kurt Schumacher in Kiel, 17 Oct. 1945, printed in Steininger, *Deutsche Geschichte 1945–1961*, i. 120.

[39] 'Kurt Schumachers Programmatische Erklärung 5.10.1945', in Grebing, Pozorski, and Schulze, *Die Nachkriegsentwicklung in Westdeutschland*, 71.

[40] 'Leitsätze zum Wirtschaftsprogramm der Sozialdemokratischen Partei Oktober 1945', ibid. 76.

strategic aim of Schumacher's not to focus the SPD's political activity only on their traditional voters, the working class.[41] However, he made this property distinction not only in order to open up the SPD to more people but also because he believed that the question of property should be seen not just as an economic problem, but also as a political one. He predicted that as long as large properties were in the hands of irresponsible and unscrupulous individuals, German democracy could not be safe because these would try to turn their economic power into political power again.[42] Schumacher blamed monopoly capitalism for the rise of Hitler because large-scale industries benefited from the orders that were placed in wartime. For Schumacher, fascism was based on Germany's economic structure, which had already been established in the late nineteenth century, and on the alliance between imperialism on the one hand, and heavy industry and large landowners on the other.[43]

The first chance to break this 'unholy union' of finance, heavy industry, and politics had been missed in 1918, and the consequence was fascism and war. Thus large-scale industry, finance, and country estates had to be nationalized to prevent the accumulation of economic power in the hands of a few capitalists and to give the state a socialist structure. Mining, heavy industry, energy production, transport, banking, and the insurance sector were seen as concentrated enough for nationalization.[44] Since they were no longer in a competitive situation, and thus not influenced by market forces, they needed to be under state control and planning.

In his declaration of October 1945 Schumacher had already stated that the experience of one country cannot simply be transferred and applied to another.[45] Schumacher advocated a third way, lying between the Russian and the American models. In a speech, Schumacher explained to his audience that the Russians had to understand that this third way had to be democratic

[41] Erich Ott, *Die Wirtschaftskonzeption der SPD nach 1945* (Marburg, 1978), 60.

[42] 'Was wollen die Sozialdemokraten? Neubau, nicht Wiederaufbau!', speech given by Kurt Schumacher in Kiel, 27 Oct. 1945, printed in Steininger, *Deutsche Geschichte 1945–1961*, i. 120.

[43] Ernst-Ulrich Huster, Gerhard Kraiker, Burkhard Scherer, *et al.*, *Determinanten der westdeutschen Restauration 1945–1949* (Frankfurt, 1972), 130.

[44] 'Leitsätze zum Wirtschaftsprogramm der Sozialdemokratischen Partei Oktober 1945', in Grebing, Pozorski, and Schulze, *Die Nachkriegsentwicklung in Westdeutschland*, 77.

[45] 'Kurt Schumachers Programmatische Erklärung 5.10.1945', ibid. 69.

because Europe needed to be democratic, and asked the Americans to accept that it needed to be socialist in order to prevent another dictatorship.[46] A third way, a free and democratic socialism, would place free individuals on a secure basis— a combination that neither capitalism nor Bolshevism could offer.[47] If this development should fail, he feared severe consequences for Germany. He pointed out that either Germany could be democratic and socialist, or the Germans would no longer be one people.[48] Democracy and socialism could not be separated because they were mutually dependent on each other.

Schumacher's analysis of the past was shared by many Germans. Victor Agartz claimed that 1918 had been a lost opportunity for a new construction on a socialist basis. He strongly influenced the Cologne programme of summer 1945 that demanded nationalization and central planning, which, in his view, were inseparably intertwined. The most important precondition was the creation of a central planning institution.[49] In the newly organized economy, central planning was to take the same role of regulator as the private aspiration to profit did in a market economy. Central planning had the task of connecting all partial plans, made by workers in industry and consumers, into one overall plan. To Agartz, nationalization did not apply only to large companies with extensive economic power, but to all enterprises which were involved in mass production. These were mining, the building industry, iron and metal production, machines, clothing, vehicle production, the chemical industry, the textile industry, the paper and printing industry, the construction industry, gas, water, and electricity supply, the insurance sector, transport, traffic, and the credit sector. Agartz believed that nationalization could be successful

---

[46] 'Proklamation des 1. Parteitages der Sozialdemokratischen Partei Deutschlands Mai 1946 Hannover', in Uffelmann, *Internationale Politik und deutsche Frage 1945–1947*, 174.

[47] Huster, Kraiker, Scherer, *et al.*, *Determinanten der westdeutschen Restauration*, 134. He saw Anglo-American reform capitalism as evidence that the capitalist system could be reformed over time by democratic institutions.

[48] Berg-Schlosser, 'Die Konstituierung des Wirtschaftssystems', 109. Speech 1946 at the SPD convention in Hanover. Huster, Kraiker, Scherer, *et al.*, *Determinanten der westdeutschen Restauration*, 130.

[49] From the economic commentary in the Cologne 'Programm der Sozialdemokratie', summer 1945, in Billstein, *Neubeginn ohne Neuordnung*, 118 ff. Victor Agartz repeated this demand in a speech on worker participation and the nationalization of primary industries given on 9 May 1946; ibid. 126–8, at 127.

only if banks were also nationalized because bonds between banks and industry were simply too close. According to Agartz, a state takeover of these companies was the only way to influence the investment activities of the entire economy. He also wanted to create powerful trade unions, and he repeated these demands one year later at the party conference in Hanover. These were the most far-reaching demands made by a leading Social Democrat.[50]

At a meeting in Wennigsen/Hanover, in October 1945, the first attempts were made to co-ordinate the activities of the leadership of the SPD in exile in London with those of the leading Social Democrats from Berlin and the Western Zones. Although the ideas of the exile and resistance groups included important insights and improvements to past programmes, they did not have a strong influence on the party's economic policy.[51] The basic economic principles were passed in October 1945. They pointed to two tendencies which made central economic planning and an active role for the state in the economy necessary. First, the trend towards monopoly capitalism meant that capitalism based on competition lost its self-regulatory mechanisms. Thus central planning and dismantling of monopolies was important to prevent a severe economic crisis. Second, economic and social policies could not be separated from each other, and thus the state played a crucial, and increasing, role in the economy.[52] The outline explained that the state, which had once oppressed the people, was now opposed to the capitalist economy, and was the public instrument for the creation of an economic system and welfare support.

Two days before the party convention on 11 May 1946 in Hanover, Schumacher repeated his extreme opinion that without a socialist economy and a democratic political system, the Germans would no longer be one people. In his speech to the party convention in Hanover, Schumacher defended Marxism as the basis of socialism. For Schumacher the most important insights of Marxism had a basis in reality, and were therefore not a historical burden for socialism. Even though he accepted other

[50] Ibid. 127, 119, 95.
[51] Ott, *Die Wirtschaftskonzeption der SPD nach 1945*, 70.
[52] 'Leitsätze zum Wirtschaftsprogramm der Sozialdemokratischen Partei Oktober 1945', in Grebing, Pozorski, and Schulze, *Die Nachkriegsentwicklung in Westdeutschland*, 75.

justifications for socialism, Schumacher found more insights and power in Marxism than in any other sociological approach. He claimed that the working class would free workers all over the world, but he did not use a narrow definition of who belonged to the working class. For Schumacher, all working people who did not use the methods of capitalist exploitation were part of the working class.[53]

Victor Agartz's speech had a different focus. He reflected on the past and pointed out that capitalism had turned into monopoly capitalism, that competition had been replaced by monopolistic 'parasites', and free entrepreneurs by cartels, syndicates, and trusts. A few banks and cartels would share out the world between them, and start demolishing the national state. Capitalism undermined societies and led to the catastrophe of fascism and war. According to Agartz, central planning was a tool for choosing the modes of production, and thus a way of influencing income distribution. Free initiative would receive support as long as it helped to improve social justice and covered risks, and did not create unwanted concentrations of power. The different partial plans had to be co-ordinated by central planning to produce a single master plan. Agartz declared that the aims of a central planned economy, which had to be under the guidance of elected representatives, were to satisfy basic needs, to guarantee the right to work, to offer a free choice of occupation, and social welfare for those who could not work. Production should serve to secure not a maximum of supply, but an optimum.[54] Furthermore, Agartz planned that no more investment should be made in arms production.

The basic principles of 1946 were similar to those adopted the year before. Capitalism was again blamed for the war and dictatorship. It was suggested, therefore, that what was required was not reform, but an entirely new social and economic organization.[55] The central features of the new economic order were to be democracy, central planning for the nationalization of transport, the money and credit supply, the insurance sector, mining,

---

[53] 'Kurt Schumacher: Aufgaben und Ziele der deutschen Sozialdemokratie', speech given at the SPD convention in Hanover in May 1946, in Huster, Kraiker, Scherer, *et al.*, *Determinanten der westdeutschen Restauration*, 363.

[54] 'Victor Agartz: Sozialistische Wirtschaftspolitik', speech given at the SPD convention in Hanover in May 1946, ibid. 370 f., 374–6.

[55] Lehmann, *Der Marshall-Plan*, 292.

the iron and steel industry, and the chemical industry—in short, of all large-scale capitalist enterprises—and a reform of agrarian land-holding.[56] The programme claimed that the nationalization plans would be adapted to each situation and industry, not imposed automatically.[57] The SPD programme stated that diversity, not a uniform *Kasernensozialismus* was the character of a socialist society. The programme also encouraged self-administered workers' and consumers' organizations to participate in the economy.[58] Small enterprises, craft workshops, and retail shops were not to be affected by nationalization, but co-operatives for the planning of common tasks above company level were to supplement the management of these small businesses. The socialist economy was to be based on central planning.[59]

In addition to central planning and nationalization, the importance of democracy was stressed. The programme declared that they could not be separated from each other because without socialism democracy would be in danger, and without democracy there would be no freedom of opinion.[60] The SPD declared that socialism was only possible if humanity and the individual were respected. Part of this concept was personal freedom in the choice of profession, and the right and duty to work for one's livelihood. Only in a society without exploitation, the programme claimed, could people enjoy their full rights and develop their personalities. Only socialism and democracy together could banish the risk of a counter-revolution.[61]

However, there was resistance within the SPD to these radical demands. For many people, Schumacher's plan to transform the SPD into a people's party did not go far enough. An argument started between the SPD centre in Hanover and the pragmatists in

---

[56] Ibid.; Uffelmann, *Internationale Politik und deutsche Frage*, 173.

[57] 'Forderungen und Ziele der Sozialdemokratischen Parteien Deutschlands, Beschlossen auf dem Parteitag in Hannover vom 9. bis 11. Mai 1946. Archiv der Sozialen Demokratie der Friedrich Ebert-Stiftung', in Johannes Volker Wagner, *Deutschland nach dem Krieg* (Bochum, 1975), 178; and Uffelmann, *Internationale Politik und deutsche Frage*, 172 f.

[58] 'Forderungen und Ziele der Sozialdemokratischen Parteien Deutschlands', in Wagner, *Deutschland nach dem Krieg*, 178; and Uffelmann, *Internationale Politik und deutsche Frage*, 172 f.

[59] 'Proklamation des 1. Parteitages der Sozialdemokratischen Partei Deutschlands Mai 1946 Hannover', in Uffelmann, *Internationale Politik und deutsche Frage*, 172 f.

[60] 'Forderungen und Ziele der Sozialdemokratischen Parteien Deutschland, Beschlossen auf dem Parteitag in Hannover vom 9. bis 11. Mai 1946', in Wagner, *Deutschland nach dem Krieg*, 30.

[61] Uffelmann, *Internationale Politik und deutsche Frage*, 172, 174.

the *Länder*, who were often in the regional government. Faced with the everyday problems of implementing a working economic policy, they advocated a British version of Keynesianism above all versions of dogmatic socialism. Politicians like Weisser, in particular, represented a free socialism (*freiheitlicher Sozialismus*) which later contributed to the concept of a social market economy and became part of party policy. In April 1947 Ernst Reuter, mayor of Berlin, wanted to abandon the dogmatism which, in his view, was represented by leading Social Democrats such as Agartz. This demand went further than Schumacher's call to open up the party.[62]

As early as 10 February 1946 the undogmatic south-west SPD under its chairman Carlo Schmid suggested that old ideas should be left behind and the ideology of class struggle abandoned in a quest for 'new shores'. Schmid supported plans for nationalization and worker participation, but rejected the Marxist analysis of society and central economic planning. Furthermore, Schmid planned to expose nationalized enterprises to competition. Wilhelm Hoegner, Bavarian Minister President and SPD chair, also followed an undogmatic direction. He wanted to strengthen the welfare state in order to reduce social differences. His programme suggested a reform rather than the establishment of a new economic order. In his inaugural speech on 22 October 1945 he did not call for nationalization. He opposed increased bureaucracy, but supported central economic planning. His aim was to overcome the old political camps that seemed to be re-emerging by opening the SPD up to new voters. In November 1945 he declared that every good Christian could be a Social Democrat without reservation, and that every Social Democrat could be a believing Christian.[63]

Wilhelm Laisen, mayor and President of the Senate of Bremen, demanded not total restructuring, but practical solutions to the problems of the present. He wanted the state to be the ally of the productive forces, and parties to compete for the best ways of raising productivity. Hoegner's policies in Bavaria matched Laisen's in Bremen. In its action programme of December 1946, the Bavarian SPD demanded the nationalization only of companies in industries of strategic importance, as part of a pragmatic reconstruction policy, rather than the start of an extensive programme of nationalization.[64]

---

[62] Lehmann, *Der Marshall-Plan*, 296.   [63] Ibid. 296 f.   [64] Ibid. 297.

However, the advocates of an undogmatic and practice-driven policy to reduce hardship were in the minority within the SPD, and they did not revolt against the official party programme. The majority of Social Democrats still accepted the Marxist analysis of society and demanded that the economic order should be changed by nationalization, economic planning, and a democratic economy.[65]

In September 1946 the SPD predicted a terrible catastrophe for Germany and demanded a political change. The SPD complained that the same forces that had caused the war were in power again in politics, the economy, and the administration, that real democracy did not exist in any of the zones, that equal rights and freedom of opinion were suppressed in the Soviet Zone, and that the Allies appointed only people with capitalist views to positions in the administration.[66]

Thus the SPD wanted to continue co-operating politically only on condition that some binding promises were made. These included an undertaking that primary industry, transport, banks, and the insurance industry would be nationalized, a promise of land reform, and confirmation that the German economic administration would participate in controlling the coal and steel industries. Furthermore, the SPD asked for an end to the dismantling of industrial sites by the Allies, and food to save the lives of millions of Germans. The Social Democrats added that they wanted to maintain the unity of Germany, and that a decentralized economy and democracy were essential for Germany.[67]

In 1947 the Social Democrats attempted to clarify their position on nationalization and how a nationalized economy would work. Twelve theses were produced and presented by a party committee on 6 January 1947,[68] and in February 1947 an SPD commission for nationalization was set up. However, their findings were vague and of little help in putting nationalization plans into practice.[69]

---

[65] Ibid. 298.

[66] 'Beschluss des Parteivorstandes und des Parteiausschusses der SPD (25.9.1946)', in Thomas Meyer, Susanne Miller, and Joachim Rohfels (eds.), *Geschichte der deutschen Arbeiterbewegung* (Bonn, 1984), pt. 2, 784 f.

[67] Ibid.

[68] Steininger, *Deutsche Geschichte 1945–1961*, ii. 337–42, at 323.

[69] Lehmann, *Der Marshall-Plan*, 292.

At the 1947 party convention in Nuremberg the 'basic princi- ples of a socialist economy' were adopted. These principles were based on a mixed economic system that still reflected both wings of the SPD. Coexistence of private and state enterprises, central economic planning with elements of the market economy, and parity participation were part of the programme.[70] These addi- tions signified a further development towards liberal economic concepts.

Schumacher promoted a 'magnet theory' which was based on the assumption that the prosperity of the Western Zones would turn the West into an economic magnet. If reunification could not be achieved politically, this magnet would have such a strong influence on East Germany, he suggested, that political rejection by the SMAD would not prevent an eventual reunification.[71]

In a publication, Agartz repeated his critique of capitalism, namely, that a danger of crisis was inherent in a capitalist econ- omy which thus carried the threat of fascism. However, he demanded that state intervention should be reduced to a mini- mum and that a decentralized economy should have space for entrepreneurial initiative which would better organize sectional as well as regional differences. Agartz saw a state-directed incomes policy, and controlled capital investment and credit policies as the main tasks of central economic planning.[72]

The SPD tried to make use of a situation in which five out of eleven Minister Presidents were Social Democrats from 1946–7 onwards. Furthermore, Social Democrats held eight Ministries of Trade and Commerce. Apart from taking care of the needs of the present situation, they aimed to start implementing the proclaimed nationalization plans.[73] Agartz insisted on the nationalization of primary industry, the public utilities, the consumption goods industries which tended towards a monop- oly, banks and the insurance sector, and transport. But in addi- tion to state ownership, co-operation was also to be supported.

---

[70] Wenzel, 'Wirtschafts- und Sozialordnung', 316.
[71] 'Kurt Schumachers "Magnet Theorie 31.5.1947" ', in Vorstand der SPD (ed.), *Acht Jahre sozialdemokratischer Kampf um Einheit, Frieden und Freiheit: Ein dokumentarischer Nachweis der gesamtdeutschen Haltung der Sozialdemokratie und ihrer Initiativen* (Bonn, 1953). See also Werner Abelshauser, 'Zur Entstehung der "Magnet-Theorie" in der Deutschlandpolitik', *Viertel- jahrshefte für Zeitgeschichte*, 7 (1979), 661.
[72] Victor Agartz, *Sozialistische Wirtschaftspolitik* (Karlsruhe, 1947), 5 ff.
[73] Berg-Schlosser, 'Die Konstituierung des Wirtschaftssystems', 110.

Agartz stressed the importance of worker participation in his concept, which was close to party programmes, but went further in respect of nationalization and planning.[74]

The concept of economic democracy was based on theories which had been developed by Fritz Naphtali in the 1920s,[75] and by Victor Agartz in the early postwar years. 'Economic democracy', as was proclaimed in October 1945, was no longer capitalism, but not yet socialism either. It was the precursor of full socialism. The main aims of economic democracy were control of economic power, greater central planning, worker participation, and increased productivity. State control and democratic participation in management were the methods which would achieve these aims.[76]

With the tendency towards monopolization, processing industries and the consumer goods industry developed toward nationalization. Equal representation was intended to reduce one-sided dependency and power relations. While a social policy based on public insurance was planned, it coexisted with private insurance in this model.[77] Farming and crafts were seen as pre-capitalist and post-capitalist forms of production respectively, which could continue to exist in a socialist economy.[78]

The concept of economic democracy, which was influenced by neo-liberal economic ideas, never played a prominent role in public discussion, perhaps because the SPD was not sure how their traditional voter groups would react to it.[79]

Aims and Limits of Liberal Economic Policy

The reorganization of the liberal parties, the Free Democratic Party (FDP), the Democratic People's Party (DVP), and the LDPD, followed a strongly regional, de-centralized, independent, and uneven pattern.[80] However, three main groups can be

---

[74] Agartz, *Sozialistische Wirtschaftspolitik*, quoted from Lehmann, *Der Marshall-Plan*, 295.

[75] Huster, Kraiker, Scherer, *et al.*, *Determinanten der westdeutschen Restauration*, 135.

[76] 'Leitsätze zum Wirtschaftsprogramm der Sozialdemokratischen Partei Oktober 1945', in 'Schumachers Programmatische Erklärung', 21 ff.

[77] Wenzel, 'Wirtschafts- und Sozialordnung', 318.

[78] 'Leitsätze zum Wirtschaftsprogramm der Sozialdemokratischen Partei Oktober 1945', in Grebing, Pozorski, and Schulze, *Die Nachkriegsentwicklung in Westdeutschland*, 78.

[79] Wenzel, 'Wirtschafts- und Sozialordnung', 318.

[80] Lehmann, *Der Marshall-Plan*, 322.

identified: the federal liberal-democratic DVP, based in the traditional centre of the liberal movement, the south-west of Germany; the free-liberal, bourgeois, anti-clerical, and centralist movement in the British Zone of Occupation; and a national democratic, strongly anti-socialist liberal right wing of the liberal parties in Hesse.[81] Not until December 1948 did the different organizations in the Western Zones unite to form one party, the FDP. Before this, they had already been expelled from the LDPD in the Soviet Zone of Occupation. The composition of the Liberal Party was very different before 1933 and after 1945. While before 1933 employees had constituted the largest faction of the party, after 1945 self-employed businessmen were more important. The latter group held the chairs of nine out of fifteen regional party organizations after 1945.[82]

The liberals were the only political movement that rejected all nationalization plans and advocated free competition right from the start of political activity after 1945.[83] Their economic policy was strongly based on the theoretical works of Wilhelm Röpke and Friedrich August von Hayek.[84] However, the difficult supply situation meant that liberal parties called for strong social policy. Thus security of basic living conditions, that is, the supply of food, clothing, housing, healthcare, and the 'creation of a real social attitude' (*Schaffung wahrer sozialer Gesinnung*), formed paragraph one of their first proclamation in July 1945.[85] Similarly, the DVP in Baden and Württemberg did not promote pure neo-liberalism, but in April 1946 declared that Germany needed a strong social ethos, while the Bavarian FDP advocated that the social insurance system should be renewed and strengthened.[86]

Confronted with the hardship caused by the wartime destruction, Theodor Heuss regarded central economic planning as necessary in the short and middle term. However, in principle he opposed central planning not only for economic reasons, but also because he claimed that it could turn into the tool of a 'total

---

[81] Ibid. 332; FDP in Bavaria, Liberal-Democratic Party LDP in Hesse, Democratic People's Party DVP in Württemberg, Steininger, *Deutsche Geschichte 1945–1961*, i. 111.

[82] Lehmann, *Der Marshall-Plan*, 337.

[83] Steininger, *Deutsche Geschichte 1945–1961*, i. 111; Grebing, Pozorski, and Schulze, *Die Nachkriegsentwicklung in Westdeutschland*, 66.

[84] Ibid.

[85] 'Aufruf der Liberal-Demokratischen Partei, undatiert (Berlin, 5. Juli 1945)', in Wagner, *Deutschland nach dem Krieg*, 195.

[86] Lehmann, *Der Marshall-Plan*, 333.

state'.[87] If the state is the only employer, no opposition is possible and therefore central planning cannot coexist with democracy, claimed Eduard Wilkenning at a Liberal Party meeting 1946.[88]

In its inaugural proclamation on 5 July 1945, the Liberal Party gave no explanation for the 'rule of tyranny' and the 'catastrophe' of the past.[89] The German people was held responsible, while no structural deficits in the political and economic constitution were mentioned. The Liberal Party's interpretation of the past was different from that of most other parties. Hitler and his regime were not seen as the ultimate result of late monopoly capitalism. Heuss called this view 'Marxist and ideological' talk.[90] The conclusion was that Marxist nationalization would have the same consequences as Nazi nationalization —the totalitarian state.[91]

The first draft programme was passed on 4 February 1946 in Opladen. Liberals from Baden, Württemberg, and the British Zone agreed that the satisfaction of basic needs was central to this situation of hardship.[92] Central planning and control were seen as necessary, but bureaucratic obstacles should be reduced, individual initiative and free competition encouraged, and private property guaranteed, because all this would lead to a better economic performance. Individual initiative and free competition should foster economic performance, and, with private property, form the basis of a working economy.[93]

The FDP's draft programme in the British Zone in 1946 made few demands on economic policy, but those that were made resembled those mentioned in earlier proclamations. Additionally, the rights to effective social policy and to work were proclaimed. Trade unions were to be set up to protect the

---

[87] Ibid. 334.

[88] Party meeting in Bad Pyrmont, 18 May 1946. Bundesarchiv, Blücher Papers, 154/1, 44.

[89] G. A. Below, O. Fischer, *et al.* (eds.), *Um ein antifaschistisch-demokratisches Deutschland: Dokumente aus den Jahren 1945–1949* (Berlin, 1968), 88.

[90] Heuss at the Drei-Königs-Treffen of the Swabian liberals, 6 Jan. 1946. Theodor Heuss, *Aufzeichnungen 1945–1947* (Tübingen, 1966), 175.

[91] Tabaczek and Altenberend, *Deutschland nach 1945*, 50. 'Programmatische Richtlinien der Frei Demokratischen Partei der britischen Zone 4.2.1946.'

[92] Lehmann, *Der Marshall-Plan*, 335.

[93] Flechtheim (ed.), *Dokumente zur parteipolitischen Entwicklung in Deutschland*, vol. ii: *Programmatik*, pt. 1, 272–4, at 273. *Programmatische Richtlinien der Freien Demokratischen Partei der britischen Zone 4.2.1946, Punkt 5* (Berlin, 1963–8).

workers. The aims of social policy were the prevention of hardship, the preservation of human dignity and personal freedom, and the securing of social peace.[94] Thus the protection of all kinds of work and the right to organize in professional associations and unions[95] were seen not as contradictions, but as preconditions for a modern market economy. These elements would help to rule out liberalism malfunctioning in a way which would reduce the role of the state to that of a 'night watchman'.

After mid-1946 the call for social policy from liberals weakened, and the need for the introduction of a free market economy, and the rejection of nationalization and central economic planning were stressed in the first party programmes. In June 1946 the DVP Baden-Württemberg in their programme called for the economy to be released, step by step, from the bonds of strong state economic policy.[96]

At the end of 1946, leading FDP politicians in the British Zone developed an economic policy draft. Once again, its central elements were private property, a free economy, and the rejection of nationalization. However, this draft was less general, and differentiated between industrial sectors. It demanded that the mining industry be run by private foundations (*Stiftungen des bürgerlichen Rechts*) to avoid a return to monopolistic tendencies and called for the strengthening of employers' rights, factory committees for large-scale enterprises, and a parity economic council for economic planning as long as planning was necessary. But this draft was turned down by the important Liberal Party in the British Zone. Thus in this form it never became part of the Liberal Party programme. A few months later, a new economic draft was passed in Bremen, and this became the core of the Liberal economic policy. In addition to a free economy, free trade, the rejection of nationalization in general, and self-administration of the economy, the prevention of economic power concentration was included in this programme.[97]

The dismantling of cartels and monopolies had already been

---

[94] Wagner, *Deutschland nach dem Krieg*, 198. 'Programmatische Richtlinien der Freien Demokratischen Partei der britischen Zone 4.2.1946', in Tabaczek and Altenberend, *Deutschland nach 1945*, 50.

[95] 'Gründungsaufruf der Liberal-Demokratischen Partei Deutschlands 5.7.1945.' Below, Fischer, *et al.* (eds.), *Um ein antifaschistisch-demokratisches Deutschland*, 88.

[96] Lehmann, *Der Marshall-Plan*, 334 f.

[97] The draft was passed in Bremen on 22 Feb. 1947. Ibid. 335 f.

demanded in passing by the FDP in the British Zone on 4 February 1946, and with more emphasis by Blücher on 10 April 1946 in Essen.[98] It turned out to be the major demand of the Liberal Party for state intervention in the free economy. The arguments against these malfunctions of the market economy are straightforward, and central to Liberal economic theories, especially those of Eucken and Böhm. However, the question of who should dismantle them was left open, as was the question of what would happen to the property of enterprises like mining which could only be run on a large scale because of technical or organizational requirements. Furthermore, it was unclear when a cartel or group of companies had to be dismantled—only if it was acting against the rules of the market, for example, if it was charging too high prices, or simply if an enterprise had the capacity to do so. The programmes did not and could not answer these question clearly. However, the main task of the state was to encourage competition by setting rules and policing them to prevent the economic or political misuse of economic power. But the state itself remained an object of suspicion for many Liberals, who did not want it to gain too much economic power.

Apart from the arguments against central planning mentioned above, some Liberals claimed that a fully centrally planned economy would lose its capacity to adjust and its ability to participate in foreign trade, which were seen as necessities for the German economy.[99]

The development of the Liberal Party in the Soviet Zone was different. In its foundation pamphlet the LDPD also demanded private property, but was not completely opposed to nationalization. However, in its view nationalization was justified only if it was in the interests of the wealth of the majority.[100] Some regional groups called for the nationalization and state control of large-scale enterprises and of mining. In 1946 Wilhelm Külz, chairman of the LDPD, supported such plans and advocated not only the dismantling of monopolies and cartels, but also the nationalization of large rural estates. He wanted to promote an economy with mainly medium-sized companies competing with

---

[98] Ibid. 337.
[99] e.g., Blücher on 22 Feb. 1947, Lehmann, *Der Marshall-Plan*, 337.
[100] Ibid. 338.

each other, but not in Manchester-style competition.[101] Only the left wing of the LDPD went so far as to advocate central economic planning even after the reconstruction period, which was not on the agenda for most Liberals in the Soviet Zone at that time.[102]

Conclusion

The SPD and CDU programmes shared a number of demands concerning economic policy and structure. These included control of strategic industries, the nationalization of raw materials extraction, especially mining, some form of central planning (much more weakly developed in the CDU concept), democracy, anti-Bolshevism, free choice of profession, and a strengthening of small and medium-sized production. Support for small farms, crafts, and trade was planned by both parties, as was worker participation. This policy can be interpreted as a move on the part of both parties away from relying on their traditional voters towards becoming peoples' parties. However, the emphasis on these elements of their programmes differed increasingly over time.

At the start, the limitation of political activity to the different Allied zones gave rise to great variety within all parties. Political regional centres were formed, and within the CDU and the SPD a confrontation began between the parties in Berlin and the Western zones. The decision of the SMAD put an end to this, and to any hopes for an imminent unification.

However, debates about economic policy continued. Disagreements within the SPD were not serious, and were between the Hanover party centre and some Social Democrats in the *Länder*, who demanded less dogmatic and more practical policies. Within the CDU, however, controversies between the conservative and the left wing covered a much wider political spectrum. In the spring of 1947 in Ahlen, the CDU passed a new programme which included the far-reaching demands of the Christian Democratic Left, who advocated Christian socialism. This was the last great victory of the CDU Left. From then on

[101] Ibid.
[102] 'Der Morgen 7.2.1947', quoted ibid.

the liberal-conservative forces around Adenauer increasingly influenced CDU programmes, turning them away from this concept. After 1947 the CDU and parts of the SPD started to advocate a mixture of the social market economy and ordo-liberalism, concepts developed in economic theory by Franz Böhm, Müller-Armack, and Walter Eucken. Even though debates about the economic order continued well after 1947, the direction had been given and the window of opportunity for other options slowly closed.

7

The Importance of the Foreign Constraint: Debates about a New Social and Economic Order in Italy, 1945–1955

LUCIANO SEGRETO

The debates about a new social and economic order in Italy had very different actors and stages, which must be considered. But these debates also took place within various frameworks. There was a domestic scene, which was the setting for the main discussion and the political struggle, and there was also an international scenario which not only influenced debates and controversies, but was a central point of the discussions themselves. These two levels will be considered separately for the sake of clarity, but there were so many points of contact and interference that it is not always easy to distinguish them.

I. *The Economic Culture of the Political Parties*

To restore democracy in Italy meant to recast the political world. The most important party of pre-fascist liberal Italy, the Liberal Party, had been reduced to a small, élitist political force. Nevertheless, some of its most representative elements played a certain part during the discussions about a new social and economic order, and especially about Italian foreign trade and payment policy. Their moral and cultural profile gave them the opportunity to introduce some of the classical positions from the ideological corpus of liberalism: the free market; the high esteem in which private enterprise was held; and the elimination, or at least a strong reduction, of state intervention. These positions had already been rejected before 1914, and they were not acceptable in a country where mass parties were taking the lead in the process of democratizing a country that had spent the previous twenty years under fascist dictatorship. Thus they remained voices crying in the wilderness. But they were so strong that some echoes reached the government and a number of other places (such as the Bank of Italy) where fundamental decisions about the economic and social future of the country were taken.[1]

The most important party, which gained a relative majority at the first postwar elections in 1946 (called to form the National Assembly which was charged with drawing up the new democratic constitution), was the Christian Democratic Party. Its economic and political culture was very much inspired by the documents issued by the Vatican in the 1930s on the social and economic question. This culture was highly critical of the role of the market and its capacity to 'self-correct' the 'mistakes' or irregularities of the economic system. The text of the encyclical *Quadragesimo Anno*, published by Pope Pius XI in 1931, in which he pointed to the degeneration of capitalism and the principle of free competition as economic aspects needing urgent correction, was still the leading interpretation of capitalism.[2] In more economic jargon, a fascist economist wrote in 1932 that the malfunctioning of the economic system was caused by such factors as 'competition, the spirit of individualism and machine society'.[3]

The individual was the starting point at the heart of the Christian Democratic Party's economic programme. The market economy was connected to the country's traditional economic structure, dominated by small and medium-sized firms based on the family. In 1937 firms with fewer than 10 employees accounted for 84.5 per cent of the total, but their employees made up only 13.9 per cent. If we consider larger firms with fewer than 50 and 100 workers respectively, the percentages changed greatly. Firms with fewer than 50 workers made up 95.4 per cent of the total and those with fewer than 100 workers, 97.7 per cent; and the percentage of workers grows to 29 per cent and 40.1 per cent respectively.[4] Shopkeepers and tradesmen belonged to the same social and economic universe. The

---

[1] C. Daneo, *La politica economica della ricostruzione 1945–1949* (Turin, 1975).

[2] F. Vito, 'La Quadragesimo Anno e i problemi dell'economia moderna', *Rivista internazionale di scienze sociali e discipline ausiliarie*, 29 (1931), 335.

[3] F. Carli, *Le crisi economiche e l'ordinamento corporativo della produzione* (Rome, 1932), 10.

[4] ISTAT, *Censimento Industriale e Commerciale 1937–1940*, Prima Serie, i, pt. 2 (Rome, 1940).

Christian Democratic Party's economic vision clearly implied a conditional acceptance of the free market and diffidence towards big companies, which the social philosophy of the Catholic Church considered a sort of parasite.[5]

The progressive overcoming of economic autarky and the increasing involvement of the Italian economy in the new international economic order were connected with a new form of workers' shareholding and the direct participation of the trade unions in the management of companies. This programme was intended to increase economic prosperity, substantially reduce class antagonism, and result in the development of a new and superior form of class co-operation, the chaotic Italian way to the German model of *Mitbestimmung* (co-determination). Finally, a reform of the tax system was the instrument of a more equitable distribution of wealth that was intended to favour social *détente* and the diffusion of prosperity.[6] The approach to the central element of a capitalist economy, the market, however, was still cautious, if not contradictory. The market was actually the focus, but not the foundation of the economic and social structure the Catholic party had in mind for postwar Italy because it required important corrections (that is, intervention) to re-establish a balance between social and economic forces. Lack of intervention meant that society risked permanent disequilibrium and would never reach social, economic, and political stability.[7]

Other, but not totally different languages were spoken by the left-wing parties. In 1945 the Communist Party was strongly in favour of economic and industrial relief. European economic interdependence could overcome the lack of many raw materials, in the meantime giving workers the chance of a place in the new Italy. Italy had to remain an industrial country: 'Our industry', said the Communist Party, 'has been created by our workers, our engineers, our technicians, and by our work, and the Partito Comunista Italiano will and must maintain and develop it. Italy cannot be united or independent without a rational and developed industry.' This programme meant radically eliminating the autarky and the parasitism of the 1920s, and increasing

---

[5] A. Giovagnoli, *La cultura democristiana: Tra chiesa cattolica e identità italiana* (Rome, 1991).

[6] F. McKitrick, 'Modernizzazione e identità sociale: artigiani tedeschi e capitalismo a metà Novecento', *Passato e Presente*, 28 (2000), no. 49, 37–67.

[7] P. Barucci 'I cattolici e il mercato', *Note di economia*, no. 3 (1998), 7-28.

state intervention in the private monopolies and the banking system (95 per cent of which was already in the hands of the state).[8]

It is clear that such a vision was very much dependent on the immediate necessities of the political struggle. The Communist Party had a more moderate approach to the question of big industrial companies, while Socialist Party opinion was that they had to be nationalized. For the Communists, economic reconstruction and recovery were much more important. This change in attitudes can also be analysed in terms of the same paradigm: the international and domestic political situation as an instrument for defining the party's new economic line. On the one hand there was the new affirmation by the Soviet Communist Party at the beginning of 1946, about the imminent struggle between the two economic and social systems.[9] On the other hand, the speculative activities of 1946 in the domestic market, and inadequate or nonexistent increases in the workers' nominal and real wages were the main elements in changing the party's attitude. And the electoral results seemed to suggest that this was the correct position. The party was becoming a real mass party, not an élite or a Bolshevik party—something really original in the world of Communist parties. Its new position was strongly to criticize the country's liberal economic management, whose main instrument was private initiative, the principal obstacle to an effective control of the market.[10]

Denunciation of the use of United Nations Rehabilitation and Relief Administration (UNNRA) aid, a demand for better economic conditions for the workers, and criticism of the lack of clear regulation of exports and of guidelines for a 'plan of development' were the main points of the new strategy. The role of the state was further encouraged, both as a technical instrument for acquiring raw materials on the international markets and for distributing them among industrial companies. The party's

[8] Luciano Barca, Franco Botta, and Alberto Zevi (eds.), *I Comunisti e l'economia italiana 1944–1974: Antologia di scritti e documenti* (Bari, 1975); M. Campus, 'L'apologia della stabilizzazione. L'attuazione dell'European Recovery Program in Italia dalla ricostruzione all'avvio del "terzo tempo" (1946–1950)' (unpublished MA thesis, University of Florence, 2002/3).

[9] R. B. Day, *Cold War Capitalism: The View from Moscow 1945–1975* (New York, 1995), 32 ff.

[10] C. Daneo, *La politica economica della ricostruzione* (Turin, 1975); R. Martinelli, *Storia del partito comunista italiano*, vol. vi: *Il 'Partito Nuovo' dalla liberazione al 18 aprile* (Turin, 1996).

Copernican revolution was complete: it abandoned co-operation to achieve a better model of economic development and replaced it—to quote the party's general secretary Palmiro Togliatti—with a 'profound social change to be made legal' .[11]

The technical instrument proposed was a currency change—a sort of financial census to find out where the country's riches were really concentrated—and the adoption of an extraordinary tax on inherited wealth and assets. The party's insistence on these proposals was evidence of the perfectionist dogmatism dominating the Italian Communist Party in economic matters. Its refusal to accept a compromise which could have led to approval for 'non-perfect solutions' paralysed the Italian Communist Party. Any other solution would have driven the party to the centre of the discussions on the country's role in the international markets and on the balance between the different social groups in Italy.[12]

Yet this approach was part of the general debate on the economic and social transformation of the country. The government's rejection of the Communist Party's proposal for a currency change stopped the Communists making any other concrete proposal for economic policy. The country displayed a powerful demand for consumption, and the parties which were able to introduce concrete proposals for prosperity and security in their political manifestos, although these proposals depended on US aid, were in a better position to capture the popular vote. On the opposition benches, the Communist Party put out a slogan that the country could find the force and the substance for economic relief in itself (not in US aid), but it only reached a part of the population. The structural weakness of Italy's economic system required a powerful foreign push whose role was both concrete and psychological. In this context the point of view of the British historian David Ellwood is understandable, when he writes that 'the only Italian government which could work was a government making sure that a constant flow of economic and financial aid' was transferred to the country.[13]

The management of consensus by the Christian Democratic

[11] P. Togliatti, 'Principi di rapporti sociali', *Rinascita*, 9 (1946), 215.

[12] M. De Cecco, 'La politica economica della ricostruzione 1945–1951', in S. J. Woolf (ed.), *Italia 1943–1950: La ricostruzione* (Rome, 1974), 293.

[13] D. Ellwood, *L'alleato nemico: La politica dell'occupazione angloamericana in Italia 1943–1946* (Milan, 1977).

Party through the myth of a 'self-generating prosperity', and thus
the awareness of being a member of an extraordinarily rich and
developed economic and social area—that is, Western Europe—
ensured an electoral victory in 1948 very much beyond what any
polls had forecast for the moderate parties, whose activity was
dependent on an external guarantee and, as we shall see in the
third section of this essay, on external legitimization.

II. *Influencing the Debate: The Technocrats of the Institute for Industrial Reconstruction (IRI)*

Turning now to the other economic and social actors, we need
to look at the role of the state-owned companies controlled by
IRI. IRI was established in 1933 with the specific target of saving
the country's biggest banking institutes by restoring their liability
and liquidity through the demobilization of the industrial share-
holdings of the mixed banks. From the start, IRI had the specific
task of financing industrial activities. Fresh capital was to come
from the private sector through fixed bonds issued by IRI itself
and covered by a state guarantee. This project was completed in
1936 by a banking law reforming the previous situation. The
decision, taken in 1937, to transform IRI into a permanent institution definitively gave the state the main function of financial
intermediary, previously played by the universal banks. The new
situation also clearly showed the absolute necessity for industrial
restructuring, and revealed the chaotic situation of the enterprises inherited from the mixed banks. The rapid passage to war
actually prevented the implementation of any programme of
reorganization and transformation of the enormous industrial
apparatus (about 40 per cent of industrial stock holdings
belonged to the state), an important sector in which the state-
controlled firms attained a quasi monopoly. The public presence
dominated mainly in the iron and steel industry, where the
enterprises of IRI (which had been controlled since 1937 by a
sector holding company, Finsider) produced 77 per cent of the
cast iron and 45 per cent of the steel, and in shipbuilding and
shipping companies, where another sector holding company,
Finmare, had been established. The state was also present in the
telecommunications sector through Stet (founded in 1934), which

headed three telephone companies (Stipel, Telve, and Timo) and accounted for 52 per cent of telephone subscribers in Italy.[14]

The main elements in the economic relief extended to the state-controlled companies in the postwar period were the creation of Finmeccanica, a holding company charged with merging the IRI firms in the engineering sector; the appointment of new top managers to AGIP, thus giving this oil company a chance to develop its activities; the new IRI statute, approved in 1948; and the Sinigallia Plan for the reconstruction and rationalization of the Finsider plants. Many of these measures reveal a new motivation to promote the general interest. From an organization point of view, the creation in 1947 of Finmeccanica, a holding company for the many state-controlled firms in the mechanical sector, of Finelettrica in 1952 for the part of the electric sector already in the hands of IRI, and of ENI, the National Agency for Hydrocarbons, in 1953, with the same role for the oil industry, confirmed the validity of the organizational choices of the 1930s.[15]

The real change was the reform of the IRI statute in 1948. Contrary to the choices made between 1945 and 1948, the new rules gave the government the right to nominate the chairman, vice-chairman, and general directors of the IRI companies, greatly limiting the managers' freedom. The managerial and/or industrial approach to the problems of the state-controlled companies was now largely subordinate to a political one, although the process was not yet specifically defined. Those decisions were taken at the end of protracted discussions between the government, the political parties, and the Allies—not about the reform of IRI, but about its very existence.

Technocrats controlled IRI's leading group. From the very beginning it marked a decisive step towards reshaping Italy's economic and industrial structure. In 1944 the IRI technocrats, more economic nationalists than fascists, prepared a document on the country's postwar economic future. The document suggested that technocratic planning, which included a strong

---

[14] E. Cianci, *Nascita dello Stato imprenditore* (Milan, 1977); L. Avagliano, *Stato e imprenditori in Italia: Le origini dell'IRI* (Salerno, 1980).

[15] M. Doria, 'Note sull'industria meccanica nella Ricostruzione', *Rivista di storia economica*, no. 1 (1987), 35–75; B. Bottiglieri, 'L'industria elettrica dalla guerra agli anni del "miracolo economico" ', in V. Castronovo (ed.), *Storia dell'industria elettrica in Italia*, iv (Rome, 1994), 61–87.

brand of neo-mercantilism, as Rolf Petri put it, was necessary for the postwar period, but it was conceived as 'guidance' and orientation for 'individual forces'. Its task was to define the 'right' industrial sectors and branches and to avoid 'dispersion of energies'. Postwar reconstruction was believed to be an opportunity for 'reorganizing' rather than 'restoring' the economy. A world divided into two large areas was correctly foreseen, as was Italy's integration into the Western alliance. Among many other points, trade liberalization was considered inevitable, at least within the Anglo-American sphere. It was reckoned a great opportunity for the country, which was so historically dependent on trade tariffs and from the 1930s on autarky. In a sense the document paved the way for the readjustment of the old neo-mercantilist strategy to the new international economic order proposed by the USA.[16]

The US mission in Rome considered the large presence of the state as an entrepreneur through IRI a decisive factor in influencing the development of restrictive business practices, especially in heavy industry.[17] All the US analyses of restrictive business practices in Italy pointed out that the origins of this attitude were to be found in the fascist regime, and especially in its economic culture, whose aim was considered to be to control the economy rather than to develop it. Considering that one of the crucial points of the US economic and cultural battle was the elimination of restrictive business practices in postwar Europe, the Allies were not by chance present at the discussions about the role of the state as an entrepreneur. The IRI technocracy was able to show that the presence of state-owned companies was a key factor in Italy's economic reconstruction and political and social stabilization. The increasing importance of the 'planners' among the European Co-operation Administration (ECA) staff both in Washington and in Rome enabled such success. The IRI was also favoured by the fact that it was considered both by the Christian Democratic Party and the Italian Communist Party as an instrument for the achievement of a better economic and social balance in Italy's industrial capitalism. Both parties,

[16] R. Petri, *Storia economica d'Italia: Dalla Grande guerra al miracolo economico (1918–1963)* (Bologna, 2001), 291 ff.; see also G. Maione, *Tecnocrati e mercanti: L'industria italiana tra dirigismo e concorrenza internazionale* (Milan, 1986).

[17] A list of the international cartels in which Italian firms were represented can be found in B. Curli, 'L'Italia, la Società delle Nazioni e la discussione sugli accordi internazionali, 1927–31', *Rivista di storia economica*, NS 7 (1990), no. 1, 45–6.

despite their different ideological background, considered the state-owned companies an important ally against the predominance of the big private groups.[18]

Thus the debate on the economic and social order in Italy developed in a direction that did not actually eliminate the left-wing opposition from the political discussion, despite its ideological approach to many questions. To overcome Italy's structural backwardness (particularly in the south of the country) became a common objective for both the government and the left-wing parties. Thus despite the dramatic social tensions, which increased greatly in 1948, a door was left open. And through this door other elements of the 1945–50 debates could still enter: the role of state-owned companies; their position in the anti-monopoly campaign (forgetting that most of these companies were by definition a monopoly); and the modernization of the national stock of industrial plant as an instrument to reinforce Italy's economic independence.[19]

III. *The Other Side of the Coin: Foreign Trade and Economic Liberalization Policy*

The main problem of the Italian ruling élite in the aftermath of the Second World War was one of legitimization. Emerging from the underground, or returning from a long exile, its members were almost unknown to the great mass of the Italian people. Before the conflict, moreover, contacts between the political exiles of the fascist period and the government representatives of Italy's new partners had been infrequent or nonexistent. There was, therefore, also the problem of gaining legitimization at international level.[20]

---

[18] S. Battilossi, 'Cultura economica e riforme nella sinistra italiana dall'antifascismo al neocapitalismo', *Studi storici*, 37 (1996), 771–811; T. Baldini, 'Dalla programmazione al "libro dei sogni" ', in *Annali dell'Istituto Ugo La Malfa*, xiii (Rome, 1998).

[19] S. Battilossi, *L'Italia nel sistema economico internazionale: Il management dell'integrazione. Finanza, industria e istituzioni 1945–1955* (Milan, 1997).

[20] E. Di Nolfo, 'Sistema internazionale e sistema politico italiano: interazione e compatibilità', in L. Graziano and S. Torrow (eds.), *La crisi italiana*, vol. i: *Formazione del regime repubblicano e società civile* (Turin, 1979), 79–112; id., 'La formazione della politica estera italiana negli anni della nascita di blocchi (l'Italia tra le superpotenze)', in R. H. Rainero, B. Vigezzi, and E. Di Nolfo, *L'Italia e la politica di potenza* (Settimo Milanese, 1988), 603–19.

From a certain point of view, the latter seemed even more complex than the former, as Italy's status as a defeated country, but from 1943 no longer an enemy, had been widely criticized by the Allied powers (especially Britain). Furthermore, the difficult process of replacing the ruling classes between summer 1943 and the end of the war, and the subsequent choice of the republic (instead of the monarchy) in the 1946 referendum had put the question in an entirely new perspective. The process of legitimizing the new leaders was accelerated by the elections of April 1948, which marked the defeat of the Fronte Popolare (Popular Front), the electoral and political coalition between the Italian Communist and the Socialist Party, and the affirmation of a series of moderate governments centred on the Christian Democratic Party. The instruments used by the moderate parties to win elections and thus remain in power for the next fifteen years (until the early 1960s, when the centrist coalition was replaced by a centre-left one with the Socialist Party in the parliamentary majority) were strategic alignment with the Western world and anti-Communism as an ideological guideline. At the same time this success was used at international level to gain the legitimization of Italy's new Western partners, especially the USA. In this case the political and ideological cement was a necessary but not a sufficient condition. To achieve that objective the Italian leaders had to use a different tool, namely, inclusion in the international organizations created by the USA for the implementation of the new international economic order, and acceptance of their policies. On the one hand, inclusion in the international organizations followed a schedule that was partly determined by Italy's gradual readmission into the Western alliance and by the shedding of its status as an occupied country; on the other, the acceptance of their policies was the result of protracted bargaining by the government, which responded to the often contradictory pressures coming from the Italian business community.[21]

Italy was officially included in the International Monetary Fund in October 1946, but became an actual member only in March 1947. In the same year it joined the OEEC, and it entered GATT

---

[21] F. Barbagallo, 'La formazione dell'Italia democratica', in *Storia dell'Italia repubblicana*, vol. i: *La costruzione della democrazia: Dalla caduta del fascismo agli anni cinquanta* (Turin, 1994), 48–130; P. Soddu, *L'Italia del dopoguerra 1947–1953: Una democrazia precaria* (Rome, 1998).

during the Annecy Conference in 1949. As for the European Payments Union, which was established in 1949, Italy, being one of the founders, did not have to be kept waiting. In the same year it also joined NATO. Thus only four years after the end of the war (and two years after the signing of the peace treaty), Italy was included in the main institutions which supported the new international politico-strategic and economic structure set up by the USA. Behind this scenario, however, lay complex political and economical processes. Formal inclusion in the Bretton Woods Agreements and in the European Payments Union alone could not have suddenly created a champion of free trade out of a country which had experienced seventy years of protectionism (the first customs duty was established in 1878) and twenty years of fascist rule, during which the protectionist system and especially state intervention in the economy had considerably strengthened. It was entirely a matter of political choice and it was strongly pursued by a restricted circle consisting of members of the government and of the economic establishment, with the Bank of Italy in the forefront. Large sections of the government parties and especially the business community were much more cautious, if not directly opposed to this point of view. They actually advocated much greater wariness as to the timing and terms of acceptance of the principles of economic and commercial liberalization.[22]

Italy still had a rather backward economic structure, with an infrastructural network considered inadequate for a modern country. Its industry was dominated by oligopolies in practically every sector, with a rate of obsolescence of machinery that was on the average higher than that of its competitors and of its European partners. The state bureaucracy was encumbered by overlapping institutions created by the fascist regime following an administrative pattern that had been inherited from the liberal period without any changes except for the multiplication of state-controlled bodies and the swelling of the ranks of clerks. Such was the picture of the country repeatedly presented by the Allied forces after 1943 and especially by the Americans after 1945 when its ruling class was anxious to be included in the Bretton Woods institutions.[23]

[22] G. Mori, 'L'economia italiana tra la fine della seconda guerra mondiale e il "secondo miracolo economico" (1945–58)', in *Storia dell'Italia repubblicana*, i. 140–91.

[23] M. Salvati, *Stato e industria nella ricostruzione: Alle origini del potere democristiano* (Milan, 1982); G. Melis, *Storia dell'amministrazione italiana 1861–1993* (Bologna, 1996), 406–8.

The suggestions made by the ECA and Mutual Security Agency (MSA) missions in Rome all pointed in the same direction. In order to modernize the country it was necessary first of all to reform the bureaucratic apparatus, and particularly the tax system; secondly, to bring the infrastructure up to date; and finally, radically to transform the industrial apparatus by getting rid of all the oligopolistic structures, both formal and informal, set up or strengthened by fascism, and by renewing productive equipment.[24] This American analysis was regarded with perplexity by many among the moderate parties in power and the Italian business community, whereas it aroused interest among the ranks of moderate reformers (in the Italian Social Democratic Party and in the Republican Party), and, despite their ideological approach, even in the parties of the Left. In this almost paradoxical situation, the design for legitimization that the new ruling classes were drawing up in those years, with all its limits, took shape. The strength of the country's new ruling élite was directly proportional to its ability to persuade the whole country to accept the general principles of the new international economic order. However, its capacity to assimilate them effectively, to translate them into real acts of government, and rationally to transform the country was inversely proportional to the resistance that a few conservative forces, hidden in the bureaucratic machinery and in many sectors of the economy, were able to exert. Full and complete acceptance of the principles of free trade would have meant, in effect, setting up a programme of reforms for which the Italian government lacked a cultural tradition (that of planning). Nor did it have the political strength to carry it through to the end. If the first limit could somehow have been overcome by imitating some other European experiences (the French one, for instance, given the common Catholic orientation of some of the government parties), it was more difficult to find a way past the second one. A serious programme of reforms would in fact have compelled the new ruling classes to make choices which would create incurable fractures within the compound of varied social forces the government was trying to bring together and which constituted its electoral basis. This put

---

[24] L. Segreto, 'The impact of the US productivity philosophy in Italy after World War II', in D. Barjot (ed.), *Productivity Missions and the Penetration of American Economic and Technological Influence after the Second World War* (Paris, 2002), 135–46.

the new international partners and especially the USA in a Catch-22 situation. To trust the new ruling classes actually involved delaying a process of reforms which, according to the pitiless analysis of the American Embassy in Rome, could no longer be put off. On the other hand, to criticize the government to the point of undermining its legitimization within the country would have lost them a suitable ally for implementing the most important part of the USA's security policy for Western Europe, namely, the containment of Communism and the retrenchment of the parties dependent on Moscow. The decade roughly from 1947 to the signing of the Treaty of Rome is therefore of the utmost importance for understanding the long-term choices Italy made in order to satisfy the political and economic requirements posed by its international position. A short examination of a few exemplary events in international economic relations will be useful in throwing light on this situation.[25]

The implementation of the Marshall Plan in Italy was characterized by repeated criticism from the Americans about the use of the counterpart funds, that is, the equivalent to the sums received in dollars, which the Italian government was required to pay out of its own pocket. This criticism climaxed in 1949 with the publication of the *Country Study*. Literature of the 1970s on the subject, in particular a contribution by Marcello de Cecco, pointed out that with this message the Americans wanted to upbraid the Italian government and the Bank of Italy for their lack of courage in undertaking a series of reforms inspired by Keynes's economic theories. The victory of Einaudi and the Bank of Italy's ideas on free trade has been interpreted as final evidence of a political choice to ban the left-wing parties from government when the economic squeeze of 1947 was about to take place. In the 1980s Piero Scoppola and Vera Zamagni moderated this politically inspired judgement, underlining especially the importance of purely economic elements in the American criticism, such as the use of unemployment funds. The most recent interpretations of the episode, like those by Carlo Spagnolo, stress the importance of the conflicts within the Truman administration and its difficult relationship with Congress, which had the last word in the decisions about

---

[25] F. Romero, 'Gli Stati Uniti in Italia: il Piano Marshall e il Patto atlantico', in *Storia dell'Italia repubblicana*, i. 241–59.

financial support of the countries included in the Marshall Plan and about its best use.[26]

The American criticism did not alter the standpoint of the Italian government on the employment of the counterpart funds. On the contrary, if anything, the episode revealed the existence of different opinions among the various branches of the ECA, which were skilfully exploited by the Italian government, as Chiarella Esposito has recently noted.[27] Rome, moreover, had another ace up its sleeve to be played against its American critics. In March 1949 the IMF expressed a positive judgement of the policy to stabilize the lira and its beneficial effects on the national budget, the balance of trade, and the balance of payments, thus giving a positive appraisal of the same policy that the ECA mission in Rome had harshly criticized.[28]

The appointment of Guido Carli, the head of the Italian Board of Change (the agency of the Bank of Italy that supervised the country's monetary policy), as Executive Director of the IMF Board was further evidence that, at least as far as monetary policy was concerned, Italy was able to offer its international partners reliability—all the more so as Carli's main rival, the Australian candidate, had been supported by a wide coalition led by Britain.[29]

However, this episode also sheds light on another factor which long played a decisive role in Italy's international economic relations of the period, namely, the prestige of a few individuals, especially from the Bank of Italy and other major banks such as the Banca Commerciale Italiana, as standard-bearers of the new image of the country in the rest of the world. This is not a matter of tracing the history of the country's political and economic relations only in the light of the contribution made by some of

[26] M. De Cecco, 'Lo sviluppo dell'economia italiana', *Rivista Internazionale di Scienze economiche e Commerciali*, 18 (1971); P. Scoppola, 'De Gasperi e la scelta politica del maggio 1947', in *Il Mulino*, no. 231, Jan.–Feb. 1974; V. Zamagni, 'Una scommessa sul futuro: l'industria italiana nella ricostruzione (1946–1952)', in Rainero, Vigezzi, and Di Nolfo, *L'Italia e la politica di potenza*, 473–95; C. Spagnolo, *La stabilizzazione incompiuta: Il Piano Marshall in Italia (1947–1952)* (Rome, 2001).

[27] C. Esposito, *America's Feeble Weapon: Funding the Marshall Plan in France and Italy, 1948–1950* (Westport, Conn., 1994).

[28] Historical Archives of the Bank of Italy (Rome), Studi, box 335, IMF, Robert Triffin, Italy's progress in 1948, Mar. 1949.

[29] G. Carli in collaboration with Paolo Peluffo, *Cinquant'anni di vita italiana* (Rome, 1992), 65–9; F. Cesarano, *Gli accordi di Bretton Woods: La costruzione di un ordine monetario internazionale* (Rome, 2000).

the key figures of its economic and financial establishment. It is necessary to point out, however, that their professional skills were often decisive in moderating judgements which would otherwise have been much more severe towards Italy. Their task was not an easy one, as they had to keep Italy closely tied to its economic partners while at the same time suggesting that Italy could meet the demands of the international economic institutions—if not in the short term, then at least in the medium or the long term. Among the bankers the most important names include Luigi Einaudi (Governor of the Bank of Italy, then Minister of the Budget, and eventually first President of the Republic), Donato Menichella (who succeeded Einaudi as Governor of the Bank of Italy), Guido Carli and Paolo Baffi, high-ranking officials of the Bank of Italy and later, in the 1960s and 1970s, also governors, and Raffaele Mattioli, President of the Banca Commerciale Italiana, who led the first Italian economic mission to the USA in 1944.[30]

In fact, it was mostly the Bank of Italy's determination to follow the IMF guidelines that assured the Allies, and in particular the USA, that despite all uncertainties, sudden halts, and political obstacles, Italy was on the right course. This is also demonstrated by the history of the law on foreign investments. This bill, approved by the Italian parliament in 1948, was regarded in the USA as the most advanced in all Europe in spite of its cumbersome procedures and the existing restrictions on the export of capital gains and the re-export of capital. This, however, did not help Italy attract much foreign (in particular, American) capital until the second half of the 1950s. The main obstacles were the existence of a market which was not yet fully developed, in particular as far as mass consumption was concerned, and a number of political restrictions, the most important of which, concerning the research and the exploitation of hydrocarbons in Italy, was never removed. Through the existence of its own agencies, first AGIP and then ENI, Italy remained the only state entitled to work in this field, and for many years this choice opened up a protracted disagreement between the USA and the American oil companies on one side

---

[30] R. Faucci, *Einaudi* (Turin, 1986); F. Cotula, C. O. Gelsomino, and A. Gigliobianco (eds.), *Donato Menichella: Stabilità e sviluppo dell'economia italiana 1946–1960*, 2 vols. (Rome, 1997); P. J. Cook, *Ugo La Malfa* (Bologna, 1999).

and the Italian government and ENI on the other. These tensions were increased by a number of decisions made by the Italian oil company which were not regarded as consonant with Western interests. In the late 1950s ENI initiated a series of contracts with oil-producing Arab countries which threatened to jeopardize the monopoly and the pattern of relations established by the multinational oil companies. Nevertheless, these tensions did not prevent considerable amounts of American capital from flowing into Italy as soon as the foreign investment law was further liberalized (1956), and, above all, after the lira returned to a regime of full convertibility (1958), thanks to the constant prodding of the Bank of Italy. Italy, which in those years experienced an economic boom with an increase in private consumption, especially of durable consumer goods, became the ideal terrain for foreign investments. In fact until the end of the 1960s this sector had a rate of growth higher than in any other Western European country.[31]

Much more controversial were two other questions which demonstrate the contradictory course the Italian government pursued in its relationship with the USA and with its ideas of reform and economic deregulation: the programmes for technical assistance and productivity, and the lifting of protectionist restrictions. In the first case scepticism prevailed, but there was a certain degree of incomprehension of what acceptance of the programmes for technical assistance and productivity would involve. The government and the political class in general did not show much interest in the initiatives presented by the Americans through the Productivity Drive. On the whole, they adopted the initial judgement expressed by industrialists and regarded them as scarcely suitable, or at least hardly adaptable to the Italian situation. Sharing the philosophy of productivity would clearly imply accepting a programme of reforms, first of all in the public administration, which touched a very sensitive point in Italy's political set-up between the 1940s and 1950s. The conclusion drawn by an ECA executive was very pessimistic: 'We have spent hundreds of millions of dollars in Italy, but that doesn't seem to have changed the social, political, and economic context in such a way as to allow us to conclusively increase its industrial produc-

---

[31] L. Segreto, 'Gli investimenti americani in Italia 1945–1963', *Studi storici*, 37 (1996), 273–316.

tivity.'[32] And ultimately they were wrong, since productivity increased remarkably during the 1950s, but following a model that was based on low salaries and low consumption. Industrialists, who were more directly concerned, were mainly attracted by two points in the productivity programme which in fact turned out to be successful, namely the processes of manager and worker training in line with the new American methods known as 'training within industry'. However, they were very unwilling to accept any change in industrial relations on the shop-floor, which would involve both workers and (non-Communist) unions in making decisions about factory policies. And above all they were firmly against the core of the American message about productivity, namely, that workers should have a share in the increased profits produced by increased productivity. According to the industrialists, workers would benefit from increased productivity as consumers, just like everyone else. It is difficult, then, at least as regards the 1950s, not to agree with the American official who wrote that Italian industrialists were interested only in 'perpetuating the myth that there is no alternative between communism and their capitalistic model based on monopolies, low salaries, limited production, high costs and high prices'.[33]

The case of the reduction of trade tariffs is the best illustration that behind the acceptance of certain principles there were different positions, all essentially concerned with national economic interest. As regards the elimination of trade quotas, Italy followed OEEC's guidelines for intra-European trade and obtained the best possible results from its participation in the European Payment Union. In this context a central role was played by the Minister for Foreign Commerce, Ugo La Malfa, one of the few Italian politicians of the time who, with the high officials of the Bank of Italy, ranks among the protagonists of the process of economic liberalization and, indirectly, of the international legitimization of the country. His main achievement was to have

[32] National Archives and Records Administration, Archives II, College Park Md, Record group 469, Office of Special Representative, Productivity and Technical Assistance Division, Country File, Italy, B. 13, Memorandum by J. T. Quinn to E. N. Flaherty, 'Technical assistance in Italy, 29.1.1951', see also Segreto, 'The impact of the US productivity philosophy', 139–40.

[33] P. D'Attorre, ' "Anche noi possiamo essere prosperi". Aiuti ERP e politiche della produttività negli anni cinquanta', *Quaderni storici*, no. 58 (Apr. 1985), 55–93; L. Segreto, 'Americanizzare o modernizzare l'economia italiana? Progetti americani e risposte italiane negli anni Cinquanta e Sessanta', *Passato e Presente*, no. 37 (1996), 55–83.

redressed the balance of payments towards Europe, which showed a very strong surplus in the early 1950s, thus opening the Italian market to imports largely through the substantial elimination of trade quotas. This decision was strongly opposed by the business community and especially by Confindustria, the Italian industrialists' association. Only constant reference to what Guido Carli defined as 'the external constraint' was able to overcome the strong resistance of the industrialists. From this point of view one can agree with Stefano Battilossi when he states that as a result of these decisions, Italy had been irreversibly changed by the events of the 1930s and 1940s.[34] However, the short-term economic rationale that led to this choice should not be underestimated, even if the ultimate explanation lies within the logic of the 'pattern of legitimization' described in the first section of this chapter. The Italian approach, in fact, was also instrumental to the pressures that the government was putting on the USA in order to receive a large Off Shore Procurements quota of the Mutual Defense Assistance Program, which could come in useful for the 1953 political elections.[35]

If Italy was a 'model pupil' in the eyes of its Western partners as far as the abolition of quotas was concerned, the same was not true as regards reduction of external tariffs. In the GATT negotiations Italy was always among the countries defending a regime of high tariffs. The disarray in the relations between the Italian delegation to the GATT conferences and the central government, and the ambiguity of the political guidelines did not help the Italian position in the negotiations. The government caved in when faced with the strong requests of the industrialists who, because of the lack of a clear-cut governmental strategy, were able decisively to shape Italian policy at the GATT conferences. The impossibility of finding an acceptable compromise between industrial and agricultural interests produced sharply contrasting pressures and suggestions, and the government was not able (or perhaps not willing) to intervene with a coherent programme of tariff cuts of its own. Once again, to mediate also meant to make choices which were bound to disappoint many people: in a word, to govern. Strong and tightly-knit as it was when facing

---

[34] Battilossi, *L'Italia nel sistema economico internazionale*.
[35] L. Sebesta, *L'Europa indifesa: sistema di sicurezza atlantico e caso italiano 1948–1955* (Florence, 1955).

the task of bringing Italy to accept the basic principles of the new international economic order, the leadership of the gang of 'liberalizers' from Carli to La Malfa had to give in when confronted with the political need not to disappoint anyone. Political considerations of this kind were mostly expressed by the Democrazia Cristiana (DC), the Christian Democratic Party, the key party of the coalition government. At this stage, in fact, the DC was mostly concerned with domestic legitimization, since international political legitimization could now be taken for granted, and in the economic field it had already displayed its ability to meet the economic standards and principles dictated by the new leaders of the Western bloc.[36]

IV. *Beyond Reconstruction: Long-Term Continuity?*

This constant attention to domestic problems or the domestic implications of international issues prevented the Italian ruling class from grasping the significance of an important phenomenon of the first half of the 1950s, namely, the strong, almost overbearing, return of Western Germany on to the international economic scene. The pattern of co-operation and interdependence which had been constructed under American supervision after the end of the war and had set the tone for the process of European economic integration was beginning to waver. Thus at the start of the process of European integration Italy was only apparently among the political protagonists, whereas from the economic point of view its position was one of substantial subordination to the current dynamics, produced by the effort of balancing the attractiveness of the German market for the entire Continent with the necessity to oppose the strength of the newly awakened giant in the heart of Europe.[37]

Rather like what had happened in the early stage of economic and commercial liberalization, the business community (including farmers and industrialists) resisted the prospect of European economic integration. This they did, paradoxically, by referring

[36] F. Fauri, 'La fine dell'autarchia: i negoziati commerciali dell'Italia dal 1947 al 1953', *Rivista di storia economica*, NS, 4 (1995).

[37] F. Fauri, *L'Italia e l'integrazione economica europea 1947–2000* (Bologna, 2001), 55–136; A. Varsori (ed.), 'L'Italia e il processo di integrazione europea: prospettive di ricerca e revisione storiografica', *Storia delle relazioni internazionali*, special issue, 13–14 (1998–9).

to the evaluations made by the Americans in the late 1940s, which described Italian backwardness, in particular in the industrial field. After much vacillation, Confindustria accepted the idea of a European Common Market, but even after its acceptance the opponents of the project (quite a few of whom were to be found among its ranks) never refrained from stressing the dangers inherent in a European perspective for an industrial sector which was still structurally weak and accustomed by decades of protectionism to ignoring the basic rules of free competition.[38]

The government regarded the European option as the best chance of giving the country's social and economic problems an international dimension. Beyond the Europeanist verbiage which the Italian ruling class employed profusely, the choice of integration was regarded, in particular by the most open-minded sectors of the political world and the economic and technocratic establishment, as the culmination of the process of international legitimization begun at the end of the 1940s with the acceptance of the Bretton Woods Agreements and the principles of economic liberalization. In the meantime, as Federico Romero has underlined, the idea of Europe was gradually transformed into a tool of nation-building which could appeal to all political parties, including the opposition parties of the extreme left wing and the extreme right wing.[39] This hegemonic diffusion of the concept of European integration did not, however, automatically produce a more enterprising attitude *vis-à-vis* the political choices offered by the European Community. Italy's lack of political and economic weight within the EEC can only partly explain this phenomenon. Rather it seems that with the construction of the EEC the process of international legitimization pursued by the Italians had somehow split into two parts: one economic (or largely economic) and the other political-diplomatic. The former would increasingly depend upon Italy's Euro-partners and Brussels, while the latter would continue to have its main interlocutor in Washington—at least until the fall of the Berlin Wall.

This 'bargained dependence', to use the image suggested by

---

[38] F. Petrini, 'Gli industriali italiani e l'integrazione economica europea', *Passato e Presente*, no. 56 (2003).

[39] F. Romero, 'L'Europa come strumento di nation-building: storia e storici dell'Italia contemporanea', *Passato e Presente*, 13 (1995), no. 36, 19–32.

David Ellwood, or 'unequal exchange', to borrow the title of a book by an Italian ex-ambassador in Moscow, Sergio Romano, about US–Italian relations,[40] rhetorically represented relations between the two countries. For the Italian governments between the end of the Second World War and the late 1980s confirmation of the international legitimization of the ruling class remained an American prerogative, certainly not a European one. Thin as it may have become with the passing of time, and enriched as it might have been by many other components, the relationship between the two countries was still centred on Italian loyalty to NATO and the resulting strategic choices, that is, on the endorsement of the American point of view on the most important international issues. In return, the American government continued to tolerate a political class which had repeatedly displayed a surprising inability to regenerate itself, or to initiate a process of economic, social, administrative, and political reform made all the more imperative by the gravity of the country's problems.

The European choice, on the other hand, was regarded as a chance to pursue the process of economic integration at the international level. But just as on many previous occasions, this process was not led by Italy and its government: the latter simply adjusted (often late and reluctantly) to the guidelines and the principles prescribed by the European Community. The business community has continued to react, as in the 1950s, with animosity, coming up with brakes, obstacles, and requests for exemptions when faced with the new foreign constraints that the government has not always supported with the necessary strength. In return, Italy's politicians have once again largely accepted the role of merely echoing the often contradictory exigencies pressed by the economic milieu. On many of the issues under debate, politicians have displayed a timidity and a carelessness which has aroused more incredulity than indignation among Italy's European partners.

There is a red thread that runs through postwar Italian history from the 1950s to the year 2001, underlining the presence of a feature common to all the Italian governments of this period, namely the importance of the foreign constraint. All the most

---

[40] S. Romano, *Lo scambio ineguale: Italia e Stati Uniti da Wilson a Clinton* (Rome, 1995).

difficult steps in Italy's monetary and economic policy—from the
reduction of the fluctuation band of the Italian lira in the EMS
from 6 to 2.25 per cent in 1990 to the meeting of the so-called
Maastricht criteria about the ratio between debt and gross
domestic product, deficit and GDP, inflation rate and interest
rates—have been taken not after an evaluation of the positive
consequences they might have for the country, but always in
response to choices made outside the country, in Brussels. Those
who have supported these steps with greatest fervour have always
wanted to force the government and the politicians to behave
'correctly' in the domain of public expenditure. One further
piece of evidence that over the last fifty years some of the basic
traits of Italian foreign economic policy have not changed is that
the most determined and consistent push in this direction has
come either from the Bank of Italy or from those technocrats
turned politicians who had a solid background in that institution
(such as Carlo Azeglio Ciampi, who was Governor of the Bank of
Italy between 1979 and 1993 and subsequently, from 1993 to
1998, Prime Minister and then Minister of Treasury, before
being elected President of the Republic, or Lamberto Dini,
General Director of the Bank of Italy and then Minister of
Treasury, Prime Minister, and finally Minister for Foreign Affairs
between 1996 and 2001), and, to a lesser extent, from politicians
who were either persuaded of the soundness of the European
choice or were convinced to make that choice by those very same
technocrats. This, at least, is a matter for rejoicing.[41]

---

[41] L. Segreto, 'Italia, Europa', *Passato e Presente*, 20 (2002), no. 56, 3–11.

8

The Modernization of France:
A New Economic and Social Order
after the Second World War?

Gérard Bossuat

The only alternative to modernization is decline

Jean Monnet[1]

Did the French Resistance want to set up a new economic and social order at the Liberation? What principles guided the political and social leadership? Was France so changed after the years of reconstruction that History could say the French people were living in a different economic and social order compared with the period before the Second World War? To answer these questions, I propose to take as my theme the idea of modernization, which in 1945 was a well-established feature of the intellectual landscape: is modernization the same thing as a new economic and social order? Did the first Modernization and Equipment Plan (the Monnet Plan) constitute a break with the past? And was American involvement in the modernization process a factor in the construction of a new economic and social order? Monnet wrote to Georges Bidault in July 1947: 'In these difficult times it is essential to keep one thing alive in the eyes of the French people, namely that the Modernization Plan is a French entity. This plan represents a hope. It shows what the lot of the French people will be, and where their country will stand in the world economically at the conclusion of the effort the plan requires of them.'[2] This key question in the history and destiny of a nation has of course been tackled by many researchers both in France and abroad, by eye-witnesses, and by former top civil servants whose views have

---

[1] Jean Monnet, *Mémoires* (Paris, 1976), 306.
[2] Vincent Auriol, *Journal du Septennat 1947–1954*, 1 (Paris, 1974), 697.

been canvassed by historians.[3] Was France renewed socially and economically? Former Treasury Director François Bloch-Lainé spoke of a 'restored' France. Finally, in terms of method, we need to look at the question of the self-representation of national power in France after the Second World War: how could the French see themselves as a great nation again after the failure of 1940? Economic affairs are affected by the social dimension and by representations of national identity. Jean Bouvier and René Girault showed conclusively that history was all-embracing. To write about groups and milieux engaged in the economic sphere is at the same time to write the history of human societies, for 'what we call "economic" mechanisms and development are embodied in individuals, groups, social milieux (including the family), firms, that is, in forces and intentions tangibly grasped and demonstrated'.[4]

Modernization, a Familiar Idea in France in 1945

De Gaulle returned to France to restore order—republican order, naturally. Thus his actions were not directed towards creating a new economic and social order. The word 'restoration' (*restauration*) in the double sense of reverting to a former order and embellishment assumed its full meaning here. Yet the desire to wipe out the defeat of 1940 could not be satisfied by a republican-style restoration. In 1945 industrial production in France had fallen to 38 per cent of its 1939 level, and 1947 was a terrible year. Shortages returned. In a book entitled *Mise en valeur*

---

[3] See above all Michel Margairaz, *L'État, les finances et l'économie: Histoire d'une conversion, 1932-1952*, Comité pour l'Histoire Économique et Financière de la France, hereafter cited as CHEFF (Paris, 1991); François Bloch-Lainé and Jean Bouvier, *La France restaurée, 1944-1954, dialogue sur les choix d'une modernization* (Paris, 1986); Philippe Mioche, *Le Plan Monnet, genèse et élaboration, 1941-1947* (Paris, 1987); Gérard Bossuat, *La France, l'aide américaine et les construction européennes, 1944-1954*, 2 vols., CHEFF (1992; 2nd edn. 1997). See also Robert Frank, 'The French Dilemma: Modernization with Dependence or Independence and Decline', in Josef Becker and Franz Knipping (eds.), *Power in Europe? Great Britain, France, Italy and Germany in a Postwar World, 1945-1950* (Berlin, 1986), 263; Robert Frank, *La Hantise du Déclin, La France, 1920-1960: Finances, défense et identité nationale* (Belin, 1994); François Bloch-Lainé, *Profession fonctionnaire, entretiens avec Françoise Carrière* (Seuil, 1976); see also the interviews with top civil servants carried out by the Ministry of Finance's CHEFF.

[4] Jean Bouvier, 'Post-scriptum, à propos de l'histoire dite "économique"', in Patrick Fridenson and André Straus (eds.), *Le Capitalisme français 19e–20e siècle: Blocages et dynamismes d'une croissance* (Paris, 1987), 400.

de la France ('Getting the best out of France'), Jean-François Gravier wrote: 'Our geographical calling is that of a great nation of 70 million people with the finest agriculture and the finest metallurgical industry in Europe.'[5] The aims expressed here were the same as those of General de Gaulle. Restoration or reconstruction was insufficient to attain greatness. More was required: modernization.

Michel Margairaz has shown that the Resistance movements had aspirations for economic and social modernization in France. These required the intervention of the state. In December 1943 the clandestine Socialist Party incorporated in its programme the creation of a Ministry of National Economy alongside the Ministry of Finance, because flexibility and imagination were needed in addition to day-to-day management of balanced budgets. State intervention was not an ideological choice; it was imposed by economic necessity, and crisis and war promoted it.[6] The modernization of France had been in the air since the 1930s in terms that could be used by the post-Second World War decision-makers. Economic planning was the instrument of French modernization from 1946. The idea was not new. Its intellectual roots lay in the planning ideas of Léon Jouhaux and Henri de Man, and in the thinking of the X-crisis group, Les Nouveaux Cahiers, and it referred to the development projects of the Vichy regime's DGEN (Direction générale à l'équipement national). The two-year start-up tranche worked out by Jean Bichelonne was published by Mendès France in 1944. Members of the Vichy organizing committees sat on the modernization commissions of the Monnet Plan. Vichy had created the tools of modernization, the Professional Research Centres (Centres de recherche professionnelle), as early as 1943. The French Petroleum Institute, INRA (Institut national de la recherche agronomique), and CEA (Commissariat à l'energie atomique) were set up in 1945, based on ideas dating from before the Liberation. During the war, the experience of the Uriage School of Management was illuminating. At Uriage (near Grenoble) the world was reinvented. Political and social

[5] The author of the famous *Paris et désert français* (Paris, 1947), Gravier brought out this second book (with the same publisher) as early as 1949.

[6] Philippe Mioche, 'Le Démarrage de l'économie française au lendemain de la guerre', *Historiens et Géographes. La IVᵉ République: Histoire, recherches et archives (357–8)* (Apr.–Aug. 1997), 423 f.

modernization was the core concern. Men such as Simon Nora and Paul Delouvrier cut their teeth there.[7] State control and economic planning lay at the heart of the thinking of those who sought solutions to the economic crisis of 1929 and to the overt political and military crisis of May 1940.

French modernization owed much to applied Keynesianism. There was a general awareness of Keynes in 1944. Simplified Keynesianism was likened to contractualized state intervention in order to increase production and distribute the fruits of growth more fairly. Young finance inspectors popularized Keynes in their intellectual and professional milieu. The general atmosphere contributed to the success of his methods, probably because the theory of the multiplier and the accelerator was particularly welcome. Practical Keynesianism was applied to the preparation of the nation's accounts. Good examples were forecast economic budgets, like the balance-sheet of the nation's accounts drawn up by Uri in 1947, the budgets of the planned economy, and the use of the exchange value of American aid. All over Europe fresh inspirations for economic activity were springing up. They came from Keynes and other 'new economists'.[8] Might not moderate inflation supply states with liquid assets for reconstruction and modernization? Should not banks take more risks? New relations between capital and labour were envisaged in a different spirit from Vichy's. The liberal Maurice Allais coined the term 'competitive economic planning' (*planisme concurrentiel*) to defend his liberal ideas.[9] Charles Rist was wholly obsolete in 1947 when he advocated establishing a free market in gold in France. Keynesian reflation gave the economic and political authorities tools with which to finance growth. And growth inevitably meant modernization. Growth called for innovation, changes, inventions, whereas recession, faced with a reduced market, was more conservative. Liberalism was less likely to produce large-scale modernization during a period of recession since it did not provide society with the means of relaunching the economy.

[7] Pierre Bitoun, *Les Hommes d'Uriage* (Paris, 1988).

[8] René Girault, 'Les Voies de la reconstruction, 1945-1949', in Dominique Barjot, Rémi Baudouï, and Danièle Voldmann (eds.), *Les Reconstructions en Europe (1945–1949)*, (Brussels, 1997), 43.

[9] Olivier Dard, 'Théoriciens et praticiens de l'économie: un changement de paradigme', in Serge Berstein and Pierre Milza (eds.), *L'Année 1947* (Paris, 1999), 112.

In 1945 many people thought that practical, New Deal-style Keynesianism could meet the aspirations of economic and social modernization in France. In Liberation France, too, men determined to modernize the country were in positions of responsibility. They were not all convinced that they were moving from Resistance to Revolution, as Claude Bourdet of *Combat* would have wished. François Bloch-Lainé spoke of a rupture created at the time of the Liberation by the coming-together of modernizers, some of whom had gone with Vichy by mistake, and Jean Monnet.[10] I doubt whether this was the 'break with the past' Bourdet had talked about.

The ideas of modernization, economic planning, state control, steering of the economy, and Keynesian reflation were in the air. Was such modernization the starting-point for a new order in France? It should be said immediately that if French society was looking to modernize, it wanted to do this on the basis of its own roots while experiencing outside influences. The wind was blowing from America. In what direction would it cause innovations to bend?

A Missed Opportunity: Mendès France

Pierre Mendès France, who became Minister of National Economy in September 1944, believed he could organize the future. However, he was not responsible for foreign economic negotiations; these were assigned to the Minister of Foreign Affairs. Mendès France prepared a long-term economic programme which he presented to the Council of Ministers on 17 November 1944. The development choices he made resembled those of the Soviet theory of economic planning. The order of priority was heavy industry, then semi-heavy industry, after that housing, and lastly consumption. He considered that nationalizations, a reduction in the money supply, a price freeze, and directed consumption were necessary for success.[11] His programme was a redistribution plan 'dictated by the shortage economy that [he predicted] was going to affect liberated France

[10] Bloch-Lainé and Bouvier, *La France restaurée, 1944–1954*, 51.
[11] Pierre Mendès France, *Œuvres complètes*, ii: *Une politique de l'économie, 1943–1954* (Paris, 1985), 55 f.

for some years to come'.[12] He assumed enormous self-denial on the part of the French.[13]

Nationalizations were an opportunity for radical moderniza-tion—for instance, by creating an integrated national electricity grid. However, the implementation of both monetary reform and nationalizations was delayed because of the equivocation of two ministers (René Pleven at Finance and Robert Lacoste at Industrial Production) and because of de Gaulle himself. Between 1945 and 1947 economic policies lacked coherence. All national-izations were an *ad hoc* response to specific conditions.[14] Bloch-Lainé did not see the currency reform affair as a Left–Right confrontation, or as pitting interventionists against liberals. He saw it as an economic decision taken under Aimé Lepercq, Pleven's predecessor at the Ministry of Finance. Exchange of large notes was technically impossible for lack of new notes in September 1944. Jean Bouvier suggests that introducing a policy of confidence, that is, a policy of borrowing, was indicative of restoration, since it was aimed at those who had liquid assets.[15] The country's financial élite (brokers and bankers) preferred the Liberation loan to compulsory exchange of notes. Roger Goetze (who at the time was Director of Algerian Finance, then moved to the Finance Commission with Mendès France, and finally became Director of the Budget in Paris from 1945 to 1956) points out that Mendès France had a reputation as a state socialist that was perhaps not to everyone's taste.[16] In other words, top civil servants were not prepared to take Mendès France's bitter pill![17]

Thus there was no consensus within the provisional govern-ment about the scale of nationalizations, or the type of economic and social modernization of France that should be undertaken. Choices were dictated by circumstances. The transformation of

---

[12] Olivier Feiertag, 'Pierre Mendès France, acteur et témoin de la planification française, 1943-1962', in Michel Margairaz (ed.), *Pierre Mendès France et l'économie, pensée et action* (Paris, 1989), 370.

[13] See Richard Kuisel, 'Pierre Mendès France et l'économie: une volonté de moder-nité', in François Bédarida and Jean-Pierre Rioux, *Mendès France et le mendésisme* (Paris, 1985), 375.

[14] Philippe Mioche, 'Le Démarrage de l'économie française au lendemain de la guerre', *Historiens et Géographes. La IVe République: Histoire, recherches et archives (357–8)*, 434.

[15] Bloch-Lainé and Bouvier, *La France restaurée, 1944–1954*, 70.

[16] Nathalie Carré de Malberg (ed.), *Entretiens avec Roger Goetze, haut fonctionnaire des Finances, Rivoli-Alger-Rivoli, 1937–1958*, CHEFF (1997), 144.

[17] Bloch-Lainé and Bouvier, *La France restaurée, 1944–1954*, 82.

the French economy and French society was the aim of differing and, probably, incompatible plans. Mendès France seems to have been the only one who knew what he wanted: financial rigour, which meant the currency reform, centralized economic planning, a diversified industrial policy, and numerous nationalizations.[18] This programme called for swift decisions. Hesitating, as the GPRF (Gouvernement provisoire de la République française, the Provisional Government of the French Republic) did, gave the old society time to rally.

The First Coherent Modernization: The 1946 Plan

De Gaulle and the GPRF modernized the country economically and socially. The provisional government introduced social security by decree in October 1945. Wage-earners were covered against the risks of sickness, industrial accident, disability, old age, and death. This was a major social modernization. The state also became France's biggest industrialist as a result of nationalizations, controlling 20 per cent of the country's economy. However, it should not be thought that a new economic order had been born, even if the industrialists and capitalists who had been sidelined did call the change 'revolutionary'. Yet citizens of the republic now had the hope of seeing the state introduce a modern social policy at the workplace and promote technological innovation. The state continued to organize the economy, employing the same technical instruments as Vichy but for a democratic political end. De Gaulle appointed Jean Monnet as Commissioner-General of the Modernization and Equipment Plan in January 1946. He accepted the Bretton Woods agreements in late 1945 in exchange for American aid that was to 'bring about the reconstruction and modernization' of France's agricultural and industrial economy.[19] The Félix Gouin government that succeeded de Gaulle in January 1946 followed the same current of innovation.[20]

---

[18] Pierre Mendès France, 'Les Causes de l'inflation', National Assembly debate, 21 Dec. 1947, in *Œuvres complètes*, ii: *Une politique de l'économie 1943–54*, 211; Philippe Mioche, 'La Planification comme réforme de structure: l'action de PMF de 1943-1945', *Histoire, Économie et Société*, 3 (1982).

[19] Fonds Jean Monnet, AMF 3/5/35, Bonnet to Byrnes, 8 Nov. 1945.

[20] Jan.–Nov. 1946.

The French government asked the USA for the means to modernize, during the Blum–Byrnes talks of February–May 1946. This three-party government (which included Communists) turned to the USA in full awareness and without compulsion. Léon Blum asked the Americans to allow France to buy German coal, to let France lower its customs duties, and to grant it supply credits. Figures were put forward: $2 billion, then $4 billion. Eximbank (the Export–Import Bank, a US governmental bank) granted only $650 million to develop the French economy but threw in commercial vessels, access to American surpluses, and a promise to help persuade the World Bank to lend France $500 million. The very basis of the modernization project called for foreign aid—something that was clearly played down, no doubt to spare the nation's feelings. Even before the announcement of the Marshall Plan, the CGT, the General Confederation of Labour, France's umbrella trade-union organization, which went along with the plan, told the National Credit Council that short-term mobilization of savings was impossible; it was looking at long-term loans. However, it did not rule out foreign credits as a back-up in order to restore the balance of payments.[21] To appreciate this, it must be remembered that in 1946 the external deficit came to several hundred million dollars! There was a general awareness that France could not modernize out of its own resources, but it was felt that opening the economy must not be allowed to wipe out whole areas of the French economy.[22]

Monnet set about launching a programme of modernization. He put in hand a coherent system of economic planning that followed a method new to France: his modernization commissions resembled the British and American working parties of the wartime economy. These eighteen modernization commissions, which brought together representatives of the employers, the civil service, and the trade unions, represented a minor revolution in social relations. Monnet was able to furnish the political authorities with arguments to justify external aid and European co-operation. The French plan demanded the country's economic independence (Monnet actually used the word), but to achieve

[21] AMF 11/2/9, or B 33213, CGT, 30 May 1947, Propositions au conseil national du Crédit pour le financement du Plan de modernization et d'équipement ('Proposals to the National Credit Council to finance the Modernization and Equipment Plan').

[22] MAE, YI 1944-49/85, reply from F. Lacoste to J.-F. Byrnes; AF, B 19951, Inter-ministerial Economic Committee, 2 Feb. 1946.

this, some provisional, productive American aid was justified. Monnet was liked because he was not an interventionist. He was 'liberal' and empirical; he bore the stamp of his wartime experiences in Britain and America. Monnet's originality was to define sectors that were priorities for modernization. Apparently he would have preferred a single sector to capture the public imagination, like Roosevelt with the American aeronautical industry. However, he defined six 'basic sectors' (*secteurs de base*, as Monnet himself called them).[23] Was there a plan? According to Pierre Dreyfus, chairman and managing director of Renault, Monnet said he did not know what a plan was. 'The Monnet Plan was to set very ambitious objectives that would enable France to demand its share of the Marshall credits. It was a "prospectus"—honest, but still a prospectus.'[24] The Plan was 'certainly the act of faith that Monnet speaks of: probably meant not so much to be realized in all its details as to announce the demands of modernization and mark out its stages'.[25] Blum's objective of negotiating American credits during his trip to Washington (the Blum–Byrnes Agreements, May 1946) gave the impression that the French plan was a glorified import programme. Alan Milward presents the plan as a temporary measure.[26] Yet French economic planning was not linked to the economic cycle: Mendès France Plan, EDF (Électricité de France) Plan, 1946 Monnet Plan, revised Monnet Plan of 1948. Monnet's deputy Hirsch wrote that the Monnet Plan was a meeting-place for ideas concerning modernization that had been around in France for a long time. Jean Fourastié has since said that Monnet 'clearly gave standard of living, the purchasing-power of wages, and comfortable living-conditions as over-riding objectives of the Plan. "A better life through improved production" (Vivre mieux en produisant mieux) was the slogan he underlined in *Le Grand espoir du XXᵉ siècle*.'[27] As he saw it, the

---

[23] Paul Delouvrier, 'Quelques souvenirs sur Jean Monnet et le premier plan de modernization et d'équipement', in Bernard Cazes and Philippe Mioche (eds.), *Modernization ou décadence, contribution à l'histoire du plan Monnet et de la planification en France*, Publications de l'Université de Provence (Aix-en-Provence, 1990), 273.

[24] Pierre Dreyfus, in Henry Rousso (ed.), *De Monnet à Massé*, Éditions du Centre National de la Recherche Scient. (Paris, 1986) 71.

[25] Jean-Paul Thuillier, 'Les Charbonnages et le plan (1942–1962)', in Rousso (ed.), *De Monnet à Massé*, 94.

[26] Alan S. Milward, 'La Planification française et la reconstruction européenne', in Cazes and Mioche (eds.), *Modernization ou décadence*, 89.

[27] Jean Fourastié, 'Témoignages sur la mise en œuvre du plan Monnet', ibid. 303.

modernization plan was a route map of France's future, which economic agents might follow. The Plan, then, was a beacon of what was to come. French economic planning changed according to circumstances and according to who was being addressed. The Plan even put an end to state economic socialism by drawing a distinction between nationalized and private sectors. In the long term, modernization could be achieved only by free enterprise and within the framework of an open economy such as the USA had been advocating since the Atlantic Charter. Jean Bouvier believed that it was reassuring after the state socialism of Vichy— and, I would add, after the theoretical interventionism of Mendès France.[28] That was, in fact, what happened. Michel Albert was able to write in 1985 that 'since Jean Monnet, the father of the Plan and the father of Europe, French economic planning has struggled incessantly against protectionism abroad and for the restoration of the workings of the market at home'.[29] The currency was placed in the service of modernization; inflation (on a moderate scale) was accepted. Monnet rejected monetary drift and economic deflation.[30] The Mayer reform of January 1948 was widely popular because it stabilized the franc without restricting the modernization effort in the process; even when orthodox liberals returned to power in the André Marie cabinet with Paul Reynaud at Finance and Joseph Laniel as Under-Secretary at the Ministry of National Economy, public investment continued.

Reactions to the Monnet Plan

This first Plan was not worked out in the atmosphere of consensus that people like to describe. The Right had split into the Republican Freedom Party (PRL, Parti républicain de la liberté, Michel Clemenceau, 1945) and the National Centre of Independents and Farmers (Centre national des Indépendants et Paysans, Roger Duchet, Antoine Pinay, 1948). The Right did not bring together the men of social change. It argued that the economy must be managed as by a prudent *paterfamilias*. Thus the

[28] Bloch-Lainé and Bouvier, *La France restaurée, 1944–1954*.

[29] Michel Albert, 'De la modernization des équipements à la modernization des comportements', in Cazes and Mioche (eds.), *Modernization ou décadence*, 204.

[30] Robert Frank, 'Contraintes monétaires et désirs de croissance et rêves européens (1931–1949)', in Fridenson and Straus (eds.), *Le Capitalisme français 19ᵉ–20ᵉ siècle*, 299.

men of the Right were prudent (too prudent) when it came to investment in modernization. As liberals, they saw themselves as the defenders of free enterprise, private property, and the small businessman. They were opposed to state intervention.[31] On the modernization commissions there were serious confrontations between the steel manufacturers of northern France and Lorraine, battles amongst motor manufacturers (Renault v. Ford-France), and between SNCF (Société national des chemins de fer, the state-owned railway company) and the road-haulage industry. The company directors on the modernization commissions were slowly won over to growth, according to Jacques Ferry, former chairman of the employers' federation of the French steel industry.[32] The ideas of growth and modernization were accepted by the administrative and political élites and in intellectual circles, but were they obvious to all industrialists and bankers? Raymond Aron said that before 1940 'opinions were virtually unanimous regarding the need to limit economic growth'.[33] Jean Fourastié believed that the notion of economic and social progress, aiming to outdo the 1938 figures, was certainly one of Monnet's ideas and was not necessarily shared by all leading circles.[34] The national employers' organization CNPF (Centre national du patronat français) was very much a fledgling body, split between bosses who backed the Plan and the vast majority of others who were horrified at the idea of state intervention. The Christian trade-union organization CFTC (Confédération français des travailleurs chrétiens) had little time for the Plan. The agricultural trade union CGA (Confédération générale de l'agriculture) was distrustful. Only the CGT agreed to work for the goals of economic planning. The banks were believed to be making only disorganized progress so far as modernization was concerned. A nationalized Banque de France might have played a pioneering role in modernization. The fact was that between 1945 and 1950 the Banque de France discount rate rose by 100 per cent to curb inflation. For the next twenty

[31] Sylvie Guillaume, 'Les Droites et la IVᵉ République', *Historiens et Géographes. La IVᵉ République: Histoire, recherches et archives (357–8)*, 239 f.
[32] Philippe Mioche, 'L'Invention du plan Monnet', in Cazes and Mioche (eds.), *Modernization ou décadence*, 39.
[33] 'Exposé de Raymond Aron, devant le groupe 1985 sur la croissance économique', 6 June 1963, ibid. 369.
[34] Fourastié, 'Témoignages sur la mise en œuvre du plan Monnet', 303.

years, the result was a law limiting credit. 'While satisfying the Minister and the issuing institute, the mechanism operated against growth.'[35] There were instances of the financing of the Plan being 'sabotaged'. EDF chairman Roger Gaspard recalled: 'My relations with the Paris banks were absolutely appalling at that time. I went looking for medium-term credit in the nationalized banks and it was refused me.'[36] As early as 1946, Monnet had sought the advice of Robert Nathan, an American expert on Roosevelt's team. In his audit, Nathan encouraged the French to modernize. He also recommended measures that have since become standard: flexibility in the employment of manpower, fiscal discipline, agreements between management and workers on economizing on manpower and raw materials, installing suggestion boxes in businesses, and profit-sharing. As Nathan saw it, the financing of modernization would come from maximizing exports, because France must not 'hypnotise itself into self-sufficiency'. He recommended the creation of an institution for granting loans.[37]

The Role of the Political Élite

Monnet did not have an exalted idea of the modernizing mindset of the civil service.[38] That was unfair because he relied on most of them—men like François Bloch-Lainé, Guillaume Guindey, Pierre-Paul Schweizer, Roger Goetze, Paul Delouvrier, and Hervé Alphand, director of Economic Affairs at the French Foreign Office, or the great ambassadors Henri Bonnet in Washington and René Massigli in London. Two ideas guided these men: modernization was the road to rebirth and hence to power, and the European ideal and foreign aid could, if used shrewdly, be harnessed in the service of French power. 'I shall preserve', wrote Vincent Auriol, the first President of the Fourth Republic, in his *Journal du Septennat*. But preserve what?

[35] Claire Andrieu, 'La Politique du crédit frein ou moteur de la modernization (1945–50)', ch. 13 of Fridenson and Straus (eds.), *Le Capitalisme français 19ᵉ–20ᵉ siècle*, 243.

[36] Quoted by Martine Bungener, 'L'Électricité et les trois premiers plans, une symbiose réussi', in Rousso (ed.), *De Monnet à Massé*, 111.

[37] Robert Nathan, 26 Aug. 1946, 'Mesures proposées en vue d'une action immédiate', in Cazes and Mioche (eds.), *Modernization ou décadence*, 332–3.

[38] Monnet, *Mémoires*, 289–90.

Not class privilege, certainly. It was a question of preserving the Republic, secularism, and France's imperial greatness, and of strengthening its security. The MRP (Mouvement républicain populaire), the Christian Democratic party set up in 1944, affirmed its modernity. Economic modernization was to be achieved in accordance with the social teachings of the Catholic Church. Its key-words were 'economic and social democracy'. The party defended nationalization, works councils, sliding wage-scales, dialogue between social partners, and regionalization.[39] In the social sphere, it promoted a policy of the family, social security, and collective bargaining. Its ministers, Georges Bidault and Robert Schuman, consistently approved of investment in modernization, but coupled it with a concern for balanced accounting (the Schuman stabilization of December 1947 being one example). Nevertheless, the aim of economic renewal was a fundamental given, and beyond discussion.

Granted, the Ministry of Finance contrived to make Monnet doubt its support. Obviously, the Ministry of Finance did not constitute a perfectly coherent entity. Budget Director Roger Goetze considered the Plan anti-liberal. According to a recent theory, the Director of External Finance, Guillaume Guindey, was suspicious of strict external balances, unwilling to take risks, and consequently resistant to the spending involved in the investments Monnet was proposing.[40] Margairaz argues that Guindey was an 'austerity liberal' and a man who agreed with Mendès France. He wanted free trade, which presupposed the disappearance of state-socialist constraints and free enterprise. However, Guindey's attitude contained contradictions. He could not be unaware of the interventionist intentions of Mendès France in 1945, or give his technical approval to the exchange of notes. The rapid introduction of free convertibility implied a restoration of élites or the birth of new entrepreneurial élites; it certainly did not imply greater equality of opportunity. Guindey resisted the managed economy, which he equated with nationalization and economic planning. Treasury Head François Bloch-Lainé had a

---

[39] 'De Gaulle et le MRP', *Espoir*, 41 (Dec. 1982), quoted in Danielle Dray-Zéraffa, 'Le MRP, parti de la Quatrième république', *Historiens et Géographes. La IVe République: Histoire, recherches et archives (357–8)*, 221.

[40] Solenne Lepage, *La Direction des Finances extérieures de 1946 à 1953, les années fondatrices ou le magistère de Guillaume Guindey* (CHEFF, 1999). For a summary, see the journal *Histoire, Economie et Société*, SEDES, 2 (1999), 255–74.

more political vision. He did not approve of the Treasury remaining the biggest bank in Paris. 'The extent of economic intervention by the state was simply the product of circumstances', he said.[41] However, whether he liked it or not, Bloch-Lainé was at the heart of the modernization process. He presided over the creation of the Investment Commission and the Modernization and Equipment Fund (Fonds de modernization et d'équipement or FME), which subsequently became the Economic and Social Development Fund (Fonds de développement économique et social or FDES), the administrative arm of the state. Speaking of his actions, he recalled that, faced with the choice between recession and inflation, he had preferred 'the latter risk to the former', and that he had 'turned liquid assets into barriers'.[42] Bloch-Lainé also created SEEF (Service des études économiques), a department attached to the Treasury with the aim of thinking about future economic performance in econometric terms and drawing up reliable national accounts (Jean Fourastié, Claude Gruson, Jacques Dumontier).[43] The goodwill of Bloch-Lainé at the head of the Treasury in respecting the government's choices assisted the emergence of a modernized, more prosperous, growth-orientated, innovative France.

The Role of Industry

The Plan was not all-encompassing, but Monnet managed to take decisive initiatives in certain sectors. Unlike the ultra-modern German steel industry in 1945,[44] the French steel industry was adversely affected by the war and had inherited earlier problems of obsolescence. First it needed to be rebuilt, but did it need modernizing?[45] 'The steel manufacturers had no collective

[41] Andrieu, 'La Politique du crédit frein ou moteur de la modernization (1945–1950)', 244.

[42] Bloch-Lainé, *Profession fonctionnaire, entretiens avec Françoise Carrière*, 106.

[43] François Fourquet, *Les Comptes de la puissance: Histoire de la comptabilité nationale et du plan* (Encres, 1980).

[44] Werner Abelshauser, 'La Reconstruction de l'Allemagne de l'ouest', in René Girault and Maurice Levy-Leboyer (eds.), *Le Plan Marshall et le relèvement économique de l'Europe*, conference held at Bercy on 21–23 March 1991, CHEFF (Paris, 1993), 421.

[45] Philippe Mioche, 'La Reconstruction de la sidérurgie européenne, 1945–1949: sérénité des uns, nouveau départ pour les autres', *Histoire, Économie et Société*, SEDES, 2 (1999), 405.

strategy', Philippe Mioche has written. 'They were living in the very short term, with all their attention on the nationalization debate.'[46] The first impetus for modernization came from the modernizers of the government—from Monnet and the Plan. Subsequently, industrialists became involved, like René Damien committing himself to the first rolling-mill at the USINOR steelworks in February 1946.

Industrialists in the motor industry, who desired modernization, welcomed the Plan. The state launched the revival of the motor industry with the Pons Plan of 1945. This sector plan was incorporated into the Modernization and Equipment Plan. The nationalization of Renault in 1945 encouraged Pierre Lefaucheux, the government-appointed chairman, to turn the publicly owned company into a social showcase. Thus industrial and social modernization went hand in hand. But this was the only even slightly convincing example of the ideals of the Resistance being implemented at last. The state-owned Renault company launched a housing programme for its workers. Peugeot followed in 1948.[47] In other words, privately owned companies lagged behind the state-owned sectors of industry in terms of social innovation. On the other hand, all industrialists supported the kind of technological innovation that resulted in the creation of the 4CV Renault, and the 2CV Citroën, both of which had been foisted on the economic planners. The four years of the war were a fertile period 'for the conception of new ways of thinking about and producing automobiles'.[48] Power transmission machines were developed by Renault from 1942 onwards and used for the 4CV in 1947. Right from the Liberation, French motor manufacturers did not hesitate to send their managerial staff to the USA. Car production was decentralized: Renault went to Flins in 1952, and Citroën to Rennes in 1953. Collective bargaining with the trade unions was introduced. The results included a third week of paid holidays and a retirement bonus at Renault and Peugeot in 1955.[49]

[46] Ibid.

[47] Jean-Louis Loubet, 'L'Industrie automobile française, un cas original?', *Histoire, Économie et Société*, SEDES, 2 (1999), 428.

[48] Patrick Fridenson, 'L'Industrie automobile: la primauté du marché', *Historiens et Géographes. La IVᵉ République: Histoire, recherches et archives*, 320.

[49] Patrick Fridenson, 'Le Plan Marshall et l'industrie automobile française', in Girault and Levy-Leboyer (eds.), *Le plan Marshall et le relèvement économique de l'Europe*, 288.

Modernization at SNCF took the form of the adoption of American rolling-stock, including 141-R steam locomotives, which were immediately available. In fact, 1,500 locomotives were ordered in 1945! In this case, modernization meant the urgent reconstruction of material capital. The Plan gave structure to SNCF's medium-term projects, such as electrification.

In the aeronautical industry, which had been preserved under the Occupation, the only work that French factories were doing in 1944 was manufacturing bottom-of-the-range German models. Change became apparent in ambitious plans to build pre-war models again and construct numerous prototypes. But quality of production was mediocre, and prices were too high. Modernization in this area was a serious failure, although the USA was offering quality, up-to-date equipment. The 'brain drain' which impoverished research departments and caused a lack of viable programmes during the war accounted for the failure of French aeronautical modernization.[50]

Electricity and energy were key sectors in the Monnet Plan. In the electricity industry, modernization required a grouping of companies. Nationalization was presented by the chairman of EDF as a sign of a pioneering spirit as opposed to the civil servant mentality.[51] The first Plan involved the structuring of a basic industry that was indispensable as far as the rest of industry was concerned. Monnet justified the rapid increase in the production and consumption of electricity by enlisting EDF in the Plan, but EDF knew what had to be done in order to modernize, which was not the case with the steel industry. EDF and SNCF became the beacons of France's recovery—nationally and internationally. Governments of the Fourth Republic pointed to Génissiat (the huge dam on the Rhône, known as the 'French Dnieprostroy' after its Russian counterpart) to prove to the world and to the French that France was on its feet again.

Monnet could not ignore the French countryside, which in 1946 was still home to 32.2 per cent of the working population. Monnet turned peasants into farmers and put them on tractors. The number of tractors and associated agricultural machinery doubled

---

[50] Claude D'Abzac-Epezy, 'La Reconstruction dans l'industrie aéronautique: l'exemple français, 1944–1946', *Histoire, Économie et Société*, SEDES, 2 (1999), 435–49.

[51] Alain Beltran, 'EDF aux temps des cathédrales des temps modernes', in *Reconstructions et modernizations, la France après les ruines, 1918 . . . 1945 . . .*, exhibition catalogue, Archives nationales (Paris, 1991), 170.

between 1945 and 1948 (from 33,000 to 68,000).[52] In other words, Monnet chose to raise production by mechanization—without thinking too much about the long-term consequences.

This Monnet-style modernization of 1946–7 did not create a new economic and social order. It was a response to the urgent needs of the time. Monnet and the political élite were aware of the role that external factors might play in modernization. Yet they were clearly incapable of predicting their appearance. Mendès France was counting on German coal for the French steel industry, but what had looked like a way forward turned out to be a dead end. The international opening-up of the French economy that was written into the Lend–Lease agreement of 28 February 1945 and the Bretton Woods Agreement of July 1944 (signed by France in late December 1945) remained conditional on the prior recovery of France. The year 1948 opened with an acknowledgement that the modernization project was not working for lack of finance. The Monnet Plan had not been properly implemented when the first accounts were drawn up: 25 per cent of the objectives for coal, 33 per cent of those for transport, and 38 per cent of those for cement had been achieved.

'An unprecedented economic turn-around' (F. Bloch-Lainé)

External factors (economic aid from the USA and the emergence of economic solidarity in western Europe) helped the initial push for modernization to succeed. Did they distort it? Modernization and growth in France from 1945 to 1950 sprang from a subtle mix of national endeavour, foreign finance, and co-operation within Europe.

Monnet had understood that American aid would make it possible to implement the Modernization and Equipment Plan and that the Plan must be European in scale. He wrote to the Prime Minister on 2 June 1948: 'We must rapidly transform our position from one of recipient of aid to one of independent contributor to a collective effort of recovery.' The Modernization Plan became France's contribution to the Programme of European Reconstruction launched by the Organization for

---

[52] Isabel Boussard, 'L'Agriculture au lendemain des guerres de 1914 et 1939', ibid. 187.

European Economic Co-operation.[53] However, Monnet had to adapt to the short term, hence he wrote: 'Co-operation is necessary, certainly, but it will come later, based on the national endeavours that preceded and paved the way for it.'[54] Advocates of economic planning were thinking more of French modernization on the 1946 model than of harmonizing trade among the countries of Europe.[55]

Having grasped that the European dimension was essential for the USA, the French believed they could channel aid to their advantage by reaching an understanding with the British. They therefore attempted to build a Franco-British project for the economic development of Europe. This failed in April 1949 because the British rejected the Long-Term European Plan.[56] The ideal was to create a Franco-British Europe into which French economic modernization would fit naturally. Britain's imperialist autarky prevented the creation of a Franco-British partnership in the Europe of the OEEC.[57] Guindey concluded: 'Europe as an alternative to American aid was an idea that made no sense.'[58] Thus the modernization of France was dependent on American aid.

The solution was to assign American aid to the French Plan in the form first of Marshall dollars earmarked for the purchase of equipment, and secondly, in the form of the exchange value in francs assigned to the Modernization and Equipment Fund (Fonds de Modernization et Équipement or FME).

A report (covering major investments only) showed that the American-sponsored ECA (European Co-operation Administration) contribution to French equipment projects fluctuated around 15 per cent.[59]

[53] AMF 11/5/1d, Monnet to Prime Minister, 2 June 1948, draft; AMF 11/5/1f, 'Memorandum of 2 Jun. 1948', repeated on 23 June 1948 (AMF 11/5/2) and sent to G. Bidault, R. Schuman, R. Mayer, V. Auriol, L. Blum, A. Marie, and P. Reynaud.

[54] F 60 ter 389, Jean Monnet to Prime Minister, 13 July 1948.

[55] F 60 ter 357, SGCI, PPS, no. 479, 14 Jan. 1949, to H. Alphand; F 60 ter 389, PPS, 14 Jan. 1949, to H. Alphand, 'Sur un conflit Hirsch/autres délégués français à l'OECE [OEEC]'.

[56] Jean Monnet, *Mémoires*, i (Livre de Poche, 1997), 404; AMF 22/3/3, Note sur l'entretien Monnet-Plowden, par Pierre Uri, 23 Apr. 1949; AN F 60 bis 476, Commissariat général du Plan, T-HH, 25 Feb. 1949, Note sur les conversations franco-britanniques.

[57] AN F 60 bis 378, H. Queuille to S. Cripps, 2 Dec. 1948.

[58] *Interview with Guillaume Guidrey* conducted by Antoine Marès and Gérard Bossuat in May 1985, IPR Paris-1.

[59] Olivier Moreau-Neret, *Valeurs étrangères: mouvements de capitaux entre la France et l'étranger depuis 1940* (Sirey, 1956).

TABLE 8.1 *Proportion of Marshall Plan dollars in the financing of major French modernizing equipment projects.*

Equipment project	Overall value in $m.	ECA contribution in $m. ERP	ECA contribution as percentage
Steel industry	226.9	70.5	31.1
Potassium mines	146.0	10.8	7.4
Oil refineries	138.4	17.4	12.6
Power stations	74.7	22.0	19.5
Air France	22.9	9.3	40.6
Other programmes	373.6	21.3	5.7
Total	982.5	151.3	15.4

Source: Gérard Bossuat, *La France, l'aide américaine et les construction européennes, 1944–1954*, 2 vols., CHEFF (1992; 2nd edn. 1997).

TABLE 8.2 *ERP (European Recovery Programme, or the Marshall Plan) aid to France by American financial years, April 1948 to September 1951 (in millions of dollars).*

	1948–9	1949–50	1950–1	Total	% of aid
Food	197.4	15.8	27.7	240.9	9.8
Energy	319.7	128.8	115.6	564.1	22.9
Raw materials	306.9	225.9	179.5	712.3	29.0
Plant	188	238.1	120.2	546.3	22.2
Miscellaneous	26.2	37.6	19.9	83.7	3.4
Freight	177.4	71	62.5	310.9	12.7
Total	1,215.6	717.2	525.4	2,458.2	100.0

Source: Ibid.

On these sums, MDAP (that is, military aid) credits came to $57.6 million. The contribution in ERP dollars for modernization equipment ($546.3 million) thus represented 22.2 per cent of the $2,458.2 million of American aid.

The decision by the ECA to assign the exchange value to the Modernization and Equipment Plan was one of the key actions of American aid, since it also contributed the francs that the economic planning programme lacked.[60] Between 10 and 15 per cent of the investments of the first Plan came from the exchange value of American aid, although the American Treasury had

---

[60] Gérard Bossuat, 'La Contre-valeur de l'aide américaine à la France et à ses territoires d'Outre-Mer: la mesure des rapports franco-américains', in Girault and Levy-Leboyer (eds.), *Le plan Marshall et le relèvement économique de l'Europe*, 177–99.

hoped initially to assign those francs to combating inflation and reducing the national debt. The exchange value represented approximately 50 per cent of the credits made available to the FME.

TABLE 8.3 *Proportion of exchange value in economic modernization (reconstitution attempt), in billions of francs.*

Sector to which assigned	Credits committed	Exchange value total	Exchange value total as %
Autonomous Reconstruction Fund [*Caisse autonome de reconstruction* or CAR]	1,045	137.6	13.4
FME and FIDES	1,027	527.0	51.3
Modernization Plan (public and private investments)	2,083	527.0	25.3
National investments	4,801	732.0	15.2

Source: Ibid.

The FME, the spearhead of modernization and the branch of the Treasury handling reconstruction and modernization investments, received the highest exchange value in 1948 and 1949. The FME granted credits to nationalized companies (Air France and various banks), to private companies, to the Overseas Territories, and to the Saar region. French and American politicians were prepared to accept that exchange value reinforced the goal of modernization. Total use of exchange value for economic development was impressive. The CGP (Commissariat Général du Plan, the state planning commission) estimated in July 1952 that the Marshall Plan had provided France with 25 per cent of its total foreign-exchange cover, 60 per cent of its dollar cover, and 50 per cent of financing in francs of productive investments.[61] If it referred to financing the FME, the CGP was correct; if it referred to the total of planned investments, it erred on the plus side. Was the Marshall Plan a happy surprise for industrialists, as one historian has written?[62]

[61] 80 AJ 17, 'Projet de mémorandum, propositions en vue de l'établissement d'un 2e plan de modernization et d'équipements', July 1952.

[62] François Caron, 'Rapport introductif aux retombés industrielles du plan Marshall', in Girault and Levy-Leboyer (eds.), *Le Plan Marshall et le relèvement économique de l'Europe*, 248.

The certainty that aid was available encouraged banks to supply medium-term credit (approximately five years) of a kind that was well suited to financing equipment needs. The Union française de Banques (Jacques de Fouchier) granted modernization loans to the small-business sector. Dollar aid and the exchange value of aid saw through major projects that Monnet had planned. A second rolling-mill (at the SOLLAC steelworks), built in 1948 (François de Wendel), had formed part of the Plan and was financed by American aid.[63] Indeed, the steel industry enjoyed three-quarters of the credits granted to the private sector, which was the clear choice of a government wishing to produce between 12 and 15 million metric tons of steel a year. The bosses subsequently said they had never believed that this would be possible because of the prohibitive cost of coal. However, encouraged by the government and by Marshall Plan credits, they modernized steel production without precipitating an economic revolution. 'The Marshall Plan did not create modernization *ex nihilo*; it assisted it.'[64] It helped the economic planners of the CGP more than those of the steel industry. The French aluminium industry, downgraded during the war, obtained high-performance plant from the USA (AC/DC converter and electrodes made with oil coke).[65] Productivity missions created lasting links between Saint-Jean de Maurienne and American industrialists.[66]

Marshall aid was one way of implementing the kind of American-style modernization wanted by the industry. However, from as early as 1950 the conversion industries were sacrificed 'on the altar of financial stabilization'.[67] In the transport sector, SNCF was able to rebuild its network, electrify it, thanks to exchange value, and go on to create such celebrated rolling-stock as the CC and BB locomotives. EDF benefited from American credits to complete or undertake construction of a network of large thermo-electric, and especially hydro-electric, power

[63] Michel Margairaz, 'Les Plans et la sidérurgie: le plan, mal nécessaire pour financer les investissements', in Rousso (ed.), *De Monnet à Massé*, 143.

[64] Philippe Mioche, 'Le Plan Marshall et la sidérurgie française', in Girault and Levy-Leboyer (eds.), *Le Plan Marshall et le relèvement économique de l'Europe*, 315.

[65] Jacques Bocquentin, 'L'Impact des deux guerres sur l'industrie française de l'aluminium', in *Reconstructions et modernizations, la France après les ruines*, 175.

[66] Jacques Bocquentin, 'État de l'industrie de l'aluminium en 1947', in Girault and Levy-Leboyer (eds.), *Le Plan Marshall et le relèvement économique de l'Europe*, 301.

[67] Margairaz, 'Les Plans et la sidérurgie', 145.

stations. The mechanization of agriculture was actually achieved in accordance with the aims of the 1946 plan. Under American pressure, Union Française benefited from development credits.

The Franco-American Modernization Model

While no new economic and social order emerged, a Franco-American development model can be described at the end of the Marshall period. In his 1946 audit, Robert Nathan wrote that 'low-cost dwellings must take priority over more expensive housing'.[68] But nobody listened to him, as one historian has suggested: 'State investments in the realm of rebuilding were proportionally lower than in the other sectors, at least until the early 1950s and even beyond.'[69] Housing was not one of the six 'basic sectors' of the Modernization and Equipment Plan. As early as 1946, experts at the Ministry of Rebuilding and Town Planning estimated requirements at 240,000 new units per year. However, this was not achieved until the second half of the 1950s. Only in 1950 did the Banque de France accept building credits for rediscounting.[70] The Americans certainly played a part in this battle over housing, albeit a difficult one to measure. On the one hand there was the quantifiable assignment of exchange value to social housing; on the other, the Americans influenced the decision that France took. The Americans wanted French workers to be decently housed to put a stop to the anti-capitalist, anti-Western propaganda of the Communists and the USSR. The Caisse des Dépôts (François Bloch-Lainé) got involved with local communities, and through the SCCI (Société centrale de construction immobilière or Central Real-Estate Construction Company) became a promoter of subsidized social housing from 1954 onwards. Social modernization also progressed via the diffusion of credit to consumption and housing.[71] The American social project was to

[68] Robert Nathan, 26 Aug. 1946, 'Mesures proposées en vue d'une action immédiate', in Cazes and Mioche (eds.), *Modernization ou décadence*, 327.

[69] Danièle Voldmann, 'L'Urbanisme de la reconstruction et la question de logement', *Historiens et Géographes. La IVᵉ République: Histoire, recherches et archives*, 308.

[70] Andrieu, 'La Politique du crédit frein ou moteur de la modernization (1945–1950)', 248.

[71] Hubert Bonin, 'Les Banques et la IVᵉ République', *Historiens et Géographes. La IVᵉ République: Histoire, recherches et archives*, 479 f.

increase workers' purchasing power, to organize a consumer society, to produce standardized consumer goods, and to create fresh social relations based on a consensus regarding the capitalist market economy.

The Americans were keen to improve social relations within companies. Aid gave them the opportunity to offer transfers of technological skills and models of human business relations to the managers, engineers, technicians, and blue-collar and white-collar employees who travelled to the USA on 'productivity missions'. For instance, the aluminium-industry mission that visited the USA from December 1950 to July 1951 received training, among other things, in management–staff relations.[72] The Americans also wanted clear increases in productivity to improve living standards and, from 1950, to provide the armaments required for the Korean War. Before the Marshall Plan productivity and relations between workers, machines, and company had been studied by Monnet and Silberman of the US Department of Labor. Jean Fourastié returned to the issue. The CGT was highly resourceful; the other trade-union organizations were suspicious. American insistence led to the creation of mixed bodies to increase productivity.[73] Barry Bingham, America's Marshall Plan representative in France in 1950, was still finding resistance to the development of a productivity programme, although AFAP (Association française d'aide à la productivité) had been set up in 1950. Productivity increased as the result of the purchase of American patents and the productivity missions. Some 300 productivity missions involving 2,700 French participants visited production units in the USA.[74] Jean Fourastié wrote that 'American dynamism triggered real enthusiasm among the approximately 4,000 trainees'.[75] Actually, to judge by accounts written on their return, the impressions formed by trainees were rather more half-hearted. In 1951 the

[72] Henri Morsel, 'La Mission française de productivité aux États-Unis de l'industrie française de l'aluminium', *Histoire, Économie et Société*, SEDES, 2 (1999), 413–17.
[73] François Caron, 'Rapport introductif aux retombés industrielles du plan Marshall', in Girault and Levy-Leboyer (eds.), *Le plan Marshall et le relèvement économique de l'Europe*, 250.
[74] See Richard Kuisel, 'The Marshall Plan in Action' *ibid*. 344; Richard Kuisel, 'L'American way of life et les missions françaises de productivité', *Vingtième siècle*, 17 (Jan.–Mar. 1988), 21-38.
[75] Fourastié, 'Témoignages sur la mise en œuvre du plan Monnet', 309. Fourastié gives the figure of productivity missions as 211 (57 for agriculture, 50 for the service sector, the rest for industry) comprising between 18 and 20 people each.

American Congress offered a specific aid package to increase productivity. Robert Buron, Secretary of State at the Ministry of Economic Affairs and Chairman of the National Productivity Committee, drew up a fresh programme of technical co-operation. The Americans insisted on increasing the level of 'equitable distribution of national income'.[76] So insistent were they, in fact, that they even managed to offend a man like Léon Gingembre, the far from anti-American chairman of the French small-business association.[77]

However, the modernization of social relations in the workplace represented a fundamental reform because of highly militant, even revolutionary trade unions and the weakness of worker purchasing-power. The stages of modernization of French business life, as seen from the USA, were increased pay, democratization of the trade-union scene, and a plurality of trade unions, not to say the 'marginalizing' of the Marxist CGT. Often, as at Poissy, this involved creating a monopoly, intolerant 'house' union. Trainees returning from productivity missions learned that increasing productivity was linked to an overall reorganization of business structures and managing social relations within the company. The American model was accepted by French employers. The American offer only had to be there, wrote Jean Bouvier, to be accepted.[78]

This Americanization of business management encouraged managers to be more open to American culture. A new French middle class, different from the *grande bourgeoisie* of the past, grew up appreciating jazz, American crime novels, and science fiction. From 1953 it read Jean-Jacques Servan-Schreiber's *l'Express*, and from 1955 it listened to the new, American-style radio station *Europe no. 1*. American sales techniques were widely accepted (the very word 'marketing' passed into the French language). Credit, advertising, and self-service shopping developed in imitation of what already existed in the USA.[79] Paperbacks and long-playing records revolutionized leisure habits around 1953. An innovative

---

[76] CE 04, Bonnet 27 July 1951, 9h, nos. 5443–8.

[77] F 60 ter 407, L. Gingembre PME to John Carmody, 12 Sept. 1951, head of the ECA's productivity section.

[78] Bloch-Lainé and Bouvier, *La France restaurée, 1944-1954*, 92.

[79] Ludovic Tournès, 'L'Américanisation de la culture française, ou la rencontre d'un modèle culturel conquérant et d'un pays au seuil de la modernité', *Historiens et Géographes. La IVᵉ République: Histoire, recherches et archives*, 253.

French company in the domestic-appliance sector, Moulinex, adopted typically American sales methods, while Coca-Cola finally became installed in France in 1953—two signs of an Americanization of taste that symbolized modernity. Was this a transformation of French society, a new economic and social order? It was not so much a revolution as a profound referential shift by a section of the population.

The USA as dispenser of economic and financial aid placed conditions on that aid: inflation must be fought and budgets must balance.[80] So it was that in 1947–8 Monnet argued in favour of a degree of budgetary discipline. Bloch-Lainé tells us that he wanted to reject *laisser-faire* in budgetary matters while still preserving growth and modernization. 'Jean Monnet being intuitive and well-advised', he wrote,[81] meaning that he was well advised by his American friends at the time when Congress was examining the European aid legislation. In 1948 Monnet advised Finance Minister Paul Reynaud (who agreed) to make a fiscal effort: 'We have the extraordinary good fortune for modernization to be made considerably easier by American aid, the net result of which will be to have the American taxpayer finance many of the investments of the modernization plan.'[82] On the other hand, in November 1948, Monnet prevented investments being reduced too abruptly and gained the support of the French branch of the ECA, which was keen to see French modernization succeed.

The French modernization process of 1945 was marked by interventionism, state socialism, nationalizations, and a broad programme of social justice for the working population. It was distinctively French. The USA contributed money but also fresh conceptions that were in fact demands: social dialogue in the workplace, balanced public finances, an export drive, material comfort for wage-earners, and high-performance technology for companies open to the industrialized world. American economic and social organization was not transplanted to France, but it did influence the economic and social organization of France during the growth years; a Franco-American modernization model emerged.

---

[80] Bossuat, *La France, l'aide américaine et les constructions européennes, 1944–1954*, ch. 10 ('Nos amis américains' ['Our American friends']), 353 f.

[81] Bloch-Lainé, *Profession fonctionnaire, entretiens avec Françoise Carrière*, 108.

[82] 74 AP 31 J. Monnet 26 Aug. 1948 to Prime Minister, Minister of Finance.

Economic circles continued to criticize a modernization process of which they were not always in control. Even in 1949, important figures and pressure groups did not always appreciate the way aid was being used. The Economic and Social Council wanted to assign the exchange value to reconstruction in order to reduce taxes, rather than to modernization. Certain figures, for a variety of reasons, attacked Monnet: Léon Gingembre, the SMB leader, felt that small and medium-sized business had been 'continually excluded' by the Plan. The US government was, in fact, aware of the presence of the American and French small-business sectors in the mechanics of the Marshall Plan. In the 20 November 1949 issue of *La Vie française*, Charles Rist launched an attack on the Plan, accusing it of destroying budgetary equilibrium. Edmond Giscard d'Estaing felt that American public opinion wanted aid to serve reconstruction rather than the financing of 'vast nationalized enterprises by the state'.[83] Until the Common Market, the employers' organization (the CNPF or Conseil national du patronat français) continued to suggest that the government 'exercise prudence and moderation' in making investments.[84] On the contrary, was Monnet not demonstrating prudence and moderation by modernizing? The modernizers sought to contain inflation and modernize nevertheless. One is still struck by the bad faith of certain figures, the blindness of others, and the widespread inability to make a dispassionate assessment of the long-term interest of all the people of France. But who, twenty years on, argues against modernization? Even the most critical voices approve the fact that the state assumed its responsibilities in the modernization process, faced as it was by an enfeebled private-capital sector that was not always proud of the compromises it had struck with the Nazi occupier. For after all, who was served by the investments made in the coalmines, EDF, GDF, or SNCF if not everyone, private and public sectors alike? It is astonishing that a man such as Edmond Giscard d'Estaing should have taken a Malthusian stance, for the Americans repeatedly pointed out that it was necessary to

[83] AMF 17/10 'Rapport du CGP de février 1950 sur les investissements dans la Presse et au Parlement'.

[84] Jean Bouvier and François Bloch-Lainé, 'Sur l'investissement de reconstruction-modernization au temps du plan Monnet', Fondation nationale des Sciences politiques/Paris (FNSP), 1981, *La France en voie de modernization, 1944–52*, conference held on 4–5 December 1981, unpublished.

finance the productive sector and to stabilize the country's finances at one and the same time. Surely there was a conspiracy amongst certain élites against the CGP, nourished by the complex way in which aid worked? Fortunately, the Plan was defended by the ruling political intelligentsia. Monnet avoided the worst, because France needed to modernize its economy.

Was a new economic and social order established in France? First, it is clear that a rapid modernization of the economy took place. One remembers the classic photographs: the electrification of the Paris–Lyons–Mediterranean line, the 141-R steam locomotives, then the electric locomotives, the hydro-electric dams of the Monnet Plan—Tignes and its famous flooded village. Small farmers now rode tractors, mechanics took the place of farriers, and the Citroën 2CV commanded the village street. A Chanel model made the Renault 4CV look good. Then there were the verbal clichés of modernization: 'la France des berceaux' (a reference to demographic growth), social security (not yet universal), leaving for holidays on the Côte d'Azur, and the transistor radio. Missing from this tableau were Jean Monnet, who was not a 'media person', the CGT, which urged workers to 'roll up their sleeves', white-collar workers putting in overtime, top civil servants who believed in the investment drive, and political leaders (Bidault, Schuman, René Mayer, Petsche, Buron, Pineau, Philip, Moch) who took decisions for modernization at the risk of being seen as reckless spenders. French society adapted in its own time. This success was due to the personal actions of company chairmen and top civil servants in certain sectors of the economy (steel, automobiles, energy, the SNCF, though not the aeronautical industry); it was due to the implementation of daring budgetary policies. The modernization of French society can also be explained in terms of external factors. Had it not been for the prestige of the Fordist model there would have been no increased productivity in France—nor, probably, the same rapid development of the middle class. Without American aid programmes to France, the modernization of all sectors of the Plan would have been delayed for years. A further factor in the change came from the determination of one exceptional man, Jean Monnet. 'The Commissioner-General of the Plan and his colleagues created a climate of ambition and optimism.'[85] A true choice was made

[85] Philippe Mioche in *Reconstructions et modernizations, la France après les ruines*, 164.

between doing nothing and acting with passion.[86] The economic and social modernization of France took place in a voluntarist environment, backed up by American aid.

But was it really a *new* economic and social order that became established in France in 1945? France entered the age of mass consumption having put in place key social innovations and essential preliminaries to technological modernization flowing from the programme adopted by the Resistance and owing nothing to the Americans. It was part of an age-old yearning for social justice by the action of the state. France did not discover growth in 1945; it rediscovered it. Refusing to treat this period as an economic and social 'break with the past', refusing to see it in terms of the birth of a new order, means, of course, admitting that the Resistance failed to create a new society.[87] The French society of the day was transformed rather than overthrown. There was a shift; it was like a society adapting to fresh times, a rebirth after a difficult period, a nation recovering its pride. The adaptation that France experienced after the Second World War was the nation's introduction to economic globalization. France was a member of GATT, it signed the Bretton Woods agreements, it opened up its territories to European investment, and in 1960 it proceeded to make its currency convertible. But all this was a far cry from a new, revolutionary economic and social order, which was something that was universally repudiated, even by the French Communist Party. We need to remember, finally, what Philippe Mioche wrote: 'The Monnet Plan was not the inventor of French modernity but one of the resonance chambers of an exceptional economic situation during which the rhythm of modernization gained pace.'[88] Mioche acknowledged that some social changes did take place as early as 1945, in accordance with the wishes of the French people, and that other, unexpected changes occurred under the influence of the American socio-economic model.

---

[86] See Bloch-Lainé and Bouvier, *La France restaurée, 1944–1954*, 53, on the choice of modernization and on social changes.

[87] Jean-Pierre Rioux wrote eloquently about the unrealizable prophecies made by the Resistance; cf. Jean-Pierre Rioux, *La France de la quatrième république, I. L'Ardeur et la necessité, 1944–1952* (Nouvelle histoire de la France contemporaine, vol. 15) (Paris, 1980), 264.

[88] Mioche, *Le Plan Monnet*, 280.

9

'War Socialism' and its Aftermath: Debates about a New Social and Economic Order in Britain, 1945–1950

JOSE HARRIS

Over the past decade it has become fashionable to suggest that, despite earlier widespread perceptions to the contrary, the Second World War made little permanent impact on the structure of government and society in Britain. Instead, it is now frequently argued that the postwar generation of historians such as Richard Titmuss, A. J. P. Taylor, Alan Bullock, and Keith Hancock were wrong in portraying the war as a unique catalyst of social and structural change.[1] In addition the postwar Labour government, despite its nationalization programme and the advent of the welfare state, is widely seen as having remained well within the traditional liberal boundaries of British political, social, and economic evolution. I have myself contributed to this debate by suggesting that the very fact of being a victor in war helped to revive and relegitimize many of Britain's long-established economic practices and political institutions—just at a moment when similar institutions and practices were being fundamentally reshaped and reconstituted (often with active British help and encouragement) elsewhere in Western Europe.[2]

In this essay, however, I want to pursue a rather different line of argument, with reference to the character of wartime and postwar political thought and ideology. A return to the archives

---

[1] R. M. Titmuss, *Problems of Social Policy* (London, 1950), esp. 506–38; A. J. P. Taylor, *English History* (Oxford, 1966), 600; Alan Bullock, *The Life and Times of Ernest Bevin*, vol. ii: *Minister of Labour* (London, 1967); W. K. Hancock and M. M. Gowing, *British War Economy* (London, 1949).

[2] Jose Harris, 'War and Social History: Britain and the Home Front during the Second World War', *Contemporary European History*, 1/1 (1992), 21–7.

and texts of the period suggests that in terms of aims and aspirations, 'war socialism' and its aftermath were in many ways much
more ambitious, radical, and far-reaching than is often supposed;
and that even critics on the right and centre of British politics in
the early 1940s were often carried along by the assumptions
behind such ideas to a far greater extent than is usually acknowledged. I shall suggest that even those historians who earlier
portrayed the war as an epoch of seminal social change often
*under*estimated the highly un-traditional, sometimes even shock-
ing, character of many views that were put forward at the time,
not just by 'war socialists', but in other, much more surprising
quarters. Despite the support given by Conservative Central
Office in 1945 to the accelerated publication of F. A. Hayek's *The
Road to Serfdom*, that eloquent and impassioned book made
surprisingly little impact in the short term on public opinion, on
discussions of high economic policy, or on critical writing about
the social and political future. Hayek's earlier and more technical writings on marginalism and the theory of prices were sometimes invoked by wartime planners in support of their claim that
tests of market efficiency could be incorporated into economic
institutions run by the state.[3] But it was only much later, with the
fading of the constraints of war and with the publication of
Hayek's more systematic philosophical works, that his views
came to be seen not just as partisan rhetoric, but as weighty
theoretical objections to the whole enterprise of war socialism,
industrial corporatism, and the expansion of state power.[4]

What were the ideas and aspirations of the 'war socialists', and
how far did they determine the boundaries of political debate in
postwar Britain? I will take as my first text that curiously under-
studied, or at least under-rated document, the Labour Party
manifesto of 1945: a document that promised the introduction of
something which it called the 'Socialist Commonwealth of Great
Britain'. 'Commonwealth' sixty years later has become a rather
vague and innocuous term, usually applied to the ceremonial
and institutional residues of the former British Empire. But in
the terminology of 1945 its frame of reference was something

---

[3] E. F. M. Durbin, *Problems of Economic Planning: Papers on Planning and Economics*
(London, 1949).

[4] F. A. Hayek, *The Constitution of Liberty* (Chicago, 1960). On the permeation of the
'constitution of liberty' theme into subsequent debate, see Ralf Dahrendorf, *Society and
Democracy in Germany* (London, 1968; original German edn. Munich, 1965).

quite different. It clearly drew upon the ideas of the dissident wartime 'Commonwealth Party', a body that had won a series of parliamentary by-elections in 1943–4 on a platform of radical protest against the coalition government's cautious and slow-moving approach to postwar social reform. And, more importantly, the term was a very obvious and deliberate verbal implant from the writings of Sidney and Beatrice Webb, who only ten years earlier had identified their ideal model of a Socialist Commonwealth in the domestic, economic, and welfare institutions of Stalinist Russia. The Webbs' *Soviet Communism: A New Civilization* has been almost invariably ridiculed by historians as a bizarre and irrelevant fantasy of the Webbs' old age. Yet despite its immense length (over a thousand pages) it went into no less than five editions between 1935 and 1947, together with numerous abbreviated and pamphlet versions. Many aspects of its portrayal of life in the Soviet Union (particularly its emphasis on universal provision of free health care, and on the role of the Red Army not just as 'heroic warriors' but as a 'school of citizenship') closely chimed with that disseminated by representatives of the British Ministry of Information after the German invasion of Russia in 1941.[5] Such accounts appeared to strike a powerful chord with wartime public opinion: Mass Observation surveys from mid-1941 through to the end of the war regularly recorded highly favourable popular responses to the Soviet Union, and Joseph Stalin as one of the three or four contemporary political leaders whom Britons most admired.[6]

Such perceptions were, of course, by no means confined to the inchoate feelings of the mass of the British public, but were widespread among the élite theorists of the postwar social reconstruction movement. Harold Laski, the most influential political scientist of his generation, writing in 1943 as an academic 'evacuee' in Clarkson Road, Cambridge, eloquently portrayed the ideals of Soviet Communism as a kind of modernist expression of the ideals of the Protestant reformation; its critique of capitalism, he claimed, was indistinguishable from that of Dickens, Ruskin, and Carlyle, its public officials were no less honourable and

---

[5] S. and B. Webb, *Soviet Communism: A New Civilisation* (3rd edn.; London, 1944); John Lawrence, *Life in Russia* (London, 1947); Dora Russell, *The Tamarisk Tree*, vol. iii: *Challenge to the Cold War* (London, 1985).

[6] Mass Observation Archive, FR 848-9, 1036; box 4 file A.

impartial (though in general much more efficient) than their counterparts in Britain and the USA. The war, in Laski's view, had forcibly impressed upon the people of Britain three of the 'great truths' about the Soviet system—the productive superiority of planning over market forces, the moral superiority of 'positive' over 'negative' liberty, and the deep psychological fulfilment to be found in conscription and public service. 'I speak, I think, for most Englishmen', Laski claimed, 'when I say that in these terrible wartime years . . . more men and women have found a genuine liberation [in compulsory public service] than was the case in the years of doubt and disillusion between 1919 and 1939.'[7] Similarly, G. D. H. Cole, in his contribution to the Fabian Society's 1943 *Plan for Britain*, portrayed the war as having empirically demonstrated the need for Soviet-style strategies in peacetime as well as in wartime planning. And he went even further than Laski in claiming that 'in a sheerly realistic sense', Russian workers 'are a great deal more free than we are, or can be until we forsake our atomism, and set out to make a determined pursuit after collective, instead of merely individualistic, values'.[8]

Such views were perhaps unsurprising among long-term quasi-Marxian theorists like Laski and Cole, but echoes of their outlook were found across a much wider range of the political spectrum. Many planning enthusiasts who wholly rejected the Labour Left's penchant for Soviet-style coercion were nevertheless close observers of, and admirers of, Russian developments in macro and micro planning.[9] R. H. Tawney in a classic article published in the 1943 *Economic History Review* invoked the disastrous impact of the abandonment of state controls at the end of the *First* World War to support the argument that government must at all costs maintain controls over all aspects of the economy at the end of the *Second*.[10] Tawney's article had originally been written in 1940 as an advisory paper for the Treasury, only to be hastily suppressed as a dangerous and subversive document; but by 1945 its central argument had become the new orthodoxy in many Whitehall departments, including to some

[7] H. Laski, *Reflections on the Revolution of our Time* (London, 1943), esp. 346–419.

[8] Fabian Society, *Plan for Britain* (London, 1943), 4, 11, and 27.

[9] W. H. Beveridge, *Planning under Socialism and other Addresses* (London, 1936); Barbara Wootton, *Freedom under Planning* (London, 1945).

[10] R. H. Tawney, 'The Abolition of Economic Controls, 1918–21', *Economic History Review*, 12 (1943), 1–30.

extent even within the Treasury itself.[11] Its message was also widely disseminated throughout the civil and military population in the format of ABCA and WEA pamphlets—making it possibly the most widely read and influential article ever to appear in a journal of academic history.

Moreover, this kind of argument went far beyond the boundaries of the Labour movement. The three major land-use inquiries of the reconstruction movement, the Barlow, Scott, and Uthwatt reports, all in some form or another endorsed the view that a large component of 'development-value' should be transferred to the community, either through direct public ownership, or through planning controls and measures of rating and general taxation.[12] The Liberal reformer William Beveridge constantly stressed that economic controls and social planning should always be subordinate to the claims of personal freedom. Nevertheless, in his *Full Employment in a Free Society* (1944) Beveridge clearly stated that private ownership of the means of production was 'not an essential citizen liberty in Britain' and could not be allowed to stand in the way of the abolition of peacetime mass unemployment. Nor can there be any doubt that Beveridge and his advisers on full employment went far beyond the Keynesian prescription of centralized fiscal and monetary management. The young 'Keynesian socialists' who shaped Beveridge's *Full Employment* report all envisaged that techniques learnt from wartime controls over supply and manpower could be permanently used to determine the distribution of population, organization of manpower, and physical location of industry after the end of the war.[13]

Such enlarged visions of the role of the state were by no means exclusively confined to the left and centre of the British political spectrum. At the very start of the war the central government's first faltering steps towards a new kind of fiscal control over the national economy had occurred under the auspices of the conservative-inclined Committee on Economic Information, headed by

[11] George Peden, *The Treasury and British Public Policy, 1906–1959* (Oxford, 2000), 345–55. On Treasury responses to Tawney's paper, see PRO, CAB 117/2 and CAB 117/40.

[12] *Royal Commission on the Distribution of the Industrial Population, Report*, Cmd. 6153, 1940 (Barlow report), 104–19; *Committee on Land Utilisation in Rural Areas, Report*, Cmd. 6378, 1942 (Scott report), 80–91; *Expert Committee on Compensation and Betterment*, Cmd. 6386, 1942 (Uthwatt report), 31–45, 54–6, 62–4, 74–81, and 135–7.

[13] *Full Employment in a Free Society* (1944), 22–3, 28–9, and 124–207.

Sir Josiah Stamp.[14] And early on in the Second World War the
Conservative Party had found itself unexpectedly and perhaps
somewhat embarrassingly encumbered by a passionate ideological champion for the cause of radical reconstruction, the refugee
Hungarian sociologist Professor Karl Mannheim. Mannheim
argued that in the modern world all traditional 'small c' conservative mechanisms for transmitting moral values and social solidarity had irretrievably broken down, and needed to be replaced
by policies of large-scale social, economic, and moral reconstruction initiated and enforced by the state. Mannheim's ideas have
often been dismissed as marginal to the mainstream of British
political thought. But his works were certainly influential among
the Conservative Research Department's wartime reconstruction
committees on such matters as youth, housing, conscription, and
education, and they continued after the war to be widely diffused
through the numerous volumes of the Routledge Library of
Social Reconstruction, of which Mannheim was the founder and
chief editor.[15]

   Moreover, despite the polemic of *The Road to Serfdom*, there is a
case for suggesting that in certain spheres Hayek himself was less
averse to a more extensive role for the state than is often
supposed. Hayek's wartime correspondence with Keynes
suggests that, although they might disagree about management
of the money supply, they did not fundamentally disagree about
such things as public provision of social insurance, workmen's
compensation, and family allowances.[16] Michael Oakeshott in
his 1947 essay 'Rationalism in politics' remarked on the degree to
which Hayek's critique of statism had absorbed and replicated
the intellectual style of his opponents—'the main significance' of
The Road to Serfdom was 'not the cogency of his doctrine but the
fact that it is a doctrine. A plan to resist all planning may be
better than its opposite, but it belongs to the same style of politics.'[17] Hayek was, in fact, an admirer of the Beveridge Plan. He

   [14] PRO, CAB 89/1, minutes and agenda of the Committee on Economic
Information, 1939–40.
   [15] Karl Mannheim, *Man and Society in an Age of Reconstruction: Studies in Modern Social
Structure* (London, 1940), and id., *Diagnosis of our Time: Wartime Essays of a Sociologist*
(London, 1943); Jose Harris, 'Political Ideas and the Debate on State Welfare 1940–45', in
H. A. L. Smith (ed.), *War and Social Change: British Society in the Second World War*
(Manchester, 1986), 233–63.
   [16] J. M. Keynes, *Collected Writings* (London, 1978), xxii. 73–4, 92, 102, and 106–7.
   [17] M. Oakeshott, *Rationalism in Politics and other Essays* (London, 1962), 26.

approved of its strongly 'contractarian' basis, and saw nothing in Beveridge's substantive proposals fundamentally incompatible with liberalism in either its political or economic forms.[18]

Ideas that derived from or had affinities with 'war socialism' were therefore widespread and hegemonic for much of the wartime era, and many people (even those who found the prospect highly distasteful) saw the future as almost inevitably taking the form of state collectivism and state direction in one form or another. Moreover, there were many reasons for supporting such a trend, other than mere inner conviction or ideology. To many the continuance of wartime controls seemed the only guarantee against a return to pre-war mass unemployment, and to many others it seemed the only route through which Britain could possibly weather the dire financial and monetary crises, and supply and materials shortages, that erupted at the end of the war. It is worth mentioning also something that is often forgotten now, but at the time was very much to the forefront of the minds of planners; this was that state collectivism seemed to offer, not simply some vague entity called 'social justice', but enormous gains in terms of reduced overhead costs, and enhanced organizational efficiency. It was estimated, for example, that a universal and uniform system of state national insurance could be run on an administrative budget of merely 3 per cent of total contributions, whereas the running costs of the commercial life assurance sector in the 1930s had been over 35 per cent of premium income, and those of companies offering employers' liability insurance over 46 per cent.[19] State ownership of heavy industries and railways seemed to open up massive possibilities for rationalization, economies of scale, and well-targeted investment, which had been quite impossible in the hotchpotch of archaic and overlapping private companies that had prevailed before the war. Similar gains were expected from the nationalization of medical care. Although planners expected a sharp short-term rise in costs in the early days of free medicine, it was envisaged that a National Health Service would in the long run help to pay for its keep by savings effected through prevention, 'rehabilitation', and medical monitoring of state benefits.[20] In stark contrast with much

---

[18] Conversation with the author, June 1980.

[19] *Social Insurance and Allied Services*, Cmd. 6404, 1942 (Beveridge Report), Appendix E, 277–86.

[20] Ibid.

discourse of the present day, public ownership was thus seen not just as 'fairer', but as a more cost-effective, businesslike, and 'rational' option than a return to private markets.

In the face of such attitudes and expectations, anti-state-interventionist arguments in the later 1940s made relatively little headway, other than at the level of literary polemic of the kind offered by George Orwell, A. P. Herbert, and Sir Ernest Benn. The collection of moderately 'liberal' *Unservile State* essays edited by George Watson—which anticipated much current debate in advocating a shift of emphasis away from the state towards civil society—did not appear in published form until 1957,[21] while the various anti-planning essays of Michael Oakeshott, though composed in the late 1940s, were largely confined to a very limited Cambridge audience until their republication in 1962. Moreover, Oakeshott's critique was more concerned with attacking the basic logic and epistemology of planning thought than with condemning state action or promoting a market alternative.[22] Similarly it was significant that when a Conservative Party critique of statism did eventually begin to emerge with the Charter movement towards the end of the 1940s, its emphasis was less on promoting market efficiency than on countering the threat to personal freedom that public ownership and monopoly were deemed to entail. At the time of the 1950 election, many of those Conservative politicians who were later to be most closely identified with free-market revivalism were moderate Butlerites and One Nation Tories. In the words of T. E. Utley, 'they expressly reserved to the State the right not only to intervene by fiscal means to control the pace at which the economy moved, but also, when necessary, to use such methods as direct import controls to achieve results which free economic activity could not. They had no doubts about its being one of the functions of government to provide for a high stable level of employment.' They were essentially 'middle of the road' men, with closer affinities to an older conservatism of paternalism and protectionism than to the neo-liberalism and notions of unrestrained competition that permeated conservatism of a slightly later era.[23]

How and why did that emphasis begin to change? To explore

---

[21] George Watson (ed.), *The Unservile State: Essays in Liberty and Welfare* (London, 1957).

[22] Oakeshott, *Rationalism in Politics*, esp. 5–42, 99–131, and 407–37.

[23] T. E. Utley, *Enoch Powell: The Man and his Writings* (London, 1968), 58–61.

this fully would require a major research programme, but I shall conclude this essay by suggesting a few fairly obvious practical factors and some slightly less obvious intellectual ones. One point that deserves further comment and exploration is the curious indifference of many 'social reconstruction' enthusiasts to the fact that Great Britain was not a self-contained industrial autarky, but a trading nation with a very large financial services sector, heavily dependent on economic movements in the rest of the world. There seemed to be a curious lacuna between British wartime thinking about *domestic* and *social* reconstruction on the one hand, and Britain's involvement in *international* and *monetary* reconstruction through the Bretton Woods negotiations on the other (even though several of the major participants in both these processes were one and the same persons). This absence of what might anachronistically be called 'joined-up' thinking was to be fraught with economic and political difficulties for the long-term future. Similarly, there was a wide range of factors in the historical circumstances of postwar Britain that led inexorably to disappointment and disenchantment with the legacy of 'war socialism'. The Soviet Union's postwar occupation and subversion of much of Eastern Europe rapidly dispelled the honeymoon atmosphere of popular wartime attitudes to Russia. Chronic postwar debt and recurrent balance of payments crises severely curtailed many of the more ambitious visions of the planning movement, while the deeply entrenched resistance of British trade unions soon put an end to the possibility, cherished by early postwar Labour ministers, that the British economy could be permanently regulated by manpower planning and controls over supply. Moreover, despite Harold Laski's claims about the wartime conversion of the British people to the cause of 'higher freedom', over the long-drawn-out era of postwar scarcity this conversion began to wear pretty thin, and, as recent research has convincingly shown, the 1950s Conservative revival was to be closely linked to Conservative success in tapping into more traditional (or 'negative') conceptions of English freedom, such as freedom to consume, freedom from regulatory controls, and freedom of private choice.[24]

The reasons for this shift at an ideological and intellectual

[24] Ina Zweiniger-Bargielowska, *Austerity in Britain: Rationing, Controls, and Consumption, 1939–1955* (Oxford, 2000), ch. 5.

level are more intangible, but there is a case for suggesting that, despite their apparent eclipse and extinction in 1945, the neo-liberals and liberal conservatives were eventually to win the propaganda war because over the *longue durée* their theorists and ideologues took the intellectual debate more seriously. This may seem an odd conclusion, in view of what I have said above about the startling radicalism of many of the 'war socialists'' proposals; but their radicalism lay in the far-reaching scope and substantive content of those proposals, not in the way in which they were slotted into a framework of wider social, political, and economic theory. Despite some immensely ambitious plans, there was no major philosophical text of the British wartime planning move-ment or of British war socialism, whereas hidden away amongst all the rhetoric and polemic there were certain important works of political theory to be found in the works of their ideological opponents. The wartime works of Laski, Cole, and the Fabian 'Plan for Britain' school, though composed with great moral fervour, were self-evidently propaganda texts which set out a shopping-list of what needed to be done, but they scarcely engaged at all with the human, institutional, logical, and 'predic-tive' problems involved in large-scale planning. Such difficulties could be glossed over in the exceptional circumstances of wartime, but gradually reasserted themselves in the postwar decades; hence the eventual percolation into public debate of Hayek's arguments against managed currencies, and of the scep-tical, anti-planning, accidentalist perspectives of Michael Oakeshott. These works dealt not just with a specific economic agenda, but with more fundamental themes such as the logical limits of socio-economic knowledge, the nature of social order, the transmission of social codes, and the inner structures of human rationality. Their political agenda included goals that many who conceded their philosophical points were reluctant to espouse in practical policies. But if taking theory seriously is an important part of politics, then in Britain at least it was the neo-liberals and conservative sceptics, and not the planners and war socialists, who seemed to get the better of later twentieth-century political argument.

PART III

Beyond the Nation-State

10

From the 'Third Force' to the Common Market: Discussions about Europe and the Future of the Nation-State in West Germany, 1945–57

WILFRIED LOTH

1945-1947: Visions of Europe between East and West

In the Third Reich conceptions of Europe for the most part presupposed the Reich's hegemony over the European continent.[1] Few ever considered a new European order not based on German hegemony, and the notion of Europe only really became interesting when the defeat of Germany began to loom. Idealists such as Helmuth Count von Moltke assumed that after the Allies' victory the peace would bring 'a uniform European sovereignty extending from Portugal to a point as far east as possible'.[2] Realists such as Friedrich Stampfer and Theodor Steltzer suggested a 'European Federation' as a means of securing a bearable peace for the Germans and, thus, of helping democracy in Germany on to a sound footing. At the same time they considered that such a federation would help Europe to assert itself against the new superpowers which threatened to rule Europe from outside.[3]

---

[1] See Paul Kluke, 'Nationalsozialistische Europaideologie', *Vierteljahrshefte für Zeitgeschichte*, 3 (1955), 240–75; Michael Salewski, 'Ideas of the National Socialist Government and Party', in Walter Lipgens (ed.), *Documents on the History of European Integration*, vol. 1: *Continental Plans for European Union 1939–1945* (Berlin, 1985), 37–178; Jürgen Elvert, ' "Germanen" und "Imperialisten": Zwei Europakonzepte aus national-sozialistischer Zeit', *Historische Mitteilungen*, 5 (1992), 161–84.

[2] 'Ausgangslage, Ziele und Aufgaben', Memorandum of 24 Apr. 1942, published in Ger van Roon, *Neuordnung im Widerstand: Der Kreisauer Kreis innerhalb der deutschen Widerstandsbewegung* (Munich, 1967), 507–17, and in part also in Walter Lipgens (ed.), *Europa Föderationspläne der Widerstandsbewegungen 1940–1945* (Munich, 1968), 111–17.

[3] Wilfried Loth, 'Rettungsanker Europa? Deutsche Europa-Konzeptionen vom Reich

Of course, the 'other Germany' that expressed itself thus represented only a minority of Germans. When German dreams of hegemony over Europe began to crumble, the vast majority clung to the hope that the anti-Hitler coalition would break apart at the very last minute. When even this hope was dashed, large parts of the nation faced material breakdown, their convictions disintegrated, and they began to question their identity.

In the vacuum that opened up, the idea of a united Europe suddenly had a broad appeal, especially among the younger generation which, after the collapse of the Reich, had the biggest problems of orientation, but also among middle-class idealists and the survivors of the old labour movement who, after the experience of catastrophe, were seeking a new approach. There were undoubtedly moments of compensation and of suppression. Surprisingly often, and in a strikingly carefree way, Germans across all political and ideological borders demanded equality for the German nation within a united Europe. Tactical considerations also played a part. They expected that the price to be paid for the lost war would be lower if an integrated confederation of European states came about soon. It would control all members and thus avoid any unilateral discrimination against Germany. The experience of collapse meant that ideas which had already been developed by the resistance in many cases were now more widely understood. Insight into the catastrophic outcome of German power politics led to the realization that security in Europe could no longer be achieved by defiant self-assertion, but only by integration into a larger community.

The number of initiatives that, at the end of the war, were directed towards 'Europe' soon made the objective of a united Europe acceptable in occupied Germany. After he toured Germany in December 1946, the Swiss journalist Ernst von Schenck reported that the German people were tired of the traditions of the nation-state and had become pacifist in principle. Among those who went beyond these common attitudes and thought positively about Germany's future prospects, there were 'not many who deliberately postulated dependence on one of the victorious powers as a way out'; rather he 'repeatedly met

bis zur Bundesrepublik', in Hans-Erich Volkmann (ed.), *Ende des Dritten Reiches, Ende des Zweiten Weltkrieges* (Munich, 1995), 201–21.

among them the notion of Europe'.[4] Indeed, no other idea was articulated more often. With the exception of the Communists, who unequivocally saw Germany's future at the side of the victorious Soviet Union, every political organization in the occupation zones saw the future of German foreign affairs within the context of the European nations growing together.[5]

In the first two years after the war, public opinion expressed a demand for Europe to become a Third Force between the two new superpowers. This reflected the insight that only a united Europe could play an independent role in world politics, and also the concern that the differences between the two main victorious powers would lead to the division of Europe and Germany. For many, the desire to prevent a Third World War, which they feared would be the outcome of the confrontation between the victorious powers, was the main reason to push for a swift union of the continent. And some considered Europe as a Third Force to be a necessary condition for the success of the postwar democratic socialism they desired.

In the *Frankfurter Hefte*, Walter Dirks and Eugen Kogon, for example, advocated a socialist European federation as a prerequisite for the success of the 'Second Republic'.[6] Martin Niemöller called for a 'United Europe' as a 'bridge between East and West', and regarded it as the only agent capable of preventing a Third World War.[7] In *Ruf*, Hans-Werner Richter proposed a socialist Europe as a way of preventing the formation of blocs.[8] From his

---

[4] *Europa* (monthly journal of the Swiss 'Europa Union'), Jan. 1947, p. 3, trans. from Walter Lipgens, *Die Anfänge der europäischen Einigungspolitik 1945–1950*, vol. 1: *1945–1947* (Stuttgart, 1977), 387; further reports on general emotions ibid. 231–40 and 386–9; on their reflection in literature see Ernst Nolte, *Deutschland und der Kalte Krieg* (Munich, 1974), 190–6.

[5] See Wilfried Loth, 'German Conceptions of Europe during the Escalation of the East–West Conflict 1945–1949', in Josef Becker and Franz Knipping (eds.), *Power in Europe? Great Britain, France, Italy and Germany in a Postwar World, 1945–1950* (Berlin, 1986), 517–36; also see the documentation in Christoph Stillemunkes, 'The Discussion on European Union in German Occupation Zones', in Walter Lipgens and Wilfried Loth (eds.), *Documents on the History of European Integration*, vol. 3: *The Struggle for European Union by Political Parties and Pressure Groups in Western European Countries 1945–1950* (Berlin, 1988), 441–65.

[6] Walter Dirks, 'Die Zweite Republik: Zum Ziel und zum Weg der Deutschen Demokratie', *Frankfurter Hefte*, 1 (1946), 12–24; see Martin Stankowski, *Linkskatholizismus nach 1945* (Cologne, 1975), 66–136.

[7] See e.g. *Official Gazette of the Protestant Church in Germany*, 1 Aug. 1947, 101–4.

[8] See esp. Hans-Werner Richter, 'Churchill und die europäische Einheit', *Der Ruf*, 1 Mar. 1947; see also Hans-Werner Richter, 'Wie entstand und was war die Gruppe 47?', in Hans A. Neunzig (ed.), *Hans-Werner Richter und die Gruppe 47* (Munich, 1979), 41–176, at 41–75.

political analysis, Richard Löwenthal drew the hope that the development of a European Third Force "beyond capitalism' could no longer be stopped.[9] For old and new supporters of an organized movement for Europe, from the Europa-Union founded by Wilhelm Heile in continuation of his Weimar activities to the Europa-Bund chaired by the former Streseman staff member Henry Bernhard, preventing a division between East and West was the foremost objective.[10]

Support for the Third Force notion was also widespread among various politicians whose thinking focused more strongly on the categories of the nation-state and thus did not stress the need for a European federation with the same urgency. Jakob Kaiser, for one, did not have much liking for federalism. Nor did he understand French security concerns, which advocated federal integration irrespective of the tensions between East and West. But he felt all the more strongly that the interests of the German people required mediation in the East–West conflict, which, he was convinced, could be brought about only by liberal socialism. For all his emphasis on Germany's function as a 'bridge', he was not only interested in maintaining the territorial unity of the former Reich, but also advocated a peace order within the framework of the United Nations and a joint community of the European nations, for which he considered the term 'United States of Europe' to be quite appropriate.[11] Other leading Christian Democrats, such as Ernst Lemmer and Josef Müller, and prominent Social Democrats such as Paul Löbe and Ernst Reuter, held similar views. Even an idealistic writer like Ulrich Noack for the time being followed the same train of thought, envisaging a 'confederation' of the continental nations with a mediating mission.[12]

By contrast, the concept of a national organization of the

[9] Paul Sering (i.e. Richard Löwenthal), *Jenseits des Kapitalismus* (Lauf bei Nürnberg, 1947; new edition Bonn, 1977); see also Hans-Peter Schwarz, *Vom Reich zur Bundesrepublik: Deutschland im Widerstreit der außenpolitischen Konzeptionen in den Jahren der Besatzungsherrschaft 1945–1949* (Neuwied, 1966; 2nd edn. Stuttgart, 1980), 568–71.
[10] See Lipgens, *Die Anfänge der europäischen Einigungspolitik*, 386–434 and 592–605.
[11] The term was first used in his speech at the CDU's Whitsun meeting in 1946: *Deutschland und die Union: Die Berliner Tagung 1946. Reden und Aussprachen* (Berlin, 1946), 18. Schwarz's account of Kaiser's concept in *Vom Reich zur Bundesrepublik* justifiably neglects this 'European' aspect in favour of 'national political objectives' (see e.g. p. 304).
[12] See Schwarz, *Vom Reich zur Bundesrepublik*, 300, 503 f. 663, 684 f.; For Noack see ibid. 355–69.

three western zones integrated into a Western alliance was, at first, acceptable only to a minority. Nor was it easily reconciled with the objective of preventing another world war, or of securing self-determination for all Germans. By the same token, it did not fit the predominantly left-wing orientation of organized politics. Basically, it could be justified only if Eastern Europe and the Soviet Zone of Occupation were given up as lost. And it became inevitable only if the threat of Soviet tyranny extending beyond the Eastern half of the European continent were presupposed.

It was precisely this concern that distinguished Konrad Adenauer, who in the long term became the most prominent supporter of Western integration, from the advocates of a Europe of the Third Force. He agreed with them on the necessity for European integration as a means of satisfying the need of Germany's neighbours for security, especially the French. He also accepted that integration was the best means to moderate the interference of the victorious powers. Like them, he fundamentally rejected the nationalist and state-worshipping traditions that focused on Bismarck's Reich as the only reference for the conduct of foreign affairs.[13] At the same time a European union, in his view, would protect Western Europe, including West Germany, from Soviet expansion. 'Asia stands at the River Elbe', he wrote in March 1946 to the Social Democrat Wilhelm Sollmann, who had emigrated to the USA. 'Only an economically and spiritually regenerated Western Europe, of which that section of Germany not occupied by Russia forms an integral part, can check the further advance of Asian spirit and power.'[14]

Moreover, this Western European federation was to be closely tied to the USA, which was to play the part of a federator and a protecting power in the formation of Western Europe. Adenauer considered such a commitment necessary because, in his view, the European democracies, even if they pooled their resources, would not, in the long run, be strong enough to resist Soviet expansionist efforts. He concluded that 'Europe could only be saved with the help of the USA'.[15] The protective function of the Western European federation, by contrast, would be limited to

[13] For the basics, see ibid. 423–79; Hans-Peter Schwarz, 'Adenauer und Europa', *Vierteljahrshefte für Zeitgeschichte*, 27 (1979), 471–523; for the operative realization on a broader basis of sources id., *Adenauer. Der Aufstieg: 1876–1952* (Stuttgart, 1986).

[14] Hans-Peter Mensing (ed.), *Adenauer: Briefe 1945–1947* (Berlin, 1983), 191.

[15] Ibid.

strengthening the West by eliminating European conflicts, and to countering American disengagement, which he always feared. It might also help to enforce specific European interests *vis-à-vis* the American leadership.

Wilhelm Röpke, a theorist of neo-liberalism who had emigrated to Switzerland, followed a similar train of thought. As early as 1945, his plea for a Western German state within the framework of a Western bloc committed to free trade was based on the 'complete separation of moral, political, social and economic principles' along the River Elbe line.[16] The Rhenish federalists around Franz Albert Kramer and the *Rheinischer Merkur* demanded a Christian federal reorganization, a settlement with their neighbours to the west, and a shift of Germany's main cultural centres to the towns on the Main, Rhine, and Danube rivers. Thus they also aimed for a Western federation which would exclude not only Prussian centralist traditions but also Soviet claims.[17] With his uncompromising rejection of all German structures, even Kurt Schumacher had basically the same aim, although he imagined Europe growing together along the lines of the Third Force.[18]

It speaks for the fascination of the Third Force concept and the substantial concern to secure peace and maintain the nation's unity that was behind it, that such notions were not, at first, well received. Not only did few dare to express such ideas so long as the occupying powers were still publicly claiming their desire to co-operate, but even when the Western zones were included in the Marshall Plan, West Germans did not enthusiastically seize on the possibilities it contained for their rise at the side of the Western powers. Instead, helplessness and a careful wait-and-see policy prevailed until the Berlin Crisis, and, at first, no one wanted to admit the consequences of the founding of the Western state. The shock triggered by the collapse of 1945 was too deeply rooted and the demonstration of the victorious powers' unity was too strong to make possible a smooth continuation of Goebbels's thesis of Western defence against the Bolshevik threat.

[16] Wilhelm Röpke, *Die deutsche Frage* (Zurich, 1945; 3rd edn., 1948), 276 f.; also see Schwarz, *Vom Reich zur Bundesrepublik*, 393–401.

[17] Ibid. 413–25.

[18] Ibid. 483–573; on the practice of Schumacher's Germany and European politics see Kurt Klotzbach, *Der Weg zur Staatspartei: Programmatik, praktische Politik und Organisation der deutschen Sozialdemokratie 1945 bis 1965* (Berlin, 1982), 66–77, 98–110, 116–21, 154–72, 194–237.

1947-1953: The Cold War and the Concept of Western Integration

With the transition to open confrontation in the Cold War during 1947, the advocates of the Third Force faced a serious dilemma. On the one hand, their interest in the welfare of the Germans living under occupation and desire for greater autonomy suggested they should support the Marshall Plan and participate actively in the beginning of reconstruction marked by Western integration. Passivity seemed all the less acceptable since the brusque Soviet rejection of the Marshall Plan and the dogmatic hardening of Soviet politics since the founding of Cominform had, at least for the foreseeable future, ruined any prospect of inter-zonal integration. On the other hand, by supporting the Marshall Plan policies the Germans ran the risk of further aggravating bloc-building and the division of Europe, which they had initially tried to prevent.

In the autumn of 1947, Carlo Schmid, at the time Social Democrat Minister of Justice in Württemberg-Hohenzollern and a professor at Tübingen, developed an alternative notion of a temporary separation of the German and the European course. This concept proposed that all the European countries which, after the Soviet veto, still had freedom of choice should use the American reconstruction programme to unite according to the idea of the Third Force. The Germans, however, were to be excluded from this process of integration until the Third Force Europe had mediated between East and West to such an extent that the division of Europe could be abolished and the integration of all four zones of occupation in a 'United States of Europe' was possible. This procedure had the further advantage that Germany could then be integrated on the basis of equal rights with the other confederating states. As soon as Europe was established, the main reasons for fearing the Germans would be gone and, therefore, unilateral measures of control would become unnecessary, whereas at the present state of thinking they still seemed unavoidable, even in Germany's Western neighbours. For the time being the Germans were to be content with 'provisional regulations, which the two world powers and the states of that forthcoming Europe considered as tolerable for all participants'. Only 'after a number of such provisional regulations

would it be possible for a reunited Germany to join this Europe—
as soon as the blocs have settled their mutual interests'.[19]

Yet this did not solve, but only postponed, the dilemma faced
by the advocates of the Third Force. Schmid almost desperately
clung to the hope that, at the last minute, the escalating confrontation could be reversed by a federation of the Western European
countries. However, he offered no answer to the question of what
was to be done if, despite all appeals, the process of mediation
failed. And *de facto*, though not fully consciously, he made a
preliminary decision in favour of Western integration. Provisional
arrangements going beyond occupation status and promoting the
federation of the Western countries suggested an adherence to the
advancement of Western Europe even if, at the same time, it led
to the deepening of the East–West division. Once stronger structures for Western Europe had been established, they would be
hard to undo and it would be almost impossible to oppose the
consolidation of the West German 'provisional arrangement'.

Some of the advocates of the Third Force rushed to promote
the integration of the three Western zones in Western Europe.
In a debate of the Heidelberg Aktionsgruppe zur Demokratie
und zum freien Sozialismus, Konrad Mommsen, for example,
replied to Schmid that the continuation of the East–West division meant that West German participation in the Marshall Plan
was inevitable: 'If these efforts [to overcome the confrontation
between East and West] should fail, as seems likely, and if we
therefore have to face two worlds—America and Soviet
Russia—the only alternative for us will be to help to settle a new
organization of the respective parts within the limits of their
environment, an organization which provides some preconditions for a new economic life.'[20] In this view all that remained of
the Third Force concept was the vague hope that despite its
commitment to the USA a united Western Europe would be
able to act more autonomously than a collection of independent
nation-states under American leadership.

[19] See the presentation of his position at the time in Carlo Schmid, *Erinnerungen*
(Berne, 1979), 297; for a basic draft see also Karl Schmid, 'Das deutsch-französische
Verhältnis und der Dritte Partner', *Die Wandlung*, 2 (1947), 792–805; further, the presentation of Schmid's ideas in Schwarz, *Vom Reich zur Bundesrepublik*, 574–85 and Schmid's
report on the activities in European politics in *Erinnerungen*, 295–9 and 417–29.

[20] 'Ruhrgebiet und Friedenssicherung: Eine Diskussion' (minutes of the conference of
10–11 Oct. 1947), *Die Wandlung*, 2 (1947), 768–92, quotation at 771.

Growing fears of Soviet expansion meant that during 1948 the concept of Western Europe gathered supporters from beyond the resigned advocates of the Third Force. For many West Germans the confrontation now made the formation of the Western bloc appear an existential necessity; at the same time an alliance with the West, for which many had hoped in vain during the last phase of the war, suddenly came within reach. For West Germany this not only suggested a faster rise than would have been conceivable under other circumstances, but the notion that at the side of the Western powers Germany would be able to push the Soviet Union out of German affairs also became more plausible. In a chapter added to the third edition of his book, *Die Deutsche Frage*, published in 1948, Röpke supported this notion,[21] and, in general, it was more often discussed.

After the experience of the Berlin Blockade in the summer of 1948, most of the original advocates of the Third Force *de facto* accepted the alternative of Western integration. Some were resigned, but most were motivated by the hope that, with the assertion of relative Western European independence *vis-à-vis* the USA, it would be possible to revise the division of Europe, or at least that of Germany, in the near future. Although Carlo Schmid suggested that the reorganization of the Western zones should be limited to forming a 'state fragment', and that the Federal Republic should delay its accession to the European Council, he gave up his fundamental resistance to German participation in a Western-orientated construction of Europe. In his efforts to mediate he was now careful to think beyond the 'present little Europe' of 'the good old Continent', 'which includes both East and West'.[22] Similarly, Walter Dirks and Eugen Kogon pleaded for the 'creation of a homogeneous legislative power starting from the West'; they strictly rejected a neutralization of Germany with reference to the dangers of Communist subversion and Soviet pressure.[23] The European

---

[21] Röpke, *Die deutsche Frage*, 337; see also p. 307.

[22] Presentation at the constituent session of the German Council of the European Movement on 13 June 1949, in Carlo Schmid, *Deutschland und der Europäische Rat* [no place, no date]; also see Schmid, *Erinnerungen*, 423 and 426–9, and his speech to the German Bundestag on 15 November 1949 setting out his basic principles in foreign affairs, *Verhandlungen des Deutschen Bundestages, 1. Wahlperiode (1949–53), 17. Sitzung*, 439–41.

[23] Eugen Kogon, 'Die Aussichten Europas', in Alfred Andersch (ed.), *Europäische Avantgarde* (Frankfurt am Main, 1949), 146–61.

groups which in February 1948 had formed the Europa-Union
came to similar conclusions. It was therefore only logical that at
their first congress in May 1949 they should elect Kogon as president and Schmid as vice-president.[24]

Jakob Kaiser was bitterly disappointed at the hardening of the
Soviet position and badly wanted to justify his own attitude in a
context that was dominated by the advocates of Western integration. Thus he gave up the idea of mediating between East and
West and hoped that the division could be overcome by
strengthening the West. In his view, the blockade of the transport routes to Berlin finally proved 'that for the Soviets only
hostility and the desire for domination mattered in their relation
with peoples and parties who do not submit to the doctrine it
propagated or who at least are not willing to serve the predominance of the Soviet Union'. Therefore, he believed, Soviet politics aimed at the submission of the whole continent. Kaiser was
convinced that the Soviets would not be able to hold their position in the Soviet Zone indefinitely; he no longer asked what
price would have to be paid for a lasting arrangement with the
Soviet power.[25]

Only a minority moved on from the concept of the Third
Force to a neutralist position: those who considered the risk of
Soviet encroachment on Western Europe to be slight and saw
the danger of East–West confrontation escalating into a Third
World War. They included the circle of intellectuals around
Hans-Werner Richter, and the Christian middle classes represented by Martin Niemöller and Ulrich Noack. Both decisively
rejected the foundation of a Western state and the formation of a
Western bloc and demanded instead the simultaneous retreat of
all occupation forces as the key to the solution of the German
question as well as to a lasting settlement for the European continent. For the moment they no longer aimed for an all-European
federation—the formation of blocs, they agreed, had advanced
too far. In order for Europe to grow together gradually, they

[24] See Wilfried Loth, 'Die Europa-Bewegung in den Anfangsjahren der
Bundesrepublik', in Ludolf Herbst, Werner Bührer, and Hanno Sowade (eds.), *Vom
Marshall-Plan zur EWG: Die Eingliederung der Bundesrepublik in die westliche Welt* (Munich,
1990), 63–77.

[25] See the collection of his comments in the second half of 1948 in Werner Conze,
Jakob Kaiser: Politiker zwischen Ost und West 1945–1949 (Stuttgart, 1969), 238–44, 247, 253;
quotation from *Der Tag* (16 Sept. 1948).

argued, the blocs should acknowledge each other and exclude Germany, and possibly even a larger central European zone, from their confrontation.[26]

In their view the Germans, rather than allies of the West against totalitarian expansion, were the potential victims of a confrontation that had come about without their doing and against their will. Thus the neutralist position soon carried nationalist and emotional overtones. Nevertheless, realistic approaches to a strategy of de-escalating the East–West conflict also came from within the neutralist camp. Noack, for example, did not retain the idealistic and vague terms of his early years, looking instead for complementary interests of East and West. He became convinced that the loss of the East German territories had to be accepted and that the Soviet problems of reconstruction should be confronted by strengthening the eastern orientation of the German economy. In return he hoped that the Soviets would renounce the Communist monopoly of power in their zone of occupation and that they would gradually soften their aggressive attitude. Under these conditions he thought the neutralization of the German-speaking central European countries possible. As a result, he expected far-reaching initiatives for reducing and overcoming the formation of blocs: 'The period of peaceful co-operation that we thereby gain will give East and West the opportunity to try out whether there is a way, within one generation, of leading the now separated paths to a politically and economically sound arrangement of interests which would push forward the advancement of mankind.'[27]

The overwhelming majority of political leaders outside the Soviet sphere of control had, in the meantime, accepted the Western European politics of strength. In May 1949 Kurt Schumacher declared that Social Democratic politics aimed to include *all* of Germany in the Marshall Plan and the North Atlantic Treaty. Six weeks later Konrad Adenauer expressed the same view.[28] Early in 1950, when the FDP for the first time stood

[26] Schwarz, *Vom Reich zur Bundesrepublik*, 351–4 and 371–84; for Noack see also Reiner Dohse, *Der Dritte Weg: Neutralitätsbestrebungen in Westdeutschland zwischen 1945 und 1955* (Hamburg, 1974), 47–55.

[27] Ulrich Noack, *Die Sicherung des Friedens durch Neutralisierung Deutschlands und seine ausgleichende weltwirtschaftliche Aufgabe* (Cologne, 1948), 4.

[28] SPD News Service, 27 May 1949, and an interview with *Echo der Woche*, 6 July 1949; both quoted in Schwarz, *Vom Reich zur Bundesrepublik*, 677.

up for the model of a federative alliance of Western Europe, the party justified this by pointing to its concern for the 'continued existence and further development of the West (*Abendland*)', and its hope for the 'peaceful return of the oppressed peoples and areas of Europe to the family of free peoples'.[29] The combination of fear of Soviet aggression and Germany's satisfaction at its new role as 'border and protective barrier of Western (*abendländisch*) culture and civilization' (in the words of the Bavarian Prime Minister Hans Ehard in April 1948[30]) meant that all that had been gained in terms of insight into the extent of the defeat and the price that had to be paid, which in the early postwar years had been more widespread, was for the most part lost.

Socially, it was the Federal Republic's young educated élite in particular that supported the turn towards a Western Europe tied closely into a community with the USA. The topos of 'the Christian West' (*Abendland*) helped this élite to overcome the distance it traditionally felt towards Western civilization and to find a common front between the Western nations in its emphasis on the need for religious renewal. In this view, the 'German catastrophe' was simply the ultimate consequence of a break with God, the spread of materialism, and the development of modern mass society. At the same time, the struggle against a 'Godless Bolshevism', pushed by a power under Asian influence outside the European culture group, was given priority as the Western nations' common task. Western authors such as José Ortega y Gasset, who emphasized the common European heritage, were highly acclaimed. The establishment of the *Karlspreis,* which the city of Aachen awarded for the first time in 1950 (to Richard Graf Coudenhove-Kalergi, founder of Paneuropa), gave the movement a focus.[31]

The Western European consensus remained superficial in three ways. First, the public did not understand all its implications. Secondly, even its supporters in the new political class had not

[29] FDP-Bundestagsfraktion, Principles for Foreign Affairs passed 26 Mar. 1950, *Freie Demokratische Korrespondenz*, no. 23/1950, 5f.

[30] Hans Ehard, *Die europäische Lage und der deutsche Föderalismus* (Munich, 1948), 20.

[31] See Guido Müller and Vanessa Plichta, 'Zwischen Rhein und Donau: Abendländisches Denken zwischen deutsch-französischen Verständigungsinitiativen und konservativ-katholischen Integrationsmodellen 1923–1957', *Journal of European Integration History*, 5/2 (1999), 17–47; Axel Schildt, 'Europa als visionäre Idee und gesellschaftliche Realität: Der westdeutsche Europadiskurs in den 50'er Jahren', in Wilfried Loth (ed.), *Das europäische Projekt zu Beginn des 21. Jahrhunderts* (Opladen, 2001), 99–117.

decided on the priorities should the maximum objective of Western integration *and* German unity not be achieved easily. And thirdly, it had not yet been decided under what conditions the Federal Republic could, should, or had to accept integration into the European community. Definitive decisions had been made only on the issue of 'rearmament', discussion of which had begun in 1950, and even then in many cases they were made subconsciously.[32] The European alternative to National Socialist politics of power and conquest continued to be ambiguous, even when there was no doubt that its core was now Western integration.

1953-1957: The End of Federalist Dreams and the Treaties of Rome

After the decision in favour of Western integration—at first discussed in terms of the European Defence Community and then realized when the Federal Republic joined NATO—the fragility of the European consensus soon became obvious.[33] In 1956 polls indicated that 75 per cent of the West German population would vote for the creation of a United States of Europe. When asked, however, if decisions on important questions made by a European parliament should be binding, only 25 per cent agreed; another 46 per cent of those questioned said that the decisions of a European parliament were to be valid only if the federal government agreed. For 73 per cent, almost one third more than four years earlier, German reunification was more important than a European alliance. The desire for a United States of Europe was in only seventh place, coming after the desire for reunification, disarmament, price stability, the return of the expellees, new housing, and wage increases. Of those questioned, 34 per cent, seven percentage points more than four years earlier, believed that they would see the unification of Western European states in a United States of Europe in their lifetime; 34 per cent no longer believed this.[34]

[32] See Wilfried Loth, 'Der Koreakrieg und die Staatswerdung der Bundesrepublik', in Josef Foschepoth (ed.), *Kalter Krieg und Deutsche Frage: Deutschland im Widerstreit der Mächte 1945–1952* (Göttingen, 1985), 335–61.

[33] For details see Wilfried Loth, 'Deutsche Europakonzeptionen in der Gründungsphase der EWG', in Enrico Serra (ed.), *Il rilancio dell'Europa e i trattati di Roma* (Milan, 1989), 585–602.

[34] *Jahrbuch der öffentlichen Meinungen 1957* (Allensbach, 1957), 342; *Jahrbuch der öffentlichen Meinung 1947–1955* (Allensbach, 1956), 341; *EMNID-Information* (Bielefeld, 1967), A 4.

In the first place, these figures reflected the opposition of those, such as Gustav Heinemann, who, after the war, had dreamed of a Europe of the Third Force between East and West, but shied away from seeing Western Europe as a glacis for the West, and rejected the Federal Republic's Western integration as the decisive step towards a deepening of the division of Europe and Germany.[35] This opposition was bigger than the SPD's repeated election defeats and the miserable failure of the Gesamtdeutsche Volkspartei would suggest. In February 1958, 36 per cent of West Germans considered it 'very important' to 'free ourselves from all military alliances and [to] remain neutral like Switzerland or Austria'. That was 3 per cent more than thought it necessary 'to ally closely and in all friendship with America, in order to make the Western world invincible', and 7 per cent more than the 29 per cent who wanted 'to build up a really strong military defence with the West, in order not to be overrun one day'. Of those questioned, 32 per cent, almost as many as the supporters of a close alliance with the USA, wanted to 'remember the purpose assigned to us by our history and geographical position—to be a bridge between East and West'; 30 per cent demanded more 'national self-confidence'; and 26 per cent spoke up for 'accepting the Russian suggestions' and 'seeing that Russia might be serious'.[36]

These polls also show that after the mid-1950s the public no longer saw European unification as having the urgency it had possessed in the founding years of the Federal Republic. For many, a closer alliance for defence against the Soviet danger no longer seemed important, because since the beginning of *détente* and the advocacy of peaceful coexistence, the Soviet Union no longer seemed as threatening as it had done during the late years of Stalin's dictatorship. In addition, the necessary protective function was now carried out by NATO, and the increasing importance of the nuclear system of deterrence meant that it could be provided only by the North Atlantic Pact and not by any conceivable European entity. By the same token, a closer alliance by now seemed necessary only in order to cast off the ties of occupation and to create tolerable relationships between

[35] See Dohse, *Der Dritte Weg*, 21–5, and Diether Koch, *Heinemann und die Deutschlandfrage* (Munich, 1972).

[36] *Jahrbuch 1958-1964*, 534.

the Federal Republic and its Western neighbours. This, too, had already been achieved by the Federal Republic's integration into NATO. Even as a replacement for national ties, Europe was needed less and less. The increasing distance from the catastrophe of 1945 and the new Federal Republic's growing economic and political success made a European reorientation appear increasingly unnecessary and unreal.

Finally, the public's alienation from the continuing integration of the Six also demonstrates the disillusionment on the part of the political forces that had originally supported Western integration. They had thought that the 'politics of strength' would resolve the conflict between the ultimate objectives of protection from the Soviet Union and German unity. Until the ratification of the Paris Treaties they had supported the decision in favour of the Western Union in the hope that the Western powers would reward their support by pursuing offensive policies for reunification, and that in the face of Western strength, the Soviet Union would retreat. In the event, neither hope materialized, and when international developments instead resulted in the *status quo* becoming entrenched, concern grew that by 'cutting oneself off within the Carolingian borders' (as the *Freie Demokratische Korrespondenz* put it in 1956),[37] the division of Germany would be further deepened. This development caused the Block der Heimatvertriebenen und Entrechteten (BHE), a party of expellees from the lost German territories in the East, to give up the idea of progressive Western European integration;[38] and for the FDP it led to a situation in which Robert Margulies, a strong supporter of free trade, was able to push through a unanimous 'No to Spaakistan'.[39]

The idea of responding to the crisis of the integration of the

---

[37] *Freie demokratische Korrespondenz*, no. 83, 6 Dec. 1956.

[38] See the declarations in the Bundestag debates of 5 July 1957 and 31 Jan. 1957, *Verhandlungen des Deutschen Bundestags: Stenographische Berichte (3. Wahlperiode 1953–1957)*, xxxv and xxxiv.

[39] This is a pun on the Spaak Report of spring 1956, named after the Belgian Foreign Minister and later General Secretary of NATO, Paul-Henri Spaak, which paved the way for the Treaty of Rome (1958). See Peter Jeutter, *EWG—kein Weg nach Europa: Die Haltung der Freien Demokratischen Partei zu den Römischen Verträgen 1957* (Bonn, 1985). For the official position of the parliamentary party see Robert Margulies's three declarations to the Bundestag, *Stenographische Berichte*, 21 Mar., 9 May, and 5 July 1957; 'No to Spaakistan' is found on a flyer written by Margulies for the 1957 Bundestag election campaign. See Jeutter, *EWG—kein Weg nach Europa*, 208.

Six by creating an economic union in this situation appeared to be a way of defusing some of its political explosiveness and of bypassing the obstacles in the path of its realization. However, it did not go down particularly well with those economic leaders and politicians who were directly affected by it. Seventy-five per cent of Germany's exports went to countries outside the community of the Six, and 72 per cent of its imports came from those countries. Therefore it was not only the neo-liberal economists led by Ludwig Erhard and Alfred Müller-Armack who opposed a community that would endanger the general process of liberalization with common external tariffs and dirigist interventions.[40] More pragmatic businessmen also wondered whether the advantages of liberalizing the home market would not be more than offset by the creation of common external tariffs which would clearly be higher than those at present imposed on imports in the Federal Republic. And the more obvious it became in the negotiations that France would insist on a number of measures to protect its uncompetitive industry and to secure the level of its social contributions, the more they feared that the instrument of the Common Market would distort competition at the expense of efficient German industry.[41] The agrarian law of 1955 had just established protection from cheap Dutch and French competition, and agrarian representatives now shied away from opening the market in any way.[42]

Initially it was the hard core of the supporters of Europe, interested in expanding the Europe of the Coal and Steel Community into an economic and political unity, who pushed the EEC through. From the point of view of Adenauer and his supporters, the Federal Republic's Western integration and,

[40] See Hanns-Jürgen Küsters, *Die Gründung der Europäischen Wirtschaftsgemeinschaft* (Baden-Baden, 1982), *passim*; the objections in Erhard's Bundestag speech of 21 Mar. 1957, *Stenographische Berichte*, cols. 11,342–5.

[41] Statement in *Wirtschaftsdienst*, 37 (1957), 128–30; ibid. for information on export and import rates for 1955. A similar argument can be found in numerous articles published by the Düsseldorf *Handelsblatt* (e.g., 18 Jan., 23 Jan., 18 Mar., and 25-26 Mar. 1957) and in opinion polls among economic leaders: 'Der Gemeinsame Markt: Eine Umfrage in der deutschen Wirtschaft', *Frankfurter Allgemeine Zeitung*, 16 Mar. 1957; Karl Albrecht, 'Gemeinsamer Markt und Freihandelszone im Urteil deutscher Wirtschaftskreise', *Außenwirtschaft*, 12 (1957), 154–69.

[42] See Paul Ackermann, *Der deutsche Bauernverband im politischen Kräftespiel der Bundesrepublik* (Tübingen, 1970), 52; Fritz Baade, *Die deutsche Landwirtschaft im gemeinsamen Markt* (Baden-Baden, 1958), 9. The agrarian lobby was taken up by the FDP; see Robert Margulies in the debate on ratification, *Stenographische Berichte*, col. 12,016 C.

thus, the strengthening of the West, was not sufficiently guaranteed by its integration into NATO. Stronger ties and a supranational decision-making centre were necessary; first, to make the Federal Republic permanently immune to the temptations of an East–West seesaw policy; secondly, in order to keep France from coming to an agreement with the Soviet Union at the expense of the Germans; and thirdly, in order to make more of the resources of Western Europe. For the most part, they agreed with the generally conservative and Catholic outlook that this Europe was likely to assume. Even if they had preferred a different outlook, they had no choice but to go along with it, in sober acknowledgement of the fact that if European unification did not start with the small circle of the Six, no progress would be made at all. Also, for the most part they knew that the development of such a centre of power in Europe would promote European independence *vis-à-vis* the American leadership or would at least serve as insurance in case American policies did not pay as much heed to West German interests as they had in the founding years of the Western alliance.[43]

It was of further importance that as the FDP and the BHE turned away from the Europe of the Six, German Social Democracy moved towards it. As the basic decisions had been made on the question of Western integration and since the Saar question was being resolved in line with the SPD's wishes, it was now much easier to show a basic willingness for integration into the EEC and EURATOM than it had been in the case of the European Coal and Steel Community and the EDC. Both the internationalization of the nuclear economy and the creation of a European market were planks in the Social Democratic platform, and even if what came out of the negotiations did not meet Social Democratic ideals, a positive vote demonstrated responsibility and the ability to rule. After the phase of futile fundamental opposition, this also matched the general trend towards adjusting to the realities of the Federal Republic. Remaining concerns about the deepening of the German and European division were brushed aside by the argument that the Common

---

[43] Anselm Doering-Manteuffel, 'Rheinischer Katholik im Kalten Krieg: Das christliche Europa in der Weltsicht Konrad Adenauers', in Martin Greschat and Wilfried Loth (eds.), *Die Christen und die Entstehung der Europäischen Gemeinschaft* (Stuttgart, 1994), 237–46.

Market would not be fully realized for another 12 to 15 years, and that inner-German trade remained untouched by external separation. This way the majority of the SPD faction of the Bundestag were persuaded to support the Treaty of Rome. Only a minority of 17 deputies, including Helmut Schmidt, voted against, because they feared that it would renew the isolation of Britain.[44]

The signing of the Treaty of Rome was facilitated by the fact that those who opposed it for economic reasons had no plausible alternative to offer. Even the fiercest opponents of a customs union of the Six had to agree that without the problematic Community of the Six, the desired European free trade area was not to be had. And some supporters of unrestricted free trade finally agreed that a mere free trade area was not enough to ensure the politically desired strengthening of the West and to secure social peace. Thus only in a few isolated cases did the objections to the EEC grow into firm opposition; most economic leaders, among them Ludwig Erhard, took what they considered 'economic nonsense'[45] with restrained resentment, and, after the inevitable signing of the treaties, concentrated on bringing about what they were really interested in: a European free trade area. Agrarian representatives, by contrast, accepted the EEC not as a necessary but as the lesser evil. It was easier to accept the prospect of market regulation in the area of the Six than the possible inclusion of agriculture in a common free trade area.[46]

Under these circumstances it was possible to push the Treaties of Rome through without the public—in part resigned and in part indifferent—taking much notice. Adenauer deliberately avoided provoking discussions on the treaty project, or including the parties and unions in the negotiations.[47] Thus it was possible to play down the differences in the cabinet and to avoid public discussion. However, the revival of the European idea, which

---

[44] Rudolf Hrbek, *Die SPD, Deutschland und Europa 1945–1957* (Bonn, 1972), 234, 255–62; Jürgen Bellers, *Reformpolitik und EWG-Strategie der SPD* (Munich, 1979) 79–91.

[45] Erhard, 15 Mar. 1957, to American journalists, quoted in Karl Kaiser, *EWG und Freihandelszone* (Leiden, 1965), 136.

[46] For general information see Karl-Heinz Neunreither, 'Wirtschaftsverbände im Prozeß der europäischen Integration', in Carl J. Friedrich (ed.), *Politische Dimensionen der europäischen Gemeinschaftsbildung* (Cologne, 1968), 358–445.

[47] They therefore complained bitterly; see e.g. Robert Margulies to the Bundestag on 21 Mar. 1957, Erich Ollenhauer, ibid., 31 Jan. 1957, and the annual reports of the BdI and DBV mentioned above.

had been the aim of the project's initiators, did not take place. The treaties, complicated and technical, were in some respects still open to further decisions. They gave cause neither for euphoric enthusiasm nor for dramatic fears. Consequently, they evoked little interest and were finally accepted as a step that was more or less in line with expectations for the future, without having much influence on them. In June 1957, shortly before the ratification of the treaties in the Bundestag, 73 per cent of those asked agreed 'in general' with 'the idea of the common European market'; only 9 per cent explicitly opposed it. However, when asked, only 64 per cent admitted having heard of the Common Market; and only 52 per cent were sure that the Federal Republic was a member.[48]

---

[48] Poll taken by the DIVO Institute, quoted in *Umfragen 1957: Ereignisse und Probleme des Jahres im Urteil der Bevölkerung*, ed. by the DIVO Institute (Frankfurt, 1958), 38–40. For further developments see Wilfried Loth, 'The German and European Unification', in Wolfgang J. Mommsen (ed.), *The Long Way to Europe: Historical Observations from a Contemporary View* (Chicago, 1994), 43–66.

11

An Instrumental and Atlantic Europe: Discussions about Foreign Policy and the Future of the Nation-State in Italy, 1945–1955

LEOPOLDO NUTI

Introduction

Italian historians have looked at their country's European policy in the early postwar years from very different perspectives, with a clear divide between historians of international relations and scholars who approach European integration from a federalist perspective. The latter have tended to stress the role of federalist movements and ideas, emphasizing their importance in shaping the decision-making process of Italian political leaders, and of Alcide De Gasperi in particular.[1] The former, by contrast, have come up with a somewhat revisionist reading of this interpretation, pointing to the continuing importance of more traditional factors—such as national interest and realist power-politics—at the root of the country's postwar foreign policy. Sometimes these trends assume a slightly grotesque tone: the federalists risk portraying Italian foreign policy as the translation of noble ideals into a coherent design inspired by the purest ambitions, while historians of international relations seem to be revelling in *schadenfreude* in denying the importance of these worthy aims and showing that the archival record reveals how each single step of Italy's European policy can be explained by factors *other* than a passionate attachment to the ideals of European integration. From their perspective, that basest of traditional factors, the

I would like to thank Bruna Bagnato, Renato Moro, and Piero Graglia for their comments on a previous version of the manuscript.

[1] For a new edition of this crucial document, see Altiero Spinelli and Ernesto Rossi, *Il manifesto di Ventotene* (Turin, 2001; photostatic reprint).

national interest, therefore once again becomes the cornerstone of any interpretation of Italian diplomatic activities.[2]

In this essay I will make no attempt to reconcile these diverging views, a daunting task which would probably attract much criticism from both sides. This essay, rather, simply provides a general overview of the debate on Europe and the future of the nation-state in Italy between 1945 and 1955, and outlines how that debate affected the shaping of Italian foreign policy. For this purpose, the essay is divided into two sections. The first analyses the key factors that shaped the Italian political discourse about the future of the country and its role in Europe in the aftermath of the Second World War and in the early years of the reconstruction (I–III). The second briefly surveys the European discourse in Italian politics and then looks at its impact on Italy's foreign policy, defining the nature and objectives of Italy's policy for Europe (IV–VIII).

I. *The Disaster of 1943*

Histories of contemporary Italy generally begin their narrative with the signing of the armistice between Italy and the Allied powers on 8 September 1943, as that date is assumed to be a conceptual watershed of fundamental importance to any understanding of postwar Italian politics. To some Italians, the armistice of 8 September 1943 did indeed mark a divide in the history of the country. All the institutions associated with the nation-state—the King, the government, and the army—collapsed or discredited themselves by their behaviour, with the partial exception of those army units which valiantly resisted the German reaction. It was almost as if the worst nightmare of the country's founding fathers, who throughout the Risorgimento had been keenly aware of the acute fragility of their creation, had come true: there was no longer an Italian state, and the successes of the 1860s and 1870s had been undone. Some historians have gone so far as to assert, in recent years, that the

---

[2] The gap between these interpretations has perhaps been made even wider by the fact that, as Federico Romero has pointed out, for a long time historians of contemporary Italy have neglected the importance of the European factor in the evolution of postwar Italy. See Federico Romero's *cri de cœur* and Paul Ginsborg's reply in *Passato e presente*, 14 (1997), nos. 36 and 37.

armistice marked the 'death of the fatherland', and that since then there has been a dearth of serious patriotic feeling in the national conscience.[3] Others have suggested that, on the contrary, the armistice gave birth to a new patriotic feeling, quite distinct from the old, which tried to resurrect the national dignity from the abyss into which the ineptitude of the fascist regime and the monarchy had consigned it. The anti-Nazi Resistance, therefore, came to be regarded as a symbol of the country's desperate attempt to regain a dignified position among the concert of the civilized nations.[4] Many historians, however, have questioned this interpretation by pointing out that the Resistance was never a majority movement. At best, they suggest, it was the expression of a vigorous minority, while most Italians sheltered in a large *zone grise* where the thing they really cared about was the end of the war.[5] Finally, yet other scholars have argued that the armistice did not mark the end of the idea of the fatherland, but that the experience of the war as a whole resulted in its politicization, each political force now claiming to be its only legitimate interpreter and the only legitimate inheritor of the patriotic tradition. In the aftermath of the war, the common vision was replaced by a Catholic interpretation of the fatherland, a Communist one, a fascist one, and so forth.[6]

The only clear-cut conclusion that we can draw from this debate is that the war sanctioned the final demise of any attempt to assert Italy's presence in the international arena by the use of force or by playing the game of power-politics in the exaggerated, virulent fashion of the fascist regime in its late years. The magnitude of the disaster in 1943 seemingly persuaded the next generation of Italian policymakers that never again should Italy try to emphasize military force as a key element of its foreign policy, a perception which was heightened by the dramatic impact of the war. It is sometimes not noticed that, apart from Russia and Yugoslavia, no other European country experienced such a prolonged period of fighting on its own soil—almost

---

[3] Ernesto Galli della Loggia, *La morte della patria: la crisi dell' idea di nazione tra Resistenza, antifascismo e Repubblica* (Rome, 1996).

[4] Claudio Pavone, *Una guerra civile: Saggio storico sulla moralità nella Resistenza* (Turin, 1994).

[5] Renzo De Felice, *Rosso e Nero* (Milan, 1995).

[6] Emilio Gentile, *La grande Italia: Ascesa e declino del mito della nazione nel ventesimo secolo* (Milan, 1997).

twenty months. France saw combat for one month in 1940 and three to four months in the summer of 1944, and even Germany experienced combat *on its own territory* only in the final stage of the war. If to this is added the double occupation, and the fact that each occupying power had on its side an Italian government that claimed to be the only legitimate representative of the country, then it becomes clear that the ravages caused by the terrifying, destructive power of modern armies were augmented by the cruelty of what amounted to a civil war between the fascists on one side and the partisans and the Italian regulars fighting alongside the Allies on the other. This caused a general revulsion against war and all things military that left a deep scar on Italian public opinion, a scar which is still clearly visible today.

II. *The Nature of the Postwar Political System*

The second consequence of the wartime disasters was that they left the domestic political scene in Italy very tense, in many instances clearly bordering on a pre-revolutionary situation. As often happens when existing institutions are entirely discredited by a defeat in war—and the Italian collapse was by no means, as we have seen, an ordinary defeat—a sizeable part of Italian society, mostly in the north of the country where the hardships of the civil war had been most intense, reacted to the events of 1943 by shifting strongly to the left and looking for a thorough overhaul of the political system.

The main beneficiaries were those mass political organizations that seemed most able to interpret the aspirations of the Italians for a renewal of their country. The Italian political system had been based, in the half-century that followed unification, on a parliament controlled by the classic loose political parties of the nineteenth century (with some exceptions, the most important of which was the Socialist Party) centred on a number of key personalities and their political clientele. The system had begun to falter in 1911 with the introduction of male universal suffrage. But only in 1919, after the Italian masses had been unprecedentedly politicized in the crucible of the First World War and forced the introduction of a new electoral system based on proportional representation, did it give way to a new political pattern based on competition between democratic parties. This brief experiment, however, lasted only a few years, and by 1925–6 it was interrupted by the fascist laws which transformed Italy into a dictatorship. At the end of the Second World War, however, the Italians did not choose to go back to the old pre-fascist political system. Rather, they structured the constitution of the new state in such a way as to give maximum power to mass political parties, which assumed a central role in the institutional life of the state. *La repubblica dei partiti*, as Pietro Scoppola has called it,[7] was thus born out of the rejection of both the fascist regime *and* its predecessor, whose image had been irreversibly tarnished by its failure to stop fascism and, to some extent, by the charge that its own shortcomings had actually prepared the advent of the dictatorship.

The political centre stage was therefore dominated by a number of key political formations that were to shape the course of Italian politics for the next fifty years—the Christian Democrats (DC), the Communists, and the Socialists. A fourth leading party of the anti-fascist Resistance, the *Partito d'azione*, which had played a crucial role in the Resistance and included some of the country's sharpest intellects, failed to take a central part precisely because it turned out to be incapable of reaching out to the masses. And the other minor forces that remained active—the Liberal party, the Republicans, the Neo-Fascists, and the Monarchists—retained a very limited following that grew only at certain critical junctures of the country's postwar history, and always to a very limited extent.

Clearly the three mass parties were separated by a number of crucial ideological factors. What all three had in common was, by and large, the concept that a mass party had to play a central role in a modern society, and the vision of how such a party should be structured and organized. They also shared a perception of the international role of the state that differed from that of their pre-fascist predecessors. All of them had an allegiance to a supranational, or non-national, identity, be it the Soviet Union and the ideals of the Communist international movement, or the Catholic Church and the Vatican, although within the DC there were many different ways in which this bond could

---

[7] Pietro Scoppola, *La repubblica dei partiti: Profilo storico della democrazia in Italia (1945–1990)* (Bologna, 1990).

be interpreted. These features came out clearly during the Constituent Assembly's discussions on the drafting of the new constitutional charter, and later on affected the shaping of the country's foreign policy to a remarkable extent. What this all meant was that for the first time in the history of the country large sectors of the political class did not have the strong attachment of their predecessors to the role of the nation-state as the central institution of the international system. And, perhaps also as a reaction to the *statolatria* of the fascist regime, this fostered a cultural climate which was much more prone than in the past to limit the importance of national sovereignty. This was clearly reflected in the drafting of two key articles (10 and 11) of the Republican constitution. One of them openly states that Italy is ready to acknowledge the sharing of national sovereignty under conditions of parity with other states, and that Italy supports those international organizations that promote peace and justice among nations.[8]

In evaluating the postwar Italian political system, one must add the strength of the revolutionary impulse created by two years of fierce anti-Nazi struggle in central and northern Italy. As the Allied forces slowly inched their way forward up the peninsula, the Italian partisans were fighting a bitter war against the Germans and their fascist allies which many saw as only the first stage of a broader effort to get rid of the *ancien régime*. The major beneficiary of this swing in the national mood was the Communist Party, which was the crucial force, although by no means the only one, in the Resistance. At the end of the war it emerged with a powerful structure, enhanced prestige, and the additional psychological advantage of being associated by most Italians with the power of the triumphant Red Army entering Berlin. This sense of an impending revolutionary threat, in spite of all the declarations of the *Partito Comunista Italiano* (PCI, the Italian Communist Party) leadership, did not entirely disappear for many years, but it was strongest in the immediate aftermath of the war and then in the period leading to the elections of 1948. It gave the Italian political struggle of the time dramatic overtones, and forced many members of the ruling élite to look beyond their national borders for all the help they could get,

---

[8] See for instance the reflections of Luciano Tosi, 'Introduzione', in id., *L'Italia e le organizzazioni internazionali: Diplomazia multilaterale nel novecento* (Padua, 1999), pp. xxii–xxviii.

and possibly for any international guarantee that could help them to stabilize the country. In assessing the Italian foreign policy of this period, therefore, it is necessary to remember the dual nature of almost all of its diplomatic moves, whose potential repercussions on the domestic scene were carefully examined before any decisions were taken. This is not tantamount to resurrecting the old theory of the 'primacy of domestic politics' over foreign policy. Rather, it is like saying that the old conceptual distinction between domestic and international becomes blurred, making it impossible to use Raymond Aron's conceptual category of 'pure diplomacy'.[9] For the interpretation of those years, on the other hand, it seems more profitable to resort to the concept of 'international civil war' that Aron applies to those periods when the traditional confrontation based on power politics is reinforced by an ideological (or religious) one.[10]

III. *A Brief Outline of Italian Foreign Policy*

The impact of the factors outlined in this brief survey, however, must be properly assessed in their relationship with other, more traditional, aspirations and concepts that continued to exert a large influence in the shaping of Italian foreign policy. First of all one has to keep in mind that, in spite of the political appointments of ambassadors such as Tarchiani, Brosio, Carandini, and Gallarati Scotti, Italian foreign policy was still largely conducted by career diplomats who had been active during the previous decades and who had been schooled in a very traditional concept of what the country's real interests were. While some were ready to acknowledge the mistakes of Mussolini's regime, and some were even prone to think in European, rather than purely national, terms, all conceived of their country's foreign policy in conventional fashion, and were not ready to abandon century-old principles for the sake of the uncharted waters of any new course. As Di Nolfo has stressed, the traditional diplomats were slow 'to grasp immediately the fundamental change in the

---

[9] In his own definition, this is traditional diplomacy that ignores what happens within another state's borders, and is concerned only with its external actions.
[10] Raymond Aron, *Gli ultimi anni del secolo* (Milan, 1984), 201.

international situation [and] the reality of bipolar politics'.[11] The Foreign Ministry's first objective, therefore, was to minimize the impact of the defeat and then to ensure the country's return into the international system on a level of parity with the other powers—if not with the superpowers, then at least with the other European nations. Once this goal had been achieved, it would be possible to discuss any alliance with Italy's traditional partners, or, even better, with what promised to be the dominant power in Western Europe, the USA.

Nationalist overtones, moreover, were not the exclusive hallmark of the diplomatic corps. While influenced by the internationalist implications of the ideologies of their own political parties, many politicians had a rather basic view of what Italy's foreign policy was to accomplish. Their somewhat rudimentary but clear aims were shared by a large majority of the Italian electorate: to avoid any humiliating loss of territory and any permanent form of discrimination, to retain control of the colonies, and to ensure equality of rights in the international system. Public opinion, in particular, would be swayed much more strongly by a negative decision on any of the above than by any bold and sweeping move to establish a new form of international co-operation. Besides, in the tense domestic situation of the early postwar years, any government that failed to deliver these results was likely to see its future seriously compromised. The Italian state that was eventually reassembled in the last two years of the war, therefore, was constantly striving to overcome its obvious inferiority complex by trying to reassert its status as a *normal* member of the international community, first by demanding the status of a co-belligerent against Nazi Germany, then by trying to avoid the punitive aspects of the peace treaty and demanding its revision, and, finally, by pushing for membership in all the international organizations that the West would try to set up, with the initial exception of the Western Union (WU).

The foreign policy that the new Italian republic adopted, therefore, was a mixture of old and new: the customary approach of traditional diplomats, the devastating consequences of defeat, and aspirations to transform the postwar international

---

[11] Ennio Di Nolfo, 'The Shaping of Italian Foreign Policy during the Formation of the East–West Blocs: Italy between the Superpowers', in id. (ed.), *Power in Europe?* (Berlin, 1990), iii. 486.

order all played a role in shaping it. Through a period of trial and error, a new pattern slowly emerged that some of the key historians of Italy's foreign policy have defined as 'the foreign policy of a middle power', that is, of a country that had finally discarded the grandiose ambitions of the past, and had partly embraced the new values of democracy, but that also intended to defend its national interests with a set of tools which only gradually would change from the traditional ones into more modern and sophisticated ones.[12]

Parallel to the acute perception of powerlessness and weakness was the awareness that Italy's future as a European country was not too bright, at least for a number of years. Paris and London would certainly not forget the 'stab in the back' of 1940; Germany was likely to be in a much worse situation than Italy for a long time; and Moscow was, to a large part of the elec-torate, a dangerous and unknown quantity. This left the USA providing the only leverage that Italian diplomacy could use to regain some of its previous standing. Not only did the USA not regard Italy as a traditional enemy, but the warm feelings of the Italo-American community for its old homeland were a precious asset for Italian diplomacy, since no American politicians could afford to alienate or neglect this group. The quest for a preferen-tial relationship with Washington thus actually began before the end of the war, and preceded the onset of the Cold War. The postwar fear of Soviet expansionism strengthened but did not create it. The armistice and co-belligerence, in short, had a twofold impact on postwar Italian thinking. They revealed both Italy's powerlessness and a possible solution to the country's predicament in a relationship with Washington.[13]

American support, moreover, seemed to many the only anti-dote to the growing strength of the Left. It should come as no

[12] See in particular Brunello Vigezzi, 'De Gasperi, Sforza, la diplomazia italiana e la politica di potenza dal tratato di pace al patto atlantico', in Ennio Di Nolfo, Romain H. Rainero, and Brunello Vigezzi (eds.), *L'Italia e la politica di potenza in Europa (1945–1950)* (Milan, 1988), 3–58.

[13] On US–Italian relations in the early postwar years, see Ennio Di Nolfo, 'The United States and Italian Communism: World War II to the Cold War', *Journal of Italian History*, 1/1 (1978), 74–94; id., *Vaticano e Stati Uniti: Dalle carte di Myron Taylor 1939–1952* (Milan, 1978); id., 'Stati Uniti e Italia tra la seconda guerra mondiale e il sorgere della guerra fredda', in *Atti del I congresso internazionale di storia americana* (Genoa, 1978); James E. Miller, *The United States and Italy, 1940–1950: The Politics and Diplomacy of Stabilization* (Chapel Hill, 1984); John L. Harper, *L'America e la ricostruzione dell'Italia, 1945–1948* (Bologna, 1987).

surprise, therefore, that long before the war was over, many an appeal had been issued by the Italian élites to Washington and London. Unless the Allies lent a hand, the domestic balance of power in Italy would be subverted when the war was over, and the likely winner of the coming struggle would be a strongly leftist party. Washington proved to be the key partner for the Italians. While London was too closely associated with the King and the most conservative sectors of Italian society, Roosevelt successfully gambled on the success of a more democratic, reform-orientated party to stem the tide of a Communist victory. Alcide De Gasperi's Christian Democrats partly fulfilled this role, thus ensuring half a century of co-operation with Washington, in default of anything more suitable.

The second outcome of the final stage of the war was therefore further to enmesh the USA in Italian affairs, and to strengthen its role as the key point of reference for the Italian ruling class, not only as a necessary ally to provide an indispensable counterweight to the resentful, if not downright hostile, European powers, but also as a major player in the country's domestic arena to prevent a revolutionary landslide.

IV. Primum vivere, *1945–1947*

The second part of this essay will show how these factors combined to influence the debate about Europe and the Italian government's European policy between 1945 and 1955. For the sake of clarity this section is subdivided into a number of periods, although of course the ebb and flow of ideas and policy was much more blurred than this somewhat simplistic division seems to suggest.

In the early postwar years Italian foreign policy focused on the achievement of one central goal, namely, to avoid a punitive peace treaty. Having fought the last two years of the war on the side of the Allies, and having suffered the Nazis' cruel repression of its Resistance movement, the Italian government expected mild treatment at the hands of its new partners. However, for a number of reasons which cannot be discussed here, the Paris peace conference soon took a turn for the worse.[14] As the outline

[14] On the Allied treatment of Italy at the peace conference see Ilaria Poggiolini,

of the treaty began to take shape, the future of the city of Trieste and the Italian colonies became increasingly gloomy, and the expectations of the Italian people suffered a dramatic setback. The government tried to persuade the victors that Italy had already paid 'its return ticket' to its proper place among civilized nations, and that it therefore deserved better treatment, but to no avail. Even if the final clauses of the treaty were not nearly as bad as the Italian media of the time suggested, they were certainly harsher than what the Italians had been led to expect by their government and, to a certain extent, by Allied wartime propaganda as well.

Concern about the treaty left little room for initiatives related to any strengthening of Italy's ties with other European countries. Besides, rather than aiming at specific countries, for domestic as well as international reasons the government tried to implement a policy of good relations with all the victorious powers. Thus in 1946, when the threat of a division in the Grand Alliance appeared on the horizon, Italy's solution was not to take sides with any possible future bloc, but to maintain good relations with both through a policy of 'open, loyal neutrality'.[15] To the extent that the obsessive concern about the peace treaty left any space to think about future international co-operation, therefore, it was a global, rather than a merely European, environment that the Italian political forces were interested in. When the Working Committee that prepared the Italian Constitution (*Commissione dei 75*) discussed the drafting of article 11, there is no doubt that the key institution its members had in mind was not any future European one, but the already existing United Nations Organization. It is interesting to note, therefore, that an early draft of article 11 which made specific mention of 'European unity' was discarded, and that the final text made reference only to 'limitations of national sovereignty necessary to a juridical system that might ensure peace and justice among nations. . . . Italy supports the international organization working for that goal.' The debate then continued in the main body

Diplomazia della transizione: Gli alleati e il problema del trattato di pace italiano (1945–1947) (Florence, 1990); Miller, *The United States and Italy*, 193–205.

[15] See the letter from PM De Gasperi to the Ambassador in London, N. Carandini, quoted by Guido Formigoni, *La democrazia cristiana e l'alleanza occidentale (1943–1953)* (Bologna, 1996), 67.

of the Constituent Assembly, where its president, Meuccio Ruini, declared that

the aspiration to European unity is a most Italian principle . . . Europe is for us a second fatherland. Yet, in this historical moment, it seems that the future international order can and must go beyond the borders of Europe. To limit oneself to these borders is not adequate in relation to those other continents, such as America, that want to participate in international organizations.[16]

This general internationalist attitude was mirrored by the vague ideas of the main political forces, where those who paid attention to specifically European projects were clearly a minority. If we look at the two largest contemporary political formations, the Christian Democrats and the Socialists, we find that, in spite of the presence among their ranks of a large number of stalwart Europeanists and in spite of their many statements about the need for a regeneration of Europe, there was a surprising lack of concrete initiatives as far as European co-operation was concerned. It is true that most political parties were still clearly influenced by the ideals of the anti-Nazi Resistance, in which the creation of a new democratic Europe had played a large part, and that therefore their plans and proclamations never failed to pay lip service in this direction.[17] Yet a closer look at their behaviour presents a different picture. As Guido Formigoni has written, inside the DC the older generation of politicians, from De Gasperi to Gonella, had a somewhat traditional vision of what the future of Italy's foreign policy should be, while among the new generations (from the Catholic Youth Federation to the followers of Piero Malvestiti) the Europeanist tension was somewhat stronger.[18] Thus when the moment came to attempt to shape a common policy with the other European Catholic parties, the Italian Christian Democrats took a rather cautious attitude. At the first postwar meeting of the representatives of the European Catholic parties, the Lucerne congress of February–March 1947, only the delegate of the Dutch Popular Catholic Party (KVP) insisted on the need for an active foreign policy

---

[16] Aldo Bernardini, 'Gli articoli 10 e 11 della costituzione italiana', in Pasquale Iuso and Adolfo Pepe (eds.), *La fondazione della repubblica, 1946–1996* (Pescara, 1999), 356.

[17] See e.g. the different proposals put forward as early as 1943 by the founding fathers of the DC, in *Atti e documenti della D.C., 1943–1967* (Rome, 1967), i. 7–9.

[18] Formigoni, *La democrazia cristiana*, 432.

supporting European unity. The Italian delegation, on the other hand, politely expressed its interest in the creation of an *international* organization of Christian Democratic parties.[19]

The picture was even bleaker inside the Italian Socialist Party. In theory this party should have been one of the strongest supporters of the creation of a new Europe. When it was re-created in August 1943, the political declaration that accompanied its rebirth expressly stated the need to create 'a free federation of states in Europe'.[20] The party also included some of the most outspoken Italian supporters of European unification, outstanding intellectuals such as Ignazio Silone, who, in the columns of his magazine, *Europa socialista*, openly advocated a united Europe, and passionate champions of European socialism such as Mario Zagari. One of the authors of the *Manifesto di Ventotene*, Eugenio Colorni, had been an authoritative member of the party until he was killed by the Nazis in Rome in 1944. These impeccable European credentials, however, were the hallmark of a minority inside the Party. The Partito Socialista di Unità Proletaria (PSIUP), later renamed Partito Socialista Italiano (PSI), did not have a strong tradition of concern for foreign policy and the majority of its members did not attach much importance to it. Although the Party leader, Pietro Nenni, had been Foreign Minister in one of De Gasperi's coalition governments from 1946 to 1947, the socialists did not give much space to the European dimension in formulating their own foreign policy. Only for a brief period, from the Florence Congress of April 1946 to the October of that same year, did the Party openly embrace the proposal of a 'unity of action of the European working class'. Then the internal struggle over the pact of unity with the Communist Party split the PSI into two factions, limiting its freedom of manœuvre for the next fifteen years.

It comes as no surprise, therefore, that when a first meeting of European socialist parties was convened by the British Independent Labour Party in London in February 1947—as Winfried Loth has described—no representatives of Italian

---

[19] Philippe Chenaux, 'Les Nouvelles Équipes internationales', in Sergio Pistone (ed.), *I movimenti per l'unità europea dal 1945 al 1954* (Milan, 1992), 240.

[20] Mario Zagari, 'La sinistra europea ieri e oggi', in Marta Petricioli (ed.), *La sinistra europea nel secondo dopoguerra 1943–1949* (Florence, 1981), 259.

Socialism attended.[21] Later, a number of Italian socialists participated in the development of the Socialist Movement for the United States of Europe, but they all came from the splinter group led by Saragat that broke with the rest of the party in January 1947.

If the two largest political forces had no clear views as to the future of Europe, the same, paradoxically, is true of the tiny group which represented the core of Europeanism among the Italian political formations, namely the *Movimento federalista europeo* (MFE). From the end of 1945, the founding father of Italian federalism, Altiero Spinelli, had left the leadership of the movement in total disagreement with the line advocated by its new head, Umberto Campagnolo, who promoted the idea of a federal Europe to include the Soviet Union, in sharp contrast to Spinelli's ideas.[22] Besides, as Sergio Pistone has written, the new leadership was 'unable to unify within the MFE, or to co-ordinate under its guidance, all the federalist associations and centres of action in Italy'.[23] Until Spinelli's return as head of the movement, therefore, the vague Europeanism of the MFE did little to improve the effectiveness of the Italian debate about Europe.

V. *The Age of Illusions, 1947–1948*

As the Cold War gained momentum with the Truman Doctrine and the launching of the Marshall Plan in the spring of 1947, the Italian debate about Europe began to take a more definite shape, although it would remain shrouded in thick clouds for two more years. If there are features common to the Italian foreign policy and the intellectual and political discourse of these years, they are the attempt to escape the strictest consequences of the rigidity of the new bipolar system that was developing, and insecurity about what exactly would be the rules of the game inside each of the two blocs.

To be sure, the launching of the Marshall Plan was greeted

---

[21] Wilfried Loth, 'Il movimento socialista per gli Stati Uniti d'Europa', in Pistone (ed.), *I movimenti per l'unità europea*, 253–4.

[22] Piero Graglia, 'Introduzione', in Altiero Spinelli, *Europa Terza Forza: Scritti 1947–1954* (Bologna, 2000), pp. xxi–xxxii.

[23] Sergio Pistone, 'Italian Political Parties and Pressure Groups in the Discussion on European Union', in *Documents on the History of European Integration* (Berlin, 1990), iii. 134–5.

with enthusiasm by almost all Italian political forces. The new initiative was presented as an important step towards the reorganization of Europe. Also, it was recognized that Italy being invited to participate showed that it had already recovered its legitimate place among the other European countries. Thus the Italian government was among the first to express its acceptance of the project. To insiders, however, it was clear from the start that what was going to happen was 'European reorganization, with American help and supervision'.[24] Ambassador Quaroni, one of the sharpest minds of postwar Italian diplomacy, clearly grasped what was at stake:

I have the impression . . . that in Italy so far we have been concerned more with the formal aspects of the issue than with the substantive one. We have been concerned more . . . with participating in the Conference of the Sixteen under conditions of parity, than with the real meaning of our membership. . . . It is, on the contrary, a political step of the utmost importance: the Marshall Plan is an anti-Russian coalition—whether a defensive or an offensive one, it depends on the Americans. But we entered it, and there is no way back. . . . *Mutatis mutandis*, it is tantamount to our membership in the Steel Pact.[25]

Similar judgements, but from the opposite perspective, were made by the opposition parties, the Socialists and the Communists, who, a few weeks before the launching of the Plan, had been expelled by the government in the first major break-up of the coalition of the anti-fascist parties after the end of the war. In a bold move, De Gasperi had decided to set up a new government which would, for the first time, rely on the support only of the moderate parties. The Marshall Plan thus came about at a critical juncture of the evolution of the Italian political system, and the enthusiasm with which the new Italian government jumped at this opportunity clearly shows its expectation that the American initiative would strengthen the new course upon which Italian politics had embarked. From the opposite side of the political spectrum, the Socialist leader was taken aback by what was happening and clearly expressed his dismay:

There is a break, a fracture of Europe. To state that in these conditions in Paris a great hope was born, is patently false. The Paris conference

---

[24] 'Quaroni a Sforza, 21 luglio 1947', in *Documenti diplomatici Italiani* (henceforth cited as DDI), series x, vol. vi, no. 206 (pp. 266–70).

[25] Ibid., no. 211, pp. 279–83.

was the greatest disappointment from the end of the war to the present day.[26]

Compared with its importance for the evolution of the Italian political system, for the reconstruction of the Italian economy, and for the opportunity it offered for strengthening Italy's relationship with Washington, the European dimension of the plan, important as it might have been, quickly lost most of its significance. It is true that the new Foreign Minister, Count Carlo Sforza, was a sincere advocate of close co-operation between the European powers, and that he never tired of publicly stating the importance of a regeneration of Europe. He was also, however, a staunch supporter of his country's co-operation with Washington, and there is no doubt that this was the factor that, more than anything else, persuaded him and De Gasperi that the Marshall Plan offered them a great opportunity.

In the following months a number of episodes confirmed that Washington had become the main point of reference for the new government's foreign policy, and that in its order of priorities, the construction of Europe occupied a lower place compared to the strengthening of this transatlantic bond. At the same Paris conference that was to launch the Marshall Plan, Count Sforza took one of his most daring gambles and publicly hinted at the possibility of creating a Franco-Italian economic union.[27] This was the first step towards what, after protracted negotiations and the intermediate signing of the Turin Protocol of March 1948, became the Franco-Italian Customs Union of 26 March 1949. Although it eventually failed (the treaty was never ratified), the project was at least as important for what it was trying to show Washington as for its actual content. There is ample evidence, in fact, that while the project had a positive impact in restoring a good atmosphere between Italy and France, both partners were fully aware of its importance in persuading the Americans that their countries were taking quite seriously the American invitation to the Western Europeans to co-operate more closely in the economic field.[28]

---

[26] Pietro Nenni to the Constituent Assembly, 30 July 1947, as quoted in Danilo Ardia, 'Il rifiuto della potenza: il partito socialista italiano e la politica di potenza in europa (1943–1950)', in Di Nolfo, Raniero, and Vigezzi (eds.), *L'Italia e la politica di potenza in Europa (1945–1950)*, 253–78.

[27] Bruna Bagnato, *Storia di una illusione europea: Il progetto di unione doganale italo-francese* (London, 1995), 11.

[28] See e.g. the conclusion of a telegram from Sforza to Tarchiani, in which the latter

Further confirmation of the rather cautious Italian approach towards its European partners is revealed by the Italian attitude *vis-à-vis* the Brussels Treaty of early 1948. After Bevin's speech in the House of Commons in January 1948, Italy watched the negotiations for the formation of a new military pact with a mixture of suspicion and distrust. The diplomats feared the impact that this new project would have on the network of initiatives developed in the previous months. Above all, however, they regarded the future military alliance envisaged by Bevin as a coalition of 'powerless powers' which could do very little to protect its members from a future Soviet onslaught. Some went as far as to suggest that Italy would be interested in joining only if it could negotiate some advantages in exchange—for instance, the return of some of its colonies.[29] To the diplomats' caution the government added its own fears lest the inclusion in a military alliance could jeopardize the outcome of the impending political elections of 18 April 1948. Finally, both the diplomats and the government were clearly aware that the crucial issue for Italy was the absence of the USA from the alliance. Once again, it was Quaroni who aptly summed up the dilemma: 'with all their good will, the help that the five European allies could give us was very little indeed; the risk [of joining] could be compensated only when the matter of an American guarantee had been cleared'.[30]

Thus Italy remained outside the Brussels Treaty, which made its future allies wonder about the reliability of its Western orientation. The Italian political leadership, however, did not fully grasp the extent of this perplexity. On the one hand, the DC's large victory at the polls persuaded De Gasperi and his partners that Italy had already made it clear to the other Western powers which camp it wanted to belong to. On the other hand, there were still a number of doubts about what the ultimate framework for Europe was going to be. The spring of 1948 witnessed a stunning sequence of events in the Western camp: the signing of the Turin Protocol for the Franco-Italian Customs Union (March

is invited to stress to the American government 'the positive contribution that the two governments were giving to the reorganization of the European continent'. 'Sforza a Tarchiani, 28 dicembre 1947', in DDI, series x, vol. vii, no. 48, pp. 59–60; or 'Quaroni a Sforza, 6 gennaio 1948', ibid., no. 76, pp. 98–9.

[29] A detailed reconstruction in Antonio Varsori, 'La scelta occidentale dell'Italia (1948–1949)', *Storia delle relazioni internazionali*, 1/1 (1985), 132–5.

[30] 'Quaroni a Sforza, 1 aprile 1948', in DDI, series x, vol. vii, no. 507, pp. 628–30.

1948); the signing of the Brussels Treaty and the creation of the Western Union on 14 March 1948; the creation of the Organization for European Economic Co-operation (OEEC) to administer the American aid coming in with the Marshall Plan, 16 April 1948; and the Hague Conference, 7–10 May, when all the Europeanist movements gathered to discuss the perspectives for the future of Europe. Then, in the autumn, there were the Interlaken meeting of the European Parliamentary Union which attempted to outline a European federal Constitution, and, in the following month, the birth of the European Movement. It is not hard, therefore, to see why the Italian government was wondering which was the right path to enhance European co-operation, or to understand why it decided to take a cautious attitude on the issue of a military alliance while actively promoting co-operative efforts in all the other sectors, and, in particular, in the economic one. The archival record conveys a strong impression that the diplomats and the government sincerely thought they were on the right track, and that they were sceptical about the WU because of its inherent limitations. They felt that what was developing was probably a sort of Europe *à la carte* in which each country could select the dimension of co-operation it thought most suitable to its interests, and that they could therefore freely opt to stay out of an alliance such as the WU without jeopardizing their overall collaboration with the other Western countries. They missed, therefore, the increasing attention that was being paid to the security dimension of European reconstruction by the other Western Europeans as well as by the USA. Influenced by their own perspective on the Second World War, and by their own perception of security, which was based more on the fear of domestic subversion than on the threat of an external attack, the Italians initially did not fully understand the importance of the new security discourse that was being developed elsewhere. Thus in the summer and autumn of 1948, when Count Sforza proposed using the OEEC further to promote the cause of European integration by turning that organization into a permanent body, he was flogging a dead horse. By then, attention had already shifted from the economic to the military field, in which Italy was being sidelined and marginalized.

It seems to me, therefore, that even if there was an instrumental quality in Italy's European policy in 1947 and 1948, there was also a large degree of uncertainty and, perhaps, of illusion.[31] The government felt it could wait and see how things evolved, and did not realize how badly the other Europeans wanted a US security guarantee. It believed it could paper over the cracks that were opening by promoting stronger economic co-operation, and perhaps it even thought it was strong enough to be able to negotiate its inclusion in the Western Union by asking for some compensation. Above all, the Italian government did not realize how the USA intended to manage the security relationship it was going to develop with its European allies. Throughout the summer and autumn, the government explored the possibility of reaching some sort of informal security deal with the USA. Until the April elections, Washington had warmly endorsed a military build-up in Italy, and was keen to offer the necessary help, thus partially justifying the subsequent Italian expectations. To their great surprise, however, the Italians found out in the summer of 1948 that this very convenient source of security was quickly drying up. And in December, during a trip to Washington, the Army Chief of Staff, General Marras, clearly saw that if Italy wanted to enjoy any further American military support it had to make a clear-cut commitment and join the almost completed Atlantic Pact.[32]

This misperception on the part of the government was, once again, reproduced in the political debate. There is a rather misleading piece of data which is often quoted to demonstrate the passionate attachment of most Italian politicians to the ideal of European integration, namely, the result of the poll organized by Count Coudenhove-Kalergi. Coudenhove-Kalergi put the question: 'Are you in favour of a European federation inside the UN?' to the freely elected European Parliaments, and 64.5 per cent of Italian deputies and senators replied in the affirmative, thus giving the impression of a massive force completely dedicated to the creation of a new Europe.[33] As Guido Formigoni

---

[31] On the instrumental nature of some of the Italian initiatives see, in particular, Ilaria Poggiolini, 'Europeismo degasperiano e politica estera dell'Italia: un'ipotesi interpretativa (1947–1949)', *Storia delle relazioni internazionali*, 1/1 (1985), 67–94.

[32] On this issue, see my own *L'esercito italiano nel secondo dopoguerra, 1945–1950: La sua ricostruzione e l'assistenza militare alleata* (Rome, 1989), and 'La missione Marras, 2–22 dicembre 1948', *Storia delle relazioni internazionali*, 3/2 (1987), 343–68.

[33] On the poll, see Martin Posselt, 'L'Unione Parlamentaren europea', in Pistone (ed.), *I movimenti per l'unità europea*, 231. Pistone seems to regard the results of the poll as a real indicator of support for the European cause. See Pistone, 'Italian Political Parties', 137.

has shown, however, for the DC the issue was far more complicated than this. First of all, the DC clearly made instrumental
use of its European policy in a number of circumstances, as
when it tried not to exaggerate the extent of its Western alignment during the election campaign by couching its policy in
ambivalent language which mixed nationalist and European
slogans and phrases.[34] Moreover, the party still had very vague
notions of what 'Europe' was going to be, and, even after the
elections, a large section of the party remained quite perplexed
about the 'Western' choice. The party newspaper insisted on
promoting nebulous 'third force' ideas, and at the Fiuggi meeting of the *Nouvelle Équipes Internationales*, the Italian participants
talked more about the *international* role of the Christian
Democrats than about any concrete *European* steps. Finally, even
the federalists inside the DC seemed to have fully accepted a
third force vision of Europe which was clearly different from the
military alliances then being debated. This vision was shared by
the *Azione Cattolica*, which advocated a Christian Europe not
framed by the contrasts between the blocs, and which also drew
some support from the Vatican, and, in particular, from *Civiltà
Cattolica*.[35] Thus inside the party those who had made a clear-cut
Western choice—Taviani, perhaps De Gasperi himself—were still
in a minority at the end of 1948.

   Similar attempts to escape from the increasing rigidity of the
Cold War are visible in the Socialist Party, and to some extent
even in the splinter group, the Social Democrats, led by
Giuseppe Saragat. Nenni had a clear grasp of the connection
between international and domestic choices, and wrote time and
again that the foreign policy Italy chose to pursue would affect
its domestic political system for many years to come. For him,
the only way to maintain total freedom of manœuvre at the
domestic level was to adopt a policy of neutrality, but this position was clearly hampered by the Unity of Action Pact with the
Communists, which made the call for a neutral foreign policy
sound rather hollow, if not entirely artificial.[36] The PSI still
believed that Italy could benefit from the Marshall Plan and
American aid without taking a pro-Western stance, even if many

[34] Formigoni, *La democrazia cristiana*, 175.
[35] Ibid. 229–30.
[36] Ardia, 'Il rifiuto della potenza', 271.

inside the Party were quick to realize that US assistance came with a clear price tag. After the electoral defeat in April 1948 a new leadership inside the Party tried for a few months to get rid of the constraints caused by the alliance with the PCI by promoting a line of 'absolute neutrality', which would put Italy in a truly intermediate position between East and West. But the new course was to be very short-lived, and the party wavered between a moderate and a stronger pro-Communist stance without any clear sense of direction.

Obviously this severely limited the PSI's ability to support any form of European co-operation. The Europe the PSI had in mind was still the whole continent without any ideological split. In this case also, it is hard to tell whether this line was a mere compromise in order not to exclude the pro-Soviet position, or whether it was the result of the Party leaders' failure to grasp the strength of the new international system that was developing, thus deluding themselves that the formation of the blocs could be easily reversed or that Italy could stay outside. Personally, I believe the latter is the more persuasive explanation if one remembers that even among the anti-Communist Socialists led by Giuseppe Saragat there was a marked aversion both to the shape that European co-operation was taking with the Western Union, and to a total identification with the 'Western' cause.

The only force which was quicker to develop a firmer grasp of what was happening was the tiny federalist movement, and this was because Altiero Spinelli returned to its leadership in June 1948. Spinelli had already developed a very positive impression of the Marshall Plan and of the US objectives in Europe, which in his view offered the Europeans a real opportunity to foster their integration. He described US foreign policy as a sort of 'enlightened' expansionism (he refused to define it as imperialism), which provided an opportunity to build Europe 'starting from the West'.[37] Without shedding too many tears about the splitting of the continent, Spinelli built up his notion of a federalist Europe to be developed under the American umbrella. In this sense, his use of the term 'third force' must be understood in the context of a clearly pro-Western Europe, and not as an independent power between the two blocs.[38] From this position,

[37] See e.g. his letter to Guido Piovene in Spinelli, *Europa Terza Forza*, 57–63.
[38] Graglia, 'Introduzione', pp. xxxix–xl.

Spinelli gave a much more favourable interpretation of Bevin's initiative than most other Italian observers. While critical of the old-fashioned conception of a military alliance between states, Spinelli could still declare the British initiative a fact of 'absolute importance' and a necessary step towards the creation of a new Europe.[39] Thus, to judge by their respective assessments of the international situation, the division into hard-nosed realists and starry-eyed idealists is quite misleading. The majority of Italian politicians still failed to grasp the process that was already under way, and it was only a tiny minority who had a keener understanding of what was happening.

VI. *Under the Atlantic Shadow, 1949–1950*

This phase of illusions about what Italy could achieve and about the possibilities of its foreign policy slowly came to an end sometime between the end of 1948 and the beginning of 1949, when the government decided to try to enter the Atlantic Pact. It was a decision that De Gasperi and Sforza took after having realized that all the other alternatives should be discarded, and even then, it is well known, Italy did not have an easy path to acceptance into the Pact.

The dominant characteristics of this phase are the emergence of a sombre realism about what could actually be achieved, and a remarkable degree of dissatisfaction and uneasiness about the new alliance. The period between March and May, in theory, seemed to demonstrate that the process of building a large network based on close co-operation was still continuing. In March the treaty for the Franco-Italian Customs Union was finally signed; in April there was the birth of the Atlantic Pact; on 5 May the Council of Europe was set up. As Antonio Varsori has noted, however, the initial enthusiasm with which Count Sforza greeted the birth of the Council of Europe was soon replaced by a more realistic appraisal of what the new institution could achieve, and in the following year Italy's European policy did not reveal any remarkable initiatives.[40]

---

[39] Altiero Spinelli, 'La Gran Bretagna e l'unità Europea', in id., *Europa Terza Forza*, 93–8.

[40] Antonio Varsori, 'L'Italia e l'integrazione europea dal Piano Marshall al Piano Pleven', in id. (ed.), *La politica estera italiana nel secondo dopoguerra (1943–1957)* (Milan, 1993), 347–8.

The two new European institutions, as a matter of fact, turned out to be far less effective than had been expected. The Customs Union continued its difficult non-life, with the French government hesitating between definitely dropping the project and vague promises of ratifying the treaty in the distant future. The Council of Europe also failed to meet initial expectations. In its first session in the summer of 1949 the Council's Consultative Assembly had suggested the creation of a 'European Pact', but in the following months it fell short of this bold initial gesture and refused to discuss the MFE's proposal to set up a 'Federal Pact' which the federalists had been promoting through a popular petition in several countries.[41]

Nor did the Atlantic Pact match up to the Italian government's initial expectations. The side benefits that Italy had expected from participating in the Pact did not materialize. The long search for a positive solution to the colonial problem came to a negative end with the decision of the United Nations Assembly in May 1949. The future of Trieste also remained unclear, and the military limitations of the peace treaty were not revised as Italy desired. As for the new structure of the Pact itself, Italy found itself not only excluded from the Standing Group, but also marginalized in the regional planning groups that the Alliance was setting up. At the very first session of the Atlantic Council in September 1949, Italy's attempt to be included in the Standing Group and in two regional planning groups was frustrated, and it was admitted only to the Southern European/Western Mediterranean group.[42]

This meagre balance did not help the government to make its choices any more popular. The Christian Democrats and the Social Democrats had gone along with the decision to enter the Atlantic Pact and had voted for its ratification in a tempestuous parliamentary debate, but within both parties there remained many who were sceptical about the wisdom of such an outright 'Western choice'. Once again, the European theme was used by the party leadership to smooth over some of the uneasiness among the rank-and-file, and in December 1949, De Gasperi

---

[41] Cinzia Rognoni Vercelli, 'L'Unione europea dei federalisti', in Pistone (ed.), *I movimenti per l'unità europea*, 194–5; Umberto Morelli, 'La campagna per il Patto di Unione federale Europea', ibid. 346–56.

[42] Nuti, *L'esercito italiano*, 214–19.

himself suggested that Veronese, Head of Catholic Action, support the federalist campaign for the transformation of the Council of Europe into a European Constituent Assembly.[43] The Socialist Party, on the other hand, dropped all pretence of neutrality and fought a dramatic campaign against the Atlantic Pact alongside the Communist Party, culminating in a fierce parliamentary debate. Nor did the PSI express any enthusiasm over the Council of Europe, which it strongly criticized.

It should come as no surprise, therefore, that the Italian government rather soberly accepted the French proposal to establish a new European authority for coal and steel. True, Count Sforza welcomed the initiative and went so far as personally to revise the Italian official declaration on the subject in order to ensure that it conveyed a feeling of warm support.[44] Less public reactions, however, actually expressed a moderate disappointment. As Bruna Bagnato has shown, the Schuman Plan was seen by some as a clear shift in French foreign policy in favour of a Franco-German, and away from a Franco-Italian *entente*.[45] In any case, the Italians had shown an interest in sharing the management of the resources of the Ruhr as early as 1947 and it quickly became clear that it would be in the national interest to participate in the new initiative. Soon the new plan became the cornerstone of a technocratic project to restructure and modernize the Italian steel industry, and the Italian delegation played an important role in the negotiations.[46] The new initiative, however, did not impress the Italian public, whose overall assessment of the results of the government's Western choices was couched in rather sceptical language.

VII. *Iron Times, 1951–1953*

The final twist in this brief survey of the Italian debate about Europe came about under the pressure of the outbreak of the Korean War in June 1950. The famous Italian initiative of late 1951 is often regarded as the single most important Italian contri-

---

[43] Formigoni, *La democrazia cristiana*, 334.
[44] Ibid. 218.
[45] Bagnato, *Storia di una illusione europea*, 217–19.
[46] Ruggero Ranieri, 'L'Italia e i negoziati del Piano Schuman', in Di Nolfo, Rainero, and Vigezzi (eds.), *L'Italia e la politica di potenza in Europa*, 548–72.

bution to the process of European integration, and as the climax of a long learning process. It is well known that after a positive reaction to the American proposal to rearm Germany in NATO, and an early sceptical response to the French counter-proposal to set up a European army, Italy changed its previous position. Not only did it join the Paris Conference where the French plan was being discussed, but at the end of 1951 it launched a bold new project for capping the creation of the EDC with a *political* community.

Federalist historians have seen this initiative as the result of the efforts of the MFE and of Spinelli in particular. The *Comitè de Vigilance* and the Central Committee of the MFE had instructed him to work on the European political leaders and persuade them to sponsor the promotion of a European Constituent Assembly. In the analysis of historians such as Daniella Preda and Cinzia Rognoni Vercelli, everything revolves around the fact that De Gasperi was strongly influenced by Spinelli's work throughout these months, and that his proposal of December 1951 cannot be explained otherwise. Other historians have pointed out, however, that De Gasperi had many other reasons to make his bold move. First, at the end of July the Truman administration had also changed its attitude toward the French project, and now expressed a more favourable evaluation.[47] Second, when he went to the Ottawa Atlantic Council in September of 1951 and subsequently to the USA, De Gasperi realized that his own personal standing had deteriorated after the protracted debate about Italian rearmament the previous year, and, above all, that a favourable solution to the problem of Trieste could not be expected in the near future. He also realized that the new American stand on the EDC offered him an excellent opportunity to place Italy in a highly favourable light in American eyes if he managed to put his country at the head of this new phase of European integration.[48]

[47] On the new US position, see Dean Acheson, *Present at the Creation: My Years in the State Department* (New York, 1969), 556–9; Edward Fursdon, *The European Defense Community: A History* (New York, 1980), 121–5; Jean Monnet, *Mémoires* (Paris, 1976), 521–5.

[48] On the possible connection between De Gasperi's US trip and his European initiative, see Pietro Pastorelli, 'La politica europeistica di De Gasperi', in id., *La politica estera italiana del dopoguerra* (Bologna, 1987), 374–5. On the US trip see also Egidio Ortona, *Anni d'America*, i: *1944–1951: La ricostruzione* (Bologna, 1984), 409–14; Acheson, *Present at the Creation*, 571–3; Alberto Tarchiani, *Dieci anni tra Roma e Washington* (Milan, 1955), 205–7; FRUS, 1951, iv: *Europe*, docs. 296–316. See also De Gasperi's own report to his cabinet on

The proposal to set up a political community, however, did not just reconcile De Gasperi's quest for American support with his own growing interest in the progress of European integration. It also allowed him to silence much of the domestic criticism that had been levelled against him by the Italian military and even his own party. The former insisted that a military federation with no clear political guidance made no sense, and that before building a European army it was necessary to set up a political Europe, while the latter had found it hard to accept the rearmament demanded by the USA after the outbreak of the Korean War, and still showed some uneasiness about the Atlantic alignment. A move which would shift the debate from the Atlantic military field to the European political one, therefore, would allow De Gasperi to muffle some of this criticism. And as a matter of fact, the strong objections that many cabinet ministers still raised against him disappeared after the Foreign Ministers of the Six approved the proposal that the future Assembly of the EDC be given the task of studying the creation of a political assembly to be elected under universal suffrage.[49]

To this more realist interpretation I would add that De Gasperi's decision must also be assessed against the background of his increasing pessimism that the Italian political system could, in its present state, survive the terrible strains to which its highly volatile internal situation subjected it. Democratic stability was constantly under attack from the Left and, to a certain extent, even from some *ad hoc* combinations of the Right. It was during these very years that De Gasperi conceived a reformation of the electoral law as a solution for strengthening the democratic centre. He hoped that it would give his party the stable majority it needed to resist these attacks—a measure that some historians have described as the first step towards the creation of a 'protected democracy'.[50] Guido Formigoni sees a contradiction between this project and De Gasperi's European policies, and

---

2 October 1951, in Archivio Centrale dello Stato (henceforth cited as ACS), series: Verbali delle riunioni del consiglio dei ministri (Meetings of the Council of Ministers).

[49] Pastorelli, 'La politica europeistica'; Riunioni del consiglio dei ministri (Meetings of the Council of Ministers), 16 and 22 Dec. 1951, 4 Jan. 1952, in ACS, Verbali delle riunioni del consiglio dei ministri.

[50] Sergio Chillè, 'I riflessi della guerra di Corea sulla situazione politica italiana degli anni 1950–1953: le origini della ipotesi degasperiana di democrazia protetta', *Storia Contemporanea*, 18 (1987), 895.

concludes that his increasing attention to domestic issues acted as a brake on a possible Italian ratification of the EDC. However, it seems to me that both the electoral reform and the European manœuvre might stem from De Gasperi's own apprehensions about the future of Italian democracy, and from his desire to protect it by creating some ironclad guarantees which would make it irreversible.

De Gasperi's initiative for a European political community thus to a certain extent epitomizes all the ambiguities of the European policy Italy had been following throughout the previous years. It was bold, innovative, daring, and it reflected some of the ideas and thoughts elaborated by the federalist movement, although it is not quite clear to what extent it was *directly* influenced by Spinelli. It is also true, however, that it had a number of other sources, both domestic and international, and that therefore, like all of Italy's previous European choices, it was instrumental in nature. To try to ascertain its dominant cause, or to try to establish a hierarchy of causes, seems to me a rather empty exercise. It was an important move precisely because it allowed De Gasperi to kill a large number of birds with just one stone. From this point of view, it was indeed a climax to all the initiatives of the previous years, reconciling Atlanticism and Europeanism, silencing many of the government's critics, and projecting Italy into a more favourable international position.

VIII. *Towards a New Europeanism?* *(1954–1955)*

De Gasperi's unexpected defeat at the elections of 1953 sealed the fate of his political experiment, and, depriving him of a stable majority in parliament, also marked the end of his political career. In the following year his successors, Pella and Scelba, adopted a more nationalist-orientated foreign policy. Although there were differences between them, both Prime Ministers made the ratification of the EDC a much lower priority than De Gasperi had done, and openly made it dependent on a favourable solution to the problem of Trieste. Then, when the EDC was finally killed by the *Assemblée Nationale*, the Italian government seemed to be more concerned about the implications this could have for the relationship between Washington and Europe than for the future of European integration itself.

As Antonio Varsori has written, Italy did not take a particularly active role during the following period, which ended with the transformation of the WU into the WEU. On the contrary, Italian diplomats seemed to be concerned with the renewed activism of the British Foreign Office and with the birth of a new *entente cordiale* between Paris and London, which could form the core of a new European security structure in which Italy would inevitably be marginalized.[51] Once again, events were being appraised in terms of a highly traditional conceptual framework, without any particular regard for the efforts of the previous years.

Conclusion

What kind of Europe was being discussed in Italy in the first decade after the war? The inescapable impression is that, with the exception of a minority and despite many deceptive appearances, it was more a rhetorical device than the object of a real, sincere attachment. It was both an *instrumental* and an *Atlantic* Europe more than anything else, since the ultimate aim of the Italian government throughout these years remained the maintenance of a firm relationship with the USA. From this point of view, it is only too easy to conclude that there were many factors that explain Italy's sponsorship of the European discussion, but that the vision of a Federal Europe was only one of them, and probably not the most important one.

And yet, having dismissed the enthusiasms of militant federalist historians, I also think it would be wrong not to take the change in Western Europe into account. True, by 1955 there was neither a European political community nor a defence community. There was, however, a network of relations and institutions which created a political landscape remarkably different from that of the past. The passing of time modifies the perspective with which we study those years. In the 1970s and the 1980s the opening of the archives revealed how small the influence of

[51] Antonio Varsori, 'Le speranze europee: come nacque la UEO', *Nuova Antologia*, n. 2164 (Oct.–Dec. 1987), 133–63.

European aspirations had been in the implementation of policy, and how strong the nation-state still was—the very institution that European integration was meant to make obsolete. It also showed that much of the old diplomatic tradition had survived in the postwar years, with all its prejudices and its *modus operandi*, in spite of the European rhetoric. Looking at those years after the early phase of archival research, however, one should examine not only continuity with the past, but also the innovations, limited as they might have been. The rescue of the nation-state, as Alan Milward has written, might have been the end result of the process of European co-operation of the early postwar years.[52] It was a nation-state that might still play a game of power politics, but at least with its Western European counterparts, it had chosen to play with a new set of tools. This seems to be the case with the European policy Italy developed throughout those years. Instrumental as it might have been, it forced Italian diplomats and policy-makers to learn how to play the game according to a new set of rules. And even if this did not amount to the creation of a new Federated Europe, it was in itself no mean achievement.

[52] Alan S. Milward, *The European Rescue of the Nation State* (Berkeley, 1992).

12

Integration or Co-operation? Europe and the Future of the Nation-State in France, 1945–1955

ELISABETH DU RÉAU

From 5 August 1943 in Algiers, Jean Monnet was thinking of the reconstruction of Europe after the Second World War and of France's role from a new perspective:

There will be no peace in Europe if states do not rebuild themselves on the basis of national sovereignty. . . . It is a question of . . . transforming the European epicentre of two world wars into an ensemble pacified by the creation of a 'European federation or entity', within which there would be neither victors nor losers, but rather partners who are equal before common law. It is up to France to initiate this development.[1]

He goes on, rather prematurely, to suggest a plan to reorganize the coal and steel industry on a European scale, and outlines a new type of relationship between the European states.

Initial thoughts which developed during the war (and, in the case of France, immediately following defeat) enabled the rapid identification of a number of important tendencies.[2] These plans, specifically French, or co-ordinated by European movements, often integrated older perspectives that had been developed after the First World War.[3]

How did this debate develop in France between the Second World War and the first stages of European construction? In this

---

[1] Jean Monnet Archives (Fonds Jean Monnet pour l'Europe FJME), 33 1/4, memorandum 5 Aug. 1943, Henri Rieben (ed.), *Des guerres européennes à l'union de l'Europe* (Lausanne, 1987), 272–385.

[2] Michel Dumoulin (ed.), *Plans des heures de guerre pour l'Europe d'après guerre (1940–1947)*, colloquium held in Brussels, 12–14 May 1993 (Brussels, 1995).

[3] Elisabeth du Réau, 'L'Europe du déclin à la reconstruction d'un après-guerre à l'autre', in Jean Vanwelkenheuizen (ed.), *Les Tumultes d'un siècle* (Brussels, 2000), 87–101.

essay I will concentrate on the political and security issues involved. Two questions come to mind. First, how did the debate on French security develop in the new international geopolitical context, from the flamboyant moment of the Liberation to the harsh reality of the Cold War (I–III)? Second, how far did this security debate contribute towards the recurrent theory of the place of nation-states in the construction of a European political space (IV–VI)?

I. *General de Gaulle's Initial Projects, Debated between 1948 and 1949*

French historiography has emphasized the importance of the preparatory work done by the French Committee for National Liberation. Recent, as yet unpublished research by a young scholar, Raphaële Ulrich-Pier, confirms the importance of the role played by René Massigli during this pioneering period in the elaboration of the initial plans regarding French security after the war. From Algiers onwards, the question of the security system to be envisaged was put in the following terms. For the postwar period French security was conceived as a three-stage system: a Franco-Soviet alliance basically directed against Germany, a type of Franco-British alliance, and finally an American commitment in the context of a future global collective security organization.[4]

It was in this frame of mind that the Franco-Soviet treaty of December 1944 was signed. General de Gaulle, anxious to eradicate the German threat for the future, considered it necessary to draw closer to the Soviet Union in the hope of gaining Moscow's solid support for the long-term weakening of Germany, given Anglo-American opinion, and also to avoid the resurgence of its German neighbour. Under this plan, as we know, the German Reich would be divided up, or would at most form a loose confederation.

However, de Gaulle and René Massigli (heavily involved in the disarmament negotiations during the inter-war period) also considered it necessary to control the USSR. The Rapallo syndrome, reactivated by the conclusion in 1939 of the

---

[4] Georges-Henri Soutou, 'Le Général de Gaulle et l'URSS, 1943–1945', *Revue d'histoire diplomatique*, 4 (1994).

Soviet–German Pact, still inspired caution in a generation of decision-makers marked by the failure of the inter-war security system. Thus, to counterbalance Moscow, they banked on a Franco-British alliance, American participation in the future UNO, and a Western bloc or group, or perhaps even federation.

This notion, which first surfaced in Algiers in the autumn of 1943, was made official by de Gaulle himself. He adopted it when, on 18 March 1944, he spoke before the Consultative Assembly of a Western grouping.[5] The idea was to gather around France the Benelux countries, perhaps Italy, and also the Saar, the Rhine, and the Ruhr regions, detached from the German Reich. This grouping could also count on Britain, and thus provide a counterweight to the USSR. Here we can see part of the system later envisaged during the building of the Western Union in March 1948 (but in a different political and diplomatic configuration).[6]

II. *The New Geopolitical and Strategic Situation of the Dunkirk and Brussels Treaties and the Beginnings of the Atlantic Pact, 1945–1949*

Between the San Francisco Conference, which marked the setting up of the UNO in June 1945, and the Washington Conference, which saw the birth of the Atlantic Alliance in April 1949, the world order, based on the cementing power of the Grand Alliance of the victors of the Second World War, was called into question.[7]

The use of nuclear arms by the USA to bring down its Japanese opponent as early as August 1945 marked the beginning of a new era, that of the nuclear arms race. This fact modified the strategic debate. Soon the Pentagon, informed of the scientific progress made by the Soviets, began to worry about the USSR's intentions, as it was a potential possessor of nuclear weapons.[8]

[5] Elisabeth du Réau (ed.), *Europe des Elites? Europe des peuples? La Construction de l'espace européen 1945–1960* (Paris, 1998). See also Raphaële Ulrich-Pier, 'René Massigli et l'Europe', ibid. 51–63.

[6] Elisabeth du Réau, 'Introduction', ibid. 12.

[7] John Lewis Gaddis, *We Now Know: Rethinking of Cold War History* (Oxford, 1997), and David Reynolds (ed.), *The Origins of the Cold War in Europe: International Perspectives* (New Haven, Conn., 1994).

[8] Georges-Henri Soutou, *La Guerre de cinquante ans: Les relations Est-Ouest 1943–1990* (Paris, 2001), 138–43.

In Europe, the perception of what represented a threat evolved rapidly between 1945 and 1947. At the beginning of 1947, those in charge of security in France and Britain agreed once again to conclude an alliance directed against Germany. The Dunkirk Treaty, signed in March 1947, provided for concerted action by the two partners in the event of aggression by Germany against either of the two signatories.[9] But as early as summer 1947, the two foreign ministers, France's Georges Bidault and Britain's Ernest Bevin, noted, on the occasion of the first Paris Conference on the Marshall Plan, that it was impossible to come to an agreement with their Soviet counterpart, Vyacheslav Molotov. At the end of this meeting, Hervé Alphand, one of the French negotiators, wrote:

4 July . . . seeing Molotov yesterday coming down the steps of the Quai d'Orsay, I told myself that we were entering a new era which could go on for a long time and even take a dangerous turn as regards peace. Henceforth, contrary to our desires, economic requirements were going to modify the nature of our links with Eastern Europe.[10]

In September 1947 the USSR created the Cominform and the split was now complete. On the Soviet side, the Shdanov report presented the situation as follows:

The further we go from the end of the war, the clearer become the two main directions of international postwar policy, corresponding to the division of the political forces operating on the world stage into two main camps: the anti-imperialist and democratic camp, and the imperialist camp.[11]

As long ago as January 1948, Western Europe had been drawing its own conclusions from this tragic division. On 22 January 1948 Ernest Bevin, Secretary of State at the Foreign Office, spoke in the House of Commons to denounce the threat posed by the attitude of the Soviet Union: 'the free nations of Western Europe should now draw closer together'.[12]

Material from the European archives available for consultation, plus all accessible evidence from personal documents and

---

[9] Elisabeth du Réau, 'Paris, Londres et les premières étapes de la construction européenne', in Michel Catala (ed.), *Histoires d'Europe et d'Amérique* (Nantes, 1999), 107–23.

[10] Hervé Alphand, *L'Étonnement d'être, Journal 1939–1973* (Paris, 1977), 201.

[11] See René Girault, Robert Frank, and Jacques Thobie, *La Loi des géants 1941–1964* (Paris, 1993), 71–5.

[12] British Archives Collection of the Public Record Office (PRO), London, FO, 371–64670.

memoirs, brings to light an important change of perspective which had taken place since 1945. After that date, thinking on European security took a more global approach. The guarantee aimed for was primarily of a military nature, and hence involved the deployment of military means adapted to the potential threat represented by the adversary. It was also economic in nature, as every defence policy presupposes an increase in arms power. This was a basic stake for the European partners, who had been drained of their life-blood, and were still dependent on the USA for their reconstruction. Finally, the struggle was also a political and an ideological one.

The view of the two camps presented by the Soviets was undoubtedly a caricature, but it symbolized the ideological stake in the new international competition. Had Europe become, as André Fontaine beautifully put it, 'a single bed holding two dreams'? It did in fact split along the line of the Iron Curtain; a shattered Europe emerged from the first confrontations of the Cold War.[13] Fortunately the Europeans involved were unaware that their continent would remain split for more than ten years!

The Brussels Pact, signed on 17 March 1948, constituted the first European initiative towards a common defence one year before the setting up of the Atlantic Alliance. The signatories— France, the three Benelux countries, and the United Kingdom— had a number of objectives. The British had specified their preoccupations on the eve of the signing of the Pact in the following words: 'Faced with the Communist threat, England suggests that moral and spiritual forces, determined to defend the Western system, be organised with the support of the Americans and the dominions.' From this first step an original objective emerged: a moral and spiritual organization of Europe in the face of the Communist threat that could endanger the European democratic system.[14]

The alliance between the Five was thus more than a military pact containing the classic clauses providing for the solidarity of the members in the event of aggression. The preamble to the text recalled the huge stakes in the struggle for the values of the Western world. The five partners were determined to 'assert

---

[13] André Fontaine, *Un seul lit pour deux rêves* (Paris, 1981).
[14] France, Ministry of Foreign Affairs (MAE), series 2, Europe 1944–1949; PRO (London), Prem. 8, Memoranda.

their faith in fundamental human rights and the worth of the human being as well as in the other principles proclaimed in the United Nations Charter'. The patrimony to be safeguarded was not only a territorial region whose integrity had to be ensured, but also of a spiritual, cultural, and political nature. For Ernest Bevin, Georges Bidault, and Paul-Henri Spaak, it was a matter of defending the democratic ideal. A union of democrats had been lacking before the war, and must prevail hereafter.[15]

As soon as certain institutions of the Western Union were set up in London on 17 April 1948, a crucial question arose: what means of action did the five Brussels Pact partners have? The Council of the Foreign Affairs Ministers, the decision-making body, set up a War Committee whose headquarters were to be in London, and which was to be assisted by a permanent Military Committee.

From July 1948, after the trial of strength launched by the USSR which had imposed the Berlin Blockade, the question of power equations on the European continent led to two main trains of thought. The Military Committee felt it necessary, even in peacetime, to ask for American military assistance involving a timeframe. Moreover, from this period, just three years after the Potsdam Conference which had specified the obligations imposed on a defeated Germany, the Chiefs of Staff of the Western Union were secretly examining the question of Germany's participation in the defence of Europe.[16]

This was how a considerable reversal took place. The potential enemy was no longer Germany, but Russia. It was now the Soviet threat that was worrying all Western strategists. 'The idea is evolving in public opinion', wrote Jean-Pierre Maury, 'of a Soviet steamroller capable of reaching the North Sea and the ocean in a few days, if not a few hours. To confront this danger, American support is vital.'[17]

The creation of the Atlantic Alliance in April 1949 was an initiative which overstepped the framework of Europe; it pointed to the decline of European nations. If the power rank of a state was judged by its capacity for defence, it was clear that no

---

[15] PRO, Archives of the Council of Western Europe 'Western Union', kept in London, WU, DGL, vol. 30.

[16] Ibid. Military Committee of 13 July 1948.

[17] J.-P. Maury, *La Construction européenne: La sécurité et la défense* (Paris, 1996), 122.

European nation alone could ensure its own security. Even within the multilateral system set up at Brussels, the study of power equations revealed the extreme vulnerability of Western Europe which, at the time, had neither an adequate arsenal of conventional weapons, nor nuclear weapons, and was therefore at the mercy of an aggressor from the East. However, during the negotiations prior to the signing of the Washington Treaty, France had emphasized the necessity of maintaining a European defence capability: 'We have to accept, without reservation, the principle of collaboration with the United States', wrote the National Defence Minister Paul Ramadier, 'without allowing ourselves to be diverted from what we are doing on the European side.'[18] However, the British delegates underlined the necessity of rapidly concluding an alliance which, thanks to the coupling of forces on either side of the Atlantic, could create a truly Euro-Atlantic synergy. After the signing of the Washington Treaty, which had brought ten European partners and two North American states (the USA and Canada) together on 4 April 1949, the Brussels Pact still remained, but its characteristic military structures were condemned to die. American aid, in fact, took the form of the presence on European soil of 400,000 men, stationed largely in the Federal Republic of Germany, and the setting up of numerous air and naval bases in the countries of the Atlantic Pact allies. After the Korean War, the North Atlantic Treaty Organization (NATO) was founded. From then on, the Western Union had no military structure of its own, but remained a forum for dialogue between European partners. For a time (until 1960) it maintained a presence in the cultural field, continuing its struggle, alongside the Council of Europe, for the defence of democratic values.

At the beginning of the 1950s, the centre of gravity of the defence of Europe shifted towards the West. Was NATO the only recourse in the event of a threat to the integrity of Western Europe? The question of German rearmament provided an opportunity to re-examine several strategic hypotheses, and it gave rise to an ambitious European plan, that of the European Defence Community (EDC).

---

[18] PRO, WU, DGI, vol 30. Account of the Consultative Council of the Western Union of 25–26 Oct. 1948.

III. *France, the EDC Controversy and the Creation of the Western*
European Union

After Mao Zedong's successes and the creation of the People's
Republic of China, then the first Communist victories in the Far
East, Western strategists feared 'the expansionism of Stalin's
Soviet Union'. Washington had misgivings, after the outbreak of
the Korean War in February 1950, about its ability to defend the
interests of the free world on two fronts, in the Far East and in
Western Europe.

In September 1950 Dean Acheson, US Secretary of State,
asked his French and British colleagues to accept German rearmament in order to enable West Germany to participate in the
defence of its own territory. Robert Schuman reacted promptly,
commenting coldly: 'Germany's malady dates too far back to
have been permanently cured.'[19] This comment reveals the
extent of French reservations. Schuman had been the architect
of Franco-German reconciliation when, in May 1950, he
proposed the plan which was to give rise to the European Coal
and Steel Community (ECSC, April 1951), but the question of
defence was a stake of an altogether different kind. On this point
his views were shared by some military experts, who soon
adopted a similar position on this matter. At the end of 1949 and
during the first quarter of 1950, the question of German rearmament was brought up on several occasions within the Western
Union. General Lechères, who represented France within the
Military Commission, was in favour of German rearmament,
but it had to take place 'within the framework of Western Union,
that is to say remain specifically European'.[20]

This was also the view held by General de Gaulle. Though
living in seclusion in Colombey, he nevertheless exerted an
authoritative influence. From this date onwards, the General
posed the problem of the security of Europe in these words: 'In
the end, Europe must become a confederation, a Europe based
on strong and independent states, and on an understanding
between France and Germany.' Within this confederation, he

[19] Quoted from Jacques Bariety, 'La Décision de réarmer l'Allemagne, l'échec de la
communauté européenne et les Accords de Paris du 23 octobre 1954 vus du côté
français', *Revue belge de philosophie et d'histoire*, 71 (1993), 354–63.

[20] PRO, WU, DG2, Debates of the Military Commission.

suggested, France and West Germany would have to play an important role, 'the limits of German action being clearly defined within the framework of the European Confederation'. Faced with the matter presented by Washington in autumn 1950, de Gaulle let it be understood that he was not totally against the rearmament of West Germany; nevertheless, the eventual participation of West German contingents had to be conceived of 'within an organized Europe . . . whose centre would be a strong and firm France'.[21]

The plan which René Pleven presented to the National Assembly on 24 October 1950 was entirely different. The French government did indeed put forward an alternative solution. Not in favour of the proposals for integrating the German army into the Atlantic Organization, Pleven set out the idea of creating a European Defence Community (EDC). This became the starting point of a very long debate which will not be examined here, but whose stakes and outcome will be referred to.

Contrary to the prevailing view, the debate on the EDC was not reduced to a Franco-German confrontation. Although the French had the greatest reservations, and although the National Assembly's rejection of the proposal on 30 August 1954 did indeed seal the fate of the EDC, opposition to the treaty also came from elsewhere, notably Germany and Italy.

The treaty which was signed on 27 May 1952 in Paris created a European Defence Community involving an integrated army under a single command, whose members guaranteed mutual assistance in the event of aggression. The United Kingdom was among the states to which an appeal was made. In the planned system, national units at division level would be integrated into a multinational army corps. But the integration was not to be total. Naval and land forces stationed for the defence of overseas territories were to remain under national control. The risk of a rebirth of German militarism was, in principle, avoided, since there were to be German soldiers, but no German army.

What autonomy did the Community have on strategic matters? This was the basic question that military experts were to examine. But the European army provided for by the treaty had no strategic autonomy. Article 18 of the treaty provided for

---

[21] Maurice Vaisse, 'Le Général de Gaulle et la défense de l'Europe', *Matériaux pour l'histoire de notre temps*, no. 29 (Oct.–Dec. 1992), 5–8.

European defence forces to be stationed during peacetime at the relevant Supreme Command under NATO (unless unanimously opposed by the Six).

During the debate in France, an initial objection was voiced by certain parliamentary deputies who favoured the construction of Europe. They criticized what they saw as a weakness, namely, that the integrated military forces were to remain outside the control of the national political authority, without being subjected to a true European political authority.[22] Pierre-Henri Teitgen commented: 'The army is at the service of a policy; how do we accept the bringing together of military forces without a common authority, without pooling together general policies under a common political authority?'[23] This criticism was genuine, for how could one conceive of a European defence without a political agency capable of defining the major orientation of the defence policy and ensuring the co-ordination of the foreign policy of the member states? The Commission provided for in the EDC Treaty did, in fact, have a managerial rather than a political role. This argument was defended by those in France and among the five signatories (the Benelux countries, Italy, and the FRG) in favour of the creation of a European Political Community. From spring 1952 to spring 1953, after the treaty setting up the EDC in Paris was signed by the Six on 27 May 1952, the debate moved on to the political issues, revolving around the plan for a European Political Community.[24]

In the preamble to the draft treaty setting up the European Political Community (EPC), the preoccupations with security were clearly set out. The members of the community were 'determined to replace their "secular rivalries" with a merging together of their basic interests by establishing institutions capable of giving direction to a now shared destiny'.[25]

Defence preoccupations had played a basic part in relaunching a debate initially started by those in favour of a federation, and particularly by the Italian Altiero Spinelli. The perspectives

---

[22] See Maury, *La Construction européenne*, 91–7.

[23] Pierre-Henri Teitgen, 'Les Étapes de l'idée européenne', in Conseil d'Etat, *Études et documents* (Paris, 1963), fasc. 17.

[24] Elisabeth du Réau, *L'Idée d'Europe au XXe siècle: Des mythes aux réalités* (Brussels, 1996; new edn., 2001), 216–17.

[25] 'Projet du traité portant statut de la Communauté européenne, 9 March 1953', in *Publications de la communauté*, Mar.–Apr. 1953.

opened up by the debate on the Political Community strengthened the prejudices of those who did not wish to see the
European community move towards federalism. Gaullist circles,
among the opponents of the treaty, denounced the risks engen-
dered by the adoption of the treaty setting up the EDC in even
stronger terms. The early opposition of Michel Debré is well
known: 'The more I think about it, the more I am convinced
that the construction of the Europe of the Schumans and the
Monnets is artificial, and even dangerous. We will not construct
Europe by denationalising it: it can only be constructed out of
nations.'[26]

This argument was in the same vein as certain objections
raised by the United Kingdom, when consulted in the initial
phase. By ratifying the treaty setting up the EDC, the signatory
states delegated their sovereignty in the fundamental area of
defence. By placing their troops under a common authority, they
would lose the basic instrument of their sovereignty. They would
no longer make decisions on the use of their forces, nor on their
equipment. The United Kingdom refused to be a member of the
EDC on this account. In France, several military experts, when
consulted, discouraged the move. 'The perfecting of new
weapons, particularly nuclear weapons, would become impossible, and national industry would be placed under the control of
the supranational Commission.'[27]

On 7 April 1954, a few months before the final debate on the
EDC, de Gaulle clarified his views at a press conference.
'Having delivered to the Community our soldiers and our policies, we would lose, as a state, every possibility of action.'[28] The
treaty setting up the European Defence Community had been
bitterly criticized in all the countries concerned, but in the spring
of 1954, the Federal Republic of Germany and the three Benelux
states had ratified its text. The matter had still not been decided
in Italy or in France.

In the end, Pierre Mendès France, who became Prime
Minister in June 1954, decided to place the draft of the treaty
before the National Assembly. The outcome of the debate of 30

[26] Letter to René Mayer, 20 Aug. 1952, quoted by Gérard Bossuat, *La France, l'aide américaine et la construction de l'Europe*, 2 vols. (Paris, 1992), ii. 881.

[27] This view was expressed in particular by General Juin, cf. du Réau, *L'Idée d'Europe*, 213, and Maury, *La Construction européenne*, 100–1.

[28] Quoted by Maury, *La Construction européenne*, 101.

August is well known. Refusing to discuss the heart of the matter, a majority of French deputies prevented the adoption of the text.[29] An ambitious plan, probably presented prematurely and containing, as we have seen, many weaknesses, had been thwarted. Did this failure mean that all European designs in defence matters were relinquished? Subsequent initiatives showed that this was not the case at all.

An alternative solution was proposed for consideration from September 1954. Since the EDC had run aground, why not make use of the Brussels Treaty and enlarge it to include Germany and Italy? This plan, conceived by Mendès France, was officially suggested by the British, and the headquarters of the Western Union were located in London.

During October, with the agreement of the Americans, who were consulted, a solution was reached whose conclusion was the signing of the Paris Agreements (on 23 October 1954), bringing into being the Western European Union. On the defence plane this new Europe thereafter included seven partners, the five earlier members of the Brussels Pact—the Benelux countries, France, and Britain—joined now by the Federal Republic of Germany and Italy. The Europe of seven countries was to have renewed institutions, since, in addition to the existing committees, it possessed a Consultative Assembly, and the Assembly of the Western European Union, whose headquarters were in Paris. The new version of the Brussels Pact also provided for co-operation in arms production, the Permanent Armaments Commission constituted in May 1955, and an Agency for the Control of Armaments, an institution whose task was to ensure that the clauses restricting German rearmament were adhered to.[30] Relations between the WEU and NATO were clearly defined: 'With a view to preventing the duplication of the work

---

[29] The adoption of the preliminary question prevented the text from being put to the vote. The voting pattern was as follows: 319 in favour of the motion (Communists, Gaullist, some of the Socialists, Radicals, and Independents); 264 against (the majority of the MRP, the remaining Socialists, Radicals, and Independents); 12 abstentions; 31 invalid.

[30] The Agency of Control of Armaments (ACA) had control over all weapons of the member countries, and set up a system of measures of confidence and transparency unprecedented between independent states. But its basic role was to ensure that the Federal Republic of Germany, which had committed itself, would, in fact, respect the clauses providing for the prohibition on its territory of the manufacture and the possession of atomic, bacteriological, and chemical weapons (ABL).

being done by the staff of NATO, the Council and the Agency will leave it to the appropriate NATO military authorities to give all information and all advice concerning military matters.'

Although the WEU was considered the European pillar of defence, its members did not enjoy real autonomy. Its strictly military structures were therefore destined to disappear, and for most of the Cold War NATO played the fundamental role in ensuring the defence of Western Europe. During the 1960s de Gaulle criticized the subordinate role of the European allies with regard to the USA, the only country which had nuclear weapons until the rise of Great Britain and France. Moreover, the British wanted to develop a special relationship with the USA while strengthening their own defence capacity. The Suez crisis in 1956 represented a major test for the NATO allies; it marked the decline of the European powers and prompted those in charge of French and British defence to re-examine their defence perspectives from the time of the Fourth Republic in France and under the Macmillan government in Britain.[31]

The creation of the Western European Union was based on a system of inter-governmental co-operation accepted by its members. Those who supported the reinforcement of European integration around political and security issues had just experienced a serious defeat, to which we must now turn.

IV. *British Proposals Regarding a Political Community*

Since the crime of 30 August, the death of the EDC has inspired an abundant historiography in France and beyond. However, the failure of the political community project has not been as closely analysed, even though it is even more revealing of the important differences of opinion regarding the process of European construction.[32]

The origins of the project are well known. The creation of a European political authority was first envisaged within the Council of Europe. And it was before the Council of Ministers in

[31] Rolf Ahmann, Adolf M. Birke, and Michael Howard (eds.), *The Quest for Stability: Problems of West European Security, 1918–1957* (Oxford, 1993). See esp. the essay by J. W. Young, 'Towards a New View of British Policy and European Unity 1945–1957', 435–62.

[32] Michel Dumoulin (ed.), *La Communauté européenne de défense: Leçons pour demain* (Brussels, 2000).

March 1952 that the British Foreign Secretary, Anthony Eden, proposed a plan to create links between the Council of Europe and other specialist authorities (the ECSA and the future EDC), in order to establish connections between the Six and the other member states of the Council. The Council of Europe would have an increasingly important role, and its political strength would be stepped up. Such a plan would allow the British to exert influence without entering the community. This project, largely inspired by Anthony Nutting, should, he wrote, allow Britain to play a decisive role in Europe, without obliging the British to become full members of the supranational club.[33]

The notes of the French Ambassador in London, René Massigli, preserved in his private archives, show that during this crucial period he tried to achieve a compromise between these opinions and those which were developing in several European capitals in reaction to Eden's proposals.[34] Indeed, a federalist counter-offensive was being organized. Although René Massigli emphasized the important role played by Paul-Henri Spaak, President of the Assembly of the CECA, the role of Altiero Spinelli was also essential in this debate, as recent research in the archives of the European Union of Federalists (UEF), kept in Florence, shows.[35] As the representative of the UEF, he suggested, at the time of the debate on the institutions of the European Defence Community, that the Common Assembly of the EDC should be of a constituent nature. During this debate, the Italian head of government, Alcide De Gasperi, proposed linking the military institution to political union. This was an idea which had already been debated in France, where it had been favourably received by several sections of society.[36] In September 1952, at the Assembly of the ECSC which had just been established, the federalists proposed to examine this project.

On 10 September in Luxembourg, the six Foreign Ministers met at the Communal Assembly to undertake the study foreseen

---

[33] Quoted by René Massigli, *Une comédie des erreurs, 1943–56* (Paris, 1978). Cf. Anthony Nutting, *Europe Will Not Wait* (London, 1960), 41.

[34] MAE, Massigli Papers, vol. 75.

[35] Historical Archives of the European Communities in Florence (AHCE). I am grateful for Jean-Marie Palayret's advice on this topic.

[36] Cf. MAE, Massigli's papers and Massigli, *Une comédie des erreurs*, 329. This information is challenged by Philippe Vial in his contribution to René Girault and Gérard Bossuat (eds.), *Europe brisée, Europe retrouvée, nouvelles réflexions sur l'unité européenne au XXe siècle* (Paris, 1994), 244.

by article 138 of the Treaty establishing the EDC. It was the starting point of the process which I will briefly describe next.[37]

V. *Ambitious Texts which put the Federal System into Perspective*

The Assembly of the ECSC, which had elected Paul-Henri Spaak as its President, joined the eight parliamentary members of the Consultative Assembly of the Council of Europe, thus making up the '*ad hoc* Assembly'. This Assembly created a Constitutional Commission of twenty-six members, presided over by the German Christian Democrat Heinrich von Brentano. The sum of the Commission's work was made known in March 1953, adopted by the '*ad hoc* Assembly', then discussed by the governments of the Six during the spring of 1953. A new Commission met from December 1953 to March 1954, and the minutes of the debates, kept in the Community archives, show the importance of the discussions regarding the future of European construction during these formative years.[38] To reread these debates at a time when the issue of the political demise of the European Union is resurfacing is extremely stimulating.

The principal aims of the project, which feature in the first title of the draft treaty (article 2), are political, security-related, and economic. The initial objective was defined as being 'to replace secular rivalries with a fusion of their essential interests by establishing institutions capable of orientating a shared destiny'. The second objective was security-related. The mission of the future political Community was to co-operate with other free nations, to guarantee the security of the member states against all aggression, and to ensure the co-ordination of the foreign policy of these member states. The final objective was economic and social, and proposed the promotion of economic expansion, the development of employment, and an improvement in the standard of living in the area concerned, which could be expanded to new partners.[39] These objectives were ambitious, and the general aims excluded no single sector. What

[37] Cf. du Réau, *L'Idée d'Europe*, 217–18. See also the best-seller, Pierre Gerbet, *La Construction de l'Europe* (3rd edn.; Paris, 1999), 148–51.

[38] AHCE, papers/archive Florence.

[39] AHCE, Florence. See also J. C. Masclet, 'Où en est l'Europe politique?', *Problèmes économiques et sociaux*, nos. 721–2 (11 Feb. 1994).

means did the project's founders intend to use? And what were the French reactions to these new proposals?

The general inspiration for the project was federal, but compromise solutions had enabled the desired consensus to be reached within the Constitutional Commission. If this Europe had lived to see the day, it would have been a vigorous community with far-reaching powers. The Parliament which votes laws through would have been made up of two chambers, the Chamber of the People, and the Senate of the People. This Parliament would have exerted real legislative power, reserved in the ECSC and later the EEC for the Commission and the Council of Ministers. It would have had real control over executive power, as it could have granted or refused its vote of confidence at Executive Council level. Executive power was given in two instances. According to the founders of the project, 'the executive organization must be characterized by the maintenance of the balance between the supranational and national elements'.

Several delegations, including the French, had insisted on maintaining the Council of Ministers as a tool of state sovereignty. The Executive Council debated the main issues, but the Council of Ministers of the states had to give its opinion in accordance with this, and, on all important questions, these opinions had to be unanimous. It was therefore very much a compromise text, but one which moved away from the initial domain, and seemed to many people to be closer to the federal system than to the inter-governmental model.[40]

VI. *French Reactions: The Failure of the Project*

From March 1953 onwards, René Massigli adopted an extremely firm stand against the project of the Constitutional Commission, as he confided to Georges Bidault. He described the Political Community project as a 'sprawling monster' which would lead France to lose its international autonomous position and its great-power-status privileges.[41]

Pierre-Henri Teitgen, a member of the Commission, made

[40] AHCE, papers/archive Florence.
[41] MAE, Massigli papers, vol. 76, Massigli to Bidault, 16 Mar. 1953.

known that he was perfectly aware of the need to limit the powers of the Executive Council in order to take into account the specific situation of the constituent states. Pflimlin, minister in charge of France's overseas territories, had asked the following question: 'In a European political community, would it be metropolitan France or the entire French Union that would have a place?' Pierre-Henri Teitgen's reply suggested the following interpretation: 'it was the French Republic, united and undivided, which would enter into a federation'.[42] And thus the fundamental debate, which would touch on the very notion of the federation, began.

This text had been welcomed by the majority of the federalists who, at the second Congress at The Hague between 8 and 10 October 1953, demonstrated their hopes of seeing the European Political Community project succeed, following criticism from the supporters of a Europe of States who announced its future failure.

In conclusion, I should like to quote the words of Michel Debré, an influential member of the Council of the Republic, extremely hostile to this text which, in his eyes, made the bad situation already foreseen by the EDC treaty even worse:

As regards the organization of Europe as described by the treaty, and as expanded by the complementary project for a Political Community, it implies at this point the disappearance of France . . . The federalists are the enemies of the nation-state and want to replace it with Community Europe. That is what is unacceptable.[43]

[42] Massigli, *Une comédie des erreurs*, 339.
[43] Michel Debré, *Trois républiques pour une France: Mémoires* (Paris, 1984, 1991), ii. 181.

13

Paying the Price of Victory?
Postwar Britain and the Ideas of
National Independence

N. Piers Ludlow

It has often been asserted that there is a direct causal link between the United Kingdom's wartime experience, and in particular its taste of military and political success, and its postwar reluctance to become involved in co-operative schemes, most notably of course, its 1950 and 1955 refusals to take its place among the founder members of the European Coal and Steel Community (ECSC) and the European Economic Community (EEC). In keeping with the theme of this volume, moreover, this causal connection reflects the way in which the nature and tone of the British debate about the nation-state and international co-operation were very different from its equivalents in France, Germany, or Italy.

Britain, the argument runs, did not experience defeat, and as a result lost faith neither in its capacity for independent national action, nor in the efficacy of its political institutions. This meant that it was much less prepared than were most of its Continental neighbours to participate willingly in the type of supranational experiments in integration and co-operation which were launched in postwar Europe. Its sovereignty and independence had not been tarnished; as a result, neither could readily be surrendered. Such a thesis is present in several of the standard accounts of Britain's postwar European policy and is perhaps best summed up by Monnet's pithy formula (and the inspiration for the title of this chapter) that Britain's failure to join the Six was 'the price of victory'.[1]

---

[1] For Monnet's comment, see Michael Charlton, *The Price of Victory* (London, 1983), 307; for another example of a book which makes use of this thesis, Hugo Young, *This Blessed Plot: Britain and Europe from Churchill to Blair* (London, 1998).

At first sight, there is indeed a powerful logic to this case. It is very difficult to deny that the debate about the nation-state and, in particular, the debate about federalism was different in Britain than it was on the Continent. A few smallish federalist groupings did exist in Britain, notably the Federal Union.[2] But despite the eminence of some of their members, they appear to have been able to exercise remarkably little influence over actual British policy-making in the postwar years. And their main hope of making a greater impact—a return to power of a Conservative Party which did seem to espouse a more enthusiastic Europeanist vision than the Labour government—turned out to be illusory. Winston Churchill's readiness to act as figurehead of the European Movement and the activism of his son-in-law, Duncan Sandys, in the early work of the movement, were representative neither of mainstream views within the party, nor of Churchill's policy intentions once he was reinstalled in No. 10 Downing St. [3] Arguably, indeed, the main domestic effect of the Conservatives' pro-European rhetoric was to make it still harder for the Foreign Secretary, Ernest Bevin, and the rest of the 1945–51 Labour government to adopt any stance which might be construed as a concession to Conservative pressure. Labour's suspicion of the 'reactionary' nature of pro-Europeanism was to culminate in the government's lack of representation at the 1948 The Hague Conference, the apogee of postwar federalist enthusiasm and an event that Sandys had been instrumental in organizing.

Britain's scepticism about the desirability and viability of a federal Europe, moreover, does seem at first to have some value in explaining the divergence between UK policy towards European integration and that of its neighbours. For a start the chronological match is all but perfect. The 'fatal' British decisions to allow some of its Continental counterparts to forge ahead with an integrative experiment without them were, after all, made in 1950 and 1955—in other words within the first postwar decade.[4] The painful rethink meanwhile, and the lengthy and undignified period during which the British sought to undo

---

[2] See Richard Mayne and John Pinder, *Federal Union: The Pioneers* (London, 1990).

[3] Sue Onslow, *Backbench Debate Within the Conservative Party and its Influence on British Foreign Policy, 1945–1957* (London, 1997), 223–7.

[4] For a powerful statement of the disastrous consequences of the 1950 decision, see Edmund Dell, *The Schuman Plan and the British Abdication of Leadership in Europe* (Oxford, 1995).

this 'error' and enter the European club, coincided with that post-Suez period in the late 1950s and 1960s when the UK had to rethink so many aspects of that world role which had seemed natural in 1945. The approach to Europe can therefore be seen as the logical corollary of decolonization, the dwindling of the Commonwealth as an economic and political system, and the renunciation of Britain's claims to be a truly global power perhaps best symbolized by the end of its 'East of Suez' military presence in 1967.[5] Such painful lessons did not need to be learnt to nearly the same extent elsewhere in Europe during the 1950s and 1960s, because they had already been absorbed in the aftermath of wartime defeat.

Second, the issue of victory or defeat in the Second World War does seem to match up very accurately with the degree of European commitment shown by the states of Western Europe after the war. All of the Six who did take part in the most far-reaching forms of European co-operation from 1950 onwards had experienced defeat, whether in 1940, 1943, or in 1945. By contrast, of those Western European countries which had not been defeated in the course of the Second World War—Britain naturally, but also Sweden, Switzerland, Spain, and Portugal—none were founder members of what was to become today's European Union and all, bar Spain, were to pioneer a much less far-reaching and radical experiment in the form of the European Free Trade Association (EFTA). A Western-Europe-wide pattern did seem to suggest, therefore, that there was a link between the trauma of wartime capitulation and a postwar readiness to engage in far-reaching institutional experiments involving the surrender (or pooling) of sovereignty. (There were of course two exceptions to this rule in the shape of Denmark and Norway, both of which *were* defeated in the Second World War, but nevertheless opted for EFTA rather than the ECSC or EEC. But neither was a big enough state seriously to undermine the pattern, and in both cases the rule-breaking behaviour could relatively easily be explained away with references to Denmark

[5] On the rethink see Wolfram Kaiser, *Using Europe, Abusing the Europeans: Britain and Europe, 1945–1963* (London, 1996); James Ellison, *Threatening Europe: Britain and the Creation of the EEC* (London, 2000); Jacqueline Tratt, *The Macmillan Government and Europe: A Study in the Process of Policy Change* (London, 1996); John Young, *Britain and European Unity, 1945–1999* (London, 2000), and N. Piers Ludlow, *Dealing with Britain: the Six and the First UK Application to the EEC* (Cambridge, 1997).

and Norway's traditional cultural, political, and economic ties to Sweden and/or Britain. With neither London nor Stockholm opting for the EEC, it would have been very difficult, politically and economically, for Copenhagen or Oslo to have done so.[6])

A third attraction of the 'price of victory' thesis, and something which is probably important in explaining both Monnet's original intentions and the way in which this idea has been adopted by more recent commentators such as Hugo Young, is that it has the great merit of attributing Britain's postwar 'no' to Europe in a chronologically specific fashion which does not suggest that Britain's longer-term cultural, political, or economic future lies outside of Europe. Monnet's line of argument was, therefore, a direct rebuke to his compatriot, Charles de Gaulle's claim, that Britain did not belong in Europe because it was 'insulaire et maritime', a global, trading power, historically and temperamentally unsuited for a continental European grouping.[7] It was an explanation that centred on the exceptional nature of Britain's postwar position—with the clear implication that as these aberrant circumstances changed, so Britain would inevitably return to its natural position as part of Europe. The 'price of victory' argument therefore has been and still is an attractive viewpoint for the pro-European, eager to see Britain pulling its weight in European institutions. It is perhaps no accident that one of its more recent appearances was in a speech given in London by Chris Patten, European Commissioner and a long-standing Europhile member of the Conservative Party.[8]

Too easy an acceptance of the price of victory thesis is hazardous, however. This does not reflect the dangers for historians of espousing an explanation with such manifest political overtones: so contentious does the subject of European integration remain, in Britain especially, that no historical argument about the building of Europe is likely to be wholly free of a political subtext. Rather it is connected with the historically flawed nature of the two central contentions of the 'price of victory'

[6] On Danish policy see Johnny Laursen, 'Next in Line: Denmark and the EEC Challenge', in Richard Griffiths and Stuart Ward (eds.), *Courting the Common Market: The First Attempt to Enlarge the European Community 1961–3* (London, 1996), 211–27; on Sweden see Mikael af Malmborg, 'The Neutral Left in the Cold: The Swedish Case for EEC Association', ibid. 263–84.

[7] Charles de Gaulle, *Discours et messages* (Paris, 1970), iv. 68.

[8] *The Independent*, 29 June 2001.

thesis, namely, that Britain's lack of enthusiasm about European integration and mistrust of federalism was primarily a result of Britain's divergent wartime experience and, secondly, that this absence of federalist fervour played a crucial role in explaining why British policy towards European integration was so different from that of the Six. Neither of these claims withstands detailed historical scrutiny.

The first problem is that the price of victory argument assumes that the only type of international co-operation that has mattered in the postwar world has been participation in supranational regional institutions within Western Europe. Britain's supposed inability to co-operate and its outdated attitudes towards the role of the nation-state are thus proven by the simple fact that the UK signed neither the Treaty of Paris setting up the ECSC nor the Treaties of Rome creating the EEC and Euratom. In fact, of course, this assertion overlooks the extent to which Britain was ready to co-operate politically and economically in the postwar world. Post-1945 Britain was *not* immune to the enthusiasm for co-operation and institution-building that swept the world. On the contrary, as is demonstrated by its status as an important founding member of the Bretton Woods bodies, the United Nations, the General Agreement on Tariffs and Trade (GATT), the North Atlantic Treaty Organization (NATO), the South-East Asian Treaty Organization (SEATO), the Baghdad Pact, and the Organization for Economic Co-operation and Development (OECD), the United Kingdom was highly active in this field and seemed to have absorbed as much as any other country the lessons of the 1930s about the dangers of unilateralism, whether economic or political, and the virtues of multilateral co-operation.

Furthermore, the British were not even open to the charge of being uninterested in European co-operation. They may not have joined the two most prominent European structures of the postwar era—the ECSC and the EEC—but they were high-profile members of multiple other European institutions: the Organization for European Economic Co-operation (OEEC), the Dunkirk and Brussels treaties, the Council of Europe, and later on the Western European Union (WEU) and EFTA. Ultimately, of course, none of these structures has fared as well as those of the European Communities and most have either faded or been absorbed. But a failure to back the right horse should not be mistaken for a refusal to attend the race-meeting at all. Postwar Britain did see itself as a major player in Europe, and regarded involvement in, and even leadership of, multilateral institutions as part and parcel of this position.[9]

A second, and still more telling, problem with the 'price of victory' argument is that it only really functions if one is prepared to overlook the striking similarities between Britain's behaviour after the Second World War and its attitudes and alignments before 1939. This is perhaps most visible at the level of Britain's trade links, which had been focused primarily on the Commonwealth ever since the abandonment of free trade in 1931 and the conclusion of the Ottawa Accords, establishing the system of Imperial Preference, the following year. That pattern of economic and commercial ties with the extra-European world which some, notably Alan Milward (unconsciously perhaps echoing de Gaulle!), have argued made any British move towards economic integration with the Continent impossible prior to the late 1960s or early 1970s, was not the product of the Second World War, but instead an inheritance from the interwar period.[10] Not all historians, admittedly, would want to go as far in the direction of economic determinism as Milward. Commercial alignments can be reversed, after all. But it is almost beyond dispute that a belief that imperial trade was likely to continue to be more rewarding than European trade was a significant factor in setting the negative tone of much of Britain's immediate postwar diplomacy towards plans for economic co-operation within Western Europe. It was, after all, the economic ministries, in the form of the Treasury and the Board of Trade, plus the Colonial Office speaking for the interests of Empire, which are generally credited with dampening Ernest Bevin's fleeting interest in the establishment of a European Customs Union.[11] Such views were not a postwar aberration, born out of the unique circumstances of the Second World War. Instead they reflected a viewpoint which had been steadily growing in Britain since the rise of Joseph Chamberlain in the late nine-

---

[9] The high degree of British involvement is the main thrust of John Young, *Britain, France and the Unity of Europe* (Leicester, 1984). See also Sean Greenwood, *The Alternative Alliance: Anglo-French Relations Before the Coming of NATO, 1944–1948* (Montreux, 1996).

[10] Milward's case was set out most clearly in the Alec Cairncross lecture, St Peter's College, Oxford, 30 Sept. 1996.

[11] Young, *Britain, France and the Unity of Europe*, 38 and 67.

teenth century and which had triumphed over Britain's more traditional free trade beliefs after the onset of the Great Depression.

Similarly, albeit perhaps slightly less convincingly, it can be argued that Britain's postwar obsession with the USA and with Atlantic relations—another set of beliefs often pointed to in explaining the United Kingdom's ambivalence towards European integration—developed in the inter-war period rather than in the aftermath of the Second World War. Certainly there is a degree of similarity between the way in which the 1930 Briand Plan was rejected in London partly on the grounds that it was anti-American, and Britain's postwar anxieties that schemes such as the Schuman Plan or the EDC would, despite the enthusiastic backing which they received from Washington, lead, in the medium term, to a lessening rather than an increase in transatlantic ties.[12] The British have repeatedly voiced the anxiety that too much European co-operation would lead, inevitably, to a de-coupling of the valuable link between the USA and Europe. Again, therefore, there is a degree of continuity of British European policy between the inter-war years and the first postwar decades which significantly erodes any confident belief in the 'price of victory' thesis.

And if the continuities with the inter-war period sit ill with Monnet's explanation, so, too, do the discontinuities. For even in those areas where change does appear to have occurred because of the Second World War, the movement, while possibly towards Europe, was rarely in the direction of that Europe which Monnet had in mind. Britain, in other words, did undergo a process of learning through its wartime experience comparable to that of its continental neighbours, but this educative phase initially pushed the UK still further away from tight European co-operation and not towards it. This is certainly true at a commercial level. The leaders of postwar Britain do seem to have realized that undue reliance on trade within the Commonwealth and Sterling Area would be unhealthy. They had thus absorbed the lesson that economic nationalism, protectionism, and the aggressive use of exchange rates had aggravated

---

[12] Robert Boyce, 'Britain and the Briand Plan, 1929–30', *European Studies Review*, 8/1 (1980), 17–45; for similar fears in 1950 see *Documents on British Policy Overseas*, Series II, iii. 291–6.

the international tensions of the inter-war period and had contributed to the outbreak of the Second World War. The medium-term priority of the Treasury especially thus became the reintegration of the British economy into a liberal global system, as far as both monetary and trade issues were concerned.[13] But this reaction to the circumstances of the previous decade—a case, in other words, of Britain being affected by the type of postwar reflection to which it is meant to have been immune—made Britain even less willing to conclude commercial arrangements within Europe, and keen to see the European-level monetary instruments formalized by the European Payments Union (EPU) replaced as soon as possible by a truly global set of structures.[14] The lessons of the 1930s in other words were taken as a rejection of all exclusive commercial arrangements, European as much as Imperial.

At a practical level, admittedly, the British were rarely able, in the immediate postwar years, to practise what they preached. The Treasury and the Board of Trade made all the right noises about free trade, but in practice presided over a system of tariffs and trade regulations which was deeply inequitable. A comment by a Board of Trade Official from 1955 captures this gap between liberal rhetoric and protectionist practice rather well.

Our difficulties really spring from the fact that we are trying to please everybody; to pacify the protectionists and to remain on terms with the free traders; to sign up with the multilateralists but to raise our hat respectfully to the system of Commonwealth Preference and Commonwealth Free Entry. When we meet two of our ill-assorted friends simultaneously—as we sometimes do—we rely on our agility and speed of mind and foot to extricate us from embarrassment. It is not a restful policy.[15]

But to the extent that British ministers and officials did genuinely want to solve this dilemma (and by and large most of them did), they wanted, throughout most of the 1940s and 1950s, to do so in a liberal direction, and they certainly did not want to complicate their predicament by placing an extra layer of

---

[13] The most up-to-date discussion of these issues is in Alan Milward, *The European Rescue of the Nation-State* (2nd edn.; London, 1999), 348–50.

[14] For a discussion of operation ROBOT, the plan which would have brought the EPU to a premature end, see Alec Cairncross, *The Economic Section 1939–1961: A Study in Economic Advising* (London, 1989), 302–22.

[15] Ellison, *Threatening Europe*, 23.

European regional co-operation on top of the residual Commonwealth arrangements.

Likewise Britain's strategic choices after the Second World War were not slavishly shaped by pre-1939 precedents, but rather were pushed by the lessons of the Second World War in a direction not entirely compatible with purely European arrangements. Compared to inter-war Britain, post-1945 London *had* almost unanimously rejected that conceit, so entangled with the appeasement policies of the 1930s, that, as a global power, Britain's security should be viewed in world rather than European terms. A comment towards the end of the war by Attlee summed it up well. 'We are not a semi-detached country, free if we will to turn our backs on Europe and look towards the Atlantic, but a continental power with a valuable land frontier . . . From our point of view, Norway, Denmark, Holland and France are necessary outposts of Britain . . . Their defence is necessary to our defence, and without us they cannot defend themselves.'[16] Britain, in other words, had accepted that it was a European power and as such could not remain aloof from major changes in the European balance of power. Its activism in the early stages of the Cold War is a clear illustration of this.[17]

Many in Britain had also concluded from the Second World War, however, that a military alliance with continental Europe *alone* would not be sufficient and that the security of the old world required the involvement of the new. As a result those largely political gestures postwar Britain did make in the direction of an alliance with the French, and then with the French and the Benelux countries (the Dunkirk and Brussels treaties respectively), were rarely wholeheartedly backed by a military establishment which, as John Baylis has shown, continued to believe that only US military force could hold the Russians at bay.[18] The 1949 establishment of NATO thus constituted a great triumph for British postwar diplomacy. The inter-war germs of Atlanticism mentioned above had, in other words, sprouted and blossomed in dramatic fashion in the postwar climate, and they

---

[16] Cited in Peter Ludlow, 'Britain and Northern Europe 1940-5', *Scandinavian Journal of History* (1979), 154.

[17] See Anne Deighton, *The Impossible Peace: Britain, the Division of Germany and the Origins of the Cold War* (Oxford, 1990).

[18] John Baylis, *The Diplomacy of Pragmatism: Britain and the Formation of NATO, 1942–9* (Basingstoke, 1993).

had done so in a fashion which all but totally overshadowed the much more fragile shoots of British Europeanism. Thus, throughout the initial postwar years, the British allowed their yearning for Atlanticism to impede any European choices which might otherwise have been made. And it was only in the later 1950s and 1960s, when the argument began to be made that it was Britain's abstention from Europe, rather than its participation which was harming the *special relationship*, that the previous British scepticism about European co-operation faded somewhat (never to die altogether).[19]

Finally, the price of victory argument attributes most of Britain's lack of enthusiasm about European integration to a distinctly British reluctance to cede national sovereignty and to co-operate as equals with its main European neighbours. This argument, too, is deeply flawed. For a start Britain's rejection of European integration was not solely, or even primarily, determined by a dislike of supranationality *per se*. Instead it was a much more complicated decision based on the belief, mentioned above, that other fora were better suited for British action than Europe, a strong sense that equality with France, Germany, or Italy within European institutions would constitute a demotion rather than a promotion, and a profound scepticism about the prospects of any far-reaching co-operative schemes.[20] Mistrust of federalism and the lack of a general cultural predisposition towards European co-operation, while important, were therefore far from the only factors playing in the minds of British decision-makers.

Secondly, the identification of different attitudes towards federalism as the crucial factor in determining whether or not countries signed up for European integration is a deeply old-fashioned way of explaining the European choice of any European state.[21] A vociferous federalist lobby may have helped that choice in some Continental countries. But unless we are to

[19] For the argument that Britain came to see a European application as an essential part of its strategy for preserving the special relationship see Kaiser, *Using Europe, Abusing the Europeans*, 130–5.

[20] For a synthesis of the reasons for which Britain rejected a European choice, see N. Piers Ludlow, 'An Absent Father? Does a Failure of Leadership Explain Britain's Rejection of Schuman Plan Leadership, May–June 1950', in *Les Pères d'Europe cinquante ans après* (Brussels, 2000), 175–95.

[21] The classic text linking federalism with subsequent European policies is Walter Lipgens, *A History of European Integration* (Oxford, 1982).

reject most of the historiography of European integration produced over the last fifteen years, with its emphasis on the pursuit of national interest rather than the eager surrender of sovereignty, it is extremely difficult to accept that it was the single determining factor in any major state.[22] Britain was thus far from unique in jealously guarding its sovereignty, unless and until the circumstances made it clearly advantageous to co-operate closely with neighbouring states. Britain's initial 'no' to Europe is therefore no more satisfactorily explained by those different attitudes towards sovereignty which may, or may not, have been born out of wartime experience, than are the European choices of those countries which did take part in the early European institutions.

In its purest form, therefore, the assertion that Britain did not become involved in European integration because its divergent wartime experience made it less ready for multilateral co-operation than its main European neighbours falls down in at least four respects. It underplays the extent to which Britain *did* become involved, both in multilateral co-operation generally, and European co-operation in particular. It ignores the fact that some of the ideas and beliefs underpinning Britain's abstention from the Community institutions were in fact much older than the Second World War. It overlooks the way in which Britain *did* learn a number of important lessons from the Second World War, and from its proximity to defeat, but that these conclusions were rather different from those learnt by Germany, France, Italy, or Benelux and initially led the UK further away from the ECSC, EDC, and EEC rather than towards them. And finally it overplays the importance of differing attitudes towards sovereignty as an explanatory factor of the divergent European choices of Britain, France, Germany, and Italy.

Does all this mean that Monnet and all those who have echoed him subsequently were just plain wrong, and that we should consign the price of victory thesis to the dustbin of history? Perhaps fortunately for the theme of this volume, it

---

[22] The texts which blazed this trail were Raymond Poidevin, *Robert Schuman: Homme d'état* (Paris, 1986); Franz Knipping and Josef Becker (eds.), *Power in Europe? Great Britain, France, Italy and Germany in a Postwar World* (Berlin, 1986); Ennio Di Nolfo, *Power in Europe II: Great Britain, France, Germany and Italy and the Origins of the EEC* (Berlin, 1992); Klaus Schwabe (ed.), *Die Anfänge des Schuman-Plans 1950–1* (Baden-Baden, 1988); and Milward, *The European Rescue of the Nation-State*.

would be highly unwise to do so. For there are at least three
ways in which Britain's heady experiences between 1939 and
1945 have shaped, if not altered fundamentally, the postwar
national debate about 'Europe'.

The first is the manner in which the wartime years gave an
enormous boost to what would otherwise have been dwindling
British pretensions to global status. Postwar Britain may have
been down on its luck financially, militarily, and even imperially,
but psychologically those who ruled it remained convinced that
they were world leaders and that the world required them to
regain the necessary clout to exercise this leadership. And
Europe was just too small, and too insignificant, a stage, especially the type of Europe which Monnet and others were building.[23] The very nomenclature so often used in the Foreign
Office, describing the institutions of the Six, as those of 'Little
Europe', although not unique to Britain, was nevertheless revealing. At the risk of caricature it might perhaps be said that for a
generation which had quite genuinely plotted the future of large
portions of the world at the wartime conferences of Teheran,
Yalta, and Potsdam, discussing cereal prices in Brussels with the
Germans and the Dutch was a difficult fate to accept. No single
career better encapsulates this change of fortune than that of Sir
Pierson Dixon, who as right-hand man to Anthony Eden and
Bevin had been present and influential at most of the key international conferences of the Second World War and its immediate aftermath, but who would find himself between 1961 and
1963 as the chief British negotiator at official level with the Six
during the United Kingdom's abortive attempt to enter the
European Community. Much of the discomfort which Dixon
was to feel in this last role, and the failings which he was to
display as a Community negotiator, can probably be traced to
the enormous change in status experienced by the country which
he represented.[24]

This was all the more so, to move on to the second influence
of the Second World War, because of the way in which the
conflict and the years that had led up to it had reconfirmed any

[23] Britain's view of the world and of its own place within it is beautifully captured by
the opening chapter of Alan Bullock, *Ernest Bevin: Foreign Secretary* (Oxford, 1985).

[24] For Dixon's own account of his career see Piers Dixon, *Double Diploma: The Life of Sir
Pierson Dixon, Don and Diplomat* (London, 1968); for a more up-to-date assessment see *The
New Dictionary of National Biography* (Oxford, forthcoming).

number of long-standing British prejudices about the reliability, political stability, economic worth, military strength, or moral attractiveness of most continental Europeans. None of these views were inventions of the 1930s or 1940s. All, indeed, were traceable back over the centuries.[25] But they were all recharged significantly by the experiences of the Second World War. And this only reinforced Britain's reluctance to throw in its lot with continental Europe, rather than with the Americans or the Commonwealth partners, all of whom had come out of the wartime years with their reputations and popularity largely enhanced rather than tarnished.

As one British diplomat recalled: 'we were highly sceptical about Europe. Europe was a collection of aliens and foreigners . . . who were erratic. They were unreliable. Some of them had let us down. Some of them had fought against us. All of them were seen, in 1948, to be liable to communist subversion and they were, quite frankly, not the sort of area that we—in contrast to the Commonwealth and all its glittering prospects as we saw it—wanted to tie ourselves down to.'[26]

Finally, the Second World War also reinforced that long-standing tendency of the British to cast themselves, in popular imagination and political rhetoric, as a gallant island nation fighting against a hostile and dangerous Europe. That this is the stuff of caricature rather than reality should be evident. But its increasing divorce from the truth has not prevented the postwar political debate about Europe from being studded with multiple references to the threat Continental tyranny poses to poor embattled British (or more usually English) liberty.[27]

The British have therefore to some extent paid the price of victory—at least in a psychological sense. In their more rational moments they have thus recognized, whether in 1945, 1950, 1961, 1967, 1970, 1973, 1975, or 2001 that co-operation with Europe is an option to be seriously considered and latterly at least to be accepted, albeit grudgingly. As a result any complete explanation of British European policy does need to investigate rather further than the frequently glib price-of-victory formula. But if

---

[25] The pedigree of these views is explored in N. Piers Ludlow, 'Us or Them? Europe in British Political Discourse', in Bo Strath and Mikael af Malmborg (eds.), *The Meanings of Europe* (Oxford, 2002).

[26] Cited in Charlton, *The Price of Victory*, 62.

[27] Examples of this type of claim can be found in Ludlow, 'Us or Them?'

far from a complete explanation, the shadow of the Second
World War has influenced and continues to influence the British
debate about Europe and has helped to keep alive a series of
national myths and self-images which ought, more rationally, to
have been jettisoned long ago.

PART IV

The Transatlantic Dimension

14

Reinterpreting the Marshall Plan: The Impact of the European Recovery Programme in Britain, France, Western Germany, and Italy (1947–1952)

From the start, the Marshall Plan had a dual nature. While it was an economic programme which aimed to facilitate Europe's return to the world market, it was also the centrepiece of an American political strategy which aimed to check isolationism and nationalism in the USA and abroad.

The aims of the European Recovery Programme (ERP), as the Marshall Plan was officially called, went well beyond the anti-Communist targets with which scholars have traditionally credited it. Its larger purpose can be understood if we consider together the economic and the political ambitions of its proponents. The literature has not yet provided such a synthesis mainly because during the Cold War and even after it historians were inclined to rationalize the dualistic character of American policy into one coherent motivation. First, so-called 'orthodox' scholars emphasized the Marshall Plan's geopolitical targets, then 'revisionist' historians looked at its economic 'imperialistic' dimension, and eventually 'post-revisionist' scholars turned to US and Western European internal policy. Whereas for the orthodox scholars the Marshall Plan was an act of American benevolence dictated by the Soviet menace, for the revisionist scholars it was an anti-Communist, hegemonic tool to isolate the Soviet Union and its affiliated parties in Western Europe. In the post-revisionist synthesis the Marshall Plan became instead a shrewd, perhaps even unnecessary, neo-corporatist productivity policy in response to the calls for assistance of frightened

European allies.[1] Yet it was not the predominance of domestic or international motivations, but the ambiguous relationship between its Janus faces which gave the programme its complexity and historical relevance.

Does the vantage point of the twenty-first century put us in a better position to assess the role of post-1945 American policy in Europe? This essay argues that the end of the bipolar world order allows us to go beyond the traditional approaches. After all, the Marshall Plan has been studied as an instrumental, though relevant, aspect of an imperial conflict for world hegemony. Today, the Marshall Plan deserves attention for itself, as the keystone in the protracted twentieth-century search for a transnational solution to the governance of capitalist interdependency. In this respect, the Marshall Plan should be regarded as a far-seeing hegemonic act which aimed to face all the major problems which hampered a capitalist stabilization after the Second Word War. To recapture such a dialectics requires us to abandon the traditional notion of a rational, stable, and coherent 'national interest' and to look instead for a capitalist 'transnational interest' of a global nature. It requires us to think of the postwar peace order as unfinished and to ponder over why, after Marshall's speech at Harvard on 5 June 1947, the world no longer looked the same.

Whatever one's view of it, Marshall's proposal was inextricably linked with the rupture between Eastern and Western Europe. Such a legacy influences our perspective on the past and still hampers a detached assessment of the foundations of the postwar capitalist society. The end of the bipolar world order forces us to reopen the issue and follow the historical relationship into which politics and economics were cast by the Marshall Plan.

[1] H. B. Price, *The Marshall Plan and its Meaning* (Ithaca, 1955), 3–4; Joseph M. Jones, *The Fifteen Weeks (February 21–June 5, 1947)* (New York, 1955); Ernst H. van der Beugel, *From Marshall Aid to Atlantic Partnership: European Integration as a Concern of American Foreign Policy* (Amsterdam, 1966), 18–35; Joyce and Gabriel Kolko, *The Limits of Power: The World and United States Foreign Policy 1945–1954* (New York, 1972); Charles L. Mee, Jr., *The Marshall Plan: The Launching of the Pax Americana* (New York, 1984); Charles P. Kindleberger, 'The American Origins of the Marshall Plan: A View From the State Department', in Charles S. Maier and Stanley Hoffman (eds.), *The Marshall Plan: A Retrospective* (Boulder, 1984), 7–14; Geir Lundestad, 'Empire by Invitation? The United States and Western Europe, 1945–1952', *Journal of Peace Research* (23 Sept. 1986), 263–77; Alan S. Milward, 'Was the Marshall Plan Necessary?', *Diplomatic History*, 13/2 (Spring 1989), 231–53.

For the above reasons, it would be a daunting task to summa-rize the impact of the ERP on four countries, not only because the Marshall Plan is one of the most studied and controversial topics in the postwar literature, but also because its impact did not necessarily coincide with its aims. It worked, but not always as the Americans and Europeans intended it to. Yet the detail required to demonstrate its paradoxes would be misplaced in this context. Thus this essay will more modestly discuss four channels through which the European Recovery Programme shaped the history of Western Europe for about five years: (1) the search for a transnational legitimacy for American informal hegemony; (2) the rescue of liberal capitalism; (3) the shaping of a compromise between social and liberal democracy; and (4) the search for an institutional solution to the crisis of the nation-state through international co-operation. In conclusion I will mention some questions which remain for future research to address.

I. *A Transnational Legitimacy for American Informal Hegemony*

To face a Communist threat was only a secondary aim of Marshall's proposal. Its main target was to unify the Western countries and prevent a division within the West. Of course, the Soviet Union would have taken advantage of any such split, but at the beginning of 1947 the Truman administration did not see the Soviet Union as the main threat to its security. The major fear was of American isolation. That danger was the product of increasing clashes of interest between the USA, the UK, France, and the Soviet Union on a number of issues, such as nuclear energy, control over key strategic areas, the German question, decolonization, freedom of trade and capital movement, and the increasing socialist orientation of many European and Asian countries.[2] The Truman administration feared particularly that

---

[2] Melvyn Leffler, *A Preponderance of Power: National Security, the Truman Administration and the Cold War* (Stanford, 1992); John Gimbel, *The Origins of the Marshall Plan* (Stanford, 1976); John W. Young, *France, the Cold War, and the Western Alliance 1944–1949: French Foreign Policy and Post-War Europe* (Leicester, 1990); Anne Deighton, *The Impossible Peace: Britain, the Division of Germany and the Origins of the Cold War* (New York, 1993); Marc Trachtenberg, 'Melvyn Leffler and the Origins of the Cold War', *Orbis*, 39/3 (Summer 1995), 439–55; Federico Romero, 'La guerra fredda nella recente storiografia americana: Definizioni e interpretazioni', *Italia Contemporanea*, no. 200 (Sept. 1995), 397–412.

an economic crisis—to which we shall return—might force the European powers to close themselves to the USA and to Cordell Hull's One World Design which represented the USA's true strategy for the postwar years.[3] Such a preoccupation is visible in the 1947 preparations for what was to become the European Recovery Programme. All of the four reports which explored the implications of an American aid programme to Europe hinged on the risk of American isolation and did not mention the Soviet Union as an immediate threat. Even the State–War–Navy Coordinating Committee's (SWNCC) report, the one most concerned with military aspects, suggested that

The United States has need of friends in the world today and particularly needs to take care that other nations do not pass under the influence of any potentially hostile nation. There are some countries which are at present in very close balance and it is to our advantage to strengthen their resolution to remain independent.[4]

To be sure, there were different opinions in the Truman administration about the extent to which Stalin was responsible for this situation. George F. Kennan's containment doctrine, about which so much has been written, was clearly based on the idea that the USSR was not the direct source of danger:

The Policy Planning Staff does not see communist activities as the root of the difficulties of western Europe. It believes that the present crisis results in large part from the disruptive effect of the war on the economic, political, and social structure of Europe and from a profound exhaustion of physical plant and of spiritual vigor. . . . The Planning Staff recognizes that the communists are exploiting the European crisis. . . . It considers, however, that American effort in aid to Europe should be directed not to the combatting of communism as such but to the restoration of the economic health and vigor of European society.[5]

---

[3] Lloyd C. Gardner, *Architects of Illusion* (Chicago, 1970); Jonathan E. Boe, *American Business: The Response to the Soviet Union 1933–1947* (New York, 1987); John L. Harper, *American Visions of Europe: Franklin D. Roosevelt, George F. Kennan, and Dean G. Acheson* (Cambridge, 1994), 29–39.

[4] *Foreign Relations of the United States* (FRUS) (Washington, DC, 1972), 1947, III, 'Appendix B', 217 [italics added].

[5] Policy with Respect to American Aid to Western Europe. Views of the Policy Planning Staff, 23 May 1947, FRUS, 1947, III, quotation at 224–5; see also George F. Kennan, 'The Sources of Soviet Conduct', *Foreign Affairs*, 25 (July 1947), 566–82; Leffler, *A Preponderance of Power*, 100 ff.

There was, therefore, an inherent ambiguity in the behaviour of the Truman administration throughout the life of the Marshall Plan. On the one hand it emphasized the threat posed by the Soviet Union as a geopolitical competitor; on the other, it exploited the public's fear of Communism in order to get aid from the US Congress and obtain from its European allies political concessions that would otherwise have been rejected. The role of the US Congress in this enterprise should not be neglected, for one of the major problems of the Truman administration was how to cope with a Republican majority in Congress which wanted to cut taxes and stop foreign aid.[6]

The resulting ambiguity of the American targets was clearly expressed in General Marshall's speech. In relative continuity with the exceedingly bold Truman Doctrine of February, the US Secretary of State called for a fight against totalitarianism and subtly referred to the Soviet Union as a menace to any liberal order. At the same time, he positively offered unconditional assistance, adding that 'the initiative, I think, must come from Europe'.

The speech was couched in such language as to induce Stalin to reject the offer. As we know, the Truman administration gambled on a Soviet denial, aware that only by offering aid to the USSR as well could the USA claim altruism and moral superiority. By putting Communism at the same level as fascism and National Socialism, Marshall's speech implicitly contested the moral relevance of Soviet participation in the war in the face of Stalin's ambivalence on Europe's destiny after 1945. The morality of American aid is not discussed by scholars as it seems secondary to its effects in terms of *realpolitik*, but it was crucial to two connected targets: obtaining domestic support for aid to Europe; and assessing US informal hegemony over Western Europe. Only an 'altruistic' act could provide moral legitimacy for the open economic order that the USA had been promoting since the Bretton Woods conference, but which did not find support among the European working classes and middle classes. Only altruistic, unconditional aid could justify America's unilateral offer outside the framework of the Four Powers and the UN,

---

[6] Robert Dahl, *Congress and Foreign Policy* (Westport, Conn., 1950); Richard N. Gardner, *Sterling–Dollar Diplomacy in Current Perspective: The Origins and the Prospects of our International Economic Order* (1956; new expanded edn. New York, 1980), ch. 1; Robert Pollard, *Economic Security and the Origins of the Cold War* (New York, 1985).

the only bodies which could legitimately administer international assistance. Only almost unconditional aid could have persuaded a war-weary Europe and its allies that isolating the Soviet Union and abandoning claims for high reparations from Germany could be a workable and acceptable policy. Only generous aid could persuade conservative European forces to accept US plans for an international free market which might be at the expense of domestic sovereignty. And only the feeling of a moral mission could induce the US Republicans to consent to permanent American involvement in Europe.

Soviet acceptance of Marshall's offer would probably have undermined the Truman administration's claim to moral and political hegemony over Western Europe, for the American policymakers would have been forced to declare openly that the Marshall Plan's aim was German recovery and denying reparations to the USSR. As the State Department disclosed to the Attlee cabinet in a secret meeting on the eve of Marshall's speech, in the event of an unwanted positive answer from the Soviet Union it was planning to deny aid to the USSR anyway. The US Assistant Secretary of State, William L. Clayton, who conceived the economic strategy of the Marshall Plan, told Bevin of the American intention to exclude the Soviet Union from aid on the basis of economic criteria. Had Stalin taken part, the USA would have argued that the USSR had enough coal, wheat, and gold to do without US aid, whereas the other Europeans and even Germany did not.[7] Essential commodities and gold aid were indeed what the State Department was, in the meantime, promising France and the UK at secret bilateral meetings.[8]

We can only speculate as to what would have happened in Europe if Stalin had accepted, but it can reasonably be suggested that the Soviet Union's control over its European satellites would have been challenged. In Western countries there would have

[7] Conversation of Clayton and Douglas, US Ambassador, with British Officials Regarding the Dollar Problem, London 24 June 1947, FRUS, 1947, III, 274–5; Second Meeting of Clayton and Ambassador with British Cabinet Members, London 25 June 1947, FRUS, 1947, III, 276–83.

[8] Memorandum of the British Embassy to the Department of State, Annex to memorandum of Conversation by the Secretary of State, 28 July 1947, FRUS, 1947, III, 45–8; Caffery to SecState, 1 July 1947, FRUS, 1947, III, 301–3; on US support in North Africa, see Marshall to Caffery, 10 June 1947, and Caffery to SecState, 20 June 1947, FRUS, 1947, V, 686–8, 690–8.

been much higher resistance to US aid than was the case, not only in the working class but also among Christian Democratic parties, which were crucial to the orientation of many continental European countries. Molotov's abandonment of the Paris Conference on 3 July 1947 was therefore a blunder. Even though his reasons can now be better understood in the light of recently published Soviet sources,[9] it was nevertheless a major mistake for two reasons. First, it showed the European working classes that the Soviet Union was not willing to soften its hegemonic claims in Eastern Europe in exchange for the economic recovery of the whole of Europe, and second, it made the Western cabinets' intention to isolate the Communists within their countries much easier to achieve.

As it provided political legitimacy for the USA's *de facto* abandonment of the UN project—that is, to solve controversies short of war within the Security Council—Marshall's gamble can be regarded as the founding act of the postwar *Western* world. Stalin's rapid retreat from the UN was another major blunder, for it strengthened the new Western identity. The borders of 'East' and 'West' were not yet as clear as they became after Molotov's refusal of the American offer. Although Churchill had foreseen the falling of an 'iron curtain' since February 1946, and the Soviet hold in Central Europe had become tighter during 1946–7, until the summer of 1947 there was no formal division of Europe. Czechoslovakia, Romania, and Hungary still enjoyed some autonomy from Moscow. As long as Stalin hoped for German reunification, he could not complete his design of exporting the Soviet model to those countries.[10] As a consequence of the split, Communist parties within Western Europe aligned with Moscow and made it impossible for trade unions to remain united in France and Italy. In Western European countries, postwar class conflict was inextricably linked to international politics. The international divide paralysed all socialist

---

[9] Scott D. Parrish, 'The Turn Toward Confrontation', and Mikhail Narinski, 'The Soviet Union and the Marshall Plan', both in *Cold War International History Project*, The Woodrow Wilson Center, Working Paper no. 9 (Mar. 1994); Vladimir O. Pechatonov, *The Big Three after World War II: New Documents on Soviet Thinking about Post War Relations with the United States and Great Britain*, The Woodrow Wilson Center, Working Paper no. 13 (July 1995); John L. Gaddis, *We Now Know: Rethinking Cold War History* (New York, 1997), 116–21; M. L. Leffler, 'The Cold War: What Do "We Now Know"?', *American Historical Review* (Apr. 1999), 501–24.

[10] Vojtech Mastny, *The Cold War and Soviet Insecurity: The Stalin Years* (Oxford, 1996).

programmes. From 1947, the struggle for direct democracy and social benefits, which were the major objectives of leftist parties, took a different direction: economic collectivism was to compromise with liberal individualism. Beyond its geopolitical dimension, the Marshall Plan was the founding act of a postwar Western identity and of its ideological values, to which we shall now turn.

II. *The Rescue of Liberal Capitalism*

To suggest that the Marshall Plan rescued Western capitalism implies the existence of a threat to it. Traditionally this danger has been identified with Soviet expansionism. This fear was widespread among liberal public opinion in the USA and in Western Europe. Whereas in the USA a growing anti-Communist wave mounted from 1944 to its McCarthyist peak in the early 1950s, on the Continent, as Ennio Di Nolfo and Jean-Jacques Becker have established, anti-Communism re-emerged from early 1946 as a reaction to the participation of Communist Parties in coalition cabinets.[11] To conservative opinion, Stalin's aggressive policy in Eastern and Central Europe combined with the menace of a powerful working class at home merged into a threat to national identity, individual freedom, and the market. Whether we look at *qualunquismo* in Italy, or even Gaullism in France, we find an underlying discourse rejecting party politics and leftist internationalism.

Although there is no doubt that a strong ideological and security conflict was taking place between the two superpowers, I would argue that the Soviet attitude was perceived in the Western world as extremely aggressive not so much because of its foreign policy, which, however erratic and ambivalent, was dominated by security concerns, as because of the challenges to Western capitalist values.[12] Since the end of the Cold War historians have been able to deconstruct the traditional Western

---

[11] Ennio Di Nolfo, *Vaticano e Stati Uniti 1939–1952: Dalle carte di Myron Taylor* (Milan, 1978), 66–7; Serge Bernstein and Jean Jacques Becker, *Histoire de l'anticommunisme en France (1917–1940)* (Paris, 1987).

[12] See e.g. the memoirs of Thomas A. Bailey, *The Marshall Plan Summer: An Eyewitness Report on Europe and the Russians in 1947* (Stanford, 1977), and Charles P. Kindleberger, *Marshall Plan Days* (Boston, 1987).

discourse of a 'Soviet threat' to a 'liberal' order and investigate its social and cultural basis. To be sure, there were several reasons for insecurity because war damage, material restrictions, memories of the front, the return of veterans, and the legacy of ideological conflicts in the 1920s and 1930s, etc. made the future uncertain. And there are still many open questions about their effect on politics. Apart from East and West Germany, we have almost ignored the repercussions of family and international dislocations on domestic policy.[13] The social history of the post-war years in Europe is yet to be written. However, politically it can be said that, overall, the legitimacy of liberal capitalism had been shaken by the combination of the 1929 crisis and the war. From 1945, a socialist wave washed over Europe and also touched the former colonies. The old world of the sovereign European nation-states was definitely disappearing and with it the foundations of European liberalism. A new society was knocking at the door. As proof of that 'great transformation', even the victory against the Axis was not enough to keep Churchill in power against British Labour's promise of a new social solidarity. The Beveridge Plan promised not only more social services but also full employment and the liberation of man from want. Labour's 1945 electoral platform expressed the search for a 'New Jerusalem': 'The nation wants food, work and homes. It wants more than that—it wants good food in plenty, useful work for all, and comfortable, labour-saving homes that take full advantage of the resources of modern science and productive industry.'[14]

How could these optimistic targets be achieved without turning capitalist society upside-down? In Scandinavian countries and in Britain, the pillar of social democratic programmes in 1945–6 was the right to work. Although social provisions for women and sickness were relevant in electoral campaigning and came into force immediately, European socialists advocated a transformation of capitalism and the inclusion of social rights

---

[13] Norman Naimark, *A History of the Soviet Zone of Occupation, 1945–1949* (Cambridge, Mass., 1995); Klaus Dietmar Henke, *Die amerikanische Besetzung Deutschlands* (Munich, 1995); Axel Schildt and Arnold Sywottek (eds.), *Modernisierung im Wiederaufbau: Die westdeutsche Gesellschaft der 50er Jahre* (Bonn, 1993).

[14] Labour Party, *Let's Face the Future: A Declaration of Labour Policy for the Consideration of the Nation* (1945), here cited from Gianni Silei, *Welfare State e socialdemocrazia: Cultura, programmi e realizzazioni in Europa occidentale dal 1945 ad oggi* (Manduria, 2000), 57.

into the workplace rather than a modern, universalist welfare state. This was social democracy in the literal sense. The programmes of the French and Italian resistance movements were critical of liberal individualism and orientated toward state control of the economy. Even the German Christian Democrats advocated nationalizations and new duties of the state towards the citizen in their *Ahlener Programm* of 1946. These promises were later absorbed into the new democratic constitutions of France, Italy, and West Germany, where private property was no longer an untouchable right and was burdened with unprecedented social duties. Nationalizations played an even larger part than the welfare state in the programmes of the British Labour Party.

After all, the political claims which came together with the post-1945 membership boom in left-wing parties and trade unions reflected the outcome of total war. Fascism had destroyed the basis for liberalism on the Continent, whereas market failures had undermined it in the UK and the USA. A renewed postwar democracy was called to perform 'better than National Socialism'.[15] After two world conflicts in thirty years, national security was to include recognition of the legitimate interests of all the people upon which the UN was to be built. This meant a search for a just peace, full employment, higher living standards, and better education for all those who had contributed to the war victory. In other words, new citizenship rights had arisen from the war, the Atlantic Charter and Roosevelt's four liberties of 1941. Yet the Great Powers could not keep their political implications under control.

As one commentator wrote: 'The 1945 leap forward is the counterpart of the sweep to the left throughout Europe, following victory over fascism . . . the tremendous role of the Soviet Union . . . and the formation of new democratic Governments with Communist representation in the majority of European countries.'[16] By 1945–6, the political struggle for a new social order had progressed far in Europe. Nationalizations in Britain, France, and the Scandinavian countries promised a new

[15] Franz Neumann, *Behemoth: The Structure and Practice of National Socialism 1933–1944* (Toronto, 1942; 2nd edn., 1944), 475–6.
[16] *Labour Monthly* (Aug. 1945), quoted by D. N. Pritt, *The Labour Government 1945–51* (London, 1963), 29; see also Chris Wrigley, 'Trade Unions, the Government and the Economy', in Terry Gourvish and Alan O'Day (eds.), *Britain since 1945* (London, 1991), 59–88.

economic order. In former fascist countries the controversy over a new economic order even contained a Communist option. Thus coalition cabinets simply put off big social reforms until a more homogenous bloc emerged. Economic recovery, although relatively fast, was not fast enough to provide the resources to resolve power conflicts about a new society. In the absence of economic resources for social concessions, the balance of power could definitely shift against capitalism. Thus the Marshall Plan intervened to stop an unwanted expansion of state intervention that might have choked the very idea of the free market.

We know that the launch of the Marshall Plan dramatically altered the balance of forces on the Continent. Yet there is still disagreement as to why. Can we agree with Alan Milward that the ERP did not really matter in European recovery, and that it was only instrumental to national recovery policies? Did it have only a propaganda impact? Was it the availability of bread, butter, and bacon that made it into a myth because this made such an impression on people living in austerity, if not outright poverty? Of course, the passage in France from a bread ration of less than 200 grams per day in 1947 to the abolition of rationing about two years later had psychological implications (even though it was not attributable only to US aid). Did coal and grain aid shipped under the Economic Co-operation Administration's (ECA) emblem decisively change political attitudes and reduce class conflict, or did the impact of US aid lie elsewhere?

The answer is that although most European people saw Marshall aid as providing the essentials for life, US assistance saved Europe from financial collapse. The Marshall Plan—or, to be more precise, the several overlapping American aid programmes that were put into place in 1947 and 1948, before and in parallel with the ERP—averted a dramatic monetary crisis. As Abelshauser and Milward have shown, Western Europe did not experience a production crisis because industrial indexes were growing too fast even in 1947. There was, instead, a major *monetary crisis in view*, prompted by a booming, pent-up demand on the part of consumers and industry.

TABLE 14.1: *Composition and financing of gold and dollar deficit of ERP countries (billion dollars)*

	1947	1948	1950	1951	1952*
A. Composition					
1. Current balance with dollar area[a]	− 7.03	− 5.15	− 1.77	− 3.19	− 2.62
2. Transactions with other areas[b]	− 1.25	− 0.13	+ 0.57	+ 0.03	− 0.08
3. Net balance of gold and dollars (= 1+2)	− 8.28	− 5.28	− 1.20	− 3.16	− 2.70
B. Financing					
4. US grants and loans[c]	+ 5.97	+ 4.78	+ 3.17	+ 2.13	+ 1.50
5. European Payments Union	−	−	− 0.07	+ 0.32	− 0.10
6. Loss of reserves (increases= −)	+ 2.31	+ 0.50	− 1.90	+ 0.71	+ 1.30

Notes
* projections on half-year data
[a] excluding *end-item* military aid but including *off-shore* aid
[b] including colonies and sterling area
[c] including ERP, MSA, Eximbank, and FMI grants and loans.

Source: OEEC, *Europe the Way Ahead: Towards Economic Expansion and Dollar Balance* (Paris, Dec. 1952).

TABLE 14.2 *Dollars provided by the USA to the rest of the world ($m. 1949 and % GNP)*

Period	1. Value ($m.)	2. Private capital, goods and services (% GNP)	3. US Gov. (% GNP)	4. Total 2+3 (% GNP)
1925‒9*	9,588	6.8	−	6.8
1932‒3*	4,833	3.6	−	3.6
1935‒9*	6,335	4.0	−	4.0
1946	15,511	3.8	2.4	6.2
1947	15,348	4.1	2.4	6.6
1948	15,675	4.6	1.8	6.4
1949	16,565	4.2	2.2	6.4

Notes: 1: prices in 1949 $m., current values, calculated on the US export prices index; 2, 3, 4: share of US GNP.
* annual average.
Source: UN, ECE, *Economic Survey of Europe in 1949*, 175.

The payment deficit that resulted from booming European demand for imports in 1946 and 1947 consumed the scarce dollar and gold reserves of the whole of Europe. As Table 14.1 shows, the greatest imbalance was with the dollar area. This was the reason for the French and Italian inflationary spiral in 1947, which prompted the failure of Blum's cabinet. Monetary crisis first struck the United Kingdom, but indirectly affected the whole Commonwealth and continental Western Europe as well.[17] Without US governmental assistance, as explained in Table 14.2, the European collapse would have taken place from 1947. Sterling's abandonment of convertibility in August 1947 was a minor ill as against the risk of the total breakdown in US–UK relations that would most likely have occurred without the IMF's extraordinary assistance to sterling and the French franc to the tune of about 1 billion dollars in the summer of 1947.[18] Not the 'One World' hoped for in 1945, but four worlds would have emerged.

Europe's monetary dependency on the dollar that weighed painfully from 1945 persuaded Western European cabinets that American aid and economic viability were more relevant than socialist targets. At the Moscow Conference in April 1947 Bevin willingly conceded to General Marshall's request to stop the socialization of Ruhr industry in the name of higher steel and coal production and a 'special relationship' with the USA. German heavy industry's return to production in private hands and the pledge of a rapid growth in production put an end to socialist experiments in the rest of Western Europe.[19]

[17] Alec K. Cairncross, *Years of Recovery: British Economic Policy 1945–1951* (London, 1985); John Killick, *The United States and European Reconstruction 1945–1960* (Edinburgh, 1997); C. Spagnolo, *La stabilizzazione incompiuta: Il Piano Marshall in Italia (1947–1952)* (Rome, 2001), ch. 1.

[18] Gardner, *Sterling–Dollar Diplomacy*, 302–3, 324–5.

[19] Marshall to Truman, *Record of Notes on the Interview with British Foreign Minister*, secret, Moscow, 5 Apr. 1947, Truman Library (TL), Gen. File, b.129, f. G. Marshall. The German coal issue had also been raised by William Clayton since the first meeting with the British cabinet: Summary of First Meeting, 24 June 1947, FRUS, 1947, III, 268–73; Clayton to SecState, 25 June 1947, FRUS, 1947, II, 932.

III. *Shaping a Compromise between Liberal Capitalism and Social Democracy*

Restoring confidence in liberal capitalism was the pillar of American cultural hegemony. Yet the US State Department was aware that a compromise with the European working class was necessary in order to implement the American Fordist model abroad. The Marshall Plan scored better in restoring confidence in liberal capitalism, whereas a compromise with the European working class remained incomplete. A compromise for growth through greater productivity was implicitly accepted by Social Democratic parties; yet a formal compromise between the USA and Western Europe was difficult to shape.

The US success was largely psychological. Whereas until early 1947 employers were on the defensive, by 1948–9 elections in Italy, France, and western Germany hinged on the return to free market and growth policies. The employers' organizations, whose private status had protected them from purges, profited from the return of managers who had compromised with fascism. The need for economic competence interrupted purges in the bureaucracy and in the business world. The free market discourse of Ludwig Erhard and the French radicals would not have had such success at the polls had it not been for the promise of American plenty behind them.[20]

The interpretation of American intentions sparked enormous controversy in newspapers and parliaments. The socialist parties suffered greatly from the rhetorical separation of politics from economics that was bolstered by the American emphasis on aid as business. Accepting that separation, the socialist parties lacked instruments to avoid the trade unions' splits that followed in 1947 and 1948. The French Socialist Party remained united but lost forever its central position in the Assemblée Nationale; the Italian Socialist Party split into several factions in the period from 1947 to 1950 and did not recover from its subordination to the Communists until the early 1960s. Both failed to win work-

---

[20] Henry W. Ehrmann, *Organized Business in France* (Princeton, 1957); Annie Lacroix-Riz, *La CGT de la Libération à la scission de 1944–1947* (Paris, 1983); ead., *Le Choix de Marianne: Les relations franco-américaines de la Libération aux débuts du plan Marshall (1944–1948)* (Paris, 1985); Udo Wengst, *Auftakt zur Ära Adenauer: Koalitionsverhandlungen und Regierungsbildung 1949* (Düsseldorf, 1985), 34–9.

ing-class support for their reformist policies, which did not exclude a compromise with Germany.[21]

The Attlee cabinet quite easily overcame the superficial opposition of the two most left-wing ministers, Bevan and Shinwell, by arguing that without US aid neither trade recovery nor social reforms would have been possible. Dalton's financial policy was already outstripping domestic resources and the Labour Party was suffering its first major setbacks. In 1947 austerity became even tighter than the year before and almost produced a rupture in the cabinet. A Gallup poll published by the *News Chronicle* in August 1947 gave the Conservatives 44.5 per cent as against 41 per cent to Labour.[22]

The British Labour Secretary Harold Laski and the former US Vice-President, Henry Wallace, questioned whether the restoration of conditions for growth, including the recovery of the Ruhr, required isolating the Soviet Union. Laski advised the German working class to respond cautiously to the US offer, but the SPD Chairman Kurt Schumacher saw the opportunity quite differently: securing the West German workers' jobs came first. To the German socialists the USA's offer appeared as 'business' and was interpreted, along with the SPD's traditional economic determinism, as a technical aid which would not prevent the final victory of socialism.[23]

The German SPD refused to recognize any connection between the Truman Doctrine and the Marshall Plan. In retrospect, there was a grain of truth in this interpretation, but no more than a small one. In fact the Truman Doctrine was conceived by the US administration to persuade a reluctant Congress to commit to Europe. Because a large section of American public opinion fiercely resisted the idea of a long-term US commitment in Europe, only Acheson's domino theory could force the Congress to change its opinion.[24] Without Congress's

[21] Wilfried Loth, *Sozialismus und Internationalismus: Die französischen Sozialisten und die Nachkriegsordung Europas 1940–1950* (Stuttgart, 1977); Marta Petriccioli (ed.), *La sinistra europea nel secondo dopoguerra (1943–1949)* (Florence, 1981).

[22] Kenneth O. Morgan, *Labour in Power 1945–1951* (Oxford, 1984), 336.

[23] Eberhard Schmidt, 'Ohne Alternativen? Thesen zum Verhältnis der westdeutschen Gewerkschaften zum Marshall-Plan', in Othmar N. Haberl and Lutz Niethammer (eds.), *Der Marshall Plan und die europäische Linke* (Frankfurt am Main, 1986), 212–16.

[24] Arthur Vandenberg, Jr. (ed.), *The Private Papers of Senator Vandenberg* (Boston, 1952), 334–6; Richard M. Freeland, *The Truman Doctrine and the Origins of McCarthyism: Foreign Policy, Domestic Policy, and Internal Security, 1946–1948* (New York, 1970; 3rd edn. 1985), ch. 2.

money, it is hard to imagine how the Truman administration would have integrated sixteen European countries and their former colonies into an open design for postwar recovery under US hegemony. And without a real or perceived Communist threat it seems unlikely that the American Congress would ever have approved the continuation of aid to Western Europe. The hearings and debates of the 81st US Congress show how difficult it was for the administration to get its project through the Republican majority that had won the 1946 elections. Confirming what Eric Hobsbawm has suggested, the Bolshevik danger therefore represented a decisive incentive to shape the Western alliance for postwar economic growth.[25]

Thus whereas the Truman Doctrine had a primarily domestic function within the USA, the Marshall Plan aimed to create a transnational Western consensus. It served to give political and cultural legitimacy to what Charles Maier has called American 'informal hegemony'. Captivated by the planning aspect of the programme, the European socialists and the SPD in particular disregarded the political side of the ERP. They did not see that the Marshall Plan embodied a subtler notion of anti-Communism than the Truman Doctrine, what historians call 'containment'. Its main proponent, George F. Kennan, realized that more than ideology was necessary to gain consensus in Europe.

If the Marshall Plan played such a contradictory role in projecting US consensual hegemony abroad, then our traditional historical perspective needs to change. The impact of the ERP in Western Europe cannot be dealt with only as a problem of 'security' or 'economics': it was one of reinterpreting American Fordism the European way. For the dual US policy was to be implemented by European political actors. They disagreed on how to interpret America, because for them America was the embodiment of industrial modernization and growth. Whatever modernization occurred would be filtered through the American experience.

The psychological role of the programme was thus enormous, although difficult to quantify. Apart from electoral behaviour, the change in public expectations which took place in 1947–8 is difficult to recapture, and we should look more closely at attitudes emerging from below in the press, literature, and personal

---

[25] Eric J. Hobsbawm, *Age of Extremes: The Short Twentieth Century* (London, 1994).

memories. We have gone further in this direction over the last two decades.[26] It is no coincidence that social and cultural features of the Marshall Plan were increasingly studied from the early 1980s because historians had raised new questions about postwar American–European relations since multipolarism had seemed possible. Similarly the building of a European Union was partly responsible for a new scholarly interest in the extent of European dependency on the USA. Thus we have several case studies on the economic and cultural features of American policy for almost all the Western European countries. What lesson can be drawn from this scholarship? Did the ERP have a 'general' impact or should we rather, more modestly, speak of many Marshall Plans, one for each of the sixteen participants?

We have learned that the Marshall Plan had very different effects on social-democratic Scandinavian countries, occupied Germany, and French anti-Communist Third Force coalitions.[27] Essays by Vibeke Sorensen, Gérard Bossuat, and Richard F. Kuisel—to mention just a few—show that it is impossible to speak either of a clear, common pattern of Americanization, or of the outright success of American production techniques and consumption models. Each country picked up the aspects of the American ideology that best applied to its own traditions and domestic balance. Irwin Wall and Chiarella Esposito have shown that the French administration rejected most of the USA's requests which could damage its domestic balance, by playing on the Communist threat. Pier Paolo D'Attorre has in turn emphasized that De Gasperi's cabinet had its own domestic targets which were not identical with the wishes of the ECA mission in Rome. Similarly, many studies on productivity have pointed out that US production techniques and Fordist strategies to overcome class conflict with the working class were often not applied for reasons of market or entrepreneurial culture.[28] Studies of labour relations,

---

[26] David Ellwood, *Rebuilding Europe: Western Europe, America and Postwar Reconstruction* (London, 1992); id. (ed.), *Hollywood in Europe: Experiences of a Cultural Hegemony* (Amsterdam, 1994); Richard F. Kuisel, *Seducing the French: The Dilemma of Americanization* (Berkeley, 1993).

[27] For a review of recent literature on countries not discussed here, such as Austria and Ireland, see Kathleen Burk, 'The Marshall Plan, Filling in Some of the Blanks', *Contemporary European History*, 10/2 (2001), 267–94.

[28] Werner Abelshauser, 'American Aid and West German Economic Recovery: A Macroeconomic Perspective', in Charles S. Maier and Günther Bischof (eds.), *The Marshall Plan and Germany: West German Development within the Framework of the European*

in particular, make us aware that the US message of plenty and higher wages was lost in countries where the unions had split precisely on the question of participating in the Marshall Plan. There employers and conservative forces reassessed old visions of class and power hierarchies. Of course, Americanization is a process which cannot be limited to the period 1947 to 1952, but we can say that the ERP was not as crucial in that time as was believed.[29]

Yet these studies demonstrate that Michael J. Hogan's argument that the American programme imposed European integration and an American neo-corporatist ideology upon a reluctant Europe goes too far, for the five years of the American programme was not long enough to 'reshape Europe the American way'. Alan Milward's emphasis on European nations' own interest in overcoming the Franco-German conflict is more persuasive, though the balance between the psychological impact of the ERP and its repercussions on European integration must still be drawn.

Is this recent body of research coherent enough to allow us to state definitely that the Marshall Plan had only a limited influence on European recovery, and that the ERP did not contribute to European integration? In my opinion, the most recent historical research suggests the contrary: the Marshall

Recovery Program (New York, 1991); Gérard Bossuat, *La France, l'aide americaine et la construction européenne 1944–1954*, Comité pour l' histoire économique et financière (Paris, 1992); Gerd Hardach, *Der Marshall-Plan: Auslandshilfe und Wiederaufbau in Westdeutschland 1948–1952* (Munich, 1994); Irwin M. Wall, *The United States and the Making of Postwar France 1945–1952* (Cambridge, 1991); Chiarella Esposito, *America's Feeble Weapon: Funding the Marshall Plan in France and Italy 1948–1950* (Westport, Conn., 1994); Pier Paolo D'Attorre, *ERP Aid and the Politics of Productivity in Italy during the 1950s*, EUI Working Papers, no. 159 (1985); Luciano Segreto, 'Americanizzare o modernizzare l'economia? Progetti americani e risposte italiane negli anni Cinquanta e Sessanta', *Passato e Presente*, 37 (1996), 55–83; Terry Gourvish and Nick Tiratsoo (eds.), *Missionaries and Managers: American Influences on European Management Education, 1945–60* (Manchester, 1998); V. Sørensen, *Denmark's Social Democratic Government and the Marshall Plan 1947–1950*, ed. Mogens Rüdiger (Univ. of Copenhagen, 2001).

[29] Charles S. Maier, 'The Politics of Productivity: Foundations of American International Economic Policy after World War II', in Peter J. Katzenstein (ed.), *Between Power and Plenty: The Foreign Economic Policies of Advanced Industrial States* (Madison, Wis., 1978), 23–49, republished in Charles S. Maier, *In Search of Stability: Explorations in Historical Political Economy* (Cambridge, 1987); Anthony Carew, *Labour under the Marshall Plan: The Politics of Productivity and the Marketing of Management Science* (Manchester, 1987); Ronald L. Filippelli, *American Labor and Postwar Italy, 1943–1953: A Study of Cold War Politics* (Stanford, 1989); Federico Romero, *The United States and the European Trade Union Movement* (Chapel Hill, 1992).

Plan was a decisive event in postwar history, one of those rare political acts which shape a new transnational context. For there is at least one common thread in the history of the ERP that brings together these apparently separate national stories: the rescue of liberal capitalism through growth policies.

In fact, even though it saved liberal capitalism, the Marshall Plan did not implement a free market. US policy did not succeed in forcing Western Europe down the narrow road of capitalist freedom. On the contrary, it gave West European cabinets the tools to control market forces, thus paving the way for the unprecedented economic expansion of the 1940s and 1950s. Paradoxically, US policy favoured state intervention, and state intervention facilitated the long-term rescue of Western capitalism.

Under the shadow of the ERP, a transition took place from the collapsed fascist, compulsory, state-corporatism model of class harmony to a state-led neo-corporatism. Ranging from what I would call a 'paternalist neo-corporatism' in Italy to an administrative inter-ministerial neo-corporatism in France, the Marshall Plan facilitated the building of tighter trilateral relations between state, employers, and anti-Communist trade unions. One of the reasons for this was the changed postwar relationship between democracy and the market. Left-wing parties and trade unions had learned from the inter-war crisis how to defend themselves against inflation and devaluation through economic controls, sliding-scale mechanisms, and guarantees against dismissal. Thus traditional liberal financial policies were not practicable in 1945–52. Another reason lay in the lasting transnational controversy about the restoration of free trade. It is not possible here to explore this issue in the depth which it deserves, but it can be recalled that there were enormous obstacles to free trade because of shortages of food, coal, raw materials, and finished products. And this was not all. Since the 1930s monetary turbulences, inconvertibility, and trade wars had produced a network of bilateral trade that could not easily be dismantled. In fact, throughout the period of reconstruction, socialist cabinets pursued inflationary policies at home in order to reconcile their electorate with firm hierarchies while boosting recovery.[30] Yet

---

[30] Geoff Eley, 'Le eredità dell'antifascismo: La costruzione della democrazia nell'Europa del dopoguerra', in Franco De Felice (ed.), *Antifascismi e Resistenze* (Rome, 1997), 461–90.

this policy weakened their countries' international economic
position because it forced governments to overvalue their currencies and therefore made them dependent on US governmental
assistance to balance their trade deficits.

In social-democratic European countries, the ERP bolstered
innovative income policies in exchange for a promise to the USA
that they would open up to the international free market one day.
The compromise between American liberalism and European
social democracy that has been crucial to the history of the twentieth century had its core in the Marshall Plan. The USA allowed
full employment policies, whereas the European countries gave
up their socialist ambitions. The socialist parties in power chose
to serve their nation instead of socialism because it was in the
nation that they saw the chance for a new democracy.

Some ambiguities in that policy can be attributed to a traditional socialist lack of attention to the relationship between
sovereignty and interdependency.[31] This inconsistency led the
Labour leadership to search for a 'special relationship' with the
USA as well as to a passive acceptance of the Bretton Woods
Treaty of summer 1944, which aimed for international free trade
but did not provide a solution to the problems of transition to
free trade and convertibility. Lord Keynes, who lost his own
battle against the US Treasury representative Harry D. White
on the structure of the monetary system, obtained from the USA
bilateral concessions to uphold the international status of the
pound and some room for manœuvre for the British cabinet's
deficit-spending policies. Yet he could not protect sterling from
pent-up import demand in the Commonwealth and Europe.[32]
The latter largely prompted the British monetary crisis of August
1947 which accelerated Britain's imperial decline, whereas the
second devaluation of the pound in September 1949 marked the
UK Labour Party's definitive retreat from a possible British lead
on European integration.[33]

Britain's decline prompted a division in Europe of which the
USA took advantage. Since the drafting of the OEEC Long-

---

[31] Donald Sassoon, *One Hundred Years of Socialism: The West European Left in the Twentieth Century* (London, 1995).

[32] John M. Keynes, *The Collected Writings*, xxvi, ed. Donald Moogridge (London, 1980), 10, 32.

[33] Michael J. Hogan, *The Marshall Plan: America, Britain and the Reconstruction of Western Europe, 1947–1952* (New York, 1987).

Term Programme for the US administration, export-orientated
countries, such as Belgium, Italy, and West Germany, declared
their disapproval of Britain's decision to keep preferential trade
with the Commonwealth instead of co-operating with them. Yet
they had to accept it.[34] To them, Britain's abandonment of
European integration meant the international isolation of socialists, whereas moderate and conservative forces greatly profited
from the Marshall Plan, not only to isolate the Left but also to
keep the domestic nationalist and reactionary Right under
control. However, even for a strong, moderate party like the
CDU in Western Germany or the DC in Italy, it was difficult to
isolate both the extreme Left and the extreme Right. By 1952,
moderates had lost control on the right in France and Italy,
while the split in the working class made it impossible to reconcile social benefits with economic development. In Germany the
working class achieved unity only by accepting the division of
the country, and economic growth plus European integration
became the only possible substitutes for a lost national identity.
In Britain, the Labour Party was forced to concede power to the
Conservatives.[35]

A major problem for moderate and reformist forces was that
Marshall aid was quantitatively too modest and qualitatively too
poor to allow Western European countries to regain their pre-
war economic position. The passage from 'maccheroni' to
'machinery' which took place between 1949 and 1950 opened a
second phase of the ERP. While the first phase had been about
saving Europe from collapse, in the second the ECA tried to
create an integrated market in order finally to resolve the
balance of payments problems of the sixteen participating countries. This is not the place to investigate the issue further, but it
may be relevant to recall that the ERP failed to achieve this
target. European integration was mainly a shield from an open
world market, forged in response to German recovery and
Western rearmament.

[34] OEEC, *Interim Report on the European Recovery Programme* (Paris, 1948), i: *Report of the Council of the Organization for European Economic Co-operation to the United States Economic Cooperation Administration on the First Stages of the European Recovery Programme*; ii: *National Programmes of Members for the Recovery Period Ending 30th June, 1952, Submitted to ECA by the Organization for European Economic Co-operation.*

[35] Henry Pelling, *Britain and the Marshall Plan* (London, 1988); Othmar N. Haberl and Lutz Niethammer (eds.), *Der Marshall Plan und die europäische Linke* (Frankfurt am Main, 1986).

Thus the Marshall Plan prompted a temporary trade-off between international liberal capitalism and domestic reformism, but did not fully stabilize the moderate, reformist forces in power in Europe. Too many issues were on the latter's agenda: decolonization, growth, social reforms, full employment, and national sovereignty. Moreover, while the ERP supported coalitions in power, its target of attaining viability by 1952 tended to shake European stability, especially when the movement for rearmament split reformist forces and favoured conservatives throughout the mid-1950s. Thus the ERP did not make US–European relations rosy, but it prevented intra-Western frictions from reaching the point of rupture, so long as the USA performed its role as financier of last resort.

IV. *An Institutional Solution to the Crisis of the Nation-State*

The record of the ERP is also controversial on European integration.[36] I wish to suggest that after the Second World War there was less need of a 'European' or an 'American' federator than many believe. Tighter European co-operation was wanted by many political actors. A major problem lay in what kind of co-operation there should be. The UK was divided between Churchill's ideas for a Europe of nations and Labour's fear of co-operating with Continental conservatives. US Republicans saw European integration as a way to rebuild a German bulwark against Communism, whereas European socialists, by contrast, saw it mostly as a device to check the German economy. In 1947 the agency which managed US aid, the ECA, bolstered European integration as a first step towards a larger world market, but in 1949 it changed its tune to allow European protectionism. De Gasperi thought of European integration as a political tool for regaining international prestige. Adenauer saw European integration as a solution to the crisis of West German political identity and was willing to pay the price, whereas Erhard disliked it as harmful to German economic interests and accepted only its rhetorical value.

[36] See e.g. Imanuel Wexler, *The Marshall Plan Revisited: The European Recovery Program in Economic Perspective* (Westport, Conn., 1983); Alan S. Milward, *The European Rescue of the Nation-State* (London, 1992); Francis H. Heller and John R. Gillingham (eds.), *The United States and the Integration of Europe: Legacies of the Postwar Era* (New York, 1996).

Given such very different versions of European integration, the Marshall Plan could not impose US wishes on Europe. But it succeeded, astonishingly, in preventing intra-Western disagreements from producing a rupture between the USA, the UK, and Western Europe. Through the OEEC it set up an institutional framework in which for the first time international multilateral co-operation appeared fruitful, even sometime against the wish of the USA. Moreover, by silently and repeatedly delaying the implementation of the Bretton Woods Treaty for an international free market, the Truman administration gave Western Europe more money and greater political elbow-room than the US Congress was willing to authorize. The ERP gave continental Western Europe the time to realize that close European co-operation was the only alternative to an international free market and to Germany's comeback on the world stage.

Conclusion

There are still many open questions on the domestic effects of US policy in Europe. We need to know more about how US assistance worked at the level of individual firms; we need to understand the interplay between regional, urban and agrarian interests and the national and international targets of the ERP. And we must still explore whether these chains of transmission produced political feedback in parliaments and cabinets.

Yet we can say that the ERP decisively shaped the political and economic history of postwar Europe. It allowed Western Europe to participate in the open economic order that had been imagined at Bretton Woods but which was in peril in 1947. The ERP saved the Bretton Woods order by putting off its implementation, prevented more nationalistic policies, and avoided a division of the Western camp into three parts. By so doing, it also stopped all 'third way' attempts.

More than a decade after 1989, it is time to emphasize that the history of the Marshall Plan cannot be treated only in geopolitical or in strictly quantitative terms. The end of the Cold War leaves us not with the 'end of history' but with many unresolved clashes within the capitalist world. What is the task of historical research today? Should we be content to deepen factual knowledge as it emerges from new archival sources, or should we also look for new frameworks of interpretation?

The contradictory impact of the ERP on Western Europe suggests that we need to broaden our traditional perspective on the Cold War as a fundamentally ideological-economic American–Soviet confrontation. We need to rethink the postwar transition from the war to the Marshall Plan and examine comparatively the society which emerged from the Second World War. Did bipolarism keep many unsettled Euro-American conflicts about social ideals, the state, and the role of individuals under control? Did the ERP stabilize Western nations faced by the Communist threat, as has been traditionally argued, or was it a tool to force a disliked peace order upon restless countries? To put it paradoxically, was the Cold War necessary to get the Marshall Plan through?

15

A Public–Private Partnership? The Cultural Policies of the US Administrations in Western Europe and the Role of the Big American Foundations

Volker R. Berghahn

The cultural policies of the USA during the early postwar decade experienced a number of ups and downs that are at the centre of this essay. These ups and downs, as we shall see in a moment, were connected, to no small degree, with shifts in the balance of power and influence in American domestic politics; but they must also be seen in the larger context of American economic and security policies with respect to Europe and the escalation of the Cold War between the Atlantic alliance and the emergent Soviet bloc.

A good deal has been written about the involvement of the USA in the economic reconstruction of Europe. Economic historians have provided plenty of statistical material on how this process unfolded in line with plans that Washington had developed long before the end of the Second World War and which would have been implemented as part of an American-inspired and American-led 'New Economic World Order' even if there had been no Cold War with the Soviets.[1]

There has also been some debate on how crucial the American contribution—symbolized by the Marshall Plan—actually was to West European reconstruction. Scholars like Alan Milward and Werner Abelshauser have asserted that the foundations of the revival had been laid before Marshall Plan aid flowed into Europe.[2] By focusing on West Germany, widely

---

[1] See e.g. Bart van Ark and Nicholas Crafts (eds.), *Quantitative Aspects of Post-War European Economic Growth* (Cambridge, 1996); Barry Eichengreen (ed.), *Europe's Postwar Recovery* (Cambridge, 1995).

[2] Alan Milward, *The Reconstruction of Western Europe, 1945–1951* (London, 1984); Werner Abelshauser, *Wirtschaft in Westdeutschland, 1945–1948* (Frankfurt, 1983).

deemed to be the main engine of European reconstruction, Abelshauser's work in particular has generated a considerable amount of argument and fresh research into the dynamics of German industrial growth. Whatever the merits of Milward's and Abelshauser's hypotheses, there can be little doubt that, if nothing else, the economic commitment of the USA to Europe gave the Europeans a strong psychological boost.

Thenceforward it was clear that the mistakes made by the Americans after the First World War, when they retreated into isolationism and left the Europeans to themselves to deal with the enormous economic and social mess that the 'Great War' had left behind, would not be repeated. Not until 1924 did those on the American side, like Norman Davis, who had always opposed retreat and advocated American help to stimulate Europe's war-exhausted economies, gain enough influence to lift the USA, if not out of its political isolationism, then at least out of its reluctance to provide loans and investments.[3] With American help it became possible to resolve the reparations issue that had poisoned international relations in the early years after 1918. This, in turn, created a better psychological climate for the private sector to come to Europe. American investors bought stocks and bonds; American companies took stakes in European firms or established their own production facilities.[4]

But the relative prosperity that the upswing of the mid-1920s created was not solid and widespread enough. The underlying structural problems of the world economy, and of Europe's national economies in particular, were too deep. In 1929 the house of cards collapsed, throwing the world into depression with mass unemployment. Politics in turn became hopelessly radicalized and polarized. By 1939 the world was again at war in a conflict unleashed by Hitler and his fascist allies which cost over 50 million lives and left Europe once more in ruins. This time, however, a generation had risen to power and influence in Washington that was determined to apply the lessons of the post-1918 experience. They not only wanted to provide aid, but also to shape and recast Europe's economic structures to make them

[3] See Davis's memo of 1921, quoted in Werner Link, *Die amerikanische Stabilisierungspolitik in Deutschland, 1921–1932* (Düsseldorf, 1972), 56.

[4] Mary Nolan, *Visions of Modernity: American Business and the Modernization of Germany* (Oxford, 1994); Frank Costigliola, *Awkward Dominion: American Political, Economic, and Cultural Relations with Europe, 1919–1933* (Ithaca, 1984).

compatible with their vision of a liberal-capitalist, multilateral Open Door world trading system.[5]

The announcement and implementation of the Marshall Plan was the most tangible proof of this American commitment to European reconstruction and, no less important, it encouraged American private investors and companies to return with their funds, technologies, and managerial know-how.[6] Even if the critics of the Marshall Plan are correct that it did not provide huge amounts of money, the programme nevertheless acted as a psychological stimulus. It in turn led the Europeans to take courage and to work towards overcoming their ancient resistance to co-operation. Above all, American aid, but also constant nudging, enabled them to put aside their understandable reservations about the reintegration of West Germany into the emergent economic community. The founding of the European Coal and Steel Community in 1951 was the first tangible result of this changed atmosphere, no doubt also propelled by the growing perception of a Soviet threat.[7]

By the late 1940s, Washington had reinforced its commitment to economic reconstruction and integration with a full return of American military power to Europe. If the early postwar pressure had been to 'send the boys home', by 1949 the perception of Soviet expansionism had resulted in an extremely strong engagement of the USA through the North Atlantic Treaty Organization (NATO). Again there has been much scholarly work on the origins and evolution of NATO and the many difficulties that its creation experienced.[8] They stemmed to no small degree from the question of West Germany's role within this security system and the reluctance of various members to contribute conventional forces in the knowledge of the deterrent protection that American nuclear power afforded them.

Yet, as in the field of economic integration, while there were setbacks, there were no reversals. Washington's commitment to

---

[5] See e.g. Detlev Junker, *Der unteilbare Weltmarkt* (Stuttgart, 1974).

[6] See e.g. Michael J. Hogan, *The Marshall Plan* (Cambridge, 1987); Hans-Jürgen Schröder (ed.), *Marshall-Plan und westdeutscher Wiederaufstieg: Positionen—Kontroversen* (Stuttgart, 1992).

[7] John Gillingham, *Coal, Steel and the Rebirth of Europe* (Cambridge, 1991).

[8] See e.g. Simon Duke and Wolfgang Krieger, *U.S. Military Forces in Europe: The Early Years, 1945–1970* (Boulder, 1993); Melvyn Leffler, *A Preponderance of Power: National Security, the Truman Administration and the Cold War* (Stanford, 1993); Catherine M. Kelleher, *Germany and the Politics of Nuclear Weapons* (New York, 1975).

Europe remained firm. By the mid-1950s the reconstruction and recasting of the West European economies had been so successful that the region experienced a veritable boom. At the same time things stabilized sufficiently on the security front for the Soviet threat to be deemed to be contained. But economy and security did not make up the whole picture of the East–West confrontation after the Second World War and the American role in it. The Cold War was not just about which side had the superior economic-technological and power-political potential for shaping the future. The conflict was also about the power of ideas and which of the two sides could mobilize the greater creative energy in cultural terms, whereby culture was defined as including not just the arts and humanities, but also scientific research and education.[9]

If it is agreed that culture, broadly defined, was just as much part of the effort as economy and security to create an Atlantic alliance and to fight the Cold War against the Soviet bloc, closer inspection reveals that American efforts in this field were more precarious than those in the economic and military sectors. There are two main reasons for this. To begin with, the culture war against the Soviet bloc was won long before the economic-technological and power-political ones. Secondly, although they were not always happy with the recipes that Washington offered them, the West Europeans were too battered economically at the end of the Second World War to be in a position to reject American economic aid. Europe's weakness also applied to military power. The Soviet threat loomed large in the late 1940s and Europe was militarily quite incapable of countering this threat without the USA.

However, when it came to the question of culture, not even the West Germans—severely compromised by the barbarities of National Socialism perpetrated in the land of 'Goethe and Schiller' and in occupied Europe—were willing to abandon what can only be called a 'superiority complex' when they viewed the USA in cultural terms. The criticisms of American culture are familiar in broad outline, as they can be heard among intellectuals and educated people in Europe to this day.[10] And they are

---

[9] The older and European definition saw high culture primarily in terms of the classical canon in the arts and humanities, frequently even excluding the avant-garde.

[10] See e.g. Richard Pells, *Not Like Us* (New York, 1997).

also quite old. They had first arisen after the turn of the century when the USA appeared in the visor of the Europeans as a major international power. They saw a crescendo after the First World War, when American popular culture and mass entertainment came to Europe on a large scale, generating enthusiasm among some, especially young people, and disdain among others, often intellectuals and older, educated people. The history of this European–American encounter has been examined in a number of excellent studies and hence need not be summarized here.[11] We will only deal with its manifestations in the two decades after the Second World War and with American cultural-policy responses to it.

The first question to be pursued at this point is how American domestic politics contributed to the above-mentioned ups and downs in Washington's cultural policy-making in Europe. In particular, we propose to discuss two aspects: first, how shifts in American public expenditure patterns affected the projection of the cultural image of the USA abroad; and second, how McCarthyism influenced American cultural policies.

Largely in response to the intellectual and cultural offensives that the Soviets launched in 1946–7, the USA ratified the Smith–Mundt Act to reinforce its foreign cultural programmes.[12] Subsequently, Washington allocated considerable sums of money to combat Communist anti-American propaganda, just as the Marshall Plan and NATO represented American counters to the perceived Soviet challenge at the economic and military levels. Thenceforth Radio Free Europe expanded its broadcasts to the East in an array of foreign languages. At the same time the influential intellectual journal *Der Monat*, founded in 1948 by the American journalist Melvin Lasky, began publication, subsidized by the Office of Military Government US and later by the US High Commission in West Germany.[13] One of the milestones in these efforts was the organization of the Congress for Cultural Freedom, first as a major conference, held in Berlin in 1950 for Europe's and America's anti-Communist intellectuals, and subsequently transformed into a permanent association of academics

---

[11] Good comparative examples in Heide Fehrenbach and Uta Poiger (eds.), *Transactions, Transgressions, Transformations* (New York, 2000).

[12] Frank Ninkovich, *The Diplomacy of Ideas: US Foreign Policy and Cultural Relations, 1938–1950* (Cambridge, Mass., 1981), 128 ff.

[13] Michael Hochgeschwender, *Freiheit in der Offensive?* (Munich, 1998).

and intellectuals that soon had branches all over Europe.[14] Finally, the proliferation of America Houses and similar cultural centres must also be seen in this context.

The outbreak of the Korean War in 1950, although it proved exceedingly expensive, did not immediately threaten the funding of these American cultural activities. In fact, Congress increased the allocation. It was only in 1953, after the Republican Party recaptured the US Congress and the presidency, that things began to change. While the approach to the Cold War had been bipartisan in the late 1940s, the ancient and deeper ideological differences between the Democrats and the Republicans in domestic politics had merely been papered over. This applied in particular to divergencies of opinion over the role of the state in the economy. Against the background of the economic crisis management that US President Franklin Roosevelt had adopted during the Depression in the 1930s, the Democrats had moved toward a moderate form of Keynesianism and welfare provision paid out of higher taxes. The mobilization of industry for the war effort had then strengthened co-operation between Washington and big business. At the end of the war, many of the Truman Administration's policy-makers, fearing a recession comparable to that immediately after the First World War, did not want to leave the revival of the postwar economy to the 'forces of the market', as suggested by many Republicans who aimed at a far-reaching disengagement of the 'state' from the capitalist economy. Believing that the government had to retain an influential role in the economy, Truman thus tried to secure continuous and steady growth through a measure of demand management, and since he held the reins of power this became official policy.[15]

More than that: when faced with a possible economic downturn in the late 1940s, this fairly cautious management no longer seemed sufficient. At this point, some of the president's advisers were prepared to resort to what has been called a 'military Keynesianism', that is, a plan to stimulate the economy by placing large government orders with the armaments industry. Using the sharpening conflict with the Soviet Union as a justification, they proposed tangible increases in military expenditure. Their

---

[14] Pierre Grémion, *L'Intelligence de l'anticommunisme* (Paris, 1995). See also Michael Hochgeschwender's essay in this volume.

[15] Robert M. Collins, *The Business Response to Keynes, 1929–1964* (New York, 1983).

considerations were encapsulated in NSC-68, the frequently cited document written for the National Security Council, which recommended that the military budget be increased to 6–7 per cent of Gross National Product (GNP).[16]

The execution of this plan was overtaken by the outbreak of the Korean War in June 1950 which, whatever its human costs, created an economic boom in the USA and Western Europe. But, inevitably perhaps, inflation began to creep into the system. Even more alarming than inflation was the fact that military expenditure was soon approaching the unacceptably high figure of 14 per cent of GNP, that is, twice the figure that NSC-68 had proposed. Economists and the business world feared that the military sector was becoming so bloated that it would change the basic structure of a free-market economy. A defence sector that was so large and powerful, went the argument, would ultimately be able to direct a liberal-capitalist economy and thus undermine the 'American way of life', as market forces could no longer fulfil their function.[17] At the end of this road lay a planned 'socialist' economy.

Thus in 1952, when the danger of a war with Communist China had appeared on the horizon, ending the Korean War became not merely a geopolitical desideratum but also an economic imperative. The business community and sections of the Republican Party wanted to scale back public expenditure, and if it was difficult to apply cuts to the defence budget while the military competition with the Soviet bloc continued, other parts of foreign-policy expenditure had to give way. Party politics began to clash. Faced with these pressures, the Democrats wanted to move from a military to a commercial Keynesianism which also preserved a modicum of welfare expenditure at home. Meanwhile the Republicans continued to push for a reduction in government expenditure which they also saw as an avenue for pursuing their traditional aim of lowering taxes.[18]

---

[16] Ernest R. May (ed.), *American Cold War Strategy: Interpreting NSC-68* (Cambridge, Mass., 1993).

[17] Quoted in Volker R. Berghahn, *The Americanization of West German Industry, 1945–1973* (New York, 1986), 267.

[18] See also *Business Week* of 12 Feb. 1949 with the following revealing statement: 'There is a tremendous social and economic difference between welfare pump priming and military pump priming . . . Military spending doesn't really alter the structure of the economy. It goes through regular channels.' Social spending, by contrast, 'makes new channels of its own. It creates new institutions. It redistributes income. It shifts demand from one industry to another. It changes the whole economic pattern.'

Their basic economic principles received a big boost at the end of 1952 when Dwight D. Eisenhower was elected the first Republican president since 1933. Funds that had hitherto been spent on cultural diplomacy abroad suddenly became targets in a Republican quest for public frugality. To be sure, all this did not happen overnight; nevertheless here lies one of the roots for the shift that set in from 1953 onwards. A first public manifestation of this change was the creation and new mission of the United States Information Agency (USIA). As the deputy director of USIA put it in October 1953: 'We do not intend to embark on a vast program for spreading all and any American art abroad.'[19] According to him, it was not merely a question of art being sent overseas that was non-experimental and 'truly representative of all American people'. The question was also: 'how far should the Government go?' This implied that the installation of a Republican president began to influence American cultural policy-making in yet another significant way. It was not related to the above-mentioned fiscal and economic considerations, but to political ideology behind which the pressures of McCarthyism can be detected. It is a theme that we shall now turn to.

The first point to be made in this connection is that anti-Communism had been deeply ingrained in American society since the Russian Revolution and had repeatedly roused local and national politicians to fervent activism. Fear of Communism was behind Washington's intervention in the Russian Civil War with the aim of throttling Bolshevism in its infancy. It had also propelled later policies to contain the influence of the Soviet regime in international politics. The German invasion of the Soviet Union in June 1941 represented a somewhat strange reversal of these earlier attitudes when Roosevelt and Stalin became allies out of necessity in their joint struggle against fascism and the Axis powers, all of which subsequently declared war on the USA following the Japanese attack on Pearl Harbor in December 1941.[20]

With the end of the Second World War in sight, some people in the Administration may have hoped as late as 1944–5 that the

---

[19] Quoted in Sigrid Ruby, '*Have We An American Art?' Präsentation und Rezeption amerikanischer Malerei im Westdeutschland und Westeuropa der Nachkriegszeit* (Weimar, 1999), 86 f.

[20] See e.g. Gerhard L. Weinberg, *The World at Arms* (Cambridge, 1994).

wartime alliance between the two countries would somehow continue in peacetime. But with the defeat of Germany and Japan, both Washington and Moscow rediscovered their old ideological and power-political differences, now reinforced by the fact that both of them had emerged as the two postwar superpowers spearheading the 'division of the world' into two hostile blocs.[21] There appears to be general agreement today that Western fears of Soviet expansionism and the proliferation of Communism were based on an overperception of both Stalin's peacetime objectives and capabilities. But the fears, however exaggerated they may appear with the benefit of hindsight, were nevertheless powerful enough to shape realities and to influence decision-making in the West. By 1947, if not before, the Cold War between East and West was in full swing, leading to an explosion of anti-Communist sentiment in the USA.

This anti-Communism did not merely take the form of Truman's much-vaunted policy of containment of the Soviet bloc, formulated by George F. Kennan as America's strategy abroad; it also unleashed the search for fifth-column Communists and fellow-travellers back home in the USA.[22] A machinery of public investigation was already in place. In the 1920s and in line with early fears of Bolshevism, the Overman Committee had probed the activities of Communists in the USA. In January 1931 the Fish Committee issued a report on 'connections between Communist aliens, blacks and free love', which tellingly reflected the scope of what was soon to become an obsession.[23] The successor to this Committee was the Special Committee on Un-American Activities of 1938 which began to list allegedly subversive government servants in Washington and elsewhere. With the general modes of operation established before the Second World War, the House of Representatives in early 1945 ratified a law which set up the House Committee on Un-American Activities, authorizing it to scrutinize '1. The extent, character and objects of un-American propaganda activities in the United States, 2. The diffusion within the United States of subversive and un-American propaganda that is instigated from foreign countries or

---

[21] Wilfried Loth, *The Division of the World* (New York, 1988).
[22] See e.g. John L. Gaddis, *Strategies of Containment* (New York, 1982).
[23] David Caute, *The Great Fear: The Anti-Communist Purge under Truman and Eisenhower* (New York, 1978), 91, also for the following quotation.

of a domestic origin and attacks the principle of the form of government as guaranteed by our Constitution, and 3. All other questions in relation thereto would aid Congress in any remedial legislation.'

With a brief that wide, this Committee, over the next few years, called hundreds of academics, journalists, teachers, trade unionists, and other professionals to testify about their alleged links with Communism and other leftist organizations, and to reveal the names of friends, colleagues, and associates who might then also be pressed through the machinery. By 1951 the witch-hunt had become so ubiquitous and the problem of Communist subversion was considered so serious that the US Senate got in on the act by establishing a subcommittee of its Judiciary Committee, the Senate Internal Security Committee (SISC). Studded with arch-conservatives whose anti-Communist agenda overlapped with their fight for Christian morals, SISC made the headlines by staging a number of well-publicized hearings of high-ranking State Department officials and others, most of whom were completely innocent of the charges brought against them.

However, the anti-Communist campaign of the 1950s is most prominently associated with the name of Joseph McCarthy, who had been given the chair of the Senate Committee on Government Operations. A zealot like many around him, McCarthy set up and became the driving force in a Sub-Committee on Investigation which thenceforth acted as the hub of a movement that was by then no longer merely pursuing suspected Communists, but included assorted liberals and New Dealers from the Roosevelt era.

Much has been written about the tactics and the violations of fundamental civil rights by McCarthy and his supporters, and research has also gone into defining what kind of a phenomenon of modern democratic politics McCarthyism actually was.[24] While the domestic ramifications of the movement are quite well known, less work has been done on the repercussions of McCarthyism on the cultural foreign policy of the new Eisenhower administration at a time when, as we have seen, the Republicans were looking for ways of reducing expenditure abroad. Although it is probably impossible to establish a direct

---

[24] See e.g. Ellen Schrecker, *Many Are the Crimes* (New York, 1998).

link in this respect, it nevertheless seems significant that McCarthy began to extend his hunt for subversives abroad, looking for American officials in Europe and elsewhere who were allegedly 'soft on communism'. One of the journalists who went on investigative trips abroad was Westbrook Pegler, a syndicated reporter for Midwestern newspapers such as the *Erie Daily Times*.

On one of his tours, Pegler went through the shelves of America House libraries in West Germany, where he discovered, among other 'subversive' authors, a biography, by Catherine Owens Pearce, of Mary Mcleod Bethune, 'a colored woman who was taken up politically by Eleanor Roosevelt'.[25] The article continued: 'She has not been cited in the records of the Committee on Un-American Activities as often as her political patroness, but her record is not too modest. There are 40 citations. In the next section to the left of the same bookcase I came on a book called "Working for Democracy. Partners, the United Nations and Youth", by Eleanor Roosevelt and Helen Ferris.' Other unacceptable titles listed by Pegler were by William McFee, Jack London, and Howard Fast. Finally he 'went to the index and found a batch of cards about two inches thick listing books by Franklin D. Roosevelt and Eleanor Roosevelt and one by Anna Roosevelt entitled "Your Pregnancy." There were collections of Roosevelt's speeches, one by Sam Rosenman and by B. D. Zevin, who is unknown to me, with a foreword by Harry Hopkins.'

Worse, Pegler's journalism and that of other newspapermen was taken so seriously that no less a person than Secretary of State John F. Dulles, himself a hardline anti-Communist, at least in his public posturing, issued an instruction to 'all IIA media services' in 18 February 1953, shortly after assuming office.[26] It decreed that 'in order to avoid all misunderstanding, no—repeat—no materials by any Communists, fellow travelers, etc., will be used under any circumstances by any IIA media'. The instruction was said to apply 'also to all USIS operations in the field', including 'specifically libraries'. Accordingly, 'librarians

[25] Quoted from a cutting of Pegler's article, which appeared in 1952 most probably in the *Erie Daily Times* in Dartmouth College Library, Shepard Stone Papers, Box IV, Folder: W. Pegler. This is the provisional cataloguing, which is likely to change, as a proper inventory of the Papers is made.

[26] Copy of the telegram ibid., Drawer 'Old Chrons.', Folder: Shepard Stone Personal.

should at once remove all books and other materials by
Communists, fellow travelers, etc., from their shelves and with-
draw any that may be in circulation'. That this measure was
taken very seriously emerges from a subsequent telegram by
James B. Conant, McCloy's successor as US High Commissioner
in Germany, which was not 'to be discussed by telephone or any
other unclassified mode of communication'.[27]

Conant's telegram announced the impending distribution of
lists 'of those authors whose works are to be removed from the
Amerika Haeuser [*sic*] and installations or institutions serviced by
them'. After receiving such lists, 'each Amerika Haus director will
personally implement the removal of Communist books or publications from every installation or agency under his supervision
including, but not (r[e]p[ea]t not) necessarily limited to the following: Amerika Haus library shelves, Amerika Haus storage shelves,
long-term loans, bookmobiles, book deposit collections, Deutsche-
Amerikanische Buechereien [*sic*]'. The removal was to be done
'with great discretion and no (rpt no) attendant publicity'.

While these orders provide further clarification for the above-
mentioned remarks by USIA deputy director Berding, the trouble was that the new policies could not be kept secret. Soon the
New York Times reported on 'Librarians Hit Book Purge; U.S.
Bans 300 Titles Abroad.'[28] The State Department, the report
continued, had admitted 'that more than 300 book titles by about
eighteen authors had been removed from United States Libraries
abroad under specific directives to rid the Government's overseas
information program of works by Communist, pro-Communist
or "controversial" writers'. Men like Dr Shepard Stone, former
Director of the Public Affairs Division in the US High
Commission, suddenly found themselves investigated on totally
false charges and suspicions.[29] They fought back, and eventually
Eisenhower, mobilized by influential former associates like John
J. McCloy, raised his voice against the 'book burners' around
McCarthy.[30] While McCarthyism ruined careers and left a great
deal of bitterness at home, it is its impact on Europe that is of
interest in the context of our analysis.

[27] Copy ibid.

[28] *New York Times*, 26 June 1953.

[29] See Volker R. Berghahn, *America and the Intellectual Cold Wars in Europe* (Princeton, 2001), 75.

[30] Quoted in the *Boston Herald*, 15 June 1953, 14.

If America Houses and other institutions had been created to project an image abroad that the USA was a leading nation not only in economic and military terms, but also in the field of culture and ideas, McCarthyism was a foreign cultural policy disaster. It is probably no exaggeration to say that no other single issue so undermined the positive impressions that America's agencies and travellers had been trying so hard to transmit during the Truman years. Before Eisenhower came to power, American cultural efforts had been supported by considerable amounts of public money. Given the negative publicity in Europe of what McCarthyism was doing to American domestic politics, those earlier efforts should have been stepped up. But the Republicans, as we have seen, wanted to cut public expenditure and the developments of 1953 were consequently a double setback to US cultural policy-making abroad.

It is tempting to argue that the damage was much smaller thanks to the major rupture that occurred on the other side of the Iron Curtain: at the time of Dulles's 'book burnings', Moscow's announcement of the death of Stalin threw the Soviet bloc into disarray. The iron fist of the dictator had disappeared and a fierce struggle for his mantle began. Meanwhile the people were growing restive. In June 1953 East German workers rose and could only be stopped by Soviet tanks.[31] Intellectual ferment also set in in Poland and Hungary, eventually resulting in the uprisings of 1956. If Stalinism with its dogmas of 'socialist realism' and Lysenkoism had ever been attractive to educated people in Eastern Europe, they were thenceforth less and less so. But in an ironic twist of events, while the culture war against the Soviet bloc was being won, another conflict gathered force. What McCarthyism had done abroad was to fan a cultural anti-Americanism which extended well beyond Western Europe's Communists and fellow-travellers. To many Europeans, American society, seemingly under the spell of McCarthyism, appeared to be on the verge of turning fascist.

Among the many non-Communist West Europeans who raised their concerned voices at this time was Eugen Gerstenmaier, an influential Christian Democrat politician in West Germany with an impeccable record as a member of the resistance movement to Hitler. Referring to McCarthy's

[31] See e.g. Arnulf Baring, *Uprising in East Germany* (Ithaca, 1972).

rampage, he said he believed that the 'Americans were going mad at home and ought to do something about . . . [their] own democracy'.[32] Meanwhile the well-known radio commentator Walter von Cube confessed in dismay that 'McCarthy makes it so easy for the world to become anti-American'.[33] He went on to tell his listeners that 'whatever may be said against America— and at present much may be said—without its help, without its initiative, even without its threats, Europe would be lost'. This is why it was time, he concluded, 'to raise one's voice in America's defense and in the defense of those who trust its leadership'.

These and similar comments from Europe found a ready echo in the views of those Democrats and Keynesians on the American side whom the Republicans had defeated at the polls but, of course, not silenced. They strongly disagreed with McCarthyism and with public expenditure cuts, in the first place for domestic reasons. Those who knew Europe well were equally concerned about the fall-out across the Atlantic—a concern shared by a man who at first sight was an unlikely ally: Allen Dulles, John Foster's brother and head of the Central Intelligence Agency (CIA).[34] The CIA's budget contained funds the expenditure of which it did not have to justify in public and so, from 1953 onwards, Dulles, instead of cutting his own funding of culture, continued to distribute monies covertly for operations that had no direct connection with the traditional fight against Communism. Rather, the CIA used some of its secret funds to help counter the negative images of American society whose roots, as we have seen, lay in inter-war Europe—images that had re-emerged after 1945 and that McCarthyism had now done much to reinforce.

These negative images not only depicted the USA as a system on the verge of a fascist-populist seizure of power by those in charge of the Un-American Activities movement; they also portrayed America as a grey, standardized, and cultureless mass society. With their traditional sense of superiority undiminished, Western European intellectuals and academics once again produced their scathing analyses of the USA begun during the inter-war years. On the left, there were the leading lights of the Frankfurt School, Theodor Adorno most prominent among

---

[32] Quoted in Berghahn, *America and the Intellectual Cold Wars*, 165.

[33] Quoted ibid.

[34] See Frances Stonor Saunders, *The Cultural Cold War: The CIA and the World of Arts and Letters* (New York, 1999).

them, who wrote in a cultural-pessimistic vein about America's current state and future prospects. On the right, the critique of American 'mass society' and 'mass culture' was articulated by former 'conservative revolutionaries' of the inter-war years like Hans Zehrer, now an influential journalist with Axel Springer's newspaper empire, or by philosophers such as Arnold Gehlen and Hans Freyer. They all had their counterparts in France, Italy, and Britain.[35]

But there was also plenty of opposition by individuals and groups in the USA whose views of existing socio-cultural realities were very different. While fighting McCarthyism, their basic image of America was fundamentally positive. To them this was not an *Unkultur*, barbaric in its superficiality. Rather it had many cultural achievements to its credit which matched and even surpassed the accomplishments of the Europeans. They pointed to American music, literature, dance, theatre, architecture, and painting, much of which they counted as part of a Western avant-garde.[36] Indeed, in their view New York had caught up with, if not even surpassed, Paris, London, and Berlin as a centre of modern culture. And what about citadels of higher learning that were at least equal to any in Europe—Harvard and MIT, Stanford and Princeton, Columbia and Caltech?

Finally, those who took an optimistic view of American society also linked high culture and popular culture, asserting the interdependence and, indeed, the inseparability of the two. They thus contradicted the notions, widespread among both educated people in Europe and among American critics like Dwight Macdonald, that popular culture was primitive.[37] For example, jazz was not some unsophisticated form of African-American music, but a genre with complex rhythms and structures requiring a high degree of musicality and virtuosity on the part of the performer, and refined knowledge and taste on the part of the listener. Accordingly, in this view America's minorities who had developed these and other art forms had immensely enriched cultural creativity, high as well as popular.[38] In short, where the

---

[35] See e.g. Jerry Z. Muller, *The Other God That Failed* (Princeton, 1987); Tony Judt, *Past Imperfect* (Berkeley, 1992).

[36] See e.g. Ruby, '*Have We An American Art?*'.

[37] See Michael Wreszin, *A Rebel in Defense of Tradition* (New York, 1994).

[38] Thus *Amerikahäuser* in West Germany organized lectures by Joachim E. Berendt and other experts to talk enthusiastically about the complexities of jazz.

cultural pessimists had seen boredom, 'other-directedness', and 'massification', their opponents spotted diversity, vivaciousness, colour, and richness.[39]

A particularly good digest of these positions may be found in the writings of Daniel Bell and other social scientists, originally produced as contributions to an internal American debate with the Macdonald camp.[40] But their arguments about American high and popular culture were also directed against the right- and left-wing critics of American society in Western Europe. The question was, though, how these interpretations were to be transmitted to Europe at a time when, despite McCarthyism's negative impact abroad, the Republicans were trying to reduce public expenditure. Although the efforts of the CIA and the newly founded USIA in the field of cultural foreign policy should not be belittled, the more crucial contribution at this point came from the big American philanthropic foundations. In other words, as the 'public sector' redefined and redirected its commitments, the 'private sector' expanded its international work along lines that proved more conducive than Republican policies to the underlying aim of changing the Europeans' minds about the USA.

From 1954–5 the Ford Foundation, above all, spent millions of dollars not only on promoting academic exchanges and scientific co-operation, but also on supporting ventures that would highlight the achievements of American high and popular culture abroad.[41]

In this private effort it proved fortuitous that with Stalin's death the unpopularity of Soviet dogmas about artistic and scientific creativity had surfaced with full force. There was a growing feeling that the Cold War in the East was being won in intellectual terms. Instead of a costly cultural offensive, all that seemed necessary was to provide Eastern European scholars and artists with opportunities to see and experience for themselves the latest developments in the West through visiting programmes. Following the revolts of students and intellectuals in Hungary and Poland in 1956, the big foundations also offered fellowships to refugees when their uprisings were suppressed.

---

[39] See e.g. David Riesman *et al.*, *The Lonely Crowd* (New Haven, 1950).
[40] See e.g. Daniel Bell, *The End of Ideology* (Glencoe, 1960).
[41] See e.g. Berghahn, *America and the Intellectual Cold Wars*, 143 ff.

The developments in the East enabled the foundations to concentrate most of their efforts at cultural diplomacy on Western Europe, and not just on the struggle against local Communists and fellow-travellers, which had been the primary focus until now. The mission was also to counter the negative images held by Europe's non-Communist intellectual and educated élites and now reinforced by the negative repercussions of McCarthyism. The European work of the big American foundations took many different forms. They supported dance companies and orchestras, exhibitions of modern art and design; they promoted exchanges and joint research projects; they sent American academics on lecture tours, paid for professorships in American Studies and supported the Salzburg Seminar; they subsidized international conferences and intellectual journals, most prominently among them *Encounter, Preuves, Der Monat,* and *Tempo Presente.*[42] These journals published essays by 'pro-Americans' who adhered to an Atlanticist vision of the West.

The foundations also gave grants to British colleges, German universities, and French research centres to study the integration of Europe, or the non-European world.[43] Thus the Ford Foundation helped St Antony's College in Oxford to launch its East Asian Centre. The project is also a good example of how the covert alliance between the foundations and Allen Dulles evolved. The latter felt that with the rise of Mao Zedong more reliable information was needed in the USA about Red China. Encouraging the Ford Foundation to give money to St Antony's College to study the Far East seemed to be a good way of killing two birds with one stone: the plan would enhance British–American relations and give leading Asianists in England additional resources for their research.

Another intriguing example is the support given to the institute of the famous Danish nuclear physicist Niels Bohr in Copenhagen, again with a nod from the CIA.[44] Apart from furthering research, the calculation was that Bohr's centre would be a good meeting place for scientists from East and West. In the age before the installation of the Red Telephone between

[42] See e.g. Grémion, *L'Intelligence de l'anticommunisme.*
[43] See Berghahn, *America and the Intellectual Cold Wars,* 201 f.
[44] See John Krige, 'The Ford Foundation, European Physics and the Cold War', *Historical Studies in the Physical and Biological Sciences,* 29 (1999), 333–61.

Washington and Moscow, it was a way of maintaining a dialogue at this influential secondary level while the nuclear arms competition and Cold War rhetoric continued in the higher echelons of diplomacy and military alliance politics.

If we look back at American cultural policy-making in the early postwar period, how are we to assess the investments that the hegemonic power of the West made to convince the Europeans that, apart from economic and military power, it also had a culture? Although the Ford Foundation's activities came under heavy criticism in the 1960s, no attempt is made here to turn these 'private sector' efforts into a sinister 'conspiracy'.[45] They have to be seen in terms of the experience of a generation of Democrats and New Dealers who came out of the Second World War and saw nothing illegitimate in this kind of activity. And, indeed, it may be argued that these and many other programmes not only fostered intellectual and cultural understanding across the Atlantic and helped to soften negative images of the USA in Western Europe, but also began to pave the way that eventually led to *détente* and the de-escalation of the East–West arms race.

None of these achievements was able to prevent the foundering, in the 1960s, of the cultural policies through which the philanthropies continued the work which the Eisenhower Administration had decided to reduce. The most immediate reason for this failure was the revelation that the Congress for Cultural Freedom (CCF), the international association of intellectuals based in Paris that had acted as the organizer and funder of many of the cultural programmes and journals, had been receiving much of its financial support from the CIA.[46] This revelation not only destroyed the CCF, but also compromised the big American foundations. Their prestige and credibility had depended on the public perception that they did not give their monies out of political considerations, but applied 'objective' criteria of superior quality and merit to their funding decisions. This image now seemed tainted and resulted in the retreat of the foundations from Europe.

This retreat was hastened by the mounting criticism of

---

[45] Peter Coleman, *The Liberal Conspiracy* (New York, 1989). Since Coleman was associated with the CCF, he may have meant this ironically.

[46] See Berghahn, *America and the Intellectual Cold Wars*, 214 ff.

American 'imperialism' in the wake of the Vietnam War. Finally, the economic crisis and the oil shock of the 1970s dramatically reduced the endowment income of the American philanthropies and hence curtailed their largess. Still, if we look back on the cultural policies of the USA during the Cold War period and the quest to change the negative images of the USA as a society and culture, it may be said that the once 'hardline' attitudes of European intellectuals and educated people have softened. Knowledge and understanding of the hegemonic power across the Atlantic that had spent so much money to convince the Europeans that it, too, was 'cultured' improved. Even if many ambivalent feelings remain, Europe's cultural anti-Americanism is no longer as powerful and one-sided as it was in the early postwar period.

16

A Battle of Ideas: The Congress for Cultural Freedom (CCF) in Britain, Italy, France, and West Germany

MICHAEL HOCHGESCHWENDER

The CCF was the outcome of international and intellectual battles at the height of the Cold War.[1] Its roots go back to the circles of intellectuals who renounced Communism because of the Great Purges of the late 1930s, Stalinist actions during the Spanish Civil War, and the Hitler–Stalin pact of 1939.[2] These small émigré circles were co-ordinated and (more or less) orchestrated by the Hungarian author Arthur Koestler, an ex-Communist himself, and, after 1947, by the US journalist Melvin J. Lasky.[3] This specific prehistory of the CCF is of great importance in so far as all the left-wing liberal,[4] anti-Communist organizations and individuals involved were avowedly internationalist.

[1] Cf. in general Peter Coleman, *The Liberal Conspiracy: The Congress for Cultural Freedom and the Struggle for the Mind of Postwar Europe* (New York, 1989); Pierre Grémion, *Intelligence de l'anticommunisme: Le Congrès pour la Liberté de la Culture à Paris, 1950-1975* (Paris, 1995); Michael Hochgeschwender, *Freiheit in der Offensive? Die Deutschen und der Kongreß für kulturelle Freiheit* (Munich, 1998); Frances Stonor Saunders, *Who Paid the Piper? The CIA and the Cultural Cold War* (London, 1999). See also Volker R. Berghahn, *America and the Intellectual Cold Wars in Europe* (Princeton, 2001), Frank Schumacher, *Kalter Krieg und Propaganda: Die USA, der Kampf um die Weltmeinung und die ideelle Westbindung der Bundesrepublik Deutschland, 1945-1955* (Trier, 2000), Stephen J. Whitfield, *The Culture of the Cold War* (Baltimore, 1991), and Walter L. Hixson, *Parting the Curtain: Propaganda, Culture, and the Cold War* (New York, 1997).

[2] François Furet, *Das Ende der Illusion: Der Kommunismus im 20. Jahrhundert* (Munich, 1996), 209–400; Anne-Marie Corbin-Schuffels, *Manès Sperber: Un combat contre la tyrannie, 1934-1960* (Berne, 1996), 15–78; Ian Hamilton, *Koestler: A Biography* (New York, 1982).

[3] Cf. Michael Hochgeschwender, 'Congress for Cultural Freedom', in John M. Spalek, Konrad Feilchenfeldt, and Sandra H. Hawrychak (eds.), *Deutschsprachige Exilliteratur seit 1933*, vol. iii: *USA* (Berne, 2002), 526–41.

[4] The notion of liberalism is used primarily in the American sense, cf. Kenneth M. Dolbeare and Linda J. Medcalf, *American Ideologies Today: Shaping the New Politics of the 1990s* (New York, 1993); Richard J. Ellis, *American Political Cultures* (New York, 1993); and Richard H. Pells, *The Liberal Mind in a Conservative Age: American Intellectuals in the 1940s and 1950s* (Middletown, 1984).

Among these groups were Jewish intellectuals from New York City,[5] the Americans for Democratic Action (ADA),[6] the American Federation of Labor, the British *Horizon* group, the Union of European Federalists (UEF), and the German group around the journal *Der Monat*. After 1945 these groups were constantly interested in co-operating, internationally and transnationally,[7] with other organizations of the non-Communist Left. Their common aim was to fight the influence of global Stalinist propaganda in a world-wide effort and on as high a level as possible.

As a result of their often relentless enthusiasm, in summer 1950, 121 intellectuals from some twenty nations of what was then called the 'free world' met in West Berlin in order symbolically to counter Communism.[8] The meeting was a response to the renewed activities of the Communists after autumn 1944, when the campaign against bourgeois 'formal democracy' had started. Since then, further successful campaigns had been initiated by the Communists, in particular the Partisans for World Peace,[9] and other fellow-travelling groups based on national neutralism, labour solidarity, anti-capitalism, and the cultural superiority of socialism. The non-Communist Left and the Western governments became afraid of losing the hearts and minds of people all over the world, especially in countries with large Communist labour movements such as France or Italy.[10] Communist propaganda appeared to be a real threat to the establishment of a postwar order based on liberal democracy, capitalism, and US hegemony. Therefore an organization, the

---

[5] Irving Howe, 'The New York Intellectuals', *Commentary*, 23 (Oct. 1968), 29–51; Hugh Wilford, *The New York Intellectuals: From Vanguard to Institution* (New York, 1995).

[6] Mary Sperling McAuliffe, *Crisis on the Left: Cold War Politics and American Liberals, 1947–1954* (Amherst, 1978); more specifically Clifton Brock, *The Americans for Democratic Action: Its Role in National Politics* (Westport, 1985).

[7] Thomas Risse-Kappen (ed.), *Bringing Transnational Relations Back In: Non-State Actors, Domestic Structures, and International Institutions* (Cambridge, 1995).

[8] Coleman, *Liberal Conspiracy*, 15–58.

[9] Lawrence S. Wittner, *One World or None: A History of the World Disarmament Movement Through 1953* (Stanford, 1993); David Caute, *The Fellow-Travellers* (New York, 1973).

[10] Jerzy Holzer, *Der Kommunismus in Europa: Politische Bewegung und Herrschaftssystem* (Frankfurt am Main, 1998), 169–208; Leszek Kolakowsi, *Die Hauptströmungen des Kommunismus*, vol. iii: *Zerfall* (Munich, 1989), 520–9. Cf. further Richard Kuisel, *Seducing the French: The Dilemma of Americanization* (Berkeley, 1993) and Richard H. Pells, *Not Like Us: How Europeams have Loved, Hated, and Transformed American Culture since World War II* (New York, 1997), 66–81.

CCF, grew out of the Berlin meeting, initially planned as a one-off event. This organization survived the rapid decline of East–West tensions after Stalin's death in 1953 and the Hungarian crisis of 1956—a remarkable feat because the CCF was the only 'agency of the Cold War' that was able to continue its work throughout the 1950s and the greater part of the 1960s. The CCF's longevity was due to the fact that it was more than just an institution of the Cold War. It also served intellectual purposes and was, at least after 1955, driven by a reformist, liberal impulse that should not be neglected.[11]

The CCF's demise in 1966–7 was brought about by a variety of factors. On the one hand, the CCF suffered from long-term structural problems. Its membership grew old and inflexible and became inept at recruiting and placing new members.[12] On the other hand, there was a short-term scandal that destroyed the organization in the end. In 1966 the New Left magazine *Ramparts* and the *New York Times* revealed that the CIA had subsidized the CCF's propaganda and intellectual activities for nearly two decades.[13] These subsidies had started in spring 1951 when the American Federation of Labor had withdrawn its financial support. While the CIA had only very randomly intervened in the CCF's actual policies, during the New Left and anti-Vietnam war protests the scandal itself sufficed to give a death-blow to the surprisingly versatile organization.[14] By 1967, when the Congress was shut down, it had national and regional chapters in almost every country of the non-Communist sphere from Australia to Uganda, from Britain to Japan. Its magazines (*Der Monat*, *Encounter*, *Cuardernos*, *Quadrant*, etc.) were widely read and considered to be of superior quality.

While the CCF's organizational efforts in the Third World, with the exception of India, were a by-product of the necessary changes after 1953 and a result of the 1955 Bandung conference (that is, the rising movement of the non-aligned nations that became influential after Stalin's death had calmed the European

---

[11] Edward Shils, 'Further Thoughts on the Congress in the 1960s', Department of Special Collections of the Regenstein Library of the University of Chicago (UoC Archives), IACF/CCF Archive, Series II, Box 5, Folder 4.

[12] Hochgeschwender, *Freiheit in der Offensive?*, 534–76.

[13] Saunders, *Piper*, 381–416.

[14] Cf. the criticism of Christopher Lasch, *The Agony of the American Left* (New York, 1969).

theatre of the Cold War), its initial activities during the highly important founding phase (1950–3) had been concentrated on Western Europe and the USA. In the following I will focus on this period of Cold War anti-Communism. In a first section, I will describe the overall goals, methods, and ideological focal points of the CCF, including the CIA's involvement in its activities. In a second section I will analyse more specifically the Congress's operations in Britain, France, Italy, and West Germany.

Goals, Methods, and Ideological Focal Points

Because of its background the CCF was a predominantly anti-Communist organization. Its activities and operations were based on a distinct interpretation of the Cold War as a transnational conflict of societies, ideas, and ideologies rather than as a traditional balance of power rivalry. Within this interpretative framework, itself an outgrowth of the experiences of many CCF members inside Willi Münzenberg's agitation and propaganda department of the Comintern in Paris of the 1930s,[15] well-written magazines and highbrow liberal propaganda were as important as battle cruisers, missiles, or marines. Conflicts were no longer decided by armies, as far as the liberal, anti-Communist intellectuals and their allies in the CIA were concerned.[16] The Cold War was an experience totally different from others, an authentic conflict *sui generis*.[17] The success of one of the involved parties depended on its ability to stabilize its own hemisphere and to destabilize the enemy's hegemonial system. Culture became an important concept;[18] it was recognized that neglecting it would weaken Western aims. The strategy had to be based on a global double containment and an aggressive intellectual roll back. Thus the early CCF primarily tried to spread intellectually sound anti-Communist propaganda as well as pro-Western, liberal-democratic ideas.[19] Social reformism had its

---

[15] Corbin-Schuffels, *Sperber*, 15–28.

[16] Schumacher, *Kalter Krieg und Propaganda*, 74–98.

[17] C. D. Jackson to Dwight D. Eisenhower, 21 Sept. 1953, ibid. 111.

[18] Akira Iriye, 'Culture and International History', in Michael J. Hogan and Thomas G. Paterson (eds.), *Explaining the History of American Foreign Relations* (Cambridge, 1991), 214–26.

[19] Memorandum by Kenneth Nordquist (1948/49), UoC Archive, *Der Monat*-Records, Box 4, Folder 2.

own value in the clash with Communist or socialist labour unionists or nationalist conservatives in Western Europe. To a certain degree, the US administrations of the Democrat Harry S. Truman and, somewhat surprisingly, the Republican Dwight D. Eisenhower shared the CCF's and CIA's interpretation of the Cold War as long as it served the strategic and hegemonial interests of the USA.

Moreover, the CIA was particularly interested in propaganda that was neither clumsy nor simplistic nor fanatical, at least as far as the CCF was concerned. There were others to do the dirty work of covert action. Michael Josselson, the CIA's field agent within the CCF international leadership in Paris, reminded the members of the organization that fanaticism alone was not enough. For nearly two decades he tried to uphold certain intellectual standards.[20] These aims were shared by the majority of the members, whether or not they knew about the CIA's involvement. It would certainly be a mistake to believe that the CCF's support through secret money[21] made the intellectuals involved change their minds politically or ideologically. Just the opposite was true. They did what they did because they wanted to do it. They felt an immense need to fight Communism and to promote liberal reformism. Only this deep commitment to a common cause allowed the whole system to survive until 1967. Contrary to the famous title of Peter Coleman's book on the CCF (*The Liberal Conspiracy*), the CCF was not a conspiracy at all. Everything it did was done openly and deliberately. The CCF's finances were partly the result of covert intelligence operations, but the organization effectively sought publicity. It did propaganda, and propaganda is by definition not a conspiratorial act. Otherwise it would miss its target.

Furthermore, this deep commitment was a logical outcome of its members' pre-war experiences of Communism and fascism. Anti-Communism in their eyes was the consequence of anti-fascism.[22] Therefore it comes as no surprise that many of the CCF's members agreed with the theory of anti-totalitarianism. To some degree, this belief in anti-totalitarianism was serious.

[20] Michael Josselson Papers, Harry Ransom Humanities Research Center at the University of Texas at Austin, Boxes 5–29.
[21] Cf. esp. Saunders, *Piper*, 103.
[22] Grémion, *Intelligence*, 31–3.

No CCF congress ended without protests being made against the Franco regime in Spain or the Salazar government in Portugal.[23] Nevertheless, Communism seemed to be a much more advanced and dangerous threat to democracy in the West, while fascism was obviously gone. The CCF intellectuals were too worried about the expansion of Stalinist Communism in Eastern Europe, China, and the Communist Parties in Western Europe to contemplate the theoretical perspectives of fascism. Even the many Jews inside the CCF believed the actual horrors and crimes of Stalinism to be a greater cause for action than the bygone atrocities of Nazism.[24]

While anti-Communist anti-totalitarianism provided the CCF with an ideological basis, it also divided the American Committee for Cultural Freedom (ACCF) and the international CCF into rival factions.[25] The first adhered to radical anti-Communism and was led by charismatic and sometimes fanatical activists, such as Arthur Koestler, James Burnham, Franz Borkenau, Sidney Hook, Max Eastman, Sol Levitas, Fritz Torberg, Margarethe Buber-Neumann, and others. Many of them, especially in the ACCF, were even willing to co-operate with McCarthy without acknowledging that the Republican Senator from Wisconsin and his supporters were destroying the very order they wanted to defend.[26] Secondly, there was a moderate faction led by calmer leaders, including Ignazio Silone, Manés Sperber, Melvin J. Lasky, the majority of the British CCF (Malcolm Muggeridge and Stephen Spender), the German CCF (Carlo Schmid and Willy Brandt), and the international leadership of the organization, headed by international secretary general Nicolas Nabokov and the executive secretary and CIA field agent, Michael Josselson.[27] In 1952–3 the latter group

---

[23] Salvador de Madariaga to Melvin J. Lasky, 20 Oct. 1950, UoC Archive, *Der Monat*-Records, Box 3, Folder 8, cf. Sidney Hook, *Out of Step: An Unquiet Life in the 20th Century* (New York, 1987), 458–9.

[24] For possible reasons cf. Peter Novick, *The Holocaust and Collective Memory: The American Experience* (London, 2000), 85–102.

[25] Hochgeschwender, *Freiheit in der Offensive?*, 265–97.

[26] Sol Levitas to Melvin J. Lasky, 7 Apr. 1952, UoC Archive, *Der Monat*-Records, Box 19, Folder 5; Daniel Bell to Melvin J. Lasky, ibid., Box 23, Folder 6; Minutes of the International Executive Committee of the CCF, 27 Nov. 1953, UoC Archive, IACF/CCF Papers, Series II, Box 3, Folder 4.

[27] Friedrich Torberg to François Bondy, 14 Jan. 1956, Wiener Stadt- und Landesbibliothek, Torberg Papers, Box 1, Folder 4.

eclipsed the radicals. It was, however, a third faction that finally overcame the radicals and secured the survival of the CCF. This faction consisted of scholars such as Michael Polanyi, Edward Shils, Raymond Aron, Daniel Bell, and Richard Löwenthal, who were much more dedicated to the technocratic style of the late 1950s and early 1960s than their more charismatic predecessors.[28] They masterfully reformed the CCF in the mid-1950s and tried hard to marry anti-Communism to liberal reformism under the heading of the 'end of ideology'.[29] After 1955 the organization was never again fixated on radical anti-Communism alone. Thereafter left-wing liberal anti-totalitarianism and reformism together formed the ideological basis of the CCF. Moreover, 1950s consensus liberalism became an important means of fulfilling the CCF's second main task: Westernization.[30]

Even during its formative years the CCF had never been an exclusively anti-Communist organization. It had operated on the basis of pre-war personal networks and had intensified and expanded them over the years. These networks were primarily composed of left-wing liberal and right-wing socialist politicians, scientists, and intellectuals. They not only helped to create a specific atmosphere of genuine personal friendship and mutual help, but also had a more practical and ideological purpose. The networks provided the people involved with a firm, substantial ideological basis that made them independent of the traditionalist Socialist International,[31] while guaranteeing them an efficient international background. The CCF's support allowed them a certain, limited opposition to the regular party machine's semi-Marxist rhetoric and practice.[32] As far as we can judge today, the CCF (and the CIA) were thereby trying to promote a cohesive Western ideology that would in the long term produce the groundwork for a fundamental reform of the Western non-

---

[28] Coleman, *Liberal Conspiracy*, 171–82.

[29] Chaim I. Waxman (ed.), *The End of Ideology Debate* (New York, 1968).

[30] On the notion of Westernization cf. Anselm Doering-Manteuffel, *Wie westlich sind die Deutschen? Amerikanisierung und Westernisierung im 20. Jahrhundert* (Göttingen, 1999).

[31] An opposing view of the Socialist International, at least with regard to anti-Communism, is presented by Donald Sassoon, *One Hundred Years of Socialism: The West European Left in the Twentieth Century* (New York, 1996), 210. His interpretation is convincing, although it does not reflect the internal ideological rivalries of the non-Communist Left.

[32] Julia Angster, 'Vom Klassenkampf zur Tarifpartnerschaft: Westernisierung in SPD und DGB, 1940–1970', *Vorgänge*, 40/2 (2001), 41–50.

Communist labour movement.[33] The final aim was to reform the parties' *Weltanschauung* with the help of the international personal networks already established, and then to transform the socialist and Social Democratic parties into *Volksparteien*, modelled on the American Democratic Party.[34] Basically, the CCF was interested in broad bipartisan coalitions in foreign policy that included conservatives and Christian Democrats as well as the non-Communist Left. As far as domestic affairs were concerned, the CCF favoured reformist labour parties that had renounced Marxist rhetoric. Thus it intentionally worked for liberal, progressive reformism all over Europe.

Although the Democratic Party, at least the ADA wing, served as a role model for this deliberate process of restructuring the European labour movement, it would not be correct to interpret this as unidirectional Americanization.[35] The CCF's ideology was never exclusively American, yet it included American traditions. Consensus liberalism[36] was certainly based on the broader American liberal-progressive movement,[37] more specifically, on the right wing of New Deal and Fair Deal liberalism.[38] The major components were liberal individualism, the common heritage of the European Enlightenment, the rule of law, Wilsonian internationalism,[39] pragmatism,[40] and urban cosmo-

---

[33] Cf. Sassoon, *One Hundred Years*, 187–274; Hochgeschwender, *Freiheit in der Offensive?*, 383–9.

[34] Carl Landauer to Harold Hurwitz, 10 Mar. 1952, UoC Archive, *Der Monat*-Records, Box 19, Folder 4.

[35] On the notion of Americanization and its impact on Europe cf. Ralph Willett, *The Americanization of Germany, 1945–1949* (London, 1989); Konrad H. Jarausch and Hannes Siegrist (eds.), *Amerikanisierung und Sowjetisierung in Deutschland, 1945–1970* (Frankfurt am Main, 1997); and Volker R. Berghahn, 'Zur Amerikanisierung der westdeutschen Wirtschaft', in Ludolf Herbst *et al.* (eds.), *Vom Marshallplan zur EWG: Die Eingliederung der Bundesrepublik Deutschland in die westliche Welt* (Munich, 1990). Cf. Philipp Gassert, 'Amerikanismus, Antiamerikanismus, Amerikanisierung', *Archiv für Sozialgeschichte*, 39 (1999), 531–61.

[36] Cf. Godfrey Hodgson, *America in Our Time: From World War II to Nixon* (New York, 1978), 67–98; Pells, *Liberal Mind*, 152–60; cf. further David Plotke, *Building a Democratic Political Order: Reshaping American Liberalism in the 1930s and 1940s* (New York, 1996).

[37] Hans Vorländer, *Hegemonialer Liberalismus: Politisches Denken und politische Kultur in den USA, 1776-1920* (Frankfurt am Main, 1997), 167–214.

[38] Steve Fraser and Gary Gerstle (eds.), *The Rise and Fall of the New Deal Order, 1930–1980* (Princeton, 1989).

[39] Frank Ninkovich, *The Wilsonian Century* (New York, 1999); Tony Smith, *America's Mission: The United States and the Worldwide Struggle for Democracy in the Twentieth Century* (Princeton, 1994).

[40] Cornel West, *The American Evasion of Philosophy: A Genealogy of Pragmatism* (Madison,

politanism.[41] These fundamentally American elements of CCF ideology were combined with an etatist view of economic issues that was legitimized by Keynesian theory.[42] This unique combination of ideological ingredients made the CCF attractive to European reformist socialists and liberals. As all these concepts were the result of a long-term, transatlantic exchange of ideas going back to the seventeenth century, consensus liberalism was *a priori* comprehensible to non-Americans. The promotion of welfare-state capitalism in particular made it possible to integrate consensus liberalism into the European etatist tradition, which had been introduced to Americans throughout the twentieth century.[43] The prominent function of European émigrés within these complex processes of exchange should not be underestimated.[44] Thus the CCF was part of a broader transatlantic transfer,[45] or a common transatlantic Westernization. Westernization nevertheless depended on pre-existing common ideological grounds and mutual convictions and values provided by the Enlightenment and liberalism. This fact was never really understood by the rather dogmatic liberals in the CCF. They tended to believe that their values and doctrines were simply the result of a universal rationality shared by any given intellectual. Hence their inability to explain convincingly why the CCF regularly failed to gain ground in the Third World, that is, in countries lacking a liberal, enlightened tradition.

The last common element to be mentioned in this context—in addition to the ideological missions of anti-Communism and consensus liberalism—is that of organization. The CCF was a perfect example of the utter inability of intellectuals to organize. The internal chaos even suggests that the CCF survived *in spite of* its organization. Theoretically, the CCF leadership in Paris, the

1989); Brian Lloyd, *Left Out: Pragmatism, Exceptionalism, and the Poverty of American Marxism, 1890–1920* (Baltimore, 1997).

[41] Hochgeschwender, *Freiheit in der Offensive?*, 68–85, 175–98, 253–64.

[42] Cf. Theodore Rosenof, *Economics in the Long Run: New Deal Theorists and their Legacies, 1933–1993* (Chapel Hill, 1997).

[43] Cf. Sassoon, *One Hundred Years*, 113–66.

[44] Claus-Dieter Krohn, 'Remigranten und Rekonstruktion', in Detlef Junker *et al.* (eds.), *Die USA und Deutschland im Zeitalter des Kalten Krieges: Ein Handbuch* (Stuttgart, 2001), 803–13.

[45] Johannes Paulmann, 'Internationaler Vergleich und interkultureller Transfer: Zwei Forschungsansätze zur europäischen Geschichte des 18. bis 20. Jahrhunderts', *Historische Zeitschrift*, 267 (1998), 649–85.

international executive committee and the international secretariat, had a strong, almost overwhelming position. It depended, however, on the goodwill of the national chapters, especially when these were financially independent of Paris. Only the magazines were normally under the strict control of the central authority, but even here, Josselson, Nabokov, and François Bondy, the magazine co-ordinator, sometimes had to give in. For example, for years Friedrich Torberg, the Austrian editor of *Forum*, never listened to Josselson's advice about a more moderate anti-Communism.[46] But the CCF also had some strengths. It was able to provide itself with a smooth machinery for producing magazines, quoting the members' most recent books and attributing to them outstanding brilliance and intellectual wit.[47] Thereby the CCF was able to shape intellectual and scientific discourses. And the members of the national chapters normally agreed with the international executive branch ideologically, which allowed the organization to act within the parameters of its regular position, even if inefficiently.

The Congress's Operations in Britain, France, Italy, and West Germany

The transnational, universal elements of the CCF's intellectual and political commitment by far outweighed national specifics. This was a consequence of the milieu that most of the members came from, and of their lifestyles. Despite a commitment to national cultures, the CCF members shared a joint heritage, the urban cosmopolitanism of the predominantly Jewish intellectuals of the late Victorian period and the early twentieth century. Wherever they found similar people, they saw chances for co-operation. London, Paris, and Rome at least partly shared the cosmopolitan traditions of New York,[48] while Berlin, let alone Frankfurt, Stuttgart, or Cologne, lacked this spirit. This was one reason for the CCF's lack of success in West Germany. The CCF's inner circle was part of an international jet-setting community that formed a Western intellectual milieu beyond

---

[46] Friedrich Torberg to François Bondy, 4 Apr. 1958, Wiener Staats- und Landesbibliothek, Torberg Papers, Box 1, Folder 4.

[47] Coleman, *Liberal Conspiracy*, 59–102.

[48] Peter Coulmas, *Weltbürger: Geschichte einer Menschheitssehnsucht* (Hamburg, 1990).

national borders. Nevertheless, it had to cope with national differences. In this section I will show how the CCF's ideology and policies were adapted to specific national situations in Britain, France, Italy, and West Germany.

In Britain the CCF did not face the problems of a strong Communist Party influence or anti-American mass movements, although in the early years some CFF members believed Communism to be a dangerous and almost all-powerful force among British intellectuals.[49] There was a certain fear that Oxford and Cambridge graduates who had studied during the 'pink decade' (1925–35) were still influenced by Marxism. A number of spy cases and the fairly relaxed attitude of British postwar society towards the Communist threat seemed to confirm this painful thought. Communist cultural hegemony, therefore, was considered to be a possibility. Thus the CCF concentrated on three major aspects:

(a) According to the CCF it was necessary for anti-Communism to regain cultural hegemony. The book *The God That Failed*, edited by the Labour politician Richard H. S. Crossman in 1949,[50] had been a first and very successful step in this direction. This eyewitness account of former Communist party members who, often after painful experiences, had broken with what they believed to be a semi-religious system, became quite influential among British intellectuals and politicians during the early years of the Cold War. It helped to destroy the myth of Communism's humanitarian aims. *The God That Failed*, however, marked the peak of anti-Communist frenzy. After the alarmist mood of the immediate postwar years had passed, the anti-Communist Left changed its means. In 1953 Irving Kristol and Stephen Spender launched the magazine *Encounter,* which became the most important high-quality journal in the Anglo-American world.[51] It specifically and outspokenly aimed to combine the British and the American intellectual debate.

(b) As the situation of liberal anti-Communism became more stable, an ideological reorganization of the British labour move-

---

[49] Coleman, *Liberal Conspiracy*, 144–6; in greater detail Hugh Wilford, '"Unwitting Assets?": British Intellectuals and the Congress for Cultural Freedom', in *Twentieth Century British History*, 11/1 (2000), 42–60; *Frankfurter Allgemeine Zeitung*, 21 Aug. 1995.

[50] Richard H. S. Crossman (ed.), *The God That Failed* (London, 1949).

[51] Coleman, *Liberal Conspiracy*, 59–80; Saunders, *Piper*, 165–89.

ment,[52] the Labour Party, and the trade unions seemed more important than endless red-baiting. From the start, the CCF had tried to rally as many right-wing labour leaders as possible, the so-called Gaitskellites. In addition to R. H. S. Crossman, Anthony Crosland, Denis Healey, and others joined the rank-and-file of the British CCF. Their common goal was a more centrist labour movement. The CCF also attempted to intensify communication with the reform-minded American consensus liberalism of the ADA in order to strengthen the intellectual, political, and socio-economic special relationship between Britain and the USA. This was quite important, because many British intellectuals and politicians agonized over the rapid loss of the Empire and the hegemonic power that their American senior partner exercised during the Suez crisis of 1956.

(c) The major instrument to guarantee this special relationship at a more intellectual level was *Encounter*, which subsequently became the CCF's most important magazine. Even *Der Monat* came second to *Encounter*. This became evident in 1958, when, after a short crisis in *Encounter*'s editorial team, Lasky switched from Berlin to London in order to save the CCF's intellectual flagship. The magazine always stressed common traditions and successfully stimulated mutually noteworthy debates. This Anglo-American emphasis explains the CFF's relative neglect of another key issue: European integration. Compared with France, Italy, and West Germany the idea of Western European integration was secondary to Anglo-American identity and cosmopolitanism in *Encounter*.

The British CCF usually only had one serious problem: it did not share the ACCF's radical anti-Communism. As early as the Berlin congress of 1950 and its aftermath, the British delegation had criticized the radicalism of the Koestler–Burnham–Hook group. Malcom Muggeridge, who later led the British Society for Cultural Freedom,[53] Alfred J. Ayer, Hugh Trevor-Roper, and others had bitterly denounced any attempt to reduce individual liberties in order to fight the enemies of freedom. From then on, their position was uncompromising.[54] This, however, happened

[52] Wilford, '"Unwitting Assets?"', 49–51.

[53] Ibid. 47–9.

[54] Hugh Trevor-Roper to Melvin J. Lasky, 28 July 1950, UoC Archive, *Der Monat*-Records, Box 5, Folder 6; Alfred J. Ayer to Melvin J. Lasky, 3 Aug. 1950, ibid., Box 1, Folder 2; *Manchester Guardian*, 10 July 1950; *New Statesman and Nation*, 22 Aug. 1950.

to be an advantage when, after Stalin's death, the CCF changed its policy toward radical anti-Communism. From then on the international leadership shared the British position. Only the Suez crisis temporarily shook relations between the British CCF and the international CCF. In 1956 Bertrand Russell, honorary president of the international CCF, left the organization in protest against Rosenberg's trial and execution in McCarthyist America.[55] This incident and the rise of the Campaign for Nuclear Disarmament and the New Left in the aftermath of 1956 weakened the influence of the CCF among British intellectuals. It is therefore difficult to evaluate the CCF's successes in Britain. On the one hand, everything that it wanted materialized. The Labour Party remained firmly anti-Communist and the special relationship was never seriously threatened. But it is impossible to quantify the role that the CCF played in these processes. Perhaps it was most important in organizing personal networks and stimulating debates between British and American intellectuals and politicians. Its role should not be overestimated.

The scope of the CCF's activities in France and Italy was rather different from in Britain.[56] As the Congress faced almost the same problems in both countries, analysing them together is justified.

(a) Unlike in Britain, in France and Italy the CCF faced powerful and influential Communist parties. During the 1950s neither the French PCF nor the Italian PCI was anything like the semi-democratized Euro-communist parties that at least the PCI turned into during the 1970s. On the contrary, they were led by staunch Stalinists and had powerful fellow-traveller organizations at their disposal. In France, for example, the Curies and Romain Rolland[57] openly supported the fellow-travelling World Peace Movement. Consequently, the CCF had to fight the influence of organized and fellow-travelling Communism, while at the same time strengthening liberal centrism and weakening the position of anti-liberal, conservative Roman Catholicism.

(b) The latter was of immense importance in both Italy and

[55] Bertrand Russell to Nicolas Nabokov, 19 Nov. 1956, UoC Archive, IACF/CCF Papers, Box 280, Folder 6. The immediate cause of Russell's step was the CCF's unwillingness to protest against the Suez Crisis.

[56] Cf. in general Grémion, *Intelligence*, 82–91; Coleman, *Liberal Conspiracy*, 140–4.

[57] Grémion, *Intelligence*, 164; cf., moreover, David Caute, *Communism and the French Intellectuals* (Worcester, 1964); Furet, *Ende der Illusion*.

France, though at different levels. The CCF never really embraced the positions of Christian Democracy with its Roman Catholic background in Western Europe. It certainly declared itself ideologically neutral and favoured some sort of political collaboration between liberals and Christian Democrats, but the majority of CCF members lacked a deeper understanding of Catholicism and Christian Democracy. Some openly despised the Church and any form of creed. There were a number of reasons for this position, which changed in the 1960s with the rising influence of such French intellectuals as Pierre Emmanuel. First, most CCF members were fundamentally sceptical about the intellectual soundness of Roman Catholicism and many Anglo-Americans shared traditional anti-Catholic prejudices. For example, Bertrand Russell threatened to leave the CCF when a Communist teacher wrote to him that the organization was financed by the Vatican.[58] Popular Catholicism in Italy, in particular, did not meet their rigid intellectual standards. They were perhaps able to accept a more subtle and refined version of neo-Thomism, as represented by the eminent French philosophers Jacques Maritain, Honorary President of the CCF, and Etienne Gilson, but otherwise Catholicism seemed vulgar. Secondly, several Congress leaders were agnostics or atheists. Sidney Hook, for example, believed that the Catholic Church was a totalitarian power, comparable with Communism and fascism—certainly not a very helpful position in Italian Catholic circles.[59] Thirdly, the liberal élitism of the CCF intellectuals made them rather uncomfortable with any form of mass involvement. In their eyes, the spiritual impact of Catholicism (and Christian Democracy) on the masses was somewhat sinister. Therefore even a shared anti-Communism did not provide the CCF's liberals and Catholic-dominated Christian Democrats with a viable basis for mutual respect and understanding. This definitely limited the political impact of the CCF in France and Italy.

(c) The CCF also had to fight the influence of nationalism, primarily in France. Here, nationalism had two faces. One

---

[58] Nicolas Nabokov to Bertrand Russell, 13 July 1954, UoC Archive, IACF/CCF Papers, Series I, Box 3, Folder 5.
[59] Cf. Hellmuth Jaesrich to Rudolf Schottlaender, 6 Apr. 1950, UoC Archive, *Der Monat*-Records, Box 5, Folder 3.

aspect was openly neutralist and based on the influential philosophy of existentialism.[60] Jean-Paul Sartre and Simone de
Beauvoir were seen as the major leaders of anti-American agitation in France. Their moral weight, supported by the influence
that existentialism had gained during the German occupation in
the Second World War, had given existentialism a central position in French intellectual life. Its impact was at least as disturbing as Communism.[61] Therefore the CCF long tried at least to
minimize Sartre's influence outside France, yet with very limited
success. Even CCF members, such as Siegfried Lenz in West
Germany, favoured Sartre's philosophy over the unspoken
primacy of pragmatism within the Congress.[62] The CCF,
however, stuck to its anti-existentialist approach with its hidden
subtext of anti-Hegelianism. Nationalism in France also had
another face, that represented by General Charles de Gaulle or
Pierre Mendès France.[63] De Gaulle's anti-Atlanticist attitude
was legendary, and the electoral successes of Gaullism frightened
parts of the CCF. For years, the debate on whether the CCF
should collaborate with de Gaulle weakened the organization. In
the end, it dedicated itself to an unequivocal Atlanticism.

(d) Fourthly, Italy and France were seen as strongholds of a
cultural anti-Americanism.[64] This was one reason for locating the
CCF's headquarters in Paris and starting the magazine *Preuves*,
edited by François Bondy.[65] The CCF tried to overcome French
and Italian prejudices about the total lack of high culture in the
USA. An important means of combining this aim with cultural
anti-Communism was the spectacular exhibition 'Masterpieces of
the Twentieth Century', organized by Nicolas Nabokov and
Michael Josselson in Paris in 1952.[66] The complex and sophisticated strategy that led to this exhibition of modern art was never
understood by the radical anti-Communists in the ACCF. In the
end, 'Masterpieces' became the keystone for eliminating the radicals' influence within the CCF. Whether the exhibition served its

---

[60] Eric Mathews, *Twentieth-Century French Philosophy* (Oxford, 1996), 58–134.
[61] Grémion, *Intelligence*, 294–304.
[62] Siefried Lenz to the author, oral communication, Hamburg 1995.
[63] Grémion, *Intelligence*, 305-16; Pells, *Not Like Us*, 193–5.
[64] Kuisel, *Seducing the French*.
[65] Grémion, *Intelligence*, 273–91; Coleman, *Liberal Conspiracy*, 53–4.
[66] Hochgeschwender, *Freiheit in der Offensive?*, 282–90; Nicolaus Sombart, *Pariser Lehrjahre, 1951–1954* (Hamburg, 1994).

main purpose, namely, to convince the French of the quality of American modern culture, is more than questionable. Similar attempts by Nabokov in Rome were even less convincing.

(e) The fifth point was less controversial. The CCF in France and Italy, more than any other Western European country, campaigned for European unification. This was easy since the CCF was able and willing to co-operate with the liberal integrationist movement, the UEF. Perhaps the CCF's moderate stance against the French war in Algeria was motivated not only by a desire to stop the French from weakening themselves in a senseless and endless war in the North African *kasbahs*,[67] but also by a will to guide the French into a liberal, Atlanticist, and integrated Europe. But this remains speculation.

In order to fulfil its complicated mission in the Latin world, the CCF did not rely only on its normal tactics. To be sure, it regularly gathered together such Atlanticist intellectuals and politicians as Raymond Aron, David Rousset, Pierre Emmanuel, René Tavernier, Ignazio Silone, Nicola Chiaromonte, Benedetto Croce, and Altiero Spinelli. But the CCF also tried another strategy. France was the only country, with the exception of India, to establish a mass cultural movement, the *Amis de la Liberté de la Culture*, with several hundred members. But even in France (and Italy) the CCF relied primarily on its traditional approach of intellectual persuasion. As far as I know, the Congress was, for instance, never involved in the covert activities of the CIA and the American Federation of Labor, designed to weaken the Communist trade unions with the help of the French or Italian mafia. In the long run, the CCF's French activities had positive results. Liberal Atlanticism in France was able to survive with the massive help of the CCF. It was, however, the publication of Alexander Solzhenitsyn's *The Gulag Archipelago* in the 1970s that drastically reduced the public influence of Communist intellectuals in the Paris mandarin milieu. Compared with France, the Italian CCF was neither a great success nor a real failure. Its major problem was the small size and lack of vitality of the non-Communist, non-Catholic liberal centre.

---

[67] 'Le Congrès pour la liberté de la culture et la tragédie algeriénne' (Mar. 1958), UoC Archive, IACF/CCF Papers, Series II, Box 1, Folder 4; John Hunt to Walter Hasenclever, 29 May 1958, ibid., Box 120, Folder 9. In February 1962 the colonialist terror organization OAS bombed the CCF building in Paris, cf. International Executive Commitee to all CCF bureaus, 19 Feb. 1962, ibid., Box 1, Folder 9.

West Germany was a specific case because of its past.[68] Both the US government and the CCF clung to a strategy of double containment,[69] involving anti-Communist, Cold War elements and reorientation ideas, based on a certain lack of trust. But while the government agencies assigned Germany a central role in their global strategy,[70] the CCF considered France, Britain, and Italy more important.[71] Even the fact that the CCF had been founded in West Berlin did not change this attitude. The Paris headquarters went so far as to accept the decline of the West German national chapter in 1953–4. After it was closed down, the West German regional chapters were not reorganized until the late 1950s, and only Manés Sperber was active enough to handle the situation.[72] As everywhere else, the central and most successful aspect of the Congress's involvement in Germany was its journal *Der Monat*,[73] postwar Germany's most important cultural magazine. On average *Der Monat* had 20,000 to 30,000 readers, many of them students, academics, scholars, politicians, and journalists. It was so important because, after twelve years of National Socialism, it was able to provide the Germans with fresh impressions from all over the world, the cultural productions of the USA, Britain, and France, and in-depth political and social analysis. When *Der Monat* took a more parochial stance in the early 1960s, it lost its momentum.[74] In accordance with the specific situation in West Germany, the German national chapter concentrated on four topics:

(a) The German CCF, with its centre in West Berlin, observed closely what happened in Communist East Germany and the Eastern bloc. This does not mean that the CCF was involved in violent secret intelligence operations. Its mode of action was

[68] Hochgeschwender, *Freiheit in der Offensive?*, 298–444.

[69] Wilfried Loth, 'Die doppelte Eindämmung: Überlegungen zur Genesis des Kalten Krieges, 1945–1947', *Historische Zeitschrift*, 238 (1984), 611–31; Frank A. Ninkovich, *Germany and the United States: The Transformation of the German Question since 1945* (Boston, 1985); Hermann-Josef Rupieper, *Der besetzte Verbündete: Die amerikanische Deutschlandpolitik, 1949–1955* (Opladen, 1991).

[70] Schumacher, *Kalter Krieg und Propaganda*, 134–72.

[71] Hochgeschwender, *Freiheit in der Offensive?*, 291–7.

[72] Minutes of the International Executive Committee, 18–19 Jan. 1958, UoC Archive, IACF/CCF Papers, Series II, Box 4, Folder 5.

[73] Margit Ketterle, 'Literatur und Politik im Nachkriegsdeutschland der Zeitschrift *Der Monat*' (MA thesis, University of Munich, 1984).

[74] Statistics of *Der Monat*, 1961–1966, UoC Archive, IACF/CCF Papers, Series II, Box 242, Folder 10.

quite different. The CCF primarily used the *Ostbüro* of the Social Democratic Party (SPD)[75] to smuggle propaganda material into East Germany, such as issues of *Der Monat* or the official US magazine *Ostprobleme*. Thus the CCF and the US authorities tried to improve the situation of the secret Social Democratic network in East Germany and, as far as possible, to persuade Communist functionaries.[76] Moreover, the German CCF regularly used the American radio network in West Berlin to broadcast speeches to the East German people. In addition, the CCF members read the Communist press and informed the Paris leadership about recent developments in the Communist world.

(b) The importance of these covert activities decreased when it became clear that the German Democratic Republic would not collapse immediately. Later, in 1951, the West German CCF focused on anti-neutralist measures and anti-Nazi activities.[77] This was possible because the Germans and the international CCF agreed that there was no Communist threat in West Germany, for the traditionally anti-Communist Germans had experienced the real-life presence of the Red Army in their own country. On the other hand, the integration of West Germany into the West was at stake and the CCF provided the means to safeguard ideological and cultural integration, thereby supporting the military, economic, and political integration encouraged by the Adenauer government and criticized by the Social Democrats. The danger of national neutralism as proposed by many traditionally nationalist German Protestants, such as Martin Niemöller or the Barthians, lay in its insistence on the primacy of unification over liberal democracy and the acceptance of US hegemony. The CCF therefore made it more difficult for Niemöller to go on foreign visits,[78] and published anti-neutralist pamphlets. The Congress was especially successful in undermining attempts by the East German minister of culture, Johannes R. Becher, to organize regular talks between authors and artists from East and West Germany under the common heading of German neutrality and

[75] Cf. Wolfgang Buschforth, *Das Ostbüro der SPD: Von der Gründung zur Berlin-Krise* (Munich, 1991).

[76] Helmut Große to François Bondy, 30 Apr. 1951, UoC Archive, IACF/CCF Papers, Series II, Box 119, Folder 8.

[77] Minutes of the German Executive Committee, 12.7.1951, Bundesarchiv Koblenz, Pechel Papers, vol. 100.

[78] Melvin J. Lasky to Nicolas Nabokov, 19 July 1951, UoC Archive, IACF/CCF Papers, Series II, Box 241, Folder 4.

unity.[79] Members of the German CCF even managed to destroy the still united German PEN centre.[80] Moreover, the West German CCF kept neo-Nazi movements under surveillance.[81] The CCF also tried to fight the Nazi heritage in Germany at a deeper level. With the help of *Der Monat*, it promoted anti-Hegelian philosophical arguments on the basis of anti-totalitarian thinking. This had an undeniable advantage. To oppose Hegelianism meant, at least in the eyes of the CCF, to fight the intellectual roots of Communism, National Socialism, and nationalism, and this meant opposing a genuinely German anti-Americanism. Therefore an intellectually sound anti-Hegelianism was interpreted as the very foundation of German cultural Westernization.

(c) As in Britain, France, and Italy, the CCF co-operated with German right-wing, reformist Social Democrats,[82] such as Carlo Schmid, leader of the German CCF chapter, Willy Brandt, a member of the international executive committee of the CCF, Ernst Reuter, ruling mayor of West Berlin, Max Brauer, mayor of Hamburg, Otto Suhr, eventually to become ruling mayor of West Berlin in the 1950s and succeeded by Willy Brandt, and others. This was particularly important because the first postwar party leader, Kurt Schumacher, was an intransigent and nationalist opponent of West Germany's integration into the Western world. The CCF therefore again combined its reformist networking with networking on behalf of European integration (Carlo Schmid was a leading member of the *Europaunion* and deputy president of the CCF, the publisher Eugen Kogon was president of the *Europaunion*). Interestingly, the CCF mainly co-operated with former members of left-wing sectarian groups, Trotskyites, ethical Socialists, *Bundists*, and others, while never relying on traditional Social Democrats from the old party machines. Even if it is an exaggeration to call the CCF responsible for the programmatic renewal of the SPD in the *Godesberger Programm* of 1959, the helpful networking of the Congress should not be underestimated.

(d) The West German CCF was perhaps the only one that was

---

[79] Minutes of the Berlin CCF chapter, May 1951, Bundesarchiv Koblenz, Pechel Papers, vol. 100.

[80] Press Statement of the German CCF, 3 Feb. 1951, UoC Archive, IACF/CCF Papers, Series II, Box 118, Folder 13.

[81] Günther Birkenfeld to François Bondy, 29 June 1951, UoC Archive, IACF/CCF Papers, Series II, Box 119, Folder 1.

[82] Hochgeschwender, *Freiheit in der Offensive?*, 383–9.

really involved in covert operations, as mentioned above. During the first year of its existence (1950–1), the CCF in West Berlin sought out and co-operated with the radically anti-Communist and subversive *Kampfgruppe gegen Unmenschlichkeit*,[83] the *Untersuchungsausschuß freiheitlicher Juristen*, and the *Ostbüro* of the SPD. This period, however, came to an end once Josselson had consolidated his power in Paris.[84] Afterwards the West German CCF worked within the guidelines of the international CCF.

Conclusion

It is difficult to assess whether the CCF's activities in Western Europe had positive or negative results, and to judge the reception of its published journals. The CCF normally supported developments that were already under way, and it worked on long-term projects. None the less, without the CCF many of these processes of social, ideological, cultural, and political change would have taken longer. In this respect the CCF can be termed a successful operation, in spite of its dysfunctional aspects, its organizational chaos, personal differences, and petty quarrels. It was only successful in the broader context of other efforts by the US government to stabilize Western Europe along the lines dictated by American liberal, capitalist hegemony, and American attempts to achieve a restrained cultural hegemony within the framework of the Cold War. In terms of class and generation, the CCF, at least in Germany and Britain, was able to reach reform-minded middle-class youth. Thereby it laid the foundation for a movement toward centre-leftist, but integrationist tendencies all over Western Europe. In fact, and paradoxically, the CCF was perhaps too successful. The very youth that had been impressed by the pro-American ideological and cultural propaganda of the CCF during the 1950s started to revolt in the 1960s. Many CCF members were unable to interpret the rise of the New Left as anything but neo-Stalinist orthodoxy. They were incapable of acknowledging that their supposed enemies were the children of their own activities.

---

[83] Kai-Uwe Merz, *Kalter Krieg als antikommunistischer Widerstand: Die Kampfgruppe gegen Unmenschlichkeit, 1948–1959* (Munich, 1987).

[84] Max Karl Graf Trauttmansdorff, 'On Working Methods in Western Germany and Berlin', Feb. 1951, UoC Archive, IACF/CCF Papers, Series II, Box 118, Folder 1.

17

'Proclaim Liberty Throughout all the Land': Berlin and the Symbolism of the Cold War

DOMINIK GEPPERT

The Cold War was fought not only with the means of classic power politics, but also with words and images. It could even be argued that rhetoric and symbolism were the real battlefields of the Cold War. After all, it differed from other conflicts precisely because in its European hot spots, at least, it was not conducted by force of arms. 'A Cold War', according to the American historian Martin J. Medhurst, 'is, by definition, a rhetorical war, a war fought with words, speeches, pamphlets, public information (or disinformation) campaigns, slogans, gestures, symbolic actions and the like.'[1]

For a long time historical research tended to neglect this dimension of the conflict and concentrated on the economic, military, and diplomatic contest between the USA and the Soviet Union. Only recently has interest started to focus on the cultural aspects of the Cold War. Historians are now paying more attention to the ideological self-perception of the combatants.[2] They are examining the networks of personal and institutional contacts on both sides of the Atlantic, and are increasingly looking beyond the circles of leading politicians and diplomats, for example, at contacts between artists, writers, and intellectuals.[3] At the same

[1] Martin J. Medhurst, 'Introduction', in id. *et al.* (eds.), *Cold War Rhetoric: Strategy, Metaphor and Ideology* (New York, 1990), p. xiv.

[2] Cf. Les K. Adler, *The Red Image: American Attitudes Toward Communism in the Cold War Era* (New York, 1991); H. W. Brands, *The Devil We Knew: Americans and the Cold War* (New York, 1993); Abbot Gleason, *Totalitarianism: The Inner History of the Cold War* (New York, 1995).

[3] Cf. Peter Coleman, *The Liberal Conspiracy: The Congress for Cultural Freedom and the Struggle for the Mind of Postwar Europe* (New York, 1989); Pierre Grémion, *Intelligence de l'anticommunisme: Le Congrès pour la Liberté de la Culture à Paris, 1950–1975* (Paris, 1995); Michael Hochgeschwender, *Freiheit in der Offensive? Die Deutschen und der Kongreß für kulturelle Freiheit* (Munich, 1998); Giles Scott-Smith, *The Politics of Apolitical Culture: The Congress for*

time attention is focusing on the forms and consequences of psychological warfare. State and private public relations work— regardless of whether this is described as cultural diplomacy or propaganda—and its influence are attracting increasing attention.[4] It is generally acknowledged by now that the world-political conflict between the USA and the Soviet Union developed not only a political-military and economic-technological dynamic but also a cultural one. As Frank Trommler has recently remarked: 'It produced its own heroes, created topics, made careers, and allowed politicians and high-ranking officers linguistically to define and dominate the problems of the present.'[5]

Protagonists on the Western side and Soviet leaders perceived the conflict between the systems as, among other things, a war of ideas in which the truth needed to be defended against lies both at home and abroad. In his Long Telegram of February 1946, George Kennan had already pointed to the significance of public opinion in the confrontation with Moscow.[6] 'This is a struggle, above all else, for the minds of men', declared US President Harry Truman four years later in a speech to the American Society of Newspaper Editors. 'We must use every means at our command, private as well as governmental, to get the truth to other peoples.'[7] This did not mean just the people of the USSR and Stalin's Eastern European satellite states. Because of what Volker Berghahn called the dual thrust of the Cold War, this also included the Western Europeans.[8]

Cultural Freedom, the CIA and Post-War American Hegemony (London, 2002); see also Hochgeschwender's chapter in this volume.

[4] Cf. Edwin Yoder, *Joe Alsop's Cold War: A Study of Journalistic Influence and Intrigue* (Chapel Hill, 1995); Scott Lucas, *Freedom's War: The American Crusade Against the Soviet Union* (New York, 1999); Jessica C. E. Gienow Hecht, *Transmission Impossible: American Journalism as Cultural Diplomacy in Postwar Germany 1945–55* (Baton Rouge, 1999); Gregory Mitrovich, *Undermining the Kremlin: America's Strategy to Subvert the Soviet Bloc, 1947–1956* (Ithaca, 2000); Arch Puddington, *Broadcasting Freedom: The Cold War Triumph of Radio Free Europe and Radio Liberty* (Lexington, 2000); Bernd Stöver, *Die Befreiung vom Kommunismus: Amerikanische Liberation Policy im Kalten Krieg 1947–1991* (Cologne, 2002).

[5] Frank Trommler, 'Neuer Start und alte Vorurteile: Die Kulturbeziehungen im Zeichen des Kalten Krieges', in Detlef Junker *et al.* (eds.), *Die USA und Deutschland im Zeitalter des Kalten Krieges 1945–90: Ein Handbuch* (Stuttgart, 2001), i. 567.

[6] George F. Kennan, 'Telegraphic Message from Moscow of 22 February 1946'; excerpts published in Kennan, *Memoirs, 1925–50* (Boston, 1967), 596–7. Cf. Wilson D. Miscamble, *George F. Kennan and the Making of American Foreign Policy, 1947–1950* (Princeton, 1992).

[7] *New York Times*, 19 Apr. 1950.

[8] Cf. Volker R. Berghahn, *America and the Intellectual Cold Wars in Europe* (Princeton, 2001), esp. 287–8. See also his essay in this volume.

The rhetorical-symbolic dimension of the Cold War was rarely as visible as it became on 24 October 1950 in Berlin. On that day, a bronze bell weighing ten tons was dedicated on Rudolph Wilde Square in front of the Schöneberger Rathaus, the West Berlin city hall.[9] 'Today, with profound reverence, we dedicate the world Freedom Bell', proclaimed General Lucius D. Clay, Military Governor of the US Occupation Zone in Germany from 1947 to 1949 and organizer of the Allied air lift in 1948–9 during the Berlin Blockade. 'May its voice lift the hearts of all freedom-loving people. From this day on, its peal will be a warning to all oppressors. It will bring confidence and courage to those who have to defend their freedom, but to those who are still in subjugation today, it will be a message of hope and sympathy.' In their speeches, the other three speakers—US Commandant of the City of Berlin Maxwell Taylor, US High Commissioner John J. McCloy, and the Governing Mayor of Berlin Ernst Reuter—also emphasized the unity of the 'free world' in the struggle against Communism. Optimism, a belief in their own strength, and, above all, the power of the USA set the tone.[10]

The speakers at this ceremony addressed a crowd of 400,000 which had assembled in Rudolph Wilde Square.[11] These people had come not only from the Western sectors, but also from East Berlin and the surrounding areas, streaming over the still open border to the square, which was still flanked by ruins. At the same time, the ceremony was directed at a world public. Two thousand radio stations transmitted the words of the speakers into the ether; 1,500 radio stations broadcast to the USA alone. Voice of America and Radio Free Europe conveyed the events to those in the Soviet sphere of power behind the Iron Curtain. The radio station in the American sector (RIAS) did the same for the territory of the GDR. In this way, the dedication of the Freedom Bell probably reached one of the largest radio audiences in history up to that date. What happened on that day in Berlin was more than a gesture of friendship toward the people

---

[9] The dedication ceremony is described in Free Europe Committee (ed.), *The Story of the World Freedom Bell* (New York, 1950) and in Senat von Berlin (ed.), *Ein Jahr Freiheitsglocke in Berlin* (Berlin, 1951).

[10] Ibid. 19, 22, 24, and 28.

[11] Two million people had already turned out to line the bell's route from the airport at Tempelhof to Schöneberg.

of West Berlin, who, with American and British help, had survived the Soviet Union's blockade of their half of the city one year previously.[12] It was a carefully stage-managed propaganda event, planned down to the last detail, which was intended to guarantee the Germans US support for the reunification of their country, and to boost the profile of the Western side in the Cold War in Europe and the USA.

The dedication of the bell, like the rhetoric and symbolism at the height of the Cold War in general, was directed at three different audiences. In the USA it was intended to alert the Americans to the threat posed by the Soviet Union and to confer legitimacy on the US government's engagement in the struggle against Communism. In Western Europe it was intended to increase confidence in the superiority and dependability of the USA, and to gain support for a common front against Bolshevism. Behind the Iron Curtain, finally, the aim was, in General Eisenhower's words, to 'intensify the will for freedom in the satellite countries . . . These countries are in the Soviet back yard, and only as their people are reminded that the outside world has not forgotten them . . . do they remain potential deterrents to Soviet aggression.'[13]

This essay will analyse the rhetoric and symbolism of the Cold War using the Berlin Freedom Bell as an example.[14] It will concentrate on three aspects: first, the people and institutions that shaped and disseminated it; secondly, the structure and leitmotivs of Cold War rhetoric and symbolism; and thirdly, how they changed in the course of the conflict of systems.

I. *Institutions and Personnel of the Crusade for Freedom*

The sponsor and initiator of the Freedom Bell was an organization named Crusade for Freedom which had been founded in

---

[12] Cf. W. Phillips Davison, *The Berlin Blockade: A Study in Cold War Politics* (Princeton, 1958); Ann and John Tusa, *The Berlin Airlift* (New York, 1988); Avi Shlaim, *The United States and the Berlin Blockade, 1948–9: A Study in Crisis Decision-Making* (Berkeley, 1983); Volker Koop, *Kein Kampf um Berlin? Deutsche Politik zur Zeit der Berlin-Blockade 1948–9* (Bonn, 1998).

[13] Quoted in Puddington, *Broadcasting Freedom*, 15.

[14] For the methodology of the historiography of rhetoric see, in addition to Medhurst *et al.* (eds.), *Cold War Rhetoric*, e.g. Wayne E. Brockriede and Robert L. Scott, *Moments in the Rhetoric of the Cold War* (New York, 1970); and Martin J. Medhurst (ed.), *Eisenhower's War of Words: Rhetoric and Leadership* (East Lansing, 1994).

1950. Its chairman was General Clay. His most important collaborators were Abbott Washburn and Nate Crabtree, who had been Publicity and Accounts Executives respectively for large businesses in Minneapolis before working for the Crusade for Freedom.[15] The organization's official purpose was to raise money in America on behalf of the National Committee for a Free Europe (NCFE), later renamed Free Europe Committee. The NCFE had officially been founded in June 1949 'by American citizens for positive action against Soviet enslavement of the satellite countries', as a leaflet put it.[16] The National Committee's objective was to look after the many exiles from Eastern Europe who had fled from Communism and arrived in Western Europe or the USA during the second half of the 1940s. It saw its main purpose as using 'the many and varied skills of exiled East Europeans in the development of programs which will actively combat Soviet domination'.[17] From early on, one of NCFE's main activities was to develop Radio Free Europe (RFE), based in Munich. Anti-Communist programmes for Eastern Europe were produced there and broadcast beyond the Iron Curtain from transmitters in Portugal.[18]

The first chairman of the NCFE was the diplomat Joseph Grew, who had been US ambassador in Buenos Aires and Tokyo. In addition to Clay, General Eisenhower and Allen Dulles, later director of the CIA, were members of the Committee, as were DeWitt C. Poole, another US diplomat; William Greene, president of the American Federation of Labor; Dewitt Wallace, the publisher of *Reader's Digest*; C. D. Jackson from the management of *Time-Life*, who replaced Grew as chairman of NCFE in 1951; Frank Altschul, a prominent New York attorney; Franklin D. Roosevelt's Attorney-General Francis Biddle; and Adolf A. Berle, another collaborator of Roosevelt's

---

[15] Cf. Sig Mickelson, *America's Other Voice: The Story of Radio Free Europe and Radio Liberty* (New York, 1983), 51–3. Washburn later became head of the United States Information Agency; cf. Stöver, *Die Befreiung vom Kommunismus*, 239.

[16] Quoted ibid. 237.

[17] Certificate of Incorporation of Committee for Free Europe, Inc., 11 May 1949; quoted in Frances Stonor Saunders, *Who Paid the Piper? The CIA and the Cultural Cold War* (London, 1999), 124.

[18] Cf. Puddington, *Broadcasting Freedom*; Mickelson, *America's Other Voice*; Allan A. Michie, *Voices Through the Iron Curtain: The Radio Free Europe Story* (New York, 1963); Robert T. Holt, *Radio Free Europe* (Minneapolis, 1958).

and former Assistant Secretary of State.[19] There were also men
such as George F. Kennan, John Foster Dulles, and Frank
Wisner who, while they were not officially members of the
NCFE, supported it with help and advice. The National
Committee could, therefore, draw on powerful members of the
American East Coast establishment in government, the military,
the world of business, the press, and trade unions. However
different the backgrounds of these men may seem at first sight,
they were bound together by many and diverse biographical ties.
Kennan, DeWitt Poole, Wisner, and Dulles had all studied at
Princeton. The last two, like Altschul and Berle, had been
lawyers in New York for a time after the war. More important
still was that they knew each other from their secret service work
at the Office for Strategic Services (OSS) during the Second
World War, when Dulles had headed the office in Switzerland,
Wisner had worked for the OSS in Romania and the Balkans,
and DeWitt C. Poole had been a high-ranking OSS officer.[20]
Via the network of former OSS colleagues, NCFE, the Crusade
for Freedom, and Radio Free Europe recruited a considerable
number of their senior staff, including Washburn and Robert E.
Lang, the first director of RFE.[21]

Not least thanks to these influential connections, the Crusade
for Freedom opened its publicity campaign successfully. On 6
September 1950 Eisenhower solemnly announced the start of the
first crusade in a national broadcast: 'We need powerful radio
stations abroad, operated without Government restriction, to tell
in vivid and convincing form about the decency and essential
fairness of democracy . . . The Crusade for Freedom will provide
for the expansion of RFE into a network of stations. They will be
given the simplest, clearest charter in the world: "Tell the
Truth".'[22] Two days later the first publicity campaign began.

---

[19] In the Second World War, C. D. Jackson had worked closely with General
Eisenhower as an expert in pyschological warfare, first in North Africa, and later in
Britain and France. After Eisenhower's election as President, Jackson was briefly his
Special Assistant for Psychological Warfare; cf. H. W. Brands, Jr., 'C. D. Jackson:
Psychological Warriors Never Die', in id., *Cold Warriors: Eisenhower's Generation and American
Foreign Policy* (New York, 1988), 117–37. For Biddle see Francis Biddle, *The Fear of Freedom*
(Garden City/NY, 1951); for Berle see Adolf A. Berle *et al.*, *Navigating the Rapids: 1918–71*
(New York, 1973). For this and the following section also see Stöver, *Die Befreiung vom
Kommunismus*, 237–40.

[20] Mickelson, *America's Other Voice*, 15–16.   [21] Ibid. 52.

[22] *New York Times*, 7 Sept. 1950.

The Freedom Bell destined for Berlin travelled all over the USA, publicizing the crusade and collecting donations before being shipped across the Atlantic with the signatures of all those who had contributed. Each person who made a donation signed a Freedom Scroll, which was to be stored in a Freedom Shrine in the West Berlin city hall. The Bell's journey began with a ticker-tape parade on Broadway before it was driven to City Hall. The accompanying TV broadcast featured an actor by the name of Ronald Reagan. Thereafter the Freedom Bell, transported sometimes by road and sometimes aboard the Freedom Train, was taken via Chicago, Denver, Los Angeles, Dallas, New Orleans, and Atlanta through twenty-six states to Washington and Philadelphia, arriving back in New York on 8 October. According to a leaflet later published by the Berlin Senate, 16 million Americans signed Freedom Scrolls during the bell's journey, and they donated a total of 1.3 million dollars.[23]

From then on, the Freedom Bell served as a striking emblem on the posters and leaflets which the Crusade for Freedom used to drum up support. On radio and TV advertisements, the peal of bells accompanied appeals to Americans to give 'truth dollars' for Radio Free Europe. Every state and every large American city had a base; special offices were set up in sixteen cities.[24] Every year the crusade was conducted under a new motto. In 1950 Eisenhower's message was: 'Fight the big lie with the big truth.' The following year it was: 'Help truth fight Communism: Join the Crusade for Freedom.'[25] Hundreds of Americans worked on the campaigns as unpaid volunteers. In the ideologically charged atmosphere at the height of the Cold War early in the 1950s, to make this sort of commitment to the Crusade for Freedom did not imply taking a pronounced political position. Rather, the organization was largely absorbed into the mainstream of the contemporary *Zeitgeist*. During the presidential election campaign in 1952, both candidates held speeches at Crusade for Freedom rallies.[26] Newspapers across the USA supported it and publicized the crusade. 'Every citizen', wrote the North Carolina *Liberty News*, for example,

[23] Senat von Berlin (ed.), *Ein Jahr Freiheitsglocke*, 8.
[24] Cf. Mickelson, *America's Other Voice*, 55.
[25] Quoted in Puddington, *Broadcasting Freedom*, 23.
[26] Stöver, *Die Befreiung vom Kommunismus*, 239.

can fight Communism by supporting 'Crusade for Freedom'! Most Americans—most citizens like those living right here in Liberty and surrounding areas—deplore Communism, but calmly shrug their shoulders with the words 'What can I do about it?' These citizens can ask the question no longer without getting an answer. A program has been set up so that every American can have an active part in fighting and crushing Communism. The program is the 'Crusade for Freedom'—its most vital weapon is Radio Free Europe . . . The Crusade is fighting Communism, the 'big lie', with TRUTH.[27]

Despite the crusade's popularity, donations always covered only part of the expenditure of RFE and the NCFE, which had generous business premises in the Empire State Building. Although from 1954 private contributions by American citizens were increasingly supplemented by large donations from businesses, the campaigns did not even generate enough income to cover the costs of the Crusade for Freedom itself. In the eleven months between April 1951 and February 1952, for example, the organization's expenditure amounted to almost 2 million dollars, whereas its income was a mere 1.75 million dollars—leaving a gap of 250,000 dollars.[28] This gap was filled from the start, and without the public knowing about it, by the US government. In addition to the 2.25 to 3.3 million dollars which the Crusade for Freedom took in annual donations in the 1950s, Washington provided between one and two million dollars per year. In time, the government subsidy settled down at 37 per cent of total outgoings.[29]

Finances for the NCFE, the Crusade for Freedom, and Radio Free Europe came from the CIA.[30] This was not an emergency solution born of necessity. From the start, it was a central aspect of the strategy behind the development of the NCFE and its subdivisions. From the point of view of the US government, there were a number of reasons for not undertaking these Cold War propaganda activities in its own name, but for controlling them indirectly while outwardly maintaining the façade of a

---

[27] *Liberty News* (North Carolina), 1 Dec. 1952; quoted in Lucas, *Freedom's War*, 102–3.

[28] Mickelson, *America's Other Voice*, 58.

[29] Figures in Puddington, *Broadcasting Freedom*, 23–4.

[30] The two older studies of Radio Free Europe do not make this connection; cf. Holt, *Radio Free Europe*; and Michie, *Voices Through the Iron Curtain*. The covert payments by the CIA were not publicly acknowledged until the early 1970s, when they ceased; cf. Puddington, *Broadcasting Freedom*, 32.

private organization. They felt that this gave them 'greater flexibility and freedom from official taboos', as C. D. Jackson wrote in 1953.[31] Radio Free Europe, nominally independent but requiring its 'policy guidelines' to be sanctioned by the CIA and the State Department, was able to take greater freedoms in its reportage. It was able to judge the Communist regimes more harshly than Voice of America, which was officially under the State Department and therefore had to take diplomatic relations with the Communist regimes of the Eastern European states into account. Early on General Clay had justified the founding of the RFE and the Crusade for Freedom by suggesting that: 'We need another voice, a voice less tempered perhaps by the very dignity of government, a tough slugging voice, if you please.'[32]

Another central consideration was that an 'independent' organization financed by the donations of American citizens would enjoy greater credibility and prestige in the USA and in Eastern Europe than an undertaking known to be financed by the American government, let alone the US secret service. After the event, Washburn freely admitted that fund raising had been only one of the aims of the Crusade for Freedom: 'The first was to acquaint citizens of the United States with efforts to preach the virtues of freedom to peoples behind the Iron Curtain. The second was to obtain some limited funding to help support the effort. A third was to provide cover so it would appear the funding was derived from the general public and not from any governmental source, particularly not from the CIA.'[33] Finally, the very nature of American ideology demanded 'a private façade' for Cold War propaganda, as Scott Lucas has aptly put it. Thus the 'state–private network', of which the Crusade was an important part, was more than a smokescreen operation. It was a sincere expression of the American ideology of freedom.[34]

II. *The Rhetoric and Symbolism of Freedom*

At the heart of the rhetoric which the Crusade for Freedom used in its advertising campaigns was the idea of freedom which

---

[31] Quoted in Lucas, *Freedom's War*, 100.
[32] Quoted in Free Europe Committee (ed.), *The Story of the World Freedom Bell*, 18.
[33] Quoted in Mickelson, *America's Other Voice*, 58.
[34] Lucas, *Freedom's War*, 3.

needed to be defended against the threat of Communism. The oath on the Freedom Scroll which millions of Americans signed on the bell's journey in 1950 read:

I believe in the inviolability and dignity of the individual human being. I believe that all people have the same God-given right to freedom. I swear to resist aggression and tyranny wherever they may appear on earth. I am proud of having participated in the Crusade for Freedom. I am proud that I have contributed to the production of the Freedom Bell, that I have signed this declaration for freedom, that my name will always be part of the Freedom Shrine in Berlin, and that I have joined the millions of men and women all over the world who hold the cause of freedom holy.[35]

The topic of freedom or liberation from the Communist yoke was also at the centre of American propaganda in respect of the Eastern European nations. 'For the peoples of the prisoner states', an internal NCFE memo for Radio Free Europe, dated 21 September 1950 read, 'everything else hinges upon the question of liberation. This is for them the vital preoccupation. Accordingly, liberation must be the predominant theme in any effective long-range program of propaganda.'[36]

At the dedication of the Freedom Bell four weeks later, speakers at the ceremony held in Rudolph Wilde Square in Berlin also put the idea of freedom at the centre of their speeches. In their short addresses, which in sum lasted only thirty minutes, the words 'frei' (free) and 'Freiheit' (freedom) occurred a total of seventy times. The USA was the refuge of freedom, its furthest outpost Berlin—'a hundred miles behind the line at which freedom ends', according to Taylor. The location of the enemy was clear: the East. There tyranny, aggression, and oppression were the order of the day. There, McCloy declared, the crimes of the Nazis were being repeated: 'concentration camps, forced labour, deportations, grotesque propaganda exercises that are called elections, and marching youth'.[37] The rhetoric of freedom was building a bridge by which the USA could pass from the anti-fascism of the wartime coalition to the anti-totalitarianism of the Cold War era. Consequently the propagandists of the NCFE

[35] Quoted in Senat von Berlin (ed.), *Ein Jahr Freiheitsglocke*, 8.
[36] Radio Free Europe—Policy Guidance Memorandum No. 1, 21 Sept. 1950; published in Puddington, *Broadcasting Freedom*, 315–22, at 316.
[37] Quoted in Senat von Berlin (ed.), *Ein Jahr Freiheitsglocke*, 19, 22.

expended a certain amount of energy in underlining the features which National Socialism and Bolshevism had in common. 'Misrepresented as a liberating movement, Bolshevik imperialism is in fact reaction incarnate', Frank Altschul, chairman of the NCFE radio committee, wrote in September 1950. 'It is Red Fascism, and should be so designated.'[38] In the year that followed, a RFE Policy Manual was devoted to the topic of Soviet anti-Semitism. 'The major aspect of Soviet anti-semitism', it said, 'is of a new kind for which the Stalinists have found the name of "anti-cosmopolitanism". This is the Soviet counterpart of Hitlerian anti-semitism. . . . The German doctrine was founded on the notion of race and "blood"; the Soviet doctrine is founded on the notion of race and history.'[39]

In the Federal Republic of Germany and in West Berlin, too, the atmosphere of the 1950s was shaped by anti-totalitarianism in a characteristic mixture of a tacitly accepted anti-Nazism and brash anti-Communism. Against this background the Freedom Bell, heard every day at noon and on Christmas Eve, and which rang in the New Year, was able to establish itself as a central part of West Berlin's self-image, and as an audible challenge to Communist atrocities. The anniversaries of the dedication were marked with ceremonies in the Berlin House of Representatives, to which US President Eisenhower sent messages of greeting, and which were addressed by the US High Commissioners (from 1955 ambassadors). Until 1954, the Freedom Bell also rang on every 26 October, the Day of POWs, when the Berlin deputies remembered the German soldiers who were still being held in Soviet camps. RIAS had an important role in popularizing the Freedom Bell, adopting the Freedom Scroll and the peal of the Freedom Bell as its trademark. It regularly broadcast the text and the peal of the bell in Berlin and the GDR—at first daily at 6 p.m., and later every Sunday at noon.

A number of associations on both sides of the Atlantic dedicated themselves to commemorating the Freedom Bell, and organized

---

[38] Radio Free Europe—Policy Guidance Memorandum No. 1, 21 Sept. 1950; published in Puddington, *Broadcasting Freedom*, 315–22, at 321. See also Thomas G. Paterson, ' "Red Fascism": The Merger of Nazi Germany and Soviet Russia in the American Image of Totalitarianism, 1930's–1950's', *American Historical Review*, 75/4 (1970), 1046–64.

[39] Radio Free Europe—Policy Manual 1951; published in Puddington, *Broadcasting Freedom*, 323–5, at 323–4. On the totalitarianism theory as the 'inner history of the Cold War' cf. Gleason, *Totalitarianism*.

various campaigns to keep its memory alive. From the end of 1950, the Vereinigung der Opfer des Stalinismus (Association of Victims of Stalinism) published a periodical entitled *Die Freiheitsglocke* (The Freedom Bell). It mainly reported crimes committed behind the Iron Curtain: expulsions from the 'Polish occupied areas' (that is, the former German territory east of the Oder–Neiße line), expropriations in the 'Soviet Occupied Zone', and German POWs in Soviet camps. The periodical's masthead contained two emblems: on the right-hand side was a German Roland, cutting through a barbed-wire fence with his raised sword, and on the left was, somewhat larger, a silhouette of the Freedom Bell. Another association, the Freunde der Freiheit (Friends of Freedom), organized an essay-writing competition for schoolchildren in the spring of 1951, as part of a programme intended 'to honour freedom for German youth'. The topic set for the competition was 'The Basic Elements of Freedom'. One entrant, whose essay can be seen in the Berlin Allied Museum today, wrote: 'I feel sorry for the many Germans who live in the Eastern Zone under Stalinist dictatorship. We all long for freedom . . . Freedom is our goal. I, too, want freedom. The Freedom Bell would swing more quickly and peal more loudly if East Germany and West Germany were united.' His efforts were rewarded with a certificate of thanks, acknowledging his 'contribution to honouring the freedom of the German and American people'.[40]

The Crusade for Freedom organized trips to Germany for contributors and supporters. Delegates from all over the USA came from many different organizations, including the American Veterans of World War II and the National Association for the Advancement of Colored People, but also the Brotherhood of Locomotive Firemen and Enginemen, the Camp Fire Girls, the Loyal Knights of the Round Table, and the Fraternal Order of Eagles.[41] Files of the Senate Chancellery in the Berlin state archive allow us to reconstruct the 1954 Crusade in detail. It began with a visit to Radio Free Europe in Munich, followed by an excursion to the German–Czech border, where the eighty-five participants released hundreds of balloons to be blown over the Socialist Republic of Czechoslovakia and Hungary. Then the delegates themselves were driven to the border, 'where each

---

[40] Exhibit in the Allied Museum in Berlin-Zehlendorf, Clayallee.
[41] Landesarchiv Berlin, Rep 2. (Senatskanzlei) Acc. 1346, Lfd. Nr. 764.

glimpsed for the first time the barbed wire, watchtowers and Communist Czechoslovak soldiers along the Iron Curtain', as a press release stated. Before the group left Bavaria for Berlin, it signed a Freedom Scroll at the airport in Munich-Riem. In it, all the delegates pledged themselves to support Radio Free Europe in its mission for the enslaved millions behind the Iron Curtain, so that resistance to Communist tyranny would grow and the will for freedom among the oppressed would be strengthened.[42] The programme in Berlin included a sightseeing tour through the Western and the Eastern part of the city, a visit to the Free University of Berlin, and a ceremony to lay a wreath on the grave of Ernst Reuter, who had died in September 1953. The climax was a reception given by the Governing Mayor of Berlin, Otto Suhr, in the West Berlin city hall, where the Freedom Bell was rung in honour of the Americans. Then they paid a visit to the Freedom Shrine in the town hall tower, and climbed up to the chamber housing the Freedom Bell. The Mayor presented the youngest delegate, a representative of the American Boy Scouts, with a small porcelain replica of the Freedom Bell, which had been the city's official gift since 1953.[43]

It was not by chance that the Crusade delegates' journey ended at the Spree. Berlin played a central part in the symbolism of the Cold War. It was no coincidence that in 1948 the Free University was established there, on the 'front line' of the Cold War, with American aid. And in June 1950 the first Congress for Cultural Freedom was quite deliberately held there.[44] From the point of view of the Federal Republic of Germany, the divided city embodied West Germany's claim to represent the whole of Germany. For the USA it symbolized America's leading role in the Cold War. Both sides saw it as the heart of what Germany and the USA shared politically, a mutuality that had been created after the war. Since October 1950, the 'symbol Berlin' had found visible expression in the Freedom Bell. The gift of the

---

[42] Radio Free Europe, Press Release (25 Oct. 1954), Landesarchiv Berlin, Rep. 02, Nr. 973.

[43] Distinguished guests, such as ambassadors, envoys, and commanding officers of the powers protecting the city, received a somewhat bigger silver replica.

[44] Cf. James F. Tent, *The Free University of Berlin: A Political History* (Bloomington, 1988); Siegward Lönnendonker, *Freie Universität: Gründung einer politischen Universität* (Berlin, 1988). For the history of the CCF see Coleman, *Liberal Conspiracy*; Grémion, *Intelligence*; Hochgeschwender, *Freiheit*.

bell was intended to link the people of Berlin to the collective memory of the USA, and to extend the spiritual home of the Americans to include the divided city. Berlin was promoted—at least symbolically—to become the USA's fifty-first state, and the USA became a substitute fatherland for the people of Berlin. 'Cold War Berlin became indeed an American city, i.e., in the perception and the rationale of parts of American society Berlin embodied a bundle of qualities which made the city a place that mirrored important historical myths and political visions of the United States', as Andreas Daum has aptly put it.[45]

The symbol of this connection had been carefully selected. It was not just any bell, but a replica of Philadelphia's Liberty Bell, whose history reached back to the last decades before the American War of Independence. In 1750 Philadelphia's city government had placed an order in the British motherland for a bell for its State House. The bell was to bear the following inscription, drawn from the Third Book of Moses: 'Proclaim Liberty throughout all the land unto all the inhabitants thereof' (Leviticus 25: 10). In the decades that followed, its voice was heard at all the important turning points of the American Revolution. It was rung when the Declaration of Independence was read out in public on 8 July 1776, at the victory over Britain seven years later, when George Washington was elected as the USA's first president in 1789, and on his death in 1799. The Liberty Bell received its name only fifty years later, when opponents of slavery conferred a new meaning on the biblical verse inscribed on it. Now it no longer referred to the freedom of the white colonists from the British motherland, but to the emancipation of their black slaves.[46]

At around the same time, the myths that still surround the bell today began to grow. Probably the most influential was George Lippard's description in his short story 'The Fourth of July', published in 1847: '[T]he echo of that bell', he wrote, 'awoke a world, slumbering in tyranny and crime! . . . the bell spoke to all

[45] Andreas W. Daum, 'America's Berlin 1945–2000: Between Myths and Visions', in Frank Trommler (ed.), *Berlin: The New Capital in the East. A Transatlantic Appraisal*, Harry and Helen Gray Humanities Program Series, 7 (Washington, DC, 2000), 49–73, at 50.

[46] Between 1839 and 1858, abolitionists from the Massachusetts Anti-Slavery Fair and from the National Anti-Slavery Bazaar published a periodical entitled *The Liberty Bell. By Friends of Freedom*. See also Martin Grove Brumbaugh and Joseph S. Walton (eds.), *Liberty Bell Leaflets: Translations and Reprints of Historical Documents* (Philadelphia, 1898–1900).

the world. That sound crossed the Atlantic—pierced the dungeons of Europe—the work shops of England—the vassal-fields of France. That Echo spoke to the slave—bade him look for his toil—and know himself a man. That Echo startled the Kings upon their crumbling thrones. That Echo was the knell of King-craft, Priest-craft and all the other crafts born of the darkness of ages, and baptized in seas of blood.'[47]

Lippard's fictional story, which was eagerly used in countless other stories and poems, contributed as much to the popularization of the Liberty Bell in the second half of the nineteenth century as the various journeys on which it was taken from 1885. The purpose of these expeditions was to heal the wounds which the Civil War had left in the 1860s, and to establish the bell as a symbol of the unity of the Union. In a railway carriage specially fitted out to carry it, the Liberty Bell was first taken to all the big cities of the South: New Orleans (1885), Atlanta (1895), Charleston/South Carolina (1902), and again New Orleans (1915).[48] The greater the success of these journeys, the more popular did the Liberty Bell become as an attraction at trade fairs and celebrations all over the country. In 1893 it was taken to Chicago for the World's Columbian Exposition; in 1904 it went to the Louisiana Purchase Exposition at St Louis; and in 1915 it went on its last big journey, to San Francisco on the West Coast.[49] At times of national crisis, the government used the bell to appeal to the people's patriotism, to invoke the memory of a glorious past, and to boost belief in the victory of their own cause. During the First World War, for example, the Wilson Administration used the popularity of the Liberty Bell to advertise war loans, which they called Liberty Loans. Twenty-seven years later, the peal of the bell announced to the Americans that the Allied forces had landed in Normandy.

Washburn and Crabtree, whose idea it had been to give Berlin a replica of the Liberty Bell, made every effort to connect the

[47] Quoted from Viktor Rosewater, *The Liberty Bell: Its History and Significance* (New York, 1926), 117.

[48] Ibid. 151–93.

[49] In the same year, the peals of the Liberty Bell opened the first transcontinental telephone line between Philadelphia and San Francisco. At the same time, the trade in bell-shaped souvenirs and objects for everyday use was booming: there were bookmarks, paperweights, lampstands, salt-cellars, and door-knockers in the shape of the Liberty Bell. And the inventor of the first gambling machine, which was put in American bars, called his invention the Liberty Bell.

Freedom Bell to the American tradition by as many links as possible. The New York industrial designer, Walter Dorwin Teague, who designed the Freedom Bell, inscribed it with a slightly edited version of a quotation from Abraham Lincoln's Gettysburg Address: 'That this world under God shall have a new birth of freedom.'[50] Above the inscription was an engraved frieze depicting 'the five races of man', who stood 'with arms outstretched passing from hand to hand the torch of freedom until one day it shall light the whole world'.[51] Above this was a laurel wreath as a symbol of peace. The bell was to be cast at the same foundry in England as the original two hundred years previously. When this proved to be impossible as the foundry no longer existed, the contract was awarded to Gilett and Johnston, Ltd., whose factory was near the original production site. The Freedom Bell's fundraising journey through the USA was also modelled on the example of the Liberty Bell and its journeyings between 1885 and 1915. A further symbolic bridge was built across the Atlantic by the hundreds of thousands of Freedom Scrolls signed by American donors which were stored in the tower of West Berlin city hall.[52]

The symbolic impact of the Freedom Bell and its message of the USA's strength and superiority were not intended to be limited to Berlin and the Germans, but were meant to cross the Iron Curtain. 'Low tide is over', announced the Governing Mayor of Berlin, Reuter, in his address at the dedication of the Freedom Bell. 'High tide has begun. This Freedom Bell, which we are today taking into the protection of our city, is a clear sign that the high tide is reaching us. It will carry us and the ideas for which we are fighting out over the walls of our small town of Berlin.'[53] The ideas to which Reuter was referring are concisely presented in Radio Free Europe's political guidelines, dated September 1950. In them, Altschul described the most important elements of the political vision which America could offer the world at the time of the Cold War: 'A rising standard of living, an ever-widening horizon of opportunity, the dignity of the individual, personal freedom and national independence in a world

---

[50] The original reads: 'That this *nation* under God shall have a new birth of freedom.'
[51] Both quotations in Free Europe Committee (ed.), *The Story of the World Freedom Bell*, 14–15.
[52] Cf. Presse- und Informationsamt des Landes Berlin, *Das Rathaus Schöneberg und die Freiheitsglocke* (4th edn.; Berlin, 1984).
[53] Quoted in Senat von Berlin (ed.), *Ein Jahr Freiheitsglocke*, 24.

at peace are ideals responsive to the deepest longings of our people. We seek these things for others no less than ourselves. Our thoughts are directed to the ever-present American vision of a brighter future.'[54]

The American conviction of mission meant that religious undertones were present from the start in the campaigns of the Crusade for Freedom and the broadcasts of Radio Free Europe. The term 'crusade' alone points to the Christian tradition.[55] References to a new struggle of the Occident against the Orient make frequent appearances in the speeches of those years. As early as 1948 John Foster Dulles, Allen's brother and later to be Eisenhower's Secretary of State, had claimed: 'For the first time since the threat of Islam a thousand years ago, Western civilization is on the defensive.'[56] The Freedom Bell as an emblem of the new East–West dispute was also derived from the Christian tradition. Clay, for example, made the quasi-religious dimension quite explicit when, in his dedication address of October 1950, he declared that although part of the world would try to close itself to the bell's voice, it would penetrate everywhere. 'It will be heard by all peoples who live and work in freedom, and want to honour the godhead.'[57] The Policy Manual for Radio Free Europe similarly says expressly: 'We believe in the brotherhood of man under the fatherhood of God.'[58] To the propagandists of the Cold War, the Christian faith was not only a central component of the USA's self-image, but also an important feature that it had in common with the oppressed peoples of Eastern Europe, something which bound it to them and separated it from atheist

---

[54] Radio Free Europe—Policy Guidance Memorandum No. 1, 21 Sept. 1950; published in Puddington, *Broadcasting Freedom*, 315–22, at 319.

[55] At the same time, the name shows that in the view of many Americans, the Cold War against the Soviet Union was an almost seamless continuation of the Second World War against National Socialist Germany. It was no coincidence that General Eisenhower entitled his memoirs *Crusade in Europe* (Garden City, 1948); cf. Mark A. Stoler, 'The Second World War in U.S. History and Memory', *Diplomatic History*, 25/3 (Summer 2001), 383–92, at 386.

[56] Address to Bond Club of New York, 6 May 1948, quoted in Puddington, *Broadcasting Freedom*, 9. In the same year the writer Stefan Heym, who had fled to the USA from Nazi Germany and soon after moved to the GDR, prophetically entitled his novel about the problems of American policy in Germany *The Crusaders* (New York, 1948).

[57] Senat von Berlin (ed.), *Ein Jahr Freiheitsglocke*, 24.

[58] Radio Free Europe—Policy Manual 1951; published in Puddington, *Broadcasting Freedom*, 323–5, at 325.

Communism. One of the 'Freedom-grams' which the NCFE
distributed among American citizens for signature before smug-
gling them into Eastern Europe stated: 'In America millions
regularly pray for an understanding between our peoples. Please
add your prayers to ours. Surely our common faith in God is the
place where hope for freedom begins.'[59]

Thus the rhetoric of freedom, which, during the first half of
the 1950s, attached itself to the Berlin Freedom Bell in innumer-
able addresses and greetings, poster campaigns, newspaper articles, and radio broadcasts, was permeated by two closely related
motifs. First, there was the struggle against the lack of freedom,
which was directed primarily against Moscow but, in line with
the basic anti-totalitarian consensus of the Cold War, also
contained an unspoken rejection of the Nazi past. Secondly, the
USA's connection with the peoples of Europe and their common
values, deriving from the Christian tradition, were stressed.
Berlin's world significance as a 'bastion' or 'bulwark of freedom'
was emphasized, and its 'heartbeat' and 'constantly beating
conscience' were symbolized by the Freedom Bell.[60] For the
Western part of Germany and Berlin, the Freedom Bell symbolized the USA's promise of protection. East of the Iron Curtain it
was interpreted as a sign of hope for American help in the struggle against Soviet rule.

III. *From Liberation Policy to* Détente

The era of the Freedom Bell as a symbol of the Western world's
will to win the Cold War was of limited duration. The first cracks
became apparent immediately after Stalin's death in March 1953.
President Eisenhower, contrary to the recommendations of some
of his advisers, did not use the disorientation in the Soviet camp
for an anti-Communist propaganda offensive, but signalled his
willingness for *détente* in his 'Chance for Peace' speech of 16 April.
During the rising in East Berlin and the GDR a few weeks later,
the US government also reacted cautiously. RIAS, the West's
most important propaganda medium for the GDR, was
instructed to use restraint in its reportage of the incipient unrest,

---

[59] Quoted in Lucas, *Freedom's War*, 103.
[60] All quotations in Senat von Berlin (ed.), *Ein Jahr Freiheitsglocke in Berlin.*

and, in particular, not to mention the General Strike which the workers of East Berlin had called for. Admittedly, the Freedom Bell was rung to commemorate the 'victims of the struggle for freedom in East Berlin', as the agenda of the Berlin House of Representatives, put it.[61] At the same time, the American army closed the West Berlin streets that led to the internal border in order to prevent indignant West Berliners from intervening in events in the Eastern sector. The USA refused Reuter, who was in Vienna at the time, a seat in a military aeroplane bound for Berlin for fear that his presence in the city could exacerbate the situation. Reuter's speech, prepared in Russian, in which he called on Soviet soldiers not to fire on defenceless German workers, was not even broadcast.[62] Even a confirmed Cold Warrior such as C. D. Jackson remarked at that time: 'The big problem we face when we call for action behind the Iron Curtain is the extent to which we are willing to back that action if serious trouble develops. It would be both immoral and inefficient to provoke massacres, which would not only kill off the best men, but would also destroy our position in the minds of the people behind the Iron Curtain.'[63]

The fundamental dilemma of psychological warfare expressed by Jackson was demonstrated to the West even more brutally three years later in Hungary. After the bloody suppression of the revolution, Radio Free Europe was criticized because some people believed it had irresponsibly contributed to the escalation of the crisis.[64] Thereupon, and not least in response to the State Department's insistence, RFE changed the guidelines governing its reportage. The relevant memoranda less frequently mentioned a policy of liberation, and more often spoke of the intention 'to foster an evolutionary development resulting in the weakening of

---

[61] Abgeordnetenhaus von Berlin, *Stenographischer Bericht: I. Wahlperiode*, 72nd (extraordinary) session, 17 June 1953, 407. On the history of the uprising, see Arnulf Baring, *Uprising in East Germany: June 17, 1953* (Ithaca, 1972); Torsten Diedrich, *Der 17. Juni 1953 in der DDR: Bewaffnete Gewalt gegen das Volk* (Berlin, 1991); Manfred Hagen, *DDR. Juni '53: Die erste Volkserhebung im Stalinismus* (Stuttgart, 1992); Ilko Sascha Kowalczuk *et al.* (eds.), *Der Tag X: 17. Juni 1953* (Berlin, 1995).

[62] Cf. Christian F. Ostermann, *United States Policy, the 17 June Uprising in the GDR, and the 'Eisenhower Packages' Program: New Evidence from German and American Archives*, Cold War International History Project, Woodrow Wilson International Center for Scholars, Working Paper No. 11 (Washington, DC, 1994).

[63] Quoted in H. W. Brands, Jr., 'C. D. Jackson: Psychological Warriors Never Die', in id., *Cold Warriors*, 124.

[64] Cf. Puddington, *Broadcasting Freedom*, 89–114.

Soviet controls and the progressive attainment of national independence'. As a realistic, short-term goal of American policy it named in respect of Czechoslovakia, for example, the setting up of a national Communist regime, 'which, though it may be in close military and political alliance with the USSR, will be able to exercise to a much greater degree than in the past independent authority and control in the direction of its own affairs'. Further, it expressly stated that it was 'neither feasible nor desirable that the U.S. run the risk of instigating either local or general hostilities [by encouraging popular resistance]'.[65]

In West Berlin on 4 November the political parties called for a rally in front of the West Berlin city hall to demonstrate solidarity with the Hungarians. 'There were certainly a hundred thousand people who assembled on that evening, a great part of them desperate and embittered', as Willy Brandt, at that time Speaker of the Berlin House of Representatives, wrote later. 'The speakers at that rally had a difficult task . . . Appeals to prudence and reason merely fell flat, the crowd wanted to see "action".' To prevent 'a wild march on the east sector', and in order to avoid an escalation of popular anger, Brandt devised a number of symbolic diversionary actions. He had already had the Freedom Bell rung several days before. Now he marched at the head of a large demonstration from the West Berlin city hall to the memorial for the victims of Stalinism on Steinplatz in West Berlin, and later, when the atmosphere on the internal city border at the Brandenburg Gate became explosive, from there to the Soviet Memorial, also on West Berlin territory, where he 'defiantly' started singing the German national anthem.[66]

The period of illusions about West Berlin's position did not finally come to an end until five years later, on 13 August 1961, when the GDR *Volksarmee* started closing the internal city border in Berlin with barbed wire, and the American, British, and French forces stood helplessly by, watching the Berlin Wall being built.[67] The shock for the Germans was all the greater because, just a few months before, on the tenth anniversary of the dedication of the Freedom Bell, they had been assured that their

[65] 1957 Czechoslovakia Country Paper, quoted ibid. 118.

[66] Willy Brandt, *My Road to Berlin* (London, 1960), 241–3.

[67] For the world political background see John C. Ausland, *Kennedy, Khrushchev and the Berlin–Cuba Crisis, 1961–64* (Oslo, 1996); Frank A. Mayer, *Adenauer and Kennedy: A Study in German–American Relations, 1961–63* (New York, 1996).

Western allies continued to stand unconditionally at their side. In retrospect, the celebration at the West Berlin city hall on 24 October 1960, at the height of the second Berlin crisis, proved to be the climax of the Cold War rhetoric whose bronze focus had been the Freedom Bell. President Eisenhower conveyed the message that the American people were determined 'to stand by Berlin and, by the side of the people of Berlin, to serve the great cause of maintaining and spreading human freedom'. Ambassador Walter C. Dowling declared that the tolling of the bell still kept the world's conscience awake. 'The Freedom Bell is a symbol, and behind this symbol lies the undiminished will of the free world to stand by this city as before—not only in thought, but also in deed.' In his address Robert Murphy, who had been political adviser to the American Military Governor in Berlin, wished the people of Berlin determination, confidence, and courage, and added: 'We will all need these qualities if, together, we want to let this Freedom Bell continue to ring in Berlin in future. And may God have mercy upon us if we allow this bell to be silenced.'[68]

In the summer of 1961, these words sounded like mockery to the people of Berlin. On 16 August hundreds of thousands again turned out in front of the West Berlin city hall. This time they carried banners with sentences like: 'Betrayed by the West?', 'Where are the protecting powers?', and 'The West is doing another Munich'. The main speaker, Willy Brandt, now Governing Mayor of Berlin, who had spoken of an 'offensive of freedom' as recently as October 1960, now faced a difficult task. He did not want to annoy the Allies, but at the same time he wanted to give his fellow citizens a feeling of security and also had to ensure that they went home peacefully without a riot. In his speech, therefore, Brandt on the one hand emphasized the significance of the Western powers: 'Without them the tanks would have kept on coming.' On the other hand, he also imposed a duty upon them: 'Berlin expects more than words.'[69] Despite Brandt's efforts, at the end the crowd called for everyone to march to the border. Brandt's adviser, Egon Bahr, had expected this and, as a precaution, had given orders for the

---

[68] All quotations from Abgeordnetenhaus von Berlin, *Stenographischer Bericht: III. Wahlperiode*, 47th session, 24 Oct. 1960, 376, 378-9.

[69] *Tagesspiegel*, 17 Aug. 1961. Cf. Diethelm Prowe, 'Der Brief Kennedys an Brandt vom 18. August 1961. Eine zentrale Quelle zur Berliner Mauer und zur Entstehung der Brandtschen Ostpolitik', *Vierteljahreshefte für Zeitgeschichte*, 33 (1985), 373-83.

Freedom Bell to be rung to drown out protests from the crowd and to calm everyone down. The symbolic power of the bell worked for the last time: the crowd dispersed peacefully. After that, however, the magic had gone; the pathos of the Cold War had been used up. A new language, other strategies and models had to be found. In his memoirs, Bahr later wrote that the building of the Berlin Wall had opened a new era in postwar German history. 'Before, we had still been able to hope that Western integration and rearmament would, in the foreseeable future, lead to reunification. Now the cementing of the division was accepted by the Allies too. Before, the politics of strength could still be presented as the only effective means of forcing German self-determination; now it was clear that they would not be used for that purpose.'[70]

The Freedom Bell was identified, probably more than any other object, with the policies of the 1950s which were increasingly perceived as a failure. In the new phase, it no longer occupied a prominent place. The ringing of the Freedom Bell on the Day of POWs had already become obsolete in 1955 when the last German soldiers had been released. And after 1960, no more commemorative services were held on the anniversary of the bell's dedication. The West Berlin city hall registered such a dramatic decline in the number of visitors to the Freedom Bell that the opening hours were reduced.[71] Even where the bell was retained as a symbol, its impact changed. The periodical published by the Association of Victims of Stalinism continued to be called *Freiheitsglocke*, but the bell had disappeared from its masthead as early as March 1961. The German Roland wielded his sword against a barbed-wire fence alone, against the background of a map of Germany showing the borders of 1937. With the logo, the journal's attitude towards the USA also changed. The Victims of Stalinism now looked with mistrust at their once loyal ally, who had proved to be an unreliable friend during the Berlin crisis. In November 1961, the *Freiheitsglocke* wrote that the Berlin crisis was 'the clearest example so far of the complacency of a policy that looks for salvation in negotiations, while action is shelved for so long that it falls off the back of the shelf'.[72]

---

[70] Egon Bahr, *Zu meiner Zeit* (Munich, 1996), 125–6.
[71] *Die Welt*, 19 June 1968.
[72] *Freiheitsglocke*, 128 (1961), 3.

Indeed, the Freedom Bell was an uncomfortable reminder to Americans and Germans alike of the passion with which they had prosecuted the struggle against the very Bolsheviks with whom they were now sitting down at the table to negotiate. The bell was hardly an appropriate symbol of a German–American friendship which was no longer based on the common struggle against a lack of freedom, but on efforts to achieve *détente*. The figure symbolizing the new mixture of firmness and a willingness to negotiate which from now on shaped the Western attitude towards the Eastern bloc was no other than John F. Kennedy, by whom the people of Berlin had felt so badly let down during the Berlin Wall crisis. On his visit to Berlin on 26 June 1963, the American president managed retrospectively to recast the crisis-management of August 1961 as a success. His statement, made in German 'Ich bin ein Berliner', captured hearts and laid the foundation for the myth-making that set in after he was assassinated on 22 November 1963. Just three days later, the square in front of West Berlin city hall where the politician had spoken his famous words was renamed John-F.-Kennedy-Platz. On the anniversary of his speech, on 26 June 1964, the murdered president's brother, Robert Kennedy, unveiled a memorial plaque placed next to the main entrance to the town hall, with a picture of the president in relief and a quotation from his appeal to the people on 25 September 1961: 'Together we shall save our planet or together we shall perish in its flames. Save it we can, and save it we must, and then shall we earn the eternal thanks of mankind and, as peacemakers, the eternal blessing of God.'[73] Peace instead of freedom, co-operation rather than antagonism were the new buzz words. A stronger contrast with the implacability of the bell's message can hardly be imagined.

IV. *Conclusion*

In conclusion, we must ask whether the efforts of the National Committee and the Crusade it initiated were crowned by success. Did the Berlin Freedom Bell achieve its purpose? If we take the reactions of the Eastern bloc as a yardstick, then we can

[73] Address to the United Nations, 25 Sept. 1961; reprinted in John F. Kennedy, *To Turn the Tide*, ed. John W. Gardner (London, 1962), 207–23, at 223.

answer this question in the affirmative. From the start, the Freedom Bell was a thorn in the side of the leadership of the Socialist Unity Party (SED). On the day of the bell's dedication, it organized a noisy but unsuccessful counter-demonstration in East Berlin. GDR newspapers spoke of the 'hunger bell' or 'death knell', or even ironically of an 'alarm clock for heroes'.[74] Hans Jendretzky, a member of the Politbüro, warned: 'The rope of the death bell will become the gallows rope for those who ring it.'[75] Unlike the terms 'peace' and 'democracy', the term 'freedom' could hardly be redefined and integrated into the Marxist world picture. The Communists therefore did not begin to argue about interpretations, but contented themselves with dark threats, scorn, and ridicule.

Even when we look at the end of the Cold War and the disintegration of the Eastern bloc, the history of the Freedom Bell appears as a success story. The way in which the Germans were unexpectedly presented with unification in 1989–90 rehabilitated the German policy of the 1950s to some extent and put the Freedom Bell back into the limelight. The collapse of the Eastern bloc and the GDR's unconditional attachment to the Federal Republic was more in line with the policies of strength of the 1950s than the theories of system convergence which many people had believed in during the 1960s and 1970s. Freedom, the market economy, and parliamentary democracy had proved to be more attractive than Communism and one-party rule, and had therefore won. Consequently, the bell in the tower of the West Berlin city hall was remembered again. At 23.55 on 2 October 1990, it rang in German unity.

However, if we do not view history from the end, a more complex, many-layered picture emerges. In the spirit of the 1960s and 1970s, characterized by *détente* and anti-anti-Communism, the Berlin bell had largely been forgotten. At the same time, rumours emerging about the CIA's financing of the NCFE and its crusade became a serious threat to the future of Radio Free Europe. Ultimately, RFE survived the many demands for it to be disbanded. It even had a second heyday during the Reagan era. However, the financing by the CIA was ignominiously ended in 1973, as were the Crusade for Freedom's advertising campaigns.

---

[74] *Tribüne*, 24 Oct. 1950.
[75] Quoted in Puddington, *Broadcasting Freedom*, 21.

Instead, the broadcaster's budget was directly controlled by the US Congress.[76]

The success or failure of the Freedom Bell as an anti-Communist emblem of the Cold War can also be measured by a completely different yardstick. In the three most dangerous crises of those years—1953, 1956, and 1961—the pealing of the bell was a successful substitute for action. In 1956 and 1961, symbolic confrontation replaced a real conflict. In 1953 it helped to contain the conflict. It helped to ensure that the Cold War of words and threatening gestures did not turn into a German civil war, or even a global nuclear war. During the precarious climax of the Cold War in the 1950s, the Berlin Freedom Bell kept up the 'free world's' will for endurance and victory in the struggle against Communism. But it also helped to avoid an uncontrolled confrontation and to maintain a Cold Peace.

[76] Ibid. 187–213.

18

'Playing Beethoven like an Indian': American Music and Reorientation in Germany, 1945–1955

TOBY THACKER

The ever-growing literature on the 'Americanization' of Germany after 1945 has frequently used jazz as a symbol, typically to refer to a congeries of supposed 'American' qualities: individuality, modernity, and cultural freedom, or conversely, commercialism, superficiality, and cultural mass-production. The deliberate introduction of American concert music in Germany after 1945 has not been analysed in similar depth. This essay will examine that programme, and assess how far it was successful. In the initial postwar period, it will place the introduction of American music in the larger framework of 'Music Control' and 'reorientation' in the American Zone of Occupation, and in the comparative context of similar programmes in the British, French, and Soviet Zones. In the period from 1949 to 1955, it will trace the patterns of indirect influence which the American government exercised in the musical life of the Federal Republic. Throughout, it will explore the various means used to promote American music, which included sponsoring performances by German musicians, broadcasting recordings and live performances, publishing articles about composers and individual works, sponsoring lecture tours, and using America Houses as distribution centres for sheet music and literature, as well as bringing American musicians to Germany to give recitals and concerts.[1]

By the early 1950s, when German authorities were largely in control of municipal orchestras and of musical programming on the radio, the American composers introduced after May 1945

[1] I am grateful to David Monod for his criticisms of a draft of this essay, and to Elizabeth Koch-Janik and Amy Beal for their earlier responses to questions about American 'Music Control' in postwar Germany.

had almost entirely dropped out of the German repertoire, in contrast to those introduced by the Soviets, British, and French. It is tempting to attribute this to widespread German ignorance of, and prejudice about, American music. This is not, though, a sufficient explanation. When analysed in detail, it becomes clear that the American programme was slow to get under way, and that other aspects of 'Music Control', notably an insistence on the rigorous denazification of German musicians, and the relatively low place of music in American priorities, also acted as negative factors. Although the American programme might be seen to have failed, by 1955 a new generation of American composers, headed by John Cage, was beginning to make a dramatic impact, if not yet with a wider public, on influential critics, programmers, and cultural officials. The extensive covert involvement of the CIA in European cultural life has been documented by Frances Stonor Saunders, and West German musical life was not unaffected by this.[2] After all, Nicolas Nabokov, the émigré Russian composer who served as General Secretary and chief informal networker for the Congress of Cultural Freedom in Western Europe after 1950, had briefly served in Germany in 1945–6 with the American Information Control Division (ICD). It would be naïve to imagine that music in the early Federal Republic was untouched by his machinations. In fact, a more important role was played by the American High Commission (HICOG), and by supporting agencies like the State Department in Washington, than by the CIA. This has been confirmed by Amy Beal's pioneering work on the American connection with Darmstadt.[3] Well before 1955, American music was presented in Germany not so much as a symbol of anti-Nazism as of anti-Communism, and it had become an important factor in the cultural Cold War. The Communist Party's 'historic decree' of 1948 condemning the Soviet Union's leading contemporary composers for 'formalism' and 'cosmopolitanism' was widely debated in both Germany and America. The American avant-garde particularly became a favourite target for Communist critics in subsequent years.[4]

---

[2] Frances Stonor Saunders, *Who Paid the Piper? The CIA and the Cultural Cold War* (London, 1999).

[3] Amy Beal, 'Negotiating Cultural Allies: American Music in Darmstadt, 1946–1956', *Journal of the American Musicological Society*, 53/1 (2000), 105–39.

[4] On the 1948 decree see Alexander Werth, *Musical Uproar in Moscow* (London, 1949), and Elizabeth Wilson, *Shostakovitch: A Life Remembered* (London, 1994), 199 ff., which

American music was not an apolitical art form planted in a neutral soil. Whatever the intentions of individual American composers, their works took on added layers of meaning at different times and in different contexts in Germany between 1945 and 1955. This was a highly charged situation, where a people intensely proud of its own musical traditions was involved in a forced exercise of national redefinition. Nor was American music received in isolation. Postwar Germany was saturated with images and ideas about America, as well as with actual products, and in certain places, American soldiers. Admiration and negative clichés were mixed in popular and academic debates about American influence. To understand how American music was received after 1945, and to assess its impact, we must be sensitive to the rapidly changing nuances of the postwar German cultural scene, and to the extraordinary flux of contending influences there.[5]

1945–1949: Music and Anti-Fascism

American planning for musical reconstruction was undertaken in close co-operation with the British at the headquarters of the Allied Expeditionary Force near Paris in March and April 1945. It was the final element in the American and British planning for 'Information Control' in postwar Germany, and should be understood as part of what was described as 'the long term task of attempting to reorient the German mind'.[6] Particular

contain verbatim translations of contemporary documents, and eyewitness accounts of developments in the Soviet Union. On the reception of the decree in the USA see Virgil Thomson's articles for the *New York Herald Tribune* on 22 Feb. 1948, 2 May 1948, and 27 Feb. 1949, reprinted in Virgil Thomson, *Music Right and Left* (New York, 1951), 154–8, 158–63, and 163–7; for Germany see above all Hans-Heinz Stuckenschmidt, 'Was ist bürgerliche Musik?', *Stimmen* (1947/8), 209–13.

[5] The reception of American music in the early GDR lies outside the scope of this essay. Suffice to say that although many underlying cultural factors there were shared with the Federal Republic, the political and institutional climate was quite different. Bizarrely, it was in some ways more favourable to American music, because the SED distinguished between 'progressive' and 'decadent' forms in American music, and was prepared to disseminate those elements it deemed progressive, like black folk music and workers' protest songs, and later the music of those composers who were considered to draw from these sources. See for an overview Sidney Finkelstein, 'Komponisten der USA', *Musik und Gesellschaft*, 5 (1957), 269–72.

[6] Institut für Zeitgeschichte, Munich, Bestand MF 260, Office of Military Government, United States (hereafter IfZ OMGUS), 5/243-2/17, Statement by Brig. Gen. Robert A. McClure, Berlin, 2 Aug. 1945. McClure was the Director of ICD.

attention was paid to the restructuring of the German repertoire. Guidelines issued in June 1945 stated:

Our main endeavour must be to introduce or re-introduce the German public to the large musical world from which they have been cut off for so long. We should encourage as soon as possible the performance of operatic, instrumental and vocal works by:

a. German composers prohibited under the Nazi regime for racial or political reasons
b. Composers from outside Germany.

Appended were lists of composers 'to be encouraged in Germany'. Many were living composers from Britain, France, and the Soviet Union; several were historical figures; but the largest group comprised thirty-five American composers. This included the then leading lights of the American scene, Aaron Copland, Samuel Barber, Walter Piston, Roy Harris, Randall Thompson, Charles Ives, and Virgil Thomson.[7]

The Americans planned to supervise German musical life through regional military government offices, staffed by 'Music Control Officers'. These men would issue licences to selected German officials and musicians, who could then put on performances. Unsuitable applicants would be excluded from employment.[8] Music officers would also give practical help, and advise on the repertoire for these concerts, acting as censors where necessary. They were expected to give similar advice to the radio stations the Americans planned to establish. This dual role was difficult to discharge, and inevitably music officers were caught in crossfire, particularly in the first years of the Occupation. Generally, they welcomed the positive side of their task, which included the introduction of American music, as this gave them opportunities to build relationships with German musicians and officials, in contrast to the hostility that 'denazification' brought in its wake.

The difficulties of implementing plans drawn up in Paris became apparent to the first Music Control Sections in the field. Immediately after the German surrender, the American Zone

[7] IfZ OMGUS 5/265-1/2, Draft Guidance on Control of Music, 8 June 1945, and IfZ OMGUS 5/243-2/1, Annex 'A', Foreign composers whose works are to be encouraged in Germany.

[8] These arrangements were formalized in SHAEF Law No. 191 Amended (1), which was publicized in the American and British Zones by Nachrichtenkontrolle Anweisung Nr. 1. See IfZ OMGUS 5/243-2/8 for copies of both.

was divided into four administrative areas. 6870th District Information Services Control Command (DISCC) was assigned to Bavaria, 6871st DISCC to Württemberg-Baden and Hesse; separate Information Control Sections were assigned to the American Sector of Berlin, and to the Bremen enclave. From the first, the Americans were overtaken by a sense of competition with the other occupiers, all of which attached great importance to the early resumption of opera and symphonic concerts as visible symbols of their commitment to high culture, and none of which were as thoroughgoing as the Americans in their determination to denazify German music. When the Americans took over Stuttgart and Karlsruhe from the French, they discovered that concerts to German audiences had already resumed in both cities.[9] By the time they arrived in Berlin they found that not only had musical life resumed, but that German organizations like the Kammer der Kunstschaffenden and the Kulturbund zur demokratischen Erneuerung Deutschlands had been licensed by the Soviets, and were already concerning themselves with the reconstruction of music.[10] By the time the Americans had repaired a medium-wave transmitter in Munich to start broadcasting in their Zone, the British in Hamburg, and the Soviets in Berlin, were well ahead of them.

Further problems were caused by the immediate demand of American Army units for entertainment. Throughout the Zone, local commanders were using German musicians to entertain their men, and had little interest in ICD's demand that they should be properly licensed. Tension between ICD and other branches of the American military, notably Special Services and the Red Cross, was a constant problem in the early period of the occupation. In Düsseldorf, before the British arrived, the municipal Opera, styled as the 'Dusseldorf Opera Stars', was offering a programme called 'Continental Varieties'.[11] The transmitter in

[9] For Karlsruhe see Bayerisches Hauptstaatsarchiv, Office of Military Government, Bavaria (hereafter BHA OMGB) 10/48-1/5, Annex to Weekly Situation Report, Film, Theatre, and Music Control Section, 6871st DISCC, 7 Aug. 1945; for Stuttgart see Generallandesarchiv Karlsruhe, Office of Military Government, Württemberg-Baden (hereafter GLAK OMGWB) 12/91-1/7, Weekly Situation Report of the Film, Theater, and Music Control Section, 6871st DISCC, 30 June 1945.

[10] See Brewster Chamberlin, *Kultur auf Trümmern: Berliner Berichte des amerikanischen Information Control Section Juli–Dezember 1945* (Stuttgart, 1979).

[11] See the poster reprinted in H. Riemenschneider, *Theatergeschichte der Stadt Düsseldorf* (Düsseldorf, 1987), ii. 260.

Munich was used to relay 'AFN programs for troop entertainment' before the Music Control Section there was able to get some time for broadcasts of orchestral and chamber music.[12] It is hardly surprising that in German cities occupied by the Americans in April and May 1945, local populations typically had their prejudices about American culture strengthened. To cap it all, music officers frequently found themselves physically isolated, lacking vehicles, fuel, and adequate telephone communications with either their colleagues in other parts of the Zone, or with ICD's headquarters.

The plan to introduce American music was thwarted by a larger problem. It seems that in 1945, although German orchestras were able fairly easily to recover their old copies of Mendelssohn overtures and Tchaikovsky symphonies to start a musical *Wiedergutmachung*, there was no American music whatsoever to actually play from. The situation in Frankfurt, where 'all the classics including Mendelssohn, and plenty of French and Russian composers' were available, was typical.[13] In contrast to the British, the Soviets, and above all the French, who quickly brought scores and parts of their own national music into Germany, the Americans were incredibly slow and ineffectual. American pieces for performance in Germany had first to be cleared by the State Department in Washington, and were then sent over on microfilm. In this form they were of course useless for actual performance. Experiments were undertaken in Munich to reproduce usable parts from microfilm, but were initially unsuccessful. At a zonal conference in September 1945, Music Officers were told to prepare to have American works copied by hand to overcome this deficit.[14] Through the autumn and winter of 1945, German orchestras played Hindemith, Bartók, Stravinsky, Shostakovich, and Prokofiev, to audiences eager for some spiritual comfort in a bleak postwar landscape. In the French Zone, a raft of individual performers and ensembles

---

[12] IfZ OMGUS 5/243-1/4, SHAEF, PWD, Semi-monthly Progress Report, 15 June 1945, 8.

[13] GLAK OMGWB 12/91-1/7, Weekly Situation Report of the Film, Theater, and Music Control Section, 6871st DISCC, 9 June 1945, Annex C. The actual performance of all American music had been banned in Germany in March 1942; see Hellmuth Hase (ed.), *Jahrbuch der deutschen Musik 1943* (Leipzig, 1943), 15.

[14] GLAK OMGWB 12/90-3/1. Preliminary Meeting of Theater-Music Officers, 20 Oct. 1945.

was brought in to play French music to 'mixed' audiences in Baden-Baden and elsewhere. From studios in Hamburg, and, after October 1945, Cologne, the Nordwestdeutscher Rundfunk (NWDR), and its new symphony orchestra under Hans Schmidt-Isserstedt were used effectively as tools for the introduction of British music. In the meantime, those Germans interested in broadening their cultural horizons had to be content to read about American music in licensed German-language journals.[15] The Americans refused to allow their own musicians to perform to German audiences. Not until December 1946 was the singer Marjorie Lawrence brought to Berlin for a trial appearance, by which time all the other occupiers had developed programmes for touring musicians.

There were other negative factors at work. Despite the images of material plenty typically associated with the American presence in postwar Germany, there was acute hardship in the American Zone before June 1948. German musicians were not immune from the hunger and poverty which characterized life for the civilian population there, and they were not, as in other Zones, given extra rations or preferential treatment with fuel and housing. Where priority was given elsewhere to restarting musical publishing, and to providing the raw materials needed for musical performance, in the American Zone the firm of Pirazzi in Offenbach was not allowed to restart production of strings 'owing to a lack of understanding on the part of Military Government'.[16] No paper was allocated to the fourteen musical publishers in the Zone before April 1947,[17] in contrast to the French Zone, where as early as November 1945 Schotts Söhne of Mainz was given a special allocation of paper 'afin de faciliter une diffusion plus grande de la musique française en Allemagne'.[18] The develop-

---

[15] See John Tasker Howard, 'Amerikanische Volksmusik im zeitgenössischen Musikschaffen', *Die Amerikanische Rundschau*, 1945, no. 3, 35–44; Aaron Copland, 'Der amerikanische Komponist von heute', *ibid.*, 1945, no. 4, 71–6; and Elliott Carter, 'Neue Musik', *ibid.*, 1946, no. 7, 86–91. See also 'Neue amerikanische Musik', *Neue Auslese*, 1946, no. 4, 123–4, which was also distributed in the British Zone. Both journals continued to run articles about American music until 1949.

[16] IfZ OMGUS 5/348-1/8, Weekly Report of Theater and Music Section for period 1 May to 8 May 1946, 2a.

[17] IfZ OMGUS 5/348-3/4, Frank, Chief Theatre and Music Section, to Clarke, Chief, Film, Theatre, and Music Branch, ICD, OMGUS, 15 Apr. 1947.

[18] Centre des Archives de l'Occupation Française en Allemagne et en Autriche, Colmar, Direction Générale des Affaires Culturelles, 490/8, Schmittlein to Délégué Supérieure pour le Gouvernement Militaire de Hesse-Palatinat, 26 Nov. 1945.

ment of American 'information centers', which might act as
venues for chamber concerts, lectures, and as music libraries, was
similarly slow to get under way. The French opened their first
information centre in Constance in July 1945, and the Soviets
were equally quick to provide a well-appointed clubhouse in
Berlin for artists.

The Americans were also committed to a higher standard of
denazification in the information media than in other areas of
public life, and this had drastic consequences for German musicians in their Zone. The Americans repeatedly, and vainly,
urged the other occupying Powers to treat compromised
German musicians with greater severity, and harassed them
about individual cases.[19] ICD published its first postwar 'White,
Grey, and Black lists' in October 1945, and its Intelligence
Section constantly revised these over the next fifteen months,
adding more and more names to the many thousands of musicians, actors, and journalists excluded from their professions.
Attention, then and since, has focused on prominent individuals
like Furtwängler and Strauss, but the internationally known stars
blacklisted by the Americans were only the tip of an iceberg. At
the height of the purge, only one per cent of professional musicians in the American Zone were officially 'available for employment'.[20] Four individual musicians were listed in the Category
'White A'.[21] Inevitably, German musicians were driven to seek
work in other Zones, particularly if they had compromised backgrounds, and the anti-American prejudices of the population
were confirmed. Suspicions that the French, the Soviets, and
even the British valued music more highly than the Americans
were strengthened.

In these circumstances, the first piece of American concert
music performed in postwar Germany was for occupation
personnel only. In September 1945 the black conductor Rudolf
Dunbar conducted the Berlin Philharmonic Orchestra in two

[19] Public Record Office, London, Foreign Office Correspondence (hereafter PRO
FO) 1005/831, Allied Control Authority, Political Directorate, Information Committee,
Minutes of the Fourth Meeting, 27 May 1946, 14–16; PRO FO 1005/832, Allied Control
Authority, Political Directorate, Information Committee, Minutes of the Fourteenth
Meeting, 14 Jan. 1947, 6.

[20] IfZ OMGUS 5/270-3/4, Virgil Thomson, 'German Culture and Army Rule', *New
York Herald Tribune* (Paris Edition), 22 Sept. 1946.

[21] IfZ OMGUS 11/47-3/25, White, Grey and Black Lists for IC Purposes, 1 June
1946.

performances of William Grant Still's *Afro-American Symphony*. The 'great excitement' that Dunbar's appearance aroused in the orchestra itself must have raised the hopes of American music officers that his visit would be followed up by American musicians.[22] They were to be disappointed. Hardliners in the American Military Government (OMGUS), notably the Political Adviser Robert Murphy, driven perhaps by a sense of the American public's demand for a 'hard peace', held up the ambitious plans put forward by ICD to bring American musicians, including specifically black musicians, to perform to German audiences. Eric Clarke, Chief of Film, Theatre, and Music Branch, complained bitterly to ICD's Director, Robert McClure in early 1946 about Murphy's unwillingness to support 'top-line performers' coming to Germany.[23] Some of America's most distinguished musicians were brushed off when they tried to help. Serge Koussevitzky wrote to Murphy in November 1946, expressing his interest in the project of musical reorientation, and asked if a French colleague could be allowed into the American Zone to gain some first-hand impressions. Murphy's reply was polite, but placed a host of difficulties in Koussevitzky's way.[24] Newell Jenkins, the Music Officer in Württemberg-Baden, was told in February 1947 that Leonard Bernstein 'was not to be considered for performances in Germany'.[25]

Not until early 1946 were music officers told of the first group of five American works 'cleared for performance in Germany'.[26] The State Department requested 'detailed reports' of every performance, particularly of public and press reaction.[27] A meeting was arranged in Frankfurt, where the conductor Bruno Vondenhoff introduced German colleagues from around the Zone to the American works.[28] Walter Piston's Suite from the ballet *The Incredible Flutist* was played in Mannheim in March

---

[22] See Chamberlin, *Kultur auf Trümmern*, 122, 127, and 142.

[23] IfZ OMGUS 5/265-1/2, Clarke to Director IC, 29 March 1946.

[24] See IfZ OMGUS POLAD 459/9, Koussevitzky to Murphy, 30 Nov. 1946, and Murphy's reply, 16 Dec. 1946.

[25] GLAK OMGWB 12/91-2/7, Hinrichsen to Jenkins, 26 Feb. 1947.

[26] IfZ OMGUS 5/265-1/2, Hills (for Director ICD) to OMG (Bavaria), Information Control Branch, 9 Jan. 1946.

[27] IfZ OMGUS 5/265-1/2, Peeples (for Director ICD) to Chief, Theatre-Music, OMG W-B, 21 Mar. 1946.

[28] GLAK OMGWB 12/91-2/7, Jenkins to Moseley, 12 Jan. 1946.

1946,[29] and Randall Thompson's 3rd Symphony was played in Frankfurt on 1 April 1946.[30] The first American piece performed in Bavaria was William Howard Schuman's 2nd String Quartet, in one of Karl Amadeus Hartmann's *Musica Viva* concerts in May, alongside Shostakovich's 5th String Quartet. Apparently the Shostakovich was very well received, but there was less enthusiasm for the Schuman, which the Music Officer for Bavaria, John Evarts, regretfully described as a 'difficult' work for the audience.[31] During the summer of 1946 the programme gained pace, and ICD was able to report on forty-seven performances of twenty-five American works around the Zone.[32] One piece introduced at this time was Barber's *Adagio*, played by the Berlin Philharmonic under Sergiu Celibidache first in Berlin in April 1946, then in Leipzig, Stuttgart, and in July at the Schwetzingen Festival. Not until January 1947, when Piston's 2nd Symphony was played in Nuremberg, could Bavarians attend a performance of any American symphonic music.[33] In February 1947 an American opera, Gian Carlo Menotti's *The Old Maid and the Thief*, was performed in Mannheim; further performances were scheduled in Berlin, Wupperthal, and Dessau. By this time, the composer Harrison Kerr had been appointed to head the Music and Art Unit of the War Department's Reorientation Branch, and had travelled to Berlin to discuss 'urgently needed U.S. music . . . for educational purposes in Germany'.[34] More American music was performed around the Zone during 1947, mainly in the newly established America Houses. Frequently these concerts were accompanied by lectures and discussions led by music officers; often the Americans targeted particular audiences, handing out free tickets to local music students.

Through 1946 and 1947, a gradually increasing number of American parts, scores, and books on music were dispatched,

---

[29] GLAK OMGWB 12/91-1/9, Heidelberg Detachment, Weekly Report, 2 Mar. 1946.

[30] IfZ OMGUS 5/348-1/8, Weekly Report of Theater and Music Section for period April 3 to 10, 1946, 10 Apr. 1946.

[31] BHA OMGB 10/48-1/5, Music Weekly Report, 31 May 1946.

[32] IfZ OMGUS 5/348-1/8, German performances of plays of US authors and music of U.S. composers, 19 June 1946, 4–5.

[33] BHA OMGB 10/48-1/5, Music Weekly Report, 18 Jan. 1947.

[34] IfZ OMGUS 5/348-1/8, Weekly Report of Theatre and Music Section for Period 11 to 18 Feb. 1947.

mostly for the Inter-Allied Music Library in Berlin, for hire to all parts of Germany. The first batch arrived in April 1946, and soon a collection of sixty works was assembled, largely on microfilm.[35] The American contribution was small in comparison to those from other Powers. By June, when preparations for the opening of the Library were well advanced, the Americans had eighty works ready, compared to two hundred Soviet, and some five to six hundred British works.[36] The Library was opened in September 1946, and was very well used. Apparently Soviet music was most frequently loaned out. As late as May 1947, the Library was still unable to supply American music for use,[37] presumably because it was only on microfilm. Ironically, the Kulturbund in the Soviet Sector of Berlin was by this time arranging performances of American chamber music, and was in fact rather more adventurous in its programming, including works by John Bitter (the Music Officer in Berlin) and Roger Sessions in 1947.[38] Another comparison shows how slow the Americans were to get actual music to amateur musicians. At a time when Evarts was reporting sadly that he had received thirty Community songbooks, and thirteen copies of songs for girls' voices from America (this in a land of choirs!),[39] the new *FDJ Liederbuch* in the Soviet Zone was being printed in greater numbers than any songbook in Western Germany.[40]

The Americans were equally slow to broadcast their own music. Initially they ran three transmitters in their zone, in Munich, Frankfurt, and Stuttgart; in September 1946 they started a limited service in Berlin, which later evolved as RIAS (Rundfunk im amerikanischen Sektor). Although there were isolated broadcasts of live and recorded performances of American music during 1946, it was not until the end of 1947,

[35] IfZ OMGUS 5/265-1/2, Peeples (for Director ICD) to Dept. of State, 11 April 1946, and 19 April 1946.

[36] IfZ OMGUS 5/348-1/8, Weekly Report of Theater and Music Section for period April 10 to 17, 1946, 17 Apr. 1946.

[37] IfZ OMGUS 5/348-3/4, Staff Meeting, 6 May 1947, 3.

[38] See the programmes for the 'Abende zeitgenössischer Musik' from 1946 to 1949 in Stiftung Archiv der Parteien und Massenorganisationen im Bundesarchiv, Berlin, DY 27/213, 215, 249, and 433.

[39] BHA OMGB 10/48-1/4, Contribution of Music Section OMGB to Education, 3 Apr. 1947.

[40] See IfZ OMGUS 5/310-3/6, Report on Textbook Evaluation, Education Branch, Office of US High Commissioner, Sept. 1950, 4.

when NBC Thesaurus Record Sets arrived in Germany, that these stations were properly equipped to include a full measure of American music in their programming.[41] A 'Catalogue of American Musical Compositions' was sent out to the stations in August 1947, and station chiefs were advised to use their local music officers to help choose appropriate works for broadcast from this.[42]

By the middle of 1947, it must have seemed that the American programme was at last achieving some success. By this time, the emphasis of ICD's work was being shifted from anti-Nazism to anti-Communism. Over the next two years, the Americans, in line with the other occupiers, devolved control of music to newly constituted regional German authorities. Music officers sought to maintain their influence with these, and to encourage them to include American music on concert programmes, but two developments in 1948 undermined this intention. First, in April, ICD's Theatre and Music Section was transferred to the Education and Cultural Relations Branch, losing the word 'Control' in its title. In October the 'political vetting' of German musicians was formally ended.[43] By this time a number of the music officers who had worked through the difficult early phase of the occupation had left Germany, and their replacements found it difficult to discharge their responsibilities with limited resources. Carlos Moseley, later President of the New York Philharmonic, replaced John Evarts as the Music Officer for Bavaria in March 1948, and his reports back from Munich, the cultural capital of the American Zone, convey a sense of enormous frustration. Various incidents reveal both the successes and failures of American policy during this period. In 1948 a 'Visiting Artists Program' was started, and the public in the American Zone could at last see some really impressive performers. Leonard Bernstein's visit to Munich in May was a huge success. Cheering crowds surrounded his car after his appearance at the

---

[41] Bundesarchiv Koblenz, Bestand Z 45F, Office of Military Government, United States (hereafter BAK OMGUS) 5/260-2/4, Shipment of NBC Thesaurus Record Sets, 19 Nov. 1947.

[42] BAK OMGUS 5/260-2/4, Catalogue of Americal Musical Compositions, sent by Lewis, Chief Radio Control Branch, to Chiefs of Radio Branch ICD in all Länder, 13 Aug. 1947.

[43] IfZ OMGUS 5/348-3/10, Agreement between E&CR and ICD on Theater-Music licensing procedure, 19 Oct. 1948.

Prinzregententheater.[44] The violinist Patricia Travers, harpsichordist Ralph Kirkpatrick, and the baritone Mack Harrell also made successful tours. Yet old prejudices were still around. One German member of the audience at a recital by the pianist Webster Aitken was overheard saying, 'He plays Beethoven like an Indian.'[45]

The second problem was caused by the currency reform, which pushed American music to the margins of the German repertoire. Before June 1948, concert tickets had been almost valueless in the black-market economy of the American Zone, and concert-going had not been restricted to the better off. So great was the demand for culture from the German public in the 'hunger years' that programmers could afford to schedule many new and unknown works, alongside regular performances of Beethoven, Brahms, and Bruckner. After June 1948, though, audience figures collapsed, and programmers felt constrained to offer only the most conservative fare. This situation was recognized by German and Allied authorities alike as a grave threat to the fragile musical infrastructure of the Western Zones. The Americans had to use what they called 'DM reorientation funds' to support alternative programmes, mainly in the America Houses. These, however, were not suitable venues for full-scale symphonic or choral performances, and, increasingly, American music was restricted to chamber music and solo recitals. These concerts evoked a range of reactions, as did similar programmes in the other Zones. There is no doubt that many individuals, particularly music students, were effectively introduced to American music and musicians in the America Houses. Others had their prejudices confirmed.

In June 1949 the functions of Theatre and Music Branch were reviewed, and it was decided to close its regional offices, leaving only a skeleton staff of three working centrally with the Education and Cultural Relations Division.[46] The composer

[44] BHA OMGB 10/48-1/3, OMGB, ICD, Monthly Summary for Period 1 May 1948 through 31 May 1948, 4.

[45] BHA OMGB 10/48-1/3, Music Section, April [Munich, 1949]. We need to be very careful in generalizing about attitudes, and should perhaps bear in mind the gentle rebuke in a German reader's letter to his 're-educators' in *Neue Auslese*, 1948, no. 6: 'Halten Sie uns Deutsche doch nicht für sooo dumm . . .'.

[46] IfZ OMGUS 5/364-2/38, Theater and Music Functions of E&CR Division, 13 July 1949.

Everett Helm, who had been appointed Music Officer in Hesse in March 1948, was particularly critical of this. In an article for the journal *Musical America* he reviewed the work of Theatre and Music Branch since 1945. Bitterly, he wrote of the 'wild maneuvering' which had characterized the reorganization of the American Occupation forces, and concluded: 'When the scramble was over, culture had lost. Theatre and Music—representing precisely the fields in which rapprochement among nations can be most easily effected—had been wiped out.'[47]

1950–1955: Music, 'Cultural Freedom', and Western Integration

In February 1954 Everett Helm surveyed the concert programmes of thirty-five West German orchestras for the American public, and noted: 'It is a matter for some astonishment that not one piece of American music is represented.'[48] By this time, other aspects of American culture, notably of popular culture, like dime novels and jazz, were far more prominent in everyday German life. In the popular press and in films, images of American clothes, cigarettes, and other trappings of an affluent lifestyle were constantly paraded before the public. The admiration for American technology and production methods was confirmed by many public opinion polls. At the same time, anti-American clichés, and formulas about a supposed absence of American high culture dominated debates about American cultural influence. Clearly the intention that the German public should get to know and to esteem the work of American composers had not been realized.

It would be mistaken to see this purely as part of a wider picture of musical conservatism or retrenchment in the early Federal Republic. After all, as Helm also noted, West German concert programmes included many works by contemporary Soviet, British, and French composers. The promotion of 'zeitgenössische Musik' was a matter of municipal and regional pride in the early Federal Republic, serving as a symbol of cultural tolerance and integration with Western Europe. The *Städtetag*, which represented all larger towns, issued guidelines on main-

---

[47] Everett Helm, 'Music in Occupied Germany', *Musical America*, Feb. 1950, 115+, 256.
[48] Id., 'West Sector Roundup', *Musical America*, Feb. 1954, 150+, 219.

taining a quota of new music in public performance.[49] Radio programmers were animated by similar sentiments and maintained a studious public commitment to international 'neue Musik', not least through the sponsorship of prestigious festivals. West German composers indeed complained formally in 1953 to the Bundestag and the Conference of Land Culture Ministers that broadcasters were unduly favouring foreign composers.[50]

The Americans also displayed an ambivalent attitude towards their own composers who were identified with the political Left. On 19 June 1953, the GDR daily *Neues Deutschland*, eager to divert attention from events in East Berlin, reported that the music of Copland, Bernstein, Sessions, Harris, Gershwin, Randall Thompson, and Virgil Thomson had been banned from America House libraries in West Germany. Even the sponsored tours of American orchestras like the Boston Symphony and the US Seventh Army Symphony ran into difficulties. From contemporary reports it does appear that German audiences were impressed by the quality of American playing, but the music itself remained a problem. Virgil Thompson wrote to Nabokov in 1955: 'Everybody, including the United States Government, is mad at the [Philadelphia] Philharmonic for playing too much Soviet music in Europe and not enough American.'[51]

The reputation and credibility of a distinctly American musical tradition was, however, being subtly asserted in a way which would have lasting consequences. Since 1946, the State Department had committed itself to working indirectly to influence the German cultural scene, and by 1955 this policy was beginning to reap dividends in the rarefied sphere of avant-garde music. Two figures are of critical importance here, the German critic Hans-Heinz Stuckenschmidt, and the American composer John Cage. Stuckenschmidt's influence as a publicist of avant-garde music from the time of his early work with the Novembergruppe in the 1920s through to the 1970s has long been

[49] BAK, Bestand 105 (Deutscher Städtetag, Verbindungsstelle Frankfurt am Main), 192, Betr.: Lage der Kulturinstitute nach der Geldneuordnung IX, 9 May 1949.
[50] Westdeutscher Rundfunk-Historisches Archiv, Cologne (hereafter WDR HAC) 10070, Niederschrift über die 27. Sitzung des Hauptausschüsses des NWDR am 5. Dezember in Hamburg, 8.
[51] Thomson to Nabokov, 8 Dec. 1955, Tom Page and Virginia Page (eds.), *Selected Letters of Virgil Thomson* (New York and London, 1988), 291. Thomson was also a member of the Congress for Cultural Freedom, and had considerable influence with both the State Department and private foundations in the USA.

recognized. Cage in the early 1950s had an aura which he has since retained, that of the most radical of the international post-war avant-garde. Curiously, although Cage and Stuckenschmidt knew one another, they were not in any sense close associates. Stuckenschmidt, prevented after 1934 by the Nazis from publishing, ended the war in American captivity, but was released in 1946 to head a 'Studio for New Music' with RIAS in Berlin. He also worked there over the next three years with the Kulturbund's Kommission Musik, helping to give its monthly chamber concerts a particular distinction. In 1947 he was licensed by the Americans to edit a musical journal, *Stimmen*, and this was used as a platform for internationalism. Stuckenschmidt was utterly opposed to the demands placed on music by the Communist Party of the Soviet Union in February 1948, and soon tired of the cultural warfare which became ever more polarized during the Berlin blockade. In September 1948 he sought work with the Department of the Army in New York, offering 'to inform the German public, through articles in *Neue Zeitung* and other periodicals concerning the importance and the achievements of musical life in the United States'.[52] In early 1949 his application was accepted, and funds were made avail-able for Stuckenschmidt to tour America to learn at first hand about its musical life. He travelled widely, going to concerts, giving lectures, and meeting composers and critics. While there he was introduced to Cage by Virgil Thomson. On his return to Germany, Stuckenschmidt resumed his role as a writer and critic. He published, in German and English, in many newspa-pers and journals, and was made a Professor at the Technische Universität in Berlin in 1953. He stayed in touch with John Evarts, who worked after 1949 for Nabokov in Paris, and later with UNESCO's International Music Council. Stuckenschmidt was also President of the German Section of the International Society for Contemporary Music.

There is no need to look for a hidden CIA connection here. Stuckenschmidt had since 1946 written for the American-licensed *Neue Zeitung*, and by the early 1950s he was an employee of the State Department, as one of the newspaper's 'Special

---

[52] Stiftung Archiv der Akademie der Künste, Berlin, Hans-Heinz-Stuckenschmidt-Archiv (hereafter SadK HHSA), Korrespondenz 2618, Application for Cultural Exchange Project, 17 Sept. 1948.

Editors'. In 1954 he was receiving an annual salary of DM 25,000. The Americans, who monitored the work of 'local employees' very closely, were well pleased with Stuckenschmidt, as indeed they might be. An 'Efficiency Report' noted that his 'performance in every important respect is superior'.[53] It was with reluctance that they terminated his contract when the paper was closed down in 1955.[54] Stuckenschmidt was, unsurprisingly, a member of the Congress for Cultural Freedom. Nabokov (who typically addressed him as 'my dear Stucki') invited him to speak on 'Music and Politics' at the Rome Festival of 20th Century Music in 1954, which was attended by many prominent German musicians. Stuckenschmidt agreed to speak only if he could represent the view that music should have nothing whatsoever to do with politics. This chimed perfectly with Nabokov's agenda, and he readily assented.[55] We should be clear that there is nothing to suggest that Stuckenschmidt altered what he wrote or said in order to please his paymasters in Washington. His commitment to atonality, to twelve-tone music, and to a genuine internationalism, was developed long before 1945, and he would undoubtedly have acted as the champion of the avant-garde in the Federal Republic without American support. It was, however, no doubt helpful that the Americans paid substantial travel and accommodation allowances; this did help him to keep in touch with a West European and American network of composers, performers, writers, publishers, and broadcasters in the 1950s.[56]

Stuckenschmidt was from 1946 associated with the Internationale Ferienkurse für Neue Musik in Darmstadt, which became by the early 1950s a very visible and audible symbol of the reconstructed post-Nazi culture of the Federal Republic. He collaborated with the Darmstadt *Kulturreferent* Wolfgang Steinecke

---

[53] SadK HHSA, Korrespondenz 276, Dept. of State, Efficiency Report, Local Employees, 1.6.1953–31.5.1954.

[54] SadK HHSA, Korrespondenz 276, HICOG, Berlin Element, Administration Division, to Stuckenschmidt, Special Editor, *Neue Zeitung*, 16 Dec. 1954.

[55] See the correspondence between Stuckenschmidt and Nabokov in SadK HHSA, Korrespondenz 293; also the Festival programme, *La Musica nel XX Secolo* (Rome, 1954). For the history of the *Neue Zeitung* in general see Jessica C. E. Gienow Hecht, *Transmission Impossible: American Journalism as Cultural Diplomacy in Postwar Germany, 1945–55* (Baton Rouge, 1999).

[56] Interestingly, Stuckenschmidt's book *Schöpfer der neuen Musik: Portraits und Studien* (Frankfurt am Main, 1958) did not refer to any American composers.

on the selection of performers and composers invited there each year.[57] Stuckenschmidt was also involved with the NWDR, particularly in Cologne. He worked closely with Herbert Eimert, the director of NWDR's electronic music studio and one of the first to compose electronic music in Germany. Eimert, who had worked for the NWDR since 1945, was also influential as a programmer, running his own 'night studio' series. One of his junior employees was Karlheinz Stockhausen. Stuckenschmidt's role was straightforward in that he introduced a new generation of American composers to people like Steinecke and Eimert, who in turn presented them to wider audiences in Germany.[58] Thus in 1950, Stuckenschmidt helped plan the visit of the New York composer Edgar Varèse to Germany.[59] Amongst other places, Varèse went to Darmstadt, where he spoke about electronic music.[60] In 1952 Stuckenschmidt and Eimert co-operated in the planning of an international 'new music' festival held in Cologne in May 1953. As part of the festival, which was consciously presented as a practical manifestation of the Federal Republic's commitment to Western integration, the NWDR triumphantly opened its new electronic music studio.[61] Other radio stations in West Germany rapidly followed suit.

John Cage's introduction in Germany was a gradual process. Ironically, his music was thought too difficult to export by the State Department. Eimert, who undoubtedly knew of Cage through Stuckenschmidt, broadcast what was probably the first performance of Cage's music in Germany in one of his night studio programmes in December 1952.[62] He corresponded with Stuckenschmidt about his intention to use a piece by Cage in the

---

[57] See the correspondence between Stuckenschmidt and Steinecke in SadK HHSA, Korrespondenz 172.

[58] The influence of this network was thoroughly resented by conservatives. We might note for example the suggestion made by Hermann Unger to Hans Joachim Moser (both of whom had done rather better before 1945 than after) to put several progressives into a Sputnik: 'Dazu müssten gebracht werden Strobel, Stuckenschmidt, Steinecke, dann wäre die deutsche Musik gerettet.' Eimert was criticized in the same letter. Staatsbibliothek zu Berlin, Musikabteilung, Nachlass 31, Hans Joachim Moser, Unger to Moser, 15 Nov. 1957.

[59] SadK HHSA, Korrespondenz 172, Steinecke to Stuckenschmidt, 25 Feb. 1950.

[60] See Beal, 'Negotiating Cultural Allies', 117–18.

[61] See the festival programme, *neues musikfest 1953. 25. bis 28. mai funkhaus köln* (Cologne, 1953), and the correspondence between Eimert and Stuckenschmidt in WDR HAC 10929, and in SadK HHSA, Korrespondenz 307, and 236.

[62] WDR HAC 10929, Eimert to Stuckenschmidt, 8 Nov. 1952.

1953 festival, but this plan fell through. In 1954 though, Cage himself arrived, accompanied (in all senses) by David Tudor. The two performed first at the Donaueschingen Festival, where their use of prepared pianos, and their conduct on stage, was greeted with 'a storm of whistles, boos, and applause'. Stuckenschmidt's analysis for *Musical America* reveals how far even from his understanding of what constituted music Cage and Tudor then were. Describing the 'sonorous materials' from the prepared piano as 'partly beautiful, partly ugly, and mostly bizarre', he declared:

I have nothing against Cage. He is a serious and courageous esoteric, concerned with new sonorous media. But he combines tonal phenomena and pauses in a groping way, without creating any form. We are perhaps glimpsing into a workshop that is producing material for film and radio sound effects.[63]

Only a small audience was exposed to Cage and Tudor in Donaueschingen, but they travelled on to Cologne, where on 19 October 1954 they recorded a programme called 'Neue Klaviermusik aus Amerika' for the NWDR, which included pieces by Morton Feldman, Christian Wolff, and Earle Brown, as well as Cage's *23'56.176* for 2 pianists.[64] While in Cologne, Cage had extensive discussions with Stockhausen, undoubtedly influencing his further development as a composer.

Cage's impact in Germany was not immediate. He indeed felt that he and Tudor had been considered as 'clowns' during their first visit to Germany.[65] When Cage returned to Darmstadt in 1958, his influence was far greater, and his position has since been consolidated by longer-term reception. Amy Beal, who has explored the construction of a narrative of American 'experimental music' in Germany after 1946 in great detail, notes how other, now little-known American theorists and composers, some of them like Holger Hagen and Everett Helm as serving Music Officers, contributed to the development of this narrative through lectures, recordings, and live performances at Darmstadt before Cage became a dominating presence there. She

[63] Hans-Heinz Stuckenschmidt, 'Modern Music Festival at Donaueschingen Shows Vivid Contrasts', *Musical America*, 15 Dec. 1954, 18+, 18.

[64] Westdeutscher Rundfunk Köln (ed.), *Zwanzig Jahre Musik im Westdeutschen Rundfunk: Eine Dokumentation der Hauptabteilung Musik 1948–1968* (no date, Cologne), 86.

[65] Joan Peyser, *Boulez: Composer, Conductor, Enigma* (London, 1977), 139.

stresses how 'the sonic choices of certain American composers challenged German definitions of art music', and concludes that 'those American composers closest to the radical sound world introduced in Darmstadt during the fifties still enjoy both historical and political pride of place within German new music circles'.[66]

In 1955 this narrative was unknown to the wider German public, but a torpedo was running. Cage, Tudor, and the avant-garde helped to provoke the reassessment in Germany of America as a land without musical traditions, which had been a goal of planners in Washington and Paris before May 1945. If other composers, notably Stockhausen and Boulez, had their own niche in the avant-garde constellation, Cage above all has been absorbed into a wider perception in which avant-garde music has served as a metaphor for a Germany remade, one which had turned its back on the past. The enduring strength of this metaphor is perhaps best represented by the scene in Edgar Reitz's *Die Zweite Heimat*, where Hermann Simon, newly arrived from the Hunsrück, observes with amazement and fascination a group of older music students in Munich preparing a piano, Cage-style, for performance. This cinematic representation is set in the mid-1960s, but actually recreates something which happened first in Germany in 1954.

In the mid-1950s the programme to introduce American music to Germany appeared to have been largely unsuccessful. More people there were talking about the 'Halbstarke' and the influence of 'Boogie-Woogie' than were debating the relative merits of Copland and Barber, or the intellectual genealogy of John Cage. In the longer term though, a foothold had been secured for American music, and since then some of the composers introduced in the OMGUS period have found a place in Germany. Cage and the avant-garde slowly carved out a space in public perception which hardly existed before 1945, and which certainly took on greater significance after 1948, when avant-garde music was understood as a symbol of both anti-Nazism and anti-Communism. It even served as the last expression of culture which might remain resistant to the commercialization of the

---

[66] Beal, 'Negotiating Cultural Allies', 124 and 127.

Wirtschaftswunder.[67] One might argue that whatever this music sounded like, its rejection of the burdens and prescriptions of the past, and its challenge to a conservative older generation of music lovers, made it the ultimate symbol of 'cultural freedom' in the early Cold War. It was ideally placed to appeal later to the rebels of 1968. We have to ask not why the American programme failed, but why it was so slow to bear fruit.

First, there was a great deal of anti-American prejudice in postwar Germany. It was genuinely difficult for many music lovers to accept that America had its own music, as distinct from jazz or something recently gleaned from European émigrés. We might observe in passing that this was an idea which other Europeans, and even many American musicians had difficulty with. There is also no doubt that in comparison with the French, the Soviets, and the British, the Americans were slow to introduce their own composers and musicians into occupied Germany, and that they did so in a less favourable context. The low priority given to musical publishing and to the manufacture of instruments, strings, and reeds, imposed practical difficulties, which were more quickly and more fully overcome in the other Zones. The rigorous American denazification of musicians also hampered the general reconstruction of musical life, and helped to foster a climate in which Americans were seen as hostile to high culture.

Such arguments of course overlook any considerations of artistic merit. One could, after all, argue that the American composers introduced to Germany after 1946 were simply not as good as those put forward by the other wartime Allies. Perhaps Copland and Barber deserve to be less well known than Shostakovich and Prokofiev, Messiaen and Poulenc, or Britten and Tippett.[68] Perhaps, on the other hand, Cage was more interesting and challenging than Boulez or Stockhausen. Works of art, in this case of music, do not, however, fall into a neutral

---

[67] See Paul Betts, 'The *Nierentisch* Nemesis in West Germany: Organic Design as West German Pop Culture', *German History*, 19/2 (2001), 185–217, 215.

[68] The New York critic Harold Schonberg wrote: 'It was hoped in those days [the 1930s] that Copland, Roy Harris, Walter Piston, William Schuman, Samuel Barber, and Virgil Thomson would spearhead the new American school. Things did not work out that way, and history will put the group (Copland excepted) in an analogous position to the Boston Classicists—worthy and skillful musicians who lacked the individuality to create a lasting body of music.' *The Lives of the Great Composers* (London, 1971), 550.

social or cultural context, and sink or swim there solely by virtue of intrinsic merit. No one country, however rich and powerful, can, even if physically occupying another, and in control of its information media, simply choose which parts of its culture it wishes to impose upon the other. The fate of American music in postwar Germany between 1945 and 1955, and the continuing changes in the way it has been perceived suggest that the whole process is rather more complicated.

There is, finally, a broader context to consider. The plan to introduce American music to Germany, however we judge it in the short term, was part of a larger scheme of 'reorientation', and this was overwhelmingly successful. Volker Berghahn has argued that by 1955 there was a conviction in the West that the intellectual Cold War had been won, and certainly there is some confirmation of this in the specific field of music in Nabokov's article for the first issue of *Encounter* in 1953, in which he mocked the bankruptcy of 'socialist realism' in music.[69] The intention to integrate the Federal Republic politically with the wider Atlantic community, and to create democratic institutions there had been realized. Internally, cultural politics in the Federal Republic had been devolved to regional and pluralistic systems of control. Music had been internationalized, and this has helped since 1955 to ensure that American music, of all kinds, is played and heard in Germany today.

---

[69] Nicolas Nabokov, 'No Cantatas for Stalin?', *Encounter* 1/1 (Oct. 1953), 49–52. Volker Berghahn, *America and the Intellectual Cold War in Europe: Shepard Stone between Philanthropy, Academy, and Diplomacy* (Princeton, 2001), 287; see also his essay in this volume.

Notes on Contributors

VOLKER R. BERGHAHN is Seth Low Professor of History and Director of the Institute for the Study of Europe at Columbia University, New York. His research interests focus on modern German history and European–American relations. He is a Fellow of the Royal Historical Society. His publications include *America and the Intellectual Cold Wars in Europe* (2001) and *The Americanization of West German Industry, 1945–1973* (1986).

GÉRARD BOSSUAT is Professor of Contemporary History at the Université de Cergy-Pontoise (Jean Monnet chair). He has written a major study on the French Fourth Republic and the construction of Europe which was published in 1992 as *La France, l'aide américaine et la construction européenne, 1944–1954* (2 vols.). He has also published a number of articles on French and European postwar history. In co-operation with the German Historical Institute in Paris he has edited *Jean Monnet, l'Europe et les chemins de la Paix* (1999). Recently he wrote *Les Fondateurs de l'Europe unie* (Paris, 2001).

ÉLISABETH DU RÉAU is Professor at the Université de Sorbonne, Paris III. She has worked extensively on Édouard Daladier and written numerous articles on French and European history in the twentieth century, especially on European integration. Her most recent publications include *Europes des élites? Europe des peuples? Nouveaux regards sur la construction européenne* (1998), and *L'Idée de l'Europe au XX siècle: Des mythes aux réalités* (1996; new edn., 2001).

FILIPPO FOCARDI is Teaching Assistant in History of International Relations at the Università Roma Tre. He has written several articles on German and Italian postwar history. His Ph.D. thesis (University of Turin, 2000) was on the German question and Italian public opinion between 1945 and 1949. At present he is working on Italian war criminals.

NORBERT FREI is Professor of Modern History at the Ruhr University in Bochum. He has published extensively on National Socialism, media history, and postwar German history. His chief publications include *Adenauer's Germany and the Nazi Past: The Politics of Amnesty and Integration* (2002), and *Der Führerstaat: Nationalsozialistische Herrschaft 1933 bis 1945* (7th edn., 2002), and he has edited *Karrieren im Zwielicht: Hitlers Eliten nach 1945* (2001; paperback edn. 2003).

DOMINIK GEPPERT joined the German Historical Institute London as a Research Fellow in 2000. His main fields of interest are German and British contemporary history, international history, and the history of the press. His most recent publications include *Thatchers konservative Revolution: Der Richtungswandel der britischen Tories 1975 bis 1979* (2002) and *Die Ära Adenauer* (2002). At present he is working on British–German press relations, 1890–1914.

DAVID GILGEN is Junior Lecturer in the Faculty of History and Philosophy at Bielefeld University. He studied economics, history, and social sciences at Frankfurt, Berlin, Dublin, and Pisa. His Ph.D. thesis, 'Entstehung und Wirkung des deutschen Patentsystems im Kaiserreich: Eine neoinstitutionalistische Analyse', was completed at the European University Institute in Florence in 2003.

JOSE HARRIS is Professor of Modern History, University of Oxford. She has published extensively on the history of social policy, and on nineteenth- and twentieth-century intellectual history. Amongst her many publications are *William Beveridge: A Biography* (2nd edn., 1997), *Private Lives, Public Spirit, 1870–1914* (1993), *Unemployment and Politics: A Study in English Social Policy, 1886–1914* (2nd edn., 1984), and an edition of Ferdinand Tönnies, *Community and Civil Society* (2001).

NICK HEWITT was Project Co-ordinator of the UK National Inventory of War Memorials at the Imperial War Museum in London between 1996 and 2002. He has written articles for various journals and contributed to features in the press, radio, and television, as well as contributing a chapter to the English

Heritage Publication *Monuments and the Millennium* (2001). He is currently Interpretation Officer on board HMS Belfast, a branch of the Imperial War Museum.

MICHAEL HOCHGESCHWENDER teaches Modern History at the University of Tübingen. His main fields of interest are the history of the USA in the nineteenth and twentieth centuries, US women's and gender history, the history of Catholicism in the USA, Westernization, and the cultural history of the Cold War. He is the author of *Freiheit in der Offensive? Die Deutschen und der Kongreß für kulturelle Freiheit* (1998).

PIETER LAGROU holds the Chair in Comparative History of States and Societies since 1914 at the Université Libre de Bruxelles. He is also a Research Fellow at the Institut d'Histoire du Temps Présent in Paris. He is the author of *The Legacy of Nazi Occupation: Patriotic Memory and National Recovery in Western Europe, 1945–1965* (2000).

WILFRIED LOTH is Professor of History at the University of Essen. His main fields of research are the history of Catholicism, Socialism, and the German Empire; twentieth-century French history; and the history of the Cold War and European integration. He has published extensively on nineteenth- and twentieth-century German and European history. His publications include *Helsinki: 1. August 1975. Entspannung und Abrüstung* (1998), *Der Weg nach Europa: Geschichte der europäischen Integration 1939–1957* (3rd edn., 1996), and *Stalins ungeliebtes Kind: Warum Moskau die DDR nicht wollte* (1994).

N. PIERS LUDLOW teaches International History at the London School of Economics. His main field of interest is the history of European integration on which he has written various articles in learned journals and chapters in books. He has also written a major study of Britain's first application for EEC membership, *Dealing with Britain: The Six and the First UK Membership Application* (1997).

LEOPOLDO NUTI is Professor of the History of International Relations at the Faculty of Political Science in Rome (Università

Roma Tre). He has published extensively on postwar Italian foreign and security policy and on US–Italian relations. His publications include *Gli stati uniti e l'apertura a sinistra* (1999), *I missili di ottobre: La storiografia Americana e la crisi cubana del 1962* (1994), and *L'esercito italiano nel secondo dopoguerra, 1945–1950* (1989).

LUCIANO SEGRETO is Professor of Economic History and the History of International Relations at the University of Florence. His main fields of interest are business history and the history of economic relations between Italy and its Western partners in the twentieth century. His publications include a study on the management of US and UK surplus left in Italy after the Second World War, *ARAR: Un'azienda statale tra mercato e dirigismo* (2001); *Marte e Mercurio: Industria bellica e sviluppo economico in Italia* (1997); and *Monte Amiata: Il mercurio italiano. Strategie internazionalie vincoli extraeconomici* (1991).

CARLO SPAGNOLO is Researcher in Contemporary History at the University of Bari. He has written various articles on the postwar history of Italy and Europe. His main fields of research are European integration and the relationship between politics and economics in the twentieth century. He has recently published a study of the Marshall Plan and the stabilization of Italian capitalism, *La stabilizzazione incompiuta: Il Piano Marshall in Italia, 1947–1952* (2001).

TOBY THACKER, University of Wales, Swansea, has recently completed a Ph.D. thesis on music and politics in Germany, 1945–1955. He has published articles on 'Dance Music in the Early GDR' and on the censorship of music in the GDR.

Index